2023 CONDOMINIUM BLUEBOOK®

FOR
CALIFORNIA

BY BRANDEN E. BICKEL

35th Edition

COMMON INTEREST
PUBLISHING

The Condominium Bluebook is published by:

C I P

Common Interest Publishing, LLC
2175 N. California Blvd., Suite 575
Walnut Creek, California 94596
Tel: (844) 296-0611
condobook@commoninterestpublishing.com
www.condobook.com

PRINTED IN THE UNITED STATES OF AMERICA

Library of Congress No. ISSN 1066-9310

ISBN 978-1-7342935-6-2

Editorial Assistance by Berding & Weil, LLP

Please Note: This publication is a compilation of statutes currently in force in California. The information contained in this book may not be sufficient to address a particular problem and the user is encouraged to consult a licensed attorney for legal advice.

For legal questions please contact Berding & Weil at 800.838.2090 or
email Jasmine Hale at jhale@berdingweil.com.

PREFACE

STATUTORY CHANGES FOR 2023

Statutory changes for 2023 are highlighted in ***bold italic type***. Reliance on past editions of *The Condominium Bluebook®* may be misleading because of subsequent changes in the law. New statutory law becomes effective January 1st of the year following enactment, unless enacted as emergency legislation, in which case it becomes effective upon enactment. All relevant regular and emergency legislation enacted by the California Legislature during the 2022 calendar year is reflected in this edition of *The Condominium Bluebook®*.

CONTENTS

APPENDIX

1

AN OVERVIEW OF CALIFORNIA COMMON INTEREST DEVELOPMENT LAW AFFECTING RESIDENTIAL AND MIXED USE COMMUNITIES

I. COMMON INTEREST DEVELOPMENTS

The term "common interest development" (or "CID") describes a form of real estate where each owner holds exclusive rights to a portion of the property typically called a unit or lot, and shared rights to portions of the property typically called the common area. A development that does not contain common area is not a CID.

Members of a homeowners' association are the owners of individual units or lots, and the terms "members" and "owners" are used interchangeably in this chapter and in most governing documents.

A. TYPES OF COMMON INTEREST DEVELOPMENTS

The most numerous forms of CIDs, and the focus of *The Condominium Bluebook*, are the condominium and the planned development. The two other types of CIDs, the stock cooperative and the community apartment, are less common, although they are governed by many of the same laws. See Civil Code §§ 4100, 4105 and 4190. A timeshare and a tenancy-in-common are not CIDs.

Hybrid common interest developments are becoming increasingly common, such as mixed-use residential and commercial condominium developments and live-work lofts. Live-work lofts typically are conventional condominiums zoned for both residential and commercial use. The mixed-use development combines a commercial (or more rarely, an industrial) component with a residential component. Often, the residential and commercial units are governed by one association. Alternatively, the commercial component is governed by a commercial association, and the residential component is governed by a residential association. In this context, the mixed-use project as a whole is often governed by a master association of which both the commercial and residential association are members.

Residential associations, and mixed-use associations that contain both residential and commercial components are governed by the Davis-Stirling Common Interest Development Act, Civil Code §§ 4000 – 6150 ("Davis Stirling Act"). Associations that are wholly commercial or industrial in nature are governed by the Commercial and Industrial Common Interest Development Act, and are not covered in this book, Civil Code §§ 6500 – 6876. (See also § 4202)

B. DIFFERENCES BETWEEN CONDOMINIUM PROJECTS, PLANNED DEVELOPMENTS AND STOCK COOPERATIVES

The determination of whether a property is developed as a condominium project or a planned development is based on the physical characteristics of the buildings. Projects with only vertically-stacked units are always condominiums. Projects with only detached homes are almost always planned developments. Projects involving horizontally attached homes, or a combination of different attached home types, can be formed as either condominiums or planned developments.

The most significant difference between condominium projects and planned developments is the distinct nature of the individually-owned and commonly group-owned portions of the property. The individually-owned portion of a condominium is called a "unit," and typically consists of interior space within a defined set of walls, floors and ceilings. Condominium owners also frequently have exclusive use of common area decks, patios, and parking areas that are associated their unit. All residential and mixed-use condominium projects are common interest developments subject to the Davis-Stirling Act.

The individually owned portion of a planned development is called a "lot," and typically consists of a piece of land and everything on it. The common area in a condominium is usually all of the structural elements of the building(s) containing the units, other than the units themselves, and all land and exterior areas. The common area in a planned development is usually limited to streets, open space, and recreational facilities. In some instances, common area is not physical property. If a planned development does not have any common area, it is not a common interest development subject to the Davis-Stirling Act. See Civil Code §4201.

Condominium projects and planned developments also differ with respect to the form of joint ownership of common area. Title to at least some portion of the common area in a condominium must be jointly held by the owners. By contrast, title to the common area in a planned development can be held by the owners in common, or can be held by the association. See Civil Code §§ 4125 and 4175.

There are marked distinctions between a stock cooperative and a condominium. A stock cooperative is a corporation formed to hold title to real property, usually an apartment building. The shareholders are given an exclusive right to occupy a portion of the property under a proprietary lease. The right of occupancy is generally made by transfer of stock in the corporation and the leasehold rights to a purchaser of a shareholder's interest. The shareholder in a stock cooperative is merely a lessee, who has a landlord-tenant relationship with the stock cooperative as the owner of the land.

II. ASSOCIATION STRUCTURE

A. LEGAL STRUCTURE OF ASSOCIATIONS

The law allows an association to be either incorporated or unincorporated. An incorporated association has a legal identity that is separate from that of its members, just as Microsoft has a legal identity that is separate from its shareholders. Unlike Microsoft, which is a for-profit corporation, an incorporated association is a non-profit corporation and its powers are limited to those normally exercised for the mutual benefit of the owners. It is exempt from certain governmental fees and taxes.

Unless the governing documents state otherwise, an unincorporated association may exercise all of the powers granted to an incorporated association under the law, with a few exceptions.

Traditionally, associations have been incorporated to protect owners from responsibility for association debts, losses and liabilities. But recent laws have extended most of these protections to owners of unincorporated associations. See Civil Code § 5805. Under current law, the advantages of incorporation are some additional protection from owner liability, ease of opening association accounts with certain banks and vendors, and qualification of the units or lots for mortgage loans from lenders that require an incorporated association. Balanced against these advantages are the costs of forming the corporation, the burden of annually filing forms with the California Secretary of State, and additional procedural formalities such as having officers and directors, and conducting formal meetings.

An unincorporated association can be incorporated by its members at any time. The process of incorporation involves amending the governing documents, preparing articles of incorporation, and filing with the California Secretary of State.

B. LAW GOVERNING THE GOVERNING DOCUMENTS

1. Statutory Law

The California State Legislature has passed numerous statutory laws governing the formation and operation of condominium and planned development associations. The most important of these laws is the Davis-Stirling Act, which is included in its entirety in Chapter 2 of this book. The Davis-Stirling Act sets out detailed requirements regarding the governing documents, including the enforcement and amendment of governing documents, operating rules, ownership rights and interests, association governance and operations, fiscal requirements, assessment collection, transfer of ownership rights, maintenance, and construction defect litigation.

The California Legislature has enacted various other statutes, many contained in the Civil Code and other California Codes, which are relevant to the creation of common interest developments and their operation. Chapters 2 through 8 of this book contain statutory provisions concerning powers and procedures of the association board of directors, association membership meetings and voting, association records and record keeping, litigation and construction defects, civil rights and restrictions, vehicle issues, and requirements for professional managers.

2. Case Law

A second important source of law governing common interest developments and their associations are the legal decisions rendered by California courts. A summary of the significant judicial decisions affecting common interest developments is contained in Chapter 9 of this book.

3. California Department of Real Estate Regulations

The California Department of Real Estate ("DRE") has also enacted various regulations that concern the development of common interest developments. However, the DRE regulations apply to common interest developments only until the developer relinquishes control to the association. Once the association is in control, only the governing documents and statutory and case law regulate the common interest development.

4. Binding Effect of Governing Documents

The law provides that the use of real property can be restricted when a document describing the restrictions is recorded with the county where the property is located. The restrictions "run with the land," meaning they apply to each owner who acquires the property after the restrictions are recorded. The map or plan, and the CC&Rs, are different types of recorded restrictions that "run with the land," and that is why they bind each and every owner of the unit or lot against which they are recorded. The articles, bylaws, and rules are not recorded, but derive their authority from state law and the CC&Rs. With the articles and bylaws, this authority arises because state law makes each owner a member of the association, subject to the association's articles and bylaws. With the rules, the binding power arises because the CC&Rs or bylaws specifically empower the association to enact additional binding restrictions in the form of rules.

C. TYPES OF GOVERNING DOCUMENTS

The term "governing documents" is used as a general reference to the entire group of legally-recognized documents that creates and controls a common interest development. The governing documents include the declaration of covenants, conditions and restrictions (often referred to as "CC&Rs"), bylaws, articles of incorporation, condominium plan or subdivision map, operating rules, and any other documents that govern the property in the association.

Every common interest development will need to revise or restate its governing documents at some point. Revision usually involves modification of existing documents by amendment. Restatement means completely replacing the existing documents with an entirely new set of governing documents. Revision and restatement will be referred to in this chapter as simply "amendment" for the sake of brevity.

When amendment of governing documents is under consideration, the documents themselves should first be consulted for amendment procedures. Most governing documents can be amended by a majority vote of the owners. Sometimes a higher (super-majority) percentage vote is required when certain provisions are given special protection against amendment, such as changing the method for allocation of assessments or voting rights among owners, altering the boundaries of exclusive use common area, or terminating the development.

1. The Declaration of Covenants, Conditions and Restrictions (often referred to as "CC&Rs")

(a) Contents of CC&Rs

CC&Rs describe the rights and obligations of the association and of each owner with respect to property. CC&Rs vary widely in content and length, but at a minimum the CC&Rs must contain a legal description of the development, a statement of the type of common interest development it is, the name of the association and any use restrictions, typically including common area use restrictions, pet regulations, and architectural controls. The CC&Rs may contain other matters such as: (1) the maintenance responsibilities of the association and the individual owners; (2) the allocation of association operating costs among the owners, and the mechanism for collecting owner payments; (3) the dispute resolution procedure; (4) enforcement powers; and (5) the rights and protections of mortgage lenders.

CC&Rs are required for all condominiums and planned developments. They are prepared by the developer's attorney, reviewed by the California Department of Real Estate (unless the project has fewer than five units or lots, in which case it is exempt from DRE review), and recorded with the county at the time a condominium project or planned development is formed. See Civil Code § 4250.

(b) Amendment of CC&Rs

CC&Rs may be amended by the members of the association as provided in the CC&Rs or as provided by statute. CC&Rs that fail to include provisions permitting amendment may be amended at any time by a simple majority vote. See Civil Code § 4270. CC&Rs that specify they are not amendable may not be amended without an order of court overriding the restriction.

(i) Amendment to Extending Term

Most CC&Rs contain an automatic renewal provision extending the term during which they are valid in increments of 5, 10 or 20 years. A typical provision states an initial term and then provides that upon expiration of the initial term, the term shall be automatically extended for successive periods of the same number of years, unless the association is terminated and it records a notice of termination with the county recorder. An automatic renewal provision does not require any action on the part of the association to trigger renewal.

Occasionally CC&Rs provide a termination date but make no provision for extension of that termination date. Without further action, the CC&Rs would expire on the termination date and the CC&Rs would then cease to have any legal effect. The state legislature determined that as a matter of public policy CC&Rs are an appropriate method of protecting common interest developments and providing financial support for the upkeep of common areas, systems and facilities, which if allowed to lapse would adversely impact the housing supply. Accordingly, the legislature enacted a statute that allows an association to extend the term or life of the development beyond the initial term even where there is no automatic renewal provision by adopting a CC&R amendment approved by a majority of the owners before the expiration of the initial term. See Civil Code § 4264. If the renewal amendment requires super-majority approval, then the association may seek approval of the amendment by court order using the procedures in Civil Code § 4275. An amendment to extend the term of CC&Rs may be used on more than one occasion, but it is simpler to adopt an automatic renewal provision as part of the first extension amendment.

(ii) Amendment Procedure

In residential and mixed use associations, approval of a proposed amendment must be done by secret ballot in accordance with the procedures set forth in Civil Code §§ 5100 – 5145. The procedures for a secret ballot election are discussed in the section entitled "Member Elections" in this chapter. Approval may be by a mail-in ballot alone. The secret ballot must be sent out at least 30 days before the voting deadline and it must be accompanied by the text of the proposed amendment. See Civil Code § 5115. There is no outside limit within which the secret ballot must be returned other than a general restriction that it must be returned within a reasonable time. There is no precise definition of a reasonable time but customary practice is to allow between 60 and 120 days for the return of the secret ballots. The voting deadline must be stated on the ballot or in the voting instructions. See Civil Code §§ 5100 – 5125 and Corp. Code §§ 7513 and 7514.

There is no clear authority whether the voting deadline can be extended by the board of directors to allow the association to obtain additional approvals, however, Civil Code section 5110 authorizes the board-appointed Inspector(s) of Election to "determine when polls shall close, consistent with the governing documents." If the board wishes to reserve the right to extend the deadline, it should at least advise the members that the deadline may be extended by the Inspector(s) in the ballot instructions.

The effective date of the amendment is after the amendment has been approved by the required percentage of members on a secret ballot vote, the approval has been certified in writing by an authorized officer of the association and the amendment has been properly recorded in each county where the development is located. A copy of the amendment must be distributed by "individual delivery" to all members as soon as possible after recording. See Civil Code § 4270.

(iii) Amendment by Court Order

Often CC&Rs require approval of more than a majority of members to amend a particular CC&R provision. Some older CC&Rs require approval of more than a majority to amend any provision of the CC&Rs. The law establishes a method for overriding a super-majority approval requirement by court order. See Civil Code § 4275.

When faced with a super-majority approval requirement, either the association or a member may petition the court for an order reducing the percentage approval requirement necessary for the amendment. The association must first put the proposed amendment to a vote of the members. If the amendment receives approval by at least a majority of the members but not the required super-majority, the court can be asked for judicial approval of the amendment without a further vote.

(iv) Amendment To Eliminate Developer-Related Provisions

The law allows an abbreviated method of eliminating developer-related CC&R provisions after the developer has terminated its onsite activities. The board of directors, with a reduced percentage approval of the members, may adopt an amendment deleting from the CC&Rs any provision which is unequivocally designed and intended to facilitate the developer's access over or across the common area for completing the construction or marketing of the development or a particular phase of the development.

In order to adopt such an amendment, the board of directors must deliver by "individual delivery" to all members a copy of the proposed amendment, and a notice of the time, date and place the board will consider adopting the amendment at a meeting open to all members. Members attending the meeting must have an opportunity to comment on the proposed amendment. All board deliberations must be conducted in open session. Once approved by the board of directors, the proposed amendment must be submitted for approval of the members on a secret ballot vote. Member approval requires only a majority of votes cast once a quorum is established. See Civil Code § 4230.

Most governing documents refer to the developer as a "declarant" because it formulated the CC&Rs, and recorded them against the property. The declarant, as the original developer, has special privileges and rights because it had virtually complete control over the content of the documents when they were prepared. It is advisable for associations to amend their governing documents to remove the developer-specific provisions as soon as the project is completely built out and sold.

(v) Amendment to Correct a Statutory Reference

The law allows the board of directors to amend a reference in the CC&Rs to a provision of the Davis-Stirling Act that has been repealed and replaced with a new provision by a board resolution and without a vote of the members. The amendment must be solely to correct the statutory reference. The amendment showing the corrected reference must be recorded with a copy of the board resolution authorizing the amendment. See Civil Code § 4235.

(vi) Amendment to Eliminate Discriminatory Restriction

The board of directors must amend by board resolution and without a member vote any provision of the CC&Rs that discriminates against any person based upon race, color, religion, sex, sexual orientation, marital status, national origin, ancestry, familial status, source of income, or disability. The restated CC&Rs showing the deletion must be recorded. See Civil Code § 4225

(vii) Special Approvals of Amendments

Certain amendments to CC&Rs may require special approvals from lenders, governmental agencies or master associations. The purpose of granting special approval rights to lenders is to allow them to participate in an amendment that might impair their security interests. These rights are usually granted only to lenders in first position or to "eligible" lenders who have given notice of a desire to participate in an amendment affecting their security interest. Governmental agencies may require participation in an amendment affecting a condition imposed by the agencies as part of the initial governmental approval of the development. Sometimes a city or county redevelopment agency will require special approval rights to achieve a planning objective. Sometimes federal agencies, such as the Department of Housing and Urban Development (HUD) or the Veterans Administration require special approval rights as a condition of providing the developer with federal financing. A master association may require approval of amendments affecting architectural restrictions under the jurisdiction of the master association.

Special approval rights are enforceable, and failure to obtain special approvals may void the amendment. When an association officer certifies that all of the requisite approvals have been obtained, the officer is certifying that all special approvals as well as member approvals have been obtained.

2. Bylaws

The bylaws describe the mechanics of association decision-making and management. Bylaws vary widely in content and length, but usually include the following: (1) number of and selection methods for officers and directors; (2) notice, meeting and voting procedures for owner and board decisions; and (3) association record keeping and reporting requirements.

Although bylaws are common for both incorporated and unincorporated associations, they are required only for incorporated associations. Bylaws for associations of owners of residential and/or mixed use properties, are initially prepared by the developer's attorney and reviewed by a government agency (unless the common interest development has fewer than five units or lots) at the time a condominium project or planned development is formed. But unlike articles and CC&Rs, bylaws are not recorded or filed with any government agency, and this makes them easier to change. See Corp. Code § 7151.

Bylaws amended by the members must be approved by the percentage of owners specified in the bylaws. If a percentage is not specified in the bylaws, then approval must be by a majority of those voting once a quorum has been established. See Corp. Code § 7150(b).

3. Articles of Incorporation

A corporation is formed by filing articles of incorporation (or simply "articles") with the California Secretary of State. The articles of an association must include the information required by both Civil Code § 4280 and Corp. Code §§ 7130 – 7132. Failure to strictly comply with both statutes will result in rejection when the articles are presented for filing with the Secretary of State. Because of the technical requirements, preparation and filing of articles should be handled by an attorney.

Civil Code § 4280 requires the articles of an association of owners of a residential and/or mixed use development to state: (1) in addition to the statement of purposes required by the Corp. Code, the corporation is formed to manage a common interest development under the Davis-Stirling Common Interest Development Act; (2) the business office of the association, if any; (3) if the business office is not onsite, the front street and nearest cross street of the physical location of the development; and (4) the name and address of the association's managing agent, if any. Corp. Code §§ 7130 – 7132 requires the articles to state: (1) the name of the corporation; (2) the statement of purpose as exactly as set forth in the statute; (3) the name and address of the association's initial agent for the service of process (i.e., the person authorized to receive legal notice; (4) the initial street address of the corporation; and (5) the initial mailing address of the corporation if different from the street address.

Sometimes the articles also contain optional language about voting, directors, amendments, and dissolution of the association. Articles are required only when an association is incorporated. Unincorporated associations sometimes have "articles of association," but these are not required. Articles for associations of owners of residential and/or mixed use developments are prepared by the developer's attorney and reviewed by the California Department of Real Estate, unless the common interest development has fewer than five units or lots.

Articles of incorporation, unless restricted to a vote by the owners, are amendable by a majority of the directors present at a duly constituted board meeting. If the articles require an owner vote, those requirements must be fulfilled. An amendment to the articles becomes effective when the association files with the California Secretary of State a certificate of amendment consisting of an officer's certificate containing the text of the amendment and attesting to its approval by the board or members. See Corp. Code §§ 7810 – 7820.

4. Condominium Plans and Subdivision Maps

The term "condominium plan," is a description or survey map of a condominium project depicting the common area, exclusive use common area and unit boundaries in three dimensional space and illustrate how a property is divided. A subdivision map, which is sometimes called a "final map" or "parcel map," is a survey map that depicts lots and common area parcel boundaries, public streets, easements and monuments within a planned development.

These documents are prepared by licensed engineers or land surveyors, reviewed by government agencies, and recorded with the county at the time the condominium project or planned development is formed. Once recorded, the drawings become connected to every deed and mortgage on every unit or lot within the property, and this connection makes changing the map or plan very difficult without the consent of everyone with an interest in the property. There can be several maps or plans recorded at different times as new portions of a project are added by a process called "annexation."

5. Operating Rules

The CC&Rs usually empower the association to adopt rules and give the rules the same binding power, although not the same priority, as the other governing documents. The rules often expand upon use restrictions relating to alterations, signage, waste disposal, parking, pets, and use of recreational facilities. The rules may not conflict with the CC&Rs, Bylaws or Articles. Association rules are not subject to any governmental review and do not need to be filed or recorded with any governmental agency.

The board of directors is responsible for adopting, amending or repealing operating rules, unless the governing documents provide otherwise. Any rules adopted by the board must be: (1) in writing; (2) within the authority of the board to make pursuant to the law and the governing documents; (3) not inconsistent with the law or the governing documents; (4) made in good faith; and (5) reasonable. See Civil Code § 4350.

For rule adoption or amendment regarding use of common areas or exclusive use common areas, architectural or aesthetic standards for alterations of a unit or lot, member discipline, delinquent assessment payment plans, and discretionary provisions for dispute resolution, and election procedures, the board must provide members with 28 days to review and comment upon the propose rule before making the rule change. The notice must contain the text of the proposed new or amended rule and its effect. The board must adopt a proposed rule change at an open board meeting after consideration of any comments by association members. Once a rule change has been approved, the board must notify all members within 15 days in writing.

To challenge an adopted rule change, 5% of the members entitled to vote may call for a special vote of the members to reverse a rule by delivering a written request to the association. Not less than 35 days nor more than 90 days after receipt of the request, the association must hold a vote of the members on whether to reverse the rule change. The written request for a special vote may not be delivered more than 30 days after the association gives written notice of the rule change. The rule change may be reversed if such action is approved by an affirmative vote of a majority of the votes cast once a quorum has been established. If the members vote to reverse the rule change, the rule change may not be re-adopted by the board for one year from the date of the vote for reversal, although the board may adopt a different rule on the same subject.

If the board determines that an immediate rule change is required to address an imminent threat to public health or safety, or an imminent risk of substantial economic loss to the association, it may make an emergency rule change, and no notice is required. An emergency rule change is effective for 120 days, unless the rule itself provides for a shorter effective period.

The procedural rules set forth in the preceding paragraphs do not apply to board decisions regarding maintenance of common areas, specific decisions not intended to apply to members generally, setting the amount of a regular or special assessment, a rule change required by law if the board has no discretion as to the substantive effect of the rule change, or the issuance of a document that merely restates existing law or the governing documents. See Civil Code §§ 4340 – 4370.

D. INTERPRETATION OF GOVERNING DOCUMENTS

1. Liberal Construction of Governing Documents

The law provides that the governing documents must be liberally construed to facilitate the operation of the common interest development. This means that a court or other adjudicative decision maker asked to determine the meaning of the governing documents will read the provisions broadly so that they may accomplish the purpose for which they were written. The law also provides that if any provisions of the governing documents are judged unenforceable or impermissible, other provisions of the governing documents that are otherwise enforceable will remain enforceable. See Civil Code § 4215.

2. Conflicts Between the Governing Documents and Statutory Law

The resolution of a conflict between the governing documents and statutory law depends upon the intent of the governmental body that enacted the statutory law. Where the statutory law contains a phrase like "notwithstanding the provisions of the declaration" or "notwithstanding anything to the contrary in the governing documents" in its text, the intent to override the governing documents is clear and the statutory law controls. Where the statutory law contains a phrase like "unless otherwise provided in the declaration" or "subject to the provisions of the governing documents" in its text, the intent not to override is clear and the governing document provision controls. Where the apparently conflicting statutory law contains no clear indication of whether it is intended to supersede conflicting provisions in governing documents, the statutory law controls. See Civil Code § 4205.

3. Conflicts Between Governing Documents

To the extent of any conflicts between the articles and the CC&Rs, the CC&Rs control. To the extent of any conflicts between the bylaws and CC&Rs or the articles, the CC&Rs and articles control. The operating rules are subordinate to the law, CC&Rs, bylaws and articles. See Civil Code § 4205.

4. Unreasonable or Unfair Governing Document Provisions

Provisions of the CC&Rs, bylaws and rules are generally upheld by the courts unless they are arbitrary, impose burdens on some residents that substantially outweigh their benefits to other residents, or violate fundamental public policy. Consult an attorney if a provision does not seem to meet these standards. For additional information, see *Nahrstedt v. Lakeside Village Condominium Assn.* (1994) 8 Cal.4th 361.

III. OWNERSHIP AND TRANSFER OF INTERESTS

A. A "UNIT" OR "SEPARATE INTEREST" IN A CONDOMINIUM PROJECT

In a condominium project, the individually owned area is called a "unit." The exact physical location of each unit within a particular project is shown on the recorded condominium plan. The plan will also contain a definition of the term "unit" as it is used for that particular project, listing the elements of the building that are part of the unit. These definitions vary significantly from project to project, and it is unwise to apply generalizations or assumptions. Instead, read and apply the definition carefully.

B. A "LOT" OR "SEPARATE INTEREST" IN A PLANNED DEVELOPMENT

In a planned development, the individually owned area is called the lot and typically consists of a piece of land and everything on it. The exact physical location of each lot within a particular project is shown on the recorded subdivision map for that development. Note that the subdivision map or CC&Rs for planned developments sometimes give neighbors and even the general public the right to cross a private lot (a type of "easement"). See Civil Code § 4175.

C. OWNERSHIP OF THE COMMON AREA

Title to the common area can be held by the association or by the owners in percentage shares as "tenants in common." The decision is made by the developer at the time the governing documents are prepared, and is very difficult to change later. To determine who owns the common area, refer to the CC&Rs. See Civil Code § 4500.

D. EXCLUSIVE USE OR RESTRICTED COMMON AREA

The term "exclusive use common area," sometime called "restricted common area'" refers to portions of a condominium project or planned development that are not within the defined boundaries of a unit or lot, but are intended to be used exclusively by less than all owners. Technically, exclusive use common area is part of the common area owned either by the association or by all of the owners, but one or more owners hold a type of easement which gives such owners exclusive usage rights. The right is typically included in the grant deed or CC&Rs and is appurtenant to the unit or lot. See Civil Code § 4145.

In addition to exclusive use common area easements designated in the CC&Rs, associations may grant exclusive use of a portion of the common area to an owner, subject to the vote and approval of the members. Unless the CC&Rs specify a different percentage, a board may grant an owner exclusive use of any portion of the common area with the approval of 67% of all association members via a secret ballot vote. There are important exceptions to this general voting requirement and the statute should be consulted. For example, a board may unilaterally grant exclusive use of a portion of the common area to accommodate a disability, to allow installation of an electric vehicle charging station, and to transfer the burden of management and maintenance of any common area that is generally inaccessible and not of general use to the other members. See Civil Code §§ 4145 and 4600.

E. USE OF THE COMMON AREA

1. By a Unit or Lot Owner

Each owner in a condominium project or planned development is equally entitled to use all common area (other than exclusive use common area) regardless of ownership or assessment percentage, unless the CC&Rs provide otherwise.

2. By Guests and Tenants

An owner's guests and tenants have the same common area usage rights as the owner unless the governing documents specifically provide otherwise.

3. Restrictions on Fees for Use of Common Area Facilities

An association may charge fees for the use of recreational facilities and refuse access without payment, provided the charge applies equally to all owners and is not specifically prohibited by the governing documents. Such fees can be initiated and adjusted by the board of directors unless the governing documents specifically require a member vote. However, a fee may not exceed the amount necessary to defray the costs for which it is levied. See Civil Code § 5600(b).

An association may also temporarily remove an owner's recreational facilities usage privileges as discipline for a violation of the governing documents. This type of discipline is permitted only if: (1) the governing documents grant the board the authority to suspend membership rights; and (2) the violating owner is given notice of the violation and a board hearing before the right to use the recreational facilities is suspended. See Civil Code § 5855.

F. PARTITION

The term "partition" refers to a court-supervised process where jointly-owned real estate is sold and the proceeds divided among the owners. Contrary to common usage, partition never involves a physical division of one parcel of real estate into multiple parcels. Partition is the law's remedy when changed circumstances or disagreements prevent co-owners from jointly managing their shared property; and, in most joint ownership arrangements, any owner can force a partition at any time. However, although the common area of condominiums and planned developments are often jointly owned, the law prohibits partition unless the project has become substantially damaged or obsolete. See Civil Code § 4610.

G. INDIVIDUAL UNIT OR LOT SPLIT OFF

By the time a condominium unit or planned development lot is sold, documents have been recorded with the county government which bind it to the rest of the project. A condominium unit in a multi-unit, vertically-stacked building can never be split off; but, if the building is substantially damaged, the law and the governing documents sometimes allow the entire project to be sold and the proceeds divided. A condominium unit or planned development lot that is not attached to other units or lots on a vertical plane, can be split off, but only with the approval of the county government as well as the percentage of owners and lenders required by the governing documents.

H. COMBINING TWO OR MORE UNITS OR LOTS

The ability of an owner to physically combine units or lots (i.e., join them together with doorways, stairs, or build a single home over two or more lots, etc.) will be determined by the architectural provisions of the CC&Rs and the local building and planning codes. In most cases, the owner will need to get association approval for these types of physical alterations as well as a building permit from a governmental agency.

I. ACCESS RIGHTS

1. Association Access to Individually Owned Units or Lots

Most CC&Rs state that the association has the right to enter any unit or lot whenever necessary to fulfill the association's duties. Among the duties that would justify entry is common area maintenance and verification of an owner's compliance with owner maintenance requirements and architectural restrictions. Often, the CC&Rs will require that the association provide advance notice of the entry except in an emergency. Entry may require a court order if the owner objects.

2. Access to Owner's Separate Interest

Except by court order, an association may not discipline an owner by denying access to the owner's unit or lot through the common area. See Civil Code § 4510.

J. RENTAL RESTRICTIONS

Rental restrictions in governing documents are generally deemed to be enforceable so long as they are not unreasonable. Rental restrictions may affect an owner's ability to obtain mortgage loans from some lenders; too many rental properties in a common interest development can have the same effect.

If a rental restriction (i.e., a CC&R provision that effectively prevents an owner from renting his or her property) is enacted after January 1, 2012, an owner will not be subject to that restriction unless the restriction was in effect when the owner purchased his or her property. See Civil Code § 4740.

A selling owner must disclose the existence of rental restrictions to any prospective purchaser of his or her property. See Civil Code § 4525.

K. TRANSFER OF OWNERSHIP

Generally associations are not required to disclose information directly to prospective purchasers but are required to provide a variety of information and documentation to selling owners so that they can make the required disclosures. The documents may be made available in hard copy or electronic form and the association may charge a reasonable fee based on the association's actual cost. See Civil Code § 4525.

The law does require the seller of a unit or lot to make extensive disclosures to prospective purchasers, and an association must provide the selling owner with the documents enumerated in Civil Code § 4525 within 10 days of receiving an owner's written request. These documents include: a copy of the governing documents; a statement regarding any rental, occupancy, residency or age restrictions in the governing documents; copies of the association financials for the most recent fiscal year; a statement of current and approved, but not yet effective, regular and special assessments; a statement of any fees or charges to be imposed on the purchaser; a notice regarding any unresolved selling owner discipline issues; and information regarding construction defects at the common interest development.

IV. PROPERTY USE AND MAINTENANCE

A. COMMON USE RESTRICTIONS

Some common use restrictions contained in the CC&Rs include requiring that the unit or lot be used primarily for residential purposes, restricting the color of window coverings visible from the street or common areas, restricting hard surface flooring, restrictions on parking boats, trailers or recreational vehicles within the property, prohibiting conversion of garages into living or recreational areas, prohibiting nuisances (activities that are noxious, illegal, annoying or offensive to a person of reasonable and normal sensitivity), and restrictions on garbage disposal and use of storage spaces.

B. PROTECTED USE RESTRICTIONS

1. Right to Display of the American Flag and For-Sale/Rent and Non-Commercial Signs

No restriction can be imposed on the display of the U.S. flag in an owner's unit, lot or exclusive common area. See Civil Code § 4705.

The association may not prohibit a sign of reasonable dimensions advertising a unit or lot for sale or rental. The association also may not prohibit non-commercial signs, posters or flags within the boundaries of a unit or lot (except for the protection of public health or safety) that are 9 square feet or less in size or non-commercial banners that are 15 square feet or less in size. The association may prohibit signs in the common area. See Civil Code §§ 712, 713 and 4710 and Government Code § 434.5.

2. Right to Keep a Pet

Governing documents adopted or amended since January 1, 2001may not prohibit an owner from keeping at least one domesticated bird, cat, dog or aquatic animal in an aquarium, but the association may enact reasonable rules and regulations, such as leashing and clean-up requirements. See Civil Code § 4715.

3. Right to Fire Retardant Roof Materials

An association may not prohibit an owner from installing at least one type of fire retardant roofing material that meets the technical requirements of California Health & Safety Code § 13132.7. See Civil Code § 4720.

4. Right to Video or Television Antenna System

An association may not prevent the installation of satellites of various types where the dish has a diagonal measurement of 36 inches or less and is located in an area within the exclusive use or control of the owner, except when the dish creates a legitimate safety concern, or the building on which it is to be installed has been designated an historical site. See Civil Code § 4725.

5. Right to Use of Low Water-Using Plants and Landscape Restrictions

An association may not prohibit an owner from installing at least one type of low water-using plants or artificial turf as a group as replacement for existing turf, and any governing document provision that prohibits or restricts compliance with a governmental water conservation program is void and unenforceable. During a drought state of emergency, associations may not fine an owner for allowing landscaping to brown due to compliance with water restrictions. However, an association may fine an owner in a community piped for reclaimed water for landscaping where the owner does not use it. See Civil Code § 4735.

6. Right to Electric Vehicle Charging Stations

Governing documents may not prohibit the installation or use of an electric vehicle charging station in an owner's designated parking space, but an association may impose reasonable restrictions on the installation and use. Approval or denial of an application to install an electric vehicle charging station must be in writing and delivered within 60 days from the date of acceptance of the application as complete or the application will be "deemed approved" as a matter of law.

The association is only required to place an electric vehicle charging station in the common area, other than exclusive use common area, if it is impossible or unreasonably expensive to place it in an owner's designated parking space. See Civil Code § 4745.

7. Right to Solar Energy Systems

Associations generally may not prevent unit or lot owners from installing solar energy systems on their separate interest. Associations may impose reasonable restrictions on the installation of solar energy systems provided they do not significantly increase the cost of the system, or significantly decrease its efficiency. See Civil Code §§ 714 and 714.1.

8. Age Restrictions

Restrictions requiring that all residents be at least a certain minimum age or satisfy certain exceptions, are permitted in developments that qualify as senior citizen housing developments. See Civil Code §§ 51.3 and 51.4.

9. Display of Religious Items

Associations may not limit or prohibit the display of religious items on the entry door or entry door frame of a member's separate interest, except as restricted in Civil Code § 1940.5. If an association is performing maintenance, repair or replacement of an entry door or door frame, the member may be required to remove a religious item while the work is performed. See Civil Code § 4706.

10. Accessory Dwelling Units

Restrictions that either effectively prohibit or unreasonably restrict the construction or use of an accessory dwelling unit ("ADU") or junior accessory dwelling unit ("JADU") on a lot zoned for single-family residential use that meets the requirements of the Government Code are void an unenforceable. However, an association may impose reasonable restrictions on ADUs and JADUs. See Civil Code § 4751.

C. IMPERMISSIBLE USE RESTRICTIONS

Statutory law explicitly prohibits housing discrimination based upon race, color, religion, sex, sexual orientation, marital status, national origin, ancestry, familial status, source of income, and disability. See Govt. Code § 12955 et seq.

D. MEMBER RESPONSIBILITY FOR TENANTS & GUESTS

A member is responsible for his or her tenant's and guest's compliance with the governing documents, and can be liable for the tenant's and guest's violations. The governing documents can require a member to incorporate all of their restrictions in a lease and provide the association with tenant information before the commencement of the rental term.

E. RESPONSIBILITY FOR DAMAGE CAUSED BY NEGLIGENCE OR MISCONDUCT

Generally each owner is responsible for repairs necessitated by the negligent or other wrongful conduct of him or herself, his or her guests, employees and contractors, the occupants of his or her unit or lot (including tenants), and the guests, employees and contractors of the occupants. Similarly, the association is generally responsible for repairs necessitated by the negligent or other wrongful conduct of its employees and contractors.

F. REMOVAL OF VEHICLES

An association may cause a parked vehicle to be removed from common area to a storage facility under any one of the following circumstances:

(1) There is displayed, in plain view at all entrances to the property, a sign not less than 17 by 22 inches in size, with lettering not less than one inch in height, prohibiting public parking and indicating that vehicles will be removed at the owner's expense, and containing the telephone number of the local traffic law enforcement agency and the name and telephone number of each towing company with which the association has a written towing authorization agreement. The sign may also indicate that a citation will be issued for the violation.

(2) The vehicle has been issued a notice of parking violation and 96 hours have elapsed since the issuance of that notice.

(3) The vehicle lacks an engine, transmission, wheels, tires, doors, windshield, or any other major part or equipment necessary to operate safely on the highways, the association has notified the local traffic law enforcement agency, and 24 hours have elapsed since that notification.

The association must provide to the tow truck operator the name and address of the owner of the vehicle, if available, and indicate the grounds for removal. The tow truck operator has certain reporting requirements, but the association also must notify by telephone or, if impractical, by the most expeditious means available, the local traffic law enforcement agency within one hour of an authorized tow. See Veh. Code § 22658.

G. MODIFICATION OF A UNIT OR LOT

CC&Rs generally contain architectural controls restricting the structural and aesthetic changes that can be made to units or lots within the common interest development. Architectural controls are generally enforceable provided that the governing documents authorize the association to enforce them, the association applies reasonable standards when it makes architectural decisions, and the association has adopted and consistently followed reasonable enforcement procedures.

1. Modification of a Condominium Unit

Without association approval, an owner of a condominium unit may make modifications within the boundaries of his or her unit that do not impair the structural integrity or common utility systems and provided the modifications comply with the other provisions of the CC&Rs. Most modifications require association approval.

2. Modification of a Lot in a Planned Development

Planned development governing documents usually require association approval for exterior improvements and alterations of a lot.

3. Reasonable Modifications to Accommodate Disability

An owner may modify his or her unit or lot, at his or her own expense, to accommodate a disabled resident. An owner may also make reasonable modifications to the common area, at his or her own expense and with association approval, if such modifications are necessary to allow the disabled resident use and enjoyment of his or her residence and the common area.

4. Association Approval Procedures

Most governing documents contain detailed procedures for the submission, consideration, and approval of proposed alterations and improvements. Alteration approval is a responsibility of the board, or architectural committee, as specified in the CC&Rs.

5. Standards for Association Approval

Associations whose governing documents require architectural review and approval before an owner can make a physical change to his or her unit or lot will optimally have a written procedure for making their decision. Such procedures will provide for prompt deadlines and a maximum time for the association to respond to an application. The association's decision must be: (1) reasonable, fair and made in good faith; (2) consistent with local ordinances and stated standards; (3) be in writing; and (4) provide an explanation for any disapproval of a proposed change and procedure for reconsideration by a board of any architectural committee denials. See Civil Code § 4765.

An association must annually provide the owners with notice of any requirements for association approval of physical changes to their property. The notice must describe the types of changes that require association approval and must include a copy of the procedure used to review and approve or disapprove a proposed change. See Civil Code §§ 4765 and 5310.

The fact that an association has permitted or approved a certain activity or alteration by a particular owner at one time does not mean that the association must in all cases permit or approve that same activity or alteration by the same or a different owner at a later time.

H. MAINTENANCE

1. Maintenance Responsibilities

The allocation of maintenance responsibilities between the individual owners and the association is usually stated in the governing documents, and varies widely from project to project. Generally, unless the governing documents state otherwise, the association is responsible for the maintenance, repair and replacement of common area, and for the repair and replacement of exclusive use common area; owners in turn are responsible for the maintenance, repair and replacement of their unit or lot, and for the cleanliness and maintenance of their exclusive use common area. See Civil Code § 4775.

2. Standards for Required Maintenance

The governing documents usually include a minimum standard for owner maintenance such as the statement "each owner shall maintain the elements of the property for which he or she is responsible in a condition which does not impair the value or desirability of other units or lots." Most governing documents also provide that if an owner fails to satisfy his or her maintenance requirements, the association may do so and assess any related expense against the responsible owner as a reimbursement assessment. Before undertaking the work itself, the association generally must provide a written warning, an opportunity to cure the problem and a board hearing.

I. MORTGAGES AND LIENS

1. Owner Default

When an owner defaults on his or her mortgage, the lender is entitled to undertake a foreclosure procedure that ultimately results in an auction-like sale of the defaulting owner's unit or lot. The lender has no recourse against the association or any other owner. The purchaser at the foreclosure sale, including a foreclosing lender, after the sale is concluded, must comply with all of the provisions of the governing documents, including the obligation to pay assessments. A foreclosure sale purchaser is not responsible for any unpaid, pre-foreclosure assessments.

2. "Mortgage Protection" Provisions in Governing Documents

Most lenders will refuse to make mortgage loans on residences within condominium projects and planned developments unless there are special provisions in the governing documents to protect them. These provisions are designed to insure that the basic rights and responsibilities associated with the residence at the time the loan is made cannot be easily changed. Most lenders review the mortgage protection provisions of the governing documents before they approve a mortgage within a condominium project or planned development.

3. Mechanics' Liens

The term "mechanics' lien" describes a document that can be recorded with the county by a contractor, laborer, or construction materials supplier who has not been paid for work performed on property. The recording of a mechanics' lien relating to a particular property effectively prevents the owner from selling or refinancing the property without either paying the bill or establishing in court that the lien is invalid. Mechanics' liens can also be foreclosed.

When construction is performed for an individual owner on his or her condominium unit or planned development lot, the owner's contractors and construction materials suppliers can record mechanics' liens against that owner's unit or lot, but cannot record mechanics' liens against the common area or against any other owner's unit or lot. An owner who learns that a mechanics' lien has been recorded against his or her unit or lot should consult an attorney. See Civil Code § 4615.

When construction is performed for the association on the common area, the association's contractors and construction materials suppliers can record mechanics' liens against the common area and every unit or lot. An owner may remove his or her condominium from a lien recorded by the association contractors or material suppliers by payment of the fraction of the total sum secured by the lien that is attributable to that owner's property.

V. ASSOCIATION GOVERNANCE

A. ASSOCIATION EXISTENCE AND POWERS

The law requires a common interest development to be managed by an association that may be incorporated or unincorporated. Unincorporated associations enjoy powers virtually identical to those granted to a incorporated association under the California Corporations Code. The association may be referred to as a "homeowners' association," an "owners' association" or a "community association." These terms are synonymous.

1. Distribution of Power and Authority

In general, the distribution of power and authority within an association is determined by the governing documents, but the law contains some restrictions on how the governing documents can distribute this power. The law presumes that most association power and authority will be exercised by a board of directors with the direct involvement of the members in only limited scenarios.

2. Differences Between Directors and Officers

The main difference between officers and directors in both incorporated and unincorporated associations is how they are selected and the nature of their responsibilities. Directors are elected by the membership and are generally responsible for decisions on major issues affecting the association, such as whether to conduct an inspection of the development for latent construction defects, whether to initiate a law suit against the developer for construction defects, adopting a budget and determining yearly regular assessments, and determining the amount that should be maintained in the reserve funds. Officers are appointed by the board of directors and are generally delegated specific responsibilities in the bylaws for association management. For example, the secretary in an association is generally responsible for taking and keeping board minutes. Where an association contracts with a professional manager to run its day-to-day operations, the manager will usually perform some or all of the duties that officers would perform in an association without a professional manager. Officers chosen by the board may be replaced by the board at any time and for any reason by a majority vote of non-interested directors. See Corp. Code § 7213(b).

3. Committees

Most governing documents authorize the formation of one or more specific committees, but the board has the authority to create committees even if that power is not specifically mentioned in the governing documents. The board has complete control over all committees, officers and managers. This means that the board decides who will serve in these capacities, and what authority they will have, subject only to restrictions in the governing documents. Unless a committee is comprised solely of directors, a committee may only be advisory. See Corp. Code §§ 7210 – 7214.

4. Compensation of Directors and Officers

While it is legal to pay directors and officers for their service unless prohibited by the governing documents, doing so can prevent a director or officer from benefiting from certain immunities and protections afforded to volunteer directors and officers. Under the law, volunteer directors and officers of properly insured associations face no personal liability for their decisions absent intentional fraud or self-dealing. Paid directors and officers can face personal liability for bad judgment and unintentional mistakes. See Civil Code § 5800.

B. NOTICE AND DELIVERY

1. Delivery of Documents to the Association

Communications may be delivered to the association via U.S. Mail sent to the attention of the person authorized to receive communications on behalf of the association and identified in the annual policy statement. If no person has been identified to receive communications to the association, then delivery should be to the president or secretary of the association. "Delivery" may also be made by one of the following methods ***only if*** the association has consented to receiving communications by that method:

(1) By email, facsimile or other electronic means.

(2) By "personal delivery" or hand delivery. If the association accepts a document by personal delivery, it must provide a written receipt acknowledging it has been received. See Civil Code § 4035

2. Delivery of Documents to Members

Communications to members must be delivered by either "individual delivery/individual notice," or "general delivery/general notice." A document that is required by the Davis-Stirling Act to be provided by individual delivery or individual notice may be delivered by one of the following methods:

(1) By first class-mail, postage prepaid, registered or certified mail, express mail, or overnight delivery by an express service carrier; or

(2) By email, facsimile, or other electronic means, only if the member has consented to receiving communications by that method of delivery.

A document that is required by the Davis-Stirling Act to be provided by general delivery or general notice may be made in one or more of the following ways:

(1) By any method provided for delivery of an "individual delivery" or "individual notice" discussed above.

(2) By inclusion in a billing statement, newsletter or other document delivered to the general membership.

(3) By posting the printed document in a prominent location accessible to all members, if the posting location has been announced in the annual policy statement.

(4) By inclusion in the association's broadcast television programming established for the purpose of distributing information to the members.

(5) By posting on an association internet website that is maintained for the purpose of distributing information to the members, so long as it is posted in a prominent location that is accessible to all members and the location was designated in the association's annual policy statement as a location where the association provides general notices.

Of note, a member may request to receive all general notices by individual delivery. See Civil Code § 4045.

3. Time of Delivery

If a document or notice is delivered by mail, delivery is complete on deposit into the United States mail. If the document or notice is delivered by electronic means, delivery is complete at the time of transmission. See Civil Code § 4050.

4. Electronic Delivery

If an association or member has consented to the receipt of written documents or notice by electronic means, the document or notice transmitted must be maintained in an electronic format capable of retention and printing by the recipient. See Civil Code § 4055.

C. BOARD MEETINGS

1. Authority to Convene and Frequency of Board Meetings

In general, the governing documents will prescribe the frequency of regular board meetings, but will allow the board to establish the exact time and place of each meeting. The governing documents usually also provide that the time and place of a regular meeting can be changed, or a special meeting can be scheduled, by the chairman of the board (if any), the president, or a specified number of directors.

2. Definition of Board Meetings

A board meeting is defined as any "congregation, at the same time and place, of a sufficient number of directors to establish a quorum of the board, to hear, discuss, or deliberate upon any item of business that is within the authority of the board." See Civil Code § 4090(a).

The board may not take action on any association business outside of a meeting. Board meetings may not be conducted via email except in emergency situations, and only if all directors agree in writing and those written consents are filed with the minutes of the meeting. The written consents may be transmitted electronically. See Civil Code § 4910.

3. Board Meetings by Audio or Video Teleconferencing

A board meeting may be held by audio or audiovisual teleconference as long as a quorum of the board is present and the attending board members are able to speak and hear one another, and all members in attendance may hear all deliberations. Except in case of declared emergencies (by a federal, state or local government) that follow the specific requirements of Civil Code § 5450, notice of a teleconference board meeting must identify at least one physical location where members can attend and participate in the meeting and at least one director or person designated by the board must be present at that location. See Civil Code § 4090(b).

For emergency situations, a physical meeting location is not required, however, in addition to the federal, state or local emergency declaration, before an association can hold a meeting entirely by teleconference (or other digital means) the association must provide individual notice to its members that the meeting is being held by teleconference, clear technical instruction on how to participate by teleconference, the phone number and email address for a person who can provide technical assistance, and a reminder that the member may request individual delivery of meeting notices. See Civil Code § 5450.

4. Notice Requirements for Regular Board Meetings

Except in case of an emergency meeting or executive session meeting, notice of the time and place of a regular board meeting must be provided to the members at least four days before the meeting, although the governing documents may require a longer notice period in which case the longer period must be observed. See Civil Code §§ 4045 and 4920.

5. Notice Requirements for Executive Session Board Meetings

If the entire meeting will be an executive session, members may not attend but are still entitled to notice of the time and place of the meeting at least two days before the meeting. Notice may be given by the same method as for a regular board meeting. See Civil Code § 4920(b)(2).

6. Notice Required for Emergency Board Meetings

The president or any two board members are permitted to call an emergency meeting without notice to the members when all of the following occur: (1) immediate attention and possible action is required; (2) the circumstances of the emergency could not have been reasonably foreseen; (3) it is impracticable to provide member notice; and (4) all directors sign a written consent if the meeting is conducted by a series of emails or other electronic transmissions. Minutes of an emergency meeting must be prepared and distributed in the same manner as minutes of regular board meetings. See Civil Code § 4923, and Corp. Code § 7211.

7. Member Attendance and Participation at Board Meetings

Members are entitled to attend all board meetings except meetings held in executive session, including meetings held by audio or audiovisual teleconference. Members must be provided an opportunity to speak at all board meetings except executive sessions, but the board may establish a reasonable time limit for member comment. Members are not entitled to participate in board deliberations. See Civil Code § 4925.

8. Standard for Board Decisions: Business Judgment Rule

The standard to which a board is held regarding discretionary management decisions is called the "business judgment rule." Under this standard, each director and the board as a whole must act in good faith and in a manner the director believes to be in the best interests of the association. Further, each director must act with the care that an ordinarily prudent person in a similar position would exercise under similar circumstances. The business judgment rule also permits boards to rely on the opinions, reports, statements and financial data provided by: (1) officers and employees of the association whom the board reasonably believes to be competent; (2) legal counsel, independent accountants and other persons as to matters which the board believes to be within such person's professional competence; and (3) a committee of the board as to matters within its designated authority, provided that the board reasonably believes the committee merits confidence. See Corp. Code § 7231.

9. Executive Session Board Meetings

A board is permitted to meet in executive session in only certain scenarios: (1) to consider litigation, (2) review contracts with third parties, (3) member discipline, (4) personnel matters, (5) to meet with counsel, (6) to meet with a member to discuss delinquent assessments at the member's request, and (7) to decide whether to foreclose on an assessment lien. Any matter discussed in executive session must be generally noted in the minutes of the next board meeting open to the members. The board must meet with a member in executive session, if requested by that member, to discuss a fine, penalty or other form of discipline. See Civil Code § 4935.

10. Board Meeting Minutes

The law requires that the association maintain minutes of all director meetings except executive sessions and that the minutes be prepared (at least in draft or summary form) within 30 days of the meeting. The association must provide copies of minutes to any member upon request and upon reimbursement of the association's cost in making the distribution. Executive session minutes, if kept, should remain confidential from all members other than board members. The governing documents usually state that the secretary is responsible for preparing the minutes, but this is frequently delegated to a property manager. See Civil Code § 4950 and Corp. Code § 8320.

The annual policy statement must inform the members of their right to obtain copies of board meeting minutes and how to do so. See Civil Code § 5310(a)(5).

11. Delegated Action Without Meeting

The activities and affairs of the association must be conducted and all powers must be exercised by or under the direction of the board. However, board action is not required for all association activities. The board may delegate the management of day-to-day activities to any person, including an officer, director, committee, or property manager, so long as all association powers are exercised at the ultimate direction of the board. The board is intended to be the policy-making body pursuant to whose overall supervision and control those who actually carry on the daily operations of the association act. See Corp. Code § 7210.

D. MEMBER MEETINGS

1. Regular and Special Member Meetings

A regular member meeting is one held on a regular schedule as prescribed in the governing documents. Most governing documents require one regular meeting (the "annual meeting") each year. A special member meeting is one that is not required by the governing documents, but rather has been convened for a special purpose. A special member meeting can be convened by the board, the chairman of the board (if any), the president, or by valid petition submitted by least 5% of the members. See Corp. Code § 7510.

2. Notice Requirements for Member Meetings

Both regular and special member meetings require a written notice to all members. The notice must include the place, time and date of the meeting, an agenda of the matters to be discussed. The notice must be by "individual delivery." Posting the notice in the common area is not sufficient for member meetings. If the notice is mailed by first class registered or certified mail, or if it is hand delivered, it must be given between 10 and 90 days before the meeting; if it is delivered by any method other than "individual delivery," it must be given between 20 and 90 days before the meeting. Notice is not required when the meeting is actually the continuation of another meeting that was adjourned within the previous 45 days as long as the time and place of the continuation meeting had been announced at the original meeting.

When a group of members, acting independently from the board, wishes to convene a special meeting, they must submit a valid petition signed by at least 5% of the membership to the board. The board must then notify all of the members of the meeting between 35 and 90 days of the request. The date of the special meeting is set by the board. See Corp. Code § 7511.

3. Quorum Requirement for Member Meetings

The governing documents generally specify the minimum amount of member voting power (the "quorum") that must be present for decisions to be made at a member meeting. The law does not specify a minimum or maximum quorum requirement, but does provide that if the governing documents permit decisions by a quorum of less than one-third of the total voting power and a quorum of less than one-third of the voting power is present at a member's meeting, the only matters that can be voted on are those mentioned in the meeting notice. The law also provides that if the governing documents fail to specify a quorum requirement, it will automatically be set at one-third of the voting power. See Corp. Code § 7512.

4. Proxy Voting

A member who cannot attend a member meeting but who wishes to vote on a matter has two choices. The member may use a mail-in ballot or give another member a proxy authorizing that member to vote on his or her behalf at the meeting. The use of proxies is of diminished importance with the application of the double-envelope secret ballot process required for certain membership votes, commencing in July 2006.

5. Member Meeting Minutes

The law requires that the association prepare and maintain minutes of all member meetings, and that these minutes be made available to members for inspection on written demand at any reasonable time for any reasonable purpose. The governing documents usually provide that the secretary is to prepare the minutes within a prescribed number of days following the meeting. See Corp. Code §§ 8320 and 8333.

E. MEMBER ELECTIONS

1. Secret Ballot Elections

The law requires that the double-envelope secret ballot process be used for the following types of membership votes: (1) the election and removal of directors; (2) the levy of a special assessment in excess of 5% of the association's budgeted gross expenses for the fiscal year or a greater than 20% increase of the annual assessment; (3) amendment of governing documents; (4) grants of exclusive use common area; and (5) any other matter expressly requiring a secret ballot election in the governing documents. See Civil Code § 5100.

Except for the meeting to count the votes, secret ballot elections may be conducted entirely by mail unless otherwise required by the governing documents.

2. Election Rules

Associations are required to adopt election operating rules pursuant to the requirements of Civil Code § 5105. Election operating rules shall not be amended less than 90 days before an election. The election operating rules shall provide for the following:

(1) Ensure that all candidates are provided equal access to association media, newsletters and that association's and other internet websites for campaign purposes, regardless of whether the candidate is supported or opposed by the board.

(2) Ensure that all candidates are provided equal access to association common area meeting space for campaign purposes at no cost to the candidate.

(3) Specify qualifications and nomination procedures for candidates for all elected positions.

(4) Specify voting rights, proxy rights and voting periods.

(5) Specify the method of selecting one or three inspectors of elections.

(6) Specify whether the inspector(s) of elections is appointed by the board, elected by the members, or selected by some other method.

(7) Allow the inspector(s) of elections to oversee the tabulation and verification of votes.

(8) Require retention of association election materials.

(9) Prohibit the denial of a ballot to a member for any reason other than not being a member at the time when ballots are distributed.

(10) Prohibit the denial of a ballot to a person with general power of attorney for a member.

(11) Require the ballot of a person with general power of attorney for a member to be counted if returned in a timely manner.

(12) Require the inspector of elections to deliver the balloting materials at least 30 days before an election to each member. See Civil Code § 5105.

3. Inspector of Elections

An association must select one or three inspector(s) of elections, and they must be an "independent third party." For the purposes of this requirement, an "independent third party" is any responsible adult, including a member of the association who is not a candidate or related to a candidate for the board, and who is not a board member or not related to a board member. An inspector may not be someone employed by or under contract with the association, unless a person in that capacity solely serves as an inspector of elections.

The duties of the inspector(s) are all of the following:

(1) Determine those entitled to vote and their voting power.

(2) Determine the authenticity, validity and effect of proxies.

(3) Receive ballots.

(4) Hear and determine challenges.

(5) Count and tabulate the votes.

(6) Determine when the polls close.

(7) Determine the election results.

(8) Perform all acts necessary for proper and fair conduct of the election.

An inspector must perform his or her duties impartially, in good faith, to the best of his or her ability and expeditiously as is practical, and in a manner that protects the interest of all members of the association. If there are three inspectors of elections, a decision by at least two of the three controls. See Civil Code § 5110.

4. Ballot Instructions

Association shall provide general notice of the procedure and deadline for submitting nominations at least 30 days before any deadline for submitting a nomination. For elections of directors (including recalls) at least 30 days before ballots are distributed (i.e., 60-days before the vote tabulation), associations must also provide general notice of the date, time and physical address where ballots are to be returned; the date time and location of the meeting at which the ballots will be counted; and a list of all candidates' names that will appear on the ballot. See Civil Code § 5115. This 60-day notice is not required for other elections such as amendments, assessments, and grants of exclusive use of the common area.

Secret ballot elections must be held as follows: ballots and two envelopes with instructions on how to return ballots must be mailed by first-class mail or delivered to every member not less than 30 days before the voting deadline. Voters may not be identified by name, address, or lot, parcel, or unit number on the ballot. The ballot itself is not signed by the voter, but is inserted into an inner-envelope that is sealed. The inner envelope is inserted into a second pre-addressed envelope that is sealed. In the upper left hand corner of the second envelope, the voter prints and signs his or her name, address, and lot, parcel, or unit number that entitles him or her to vote. The second envelope is addressed to the address designated by the inspector(s) of elections, and may be mailed or hand delivered. The member may request a receipt upon hand delivery.

Each ballot received by the inspector(s) is treated as a voter present at a member meeting for the purposes of establishing a quorum. See Civil Code § 5115.

5. Tabulation of Ballots

All votes must be counted by or under the supervision of the inspector(s) in an open meeting of the board or members. Any member may witness the counting of ballots. No one, including the property manager, may open a secret ballot before the meeting at which all of the ballots are opened and counted. The results must be promptly reported to the board, recorded in the minutes of the next board meeting and available for review by the members. Within 15 days of the election, the board must notify all members of the election results. The ballots, signed voter envelopes, voter list, proxies, and candidate registration list must remain in the custody of the inspector(s) or at a location designated by the inspector(s) until they are counted and then safely stored for no less than one year, at which time custody should be transferred to the association and be handled under the association's standard record retention policy. See Civil Code §§ 5120 and 5125.

6. Prohibition Against Using Association Funds for Campaign Purposes

The law prohibits the use of association funds for campaign purposes in the election of directors. For additional information, see Civil Code § 5135.

F. ELECTION AND REMOVAL OF DIRECTORS

1. Director Requirements and Qualifications

An association shall disqualify a person from a nomination as a candidate for not being a member of the association at the time of the nomination, subject to certain exceptions. See subsection (b) of Civil Code § 5105. The governing documents can also require that directors have certain qualifications so long as the qualifications are reasonable and that members are allowed to nominate themselves as candidates for the board. Some governing documents require directors be residents as well as members, or that a director be a member in good standing. Additional qualification criteria that associations commonly use are listed in Civil Code § 5105.

2. Length of Director Terms and Staggered or Concurrent Terms

The length of the directors' terms is usually specified in the governing documents. By law, however, directors' terms may not exceed four years. If the governing documents do not specify term length, the law provides that it will be one year. It is not necessary for all directors to have terms of the same length, or for all directors' terms to expire in the same year. Frequently, the governing documents provide for staggered terms, so that fewer than all of the board seats are open to election at one time providing continuity in transition. See Corp. Code § 7220.

3. Removal of Directors Before Expiration of Term

Members may vote to recall a director by submitting a valid petition signed by at least 5% of the membership. See Corp. Code § 7510(e).

A director may also be removed by the other directors, but only in narrow circumstances when there is cause for removal, such as mental incapacity and felony conviction, or for failing to attend a specified number of board meetings, if at the time the director was elected, the bylaws provided that a director may be removed on that basis. See Corp. Code § 7221(a).

4. Director Vacancies

The method of selecting a director to fill a vacancy following a resignation or removal is usually prescribed in the governing documents. If the governing documents are silent on the issue, a vacancy created by resignation is filled by a board vote, and a vacancy created by removal is filled by owner vote (regardless of whether the removal was executed by the owners or by the board). See Corp. Code § 7224.

G. RECORD INSPECTION

1. Association Records

"Association records" are defined as all of the following:

(1) Any financial documents required by statute to be provided to a member on an annual basis (see Civil Code §§ 5300 et seq., 5565 and 5810).

(2) Any financial documents required to be provided as part of a transfer disclosure (see Civil Code §§ 4525).

(3) Interim financial statements (balance sheet, income and expense statement, budget comparison, general ledger).

(4) Executed contracts (except privileged contracts).

(5) Written board approvals of vendor or contractor proposals or invoices.

(6) Federal and state income tax returns.

(7) Reserve account statements and records.

(8) Agendas and minutes of board, member and committee meetings (excluding executive session meetings).

(9) Membership lists, including name, property address and mailing address.

(10) Check registers.

(11) The governing documents.

(12) Accounting of funds borrowed from reserves for litigation.

(13) Enhanced association records.

(14) Association election materials.

See Civil Code §5200(a)

2. Enhanced Association Records

"Enhanced association records" are defined as all of the following:

(1) Invoices, receipts and canceled checks of the association.

(2) Approved purchase orders.

(3) Credit card statements for accounts held in the association's name.

(4) Statements for services rendered.

(5) Reimbursement requests submitted to the association.
See Civil Code § 5200(b)

3. Inspection Rights

Members, or their designated representatives, have the right to inspect and copy "association records" and "enhanced association records." The requested records must be made available at the association's onsite business office or, if there is no such office, at a place where the member and association agree. If the member and association cannot agree on such a place, the association can satisfy the request by delivering copies to the member by "individual delivery." If the member submits a request for specifically identified records, the association can also satisfy the request by delivering copies to the member by "individual delivery."

The association must make association records and enhanced association records available for inspection and copying but it is not required to copy documents at a member's request. The member may retain his or her own copy service to perform the task. If the association chooses to copy documents at a member's request, it may charge the member for the actual copying cost provided the member has agreed to pay the cost in advance. The association may also charge the member for personnel time actually spent in redacting the records at the rate of $10 per hour, not to exceed $200 per request, provided the member has agreed to pay the cost in advance.

The member may request that specifically identified records be delivered by electronic transmission or machine-readable storage media so long as the records can be transmitted in a redactable, read-only format, such as a PDF. If this method of delivery is chosen, the association may charge the member only the direct cost of producing a copy of the record in an electronic format. See Civil Code § 5205.

4. Time Periods for Record Production

Association records for the current fiscal year must be made available within 10 business days of a request. Association records for the previous two fiscal years must be made available within 30 calendar days of a request. See Civil Code § 5210.

Minutes of board and member meetings must be maintained permanently and made available within 30 days of a request. Minutes of committees with decision making authority must be maintained permanently and made available within 15 days following approval, but only for committee meetings held after January 1, 2007. See Civil Code § 5210.

Membership lists must be made available within 5 business days of a request. See Civil Code § 5210 and Corp. Code § 8330.

5. Withholding or Redacting Information

The association may withhold or redact information that is likely to lead to identity theft or fraud, is likely to compromise the privacy of another owner, is privileged under law or is otherwise protected by statute. Examples of protected information are personal identification information (i.e., social security numbers, tax identification numbers, driver's license numbers, credit card numbers, bank account numbers, etc.), personal disciplinary records, personal delinquent assessment records, executive session records, personnel records and interior architectural and security system plans. But the association may not withhold information pertaining to compensation paid to employees, contractors or vendors. The association must provide a written explanation for withholding information if requested by a member and the association bears the burden of demonstrating in court that withholding was justified. A member is prohibited from making commercial or any other use of association records that does not pertain to the owner's interest as an owner.

6. Access to Membership Lists

The association must maintain a membership list which contains members' names, property address, mailing address (if different than the property address), and email addresses (if the member provided to the association per Civil Code § 4041. If an owner has opted out of having their contact information included in the membership list pursuant to Civil Code § 5220, the association needs to provide an alternative way to communicate with those owners who opt out of the membership list. The list need not include members' telephone numbers, fax numbers, or other contact information. Members must be notified of the name and address (and, if desired, also the email address) of the person designated to receive the association's official communications, including a request for a membership list, as part of the annual policy statement, and a copy of the list must be provided to owners upon receipt of a proper request. A member who desires to opt out of sharing his or her contact information (name, property address, mailing address, and/or email address) on the membership list must notify the association in writing of his or her desire and specify that he or she prefers to be contacted by the association's alternative process. Civil Code § 5220 and Corp. Code § 8330.

A member requesting a membership list must state the purpose of the request and it must be reasonably related to the member's interest in the association. It is misuse for a member to sell a membership list, use it for commercial purposes, or use it for any other purpose unrelated to the member's interest in the association. If the association believes the member will improperly use the list, it may deny access to the list but if there is a legal challenge the association will have the burden of proving the member used or intended to use the list for an improper purpose. See Civil Code § 5225.

H. ANNUAL DISCLOSURES

The law imposes strict record keeping and reporting requirements on associations, and the governing documents often impose even more stringent requirements. Some of the records and reports must be distributed to the owners automatically on a prescribed schedule, and the remainder must be available to owners upon request. The following is a summary of the minimum requirements imposed by law, organized by general category.

1. Annual Budget Report

The association must prepare and distribute to its members an annual budget report each year 30 to 90 days before the end of its fiscal year. Unless the governing documents impose additional requirements, the annual budget report shall include all of the following:

(1) A pro forma operating budget, showing the estimated revenue and expenses on an accrual basis.

(2) A summary of the association's reserves prepared in the form specified by statute.

(3) A summary of the reserve funding plan prepared in the form specified by statute and a notice to members that the full reserve study plan is available upon request.

(4) A statement whether the board has decided to defer repairs of any major component included in the reserve study and the justification for the deferral.

(5) A statement whether the board has determined or anticipates the levy of one or more special assessments will be necessary to meet reserve requirements and, if so, the estimated amount of such assessments, due date(s) and duration.

(6) A statement as to the mechanism(s) the board will use to fund reserves, including assessments, borrowing, use of other assets, or deferral of repairs.

(7) A general statement about the procedures used to calculate and establish reserves in the form specified by statute.

(8) A statement as to whether the association has any outstanding loans with an original term of more than one year, including the payee, interest rate, outstanding balance, annual payment, and when the loan matures.

(9) A summary of the association's insurance policies with particular details and language specified by statute.

(10) If the development is a condominium project, a statement regarding its status as a Federal Housing Administration (FHA)-approved condominium project, with particular details and language specified by statute.

(11) If the development is a condominium project, a statement regarding its status as a federal Department of Veterans Affairs (VA)-approved condominium project, with particular details and language specified by statute.

(12) A copy of the completed "Charges For Documents Provided" identified in Civil Code § 4528.

See Civil Code § 5300.

2. Annual Policy Statement

The association must prepare and distribute to its members an annual policy statement each year 30 to 90 days before the end of its fiscal year. The annual policy statement shall include all of the following:

(1) The name and address of the person designated to receive official communications to the association.

(2) A statement explaining that a member may have notices addressed to two different addresses.

(3) The location designated for posting a "general notice," if one exists.

(4) Notice of a member's right to receive general notices by "individual delivery."

(5) Notice of a member's right to receive copies of meeting minutes.

(6) A statement of assessment collection policy in the language specified in Civil Code 5730.

(7) A statement describing the association's enforcement policies for collection of delinquent assessments.

(8) A statement describing the association's discipline policies, including its schedule of penalties.

(9) A summary of the association's dispute resolution procedures.

(10) A summary of any requirements for association approval of a physical change to the property.

(11) The mailing address for overnight payment of assessments.

(12) Any other documents the board decides appropriate for inclusion.

Both the annual budget report and policy statement must be delivered to the members by "individual delivery" and may be provided either in full or in summary with a disclosure that a member may obtain a copy of the full report by a written request to the association. See Civil Code §§ 5310, 5320 and 5730.

I. DIRECTOR CONFLICT OF INTEREST

The Davis-Stirling Act incorporates provisions of the Corporations Code regarding conflicts of interest, and imposes restrictions on transactions between an association and a director, and between an association and a committee member. Transactions between an association and a director or a committee member in which the member has a material financial interest, or between an association and an entity in which the member has a material financial interest, are valid if the transaction is approved or ratified in one of the following three ways:

(1) The material facts of the transaction and the member's interest are fully disclosed to the other members and the transaction is approved or ratified by a majority of a quorum of the membership in good faith and without the interested member's vote.

(2) The material facts of the transaction and the member's interest are fully disclosed to the board, the transaction is approved or ratified by the board, excluding the interested member's vote, and the transaction is just and reasonable to the association.

(3) The interested member asserting the validity of the transaction proves it was just and reasonable to the association at the time it was approved or ratified.

Additionally, a director or a committee member may not vote on any of the following matters in which he or she has an interest in the outcome:

(1) A decision whether to discipline the interested member.

(2) A decision whether to levy an assessment on the interested member for damage to the common area or association property.

(3) A decision whether to approve a delinquent assessment payment plan for the interested member.

(4) A decision whether to foreclose a lien against the interested member's property.

(5) A decision whether to approve a physical change in the separate interest of the interested member.

(6) A decision whether to grant exclusive use of common area to the interested member. See Civil Code § 5350.

J. MANAGING AGENT

1. Definition

A managing agent is a person or entity, such as a property management company, who for compensation or the expectation of compensation, exercises control over the assets of an association. However, the term "managing agent" does not include any full-time employee of the association, an attorney acting within the scope of the attorney's license, or any regulated financial institution operating within the normal course of its regulated business practice. See Civil Code §§ 4158 and 5385, and Bus. & Prof. Code §§ 11500 et seq.

2. Services Typically Provided by Professional Managers

Professional managers offer a wide variety of services to associations including accounting, budgeting, record keeping, assessment collection, bill payment, meeting coordination, and facilitation of common area maintenance. Associations choose from among the services available, and enter into a contract with the manager describing the scope of work. The management contract should also include the fee, the duration of the arrangement, and the circumstances under which the arrangement can be terminated before the contract expires. Some governing documents limit the duration of management agreements or require specific early termination provisions.

While the law allows many association functions to be delegated to a professional manager, certain association functions cannot be delegated. Non-delegable functions typically include borrowing money, levying assessments, making capital expenditures in excess of budgeted amounts, and imposing discipline for violation of the governing documents. See Corp. Code § 7210.

3. Disclosure Requirements

Association managers are not required to be licensed, but they must provide extensive written disclosures to the board of directors within 90 days before entering into a management agreement with the homeowners' association. The disclosures must include a written statement containing all of the following:

(1) The names and addresses of the owner(s) of the managing agent. If the managing agent is a corporation, the names and business addresses of the directors, officers and shareholders holding more than 10% of the shares.

(2) A list of all relevant licenses (e.g., real estate, accounting, engineering, construction, architectural, etc.) issued by the State of California and currently in effect and held by the owner(s) of the managing agent. As to each license, the dates the license is valid and the name of the licensee is also required.

(3) A list of all relevant professional certifications (e.g., professional common interest development manager, real estate, accounting, engineering, construction, architectural, etc.) held by the owner(s) of the managing agent. As to each professional certification, the name of the issuing entity, the nature of the certification, the dates the certification is valid and the name of the certificate recipient.

(4) Disclosure of any business or company in which the association manager has any ownership interests, profit-sharing arrangements, or other monetary incentives.

(5) Referral fees or other monetary benefits the association manager receives from third-party providers distributing documents pursuant to Civil Code §§ 4528 and 4530.

See Civil Code § 5375.

In addition, any prospective association manager must disclose in writing any potential conflict of interest when presenting a bid for service to an association's board. See Civil Code § 5375.5.

4. Restrictions on Manager's Handling of Funds

The law imposes stringent requirements on managers that handle association funds to prevent commingling and fraud. In general, a managing agent must deposit funds received on behalf of an association into an association account or into a trust account maintained by the managing agent in a bank, saving association or credit union in California insured by the federal government. See Civil Code § 5380.

K. INFORMATION STATEMENT FILED WITH SECRETARY OF STATE

An incorporated association must file with the California Secretary of State a "Statement of Information" on Form SI-100 at the time it files its articles of incorporation and every two years thereafter. The statement must include the following: (1) the name of the non-profit corporation; (2) the business address of the association or the front street and nearest cross street of the physical location of the property; and (3) the name and address of the association's officers and agent for service of process.

Every other year thereafter, an association, whether incorporated or unincorporated, must file with the California Secretary of State a "Statement by Common Interest Development Association" on Form SI-CID which contains the following information: (1) a statement that the association was formed to manage a common interest development under the Davis-Stirling Act; (2) the name of the association; (3) the street address of the association; (4) the name and address of the association's business office or responsible officer or managing agent; (5) the name, address, and daytime telephone number or e-mail address of the president of the association; (6) the name, street address, and daytime telephone number of the managing agent; (7) the name of each city and county in which the development is physically located; (8) if in an unincorporated area, the city in closest proximity to the development; (9) the front street and nearest cross street of the physical location of the development; (10) the type of common interest development (i.e., condominium, planned development, stock cooperative, etc.); and (11) the number of separate interests (i.e., units, lots, cooperative apartments, etc.). In addition, an association must notify the Secretary of State of any change in the street address of the association's office or managing agent within 60 days of the change. All but the information regarding the contact information for the president of an association is available for public inspection. Both Form SI-100 and Form SI-CID are available online at the Secretary of State's website at https://www.sos.ca.gov/business-programs/business-entities/forms/.

Failure to file by a corporate association will result in the suspension of the association's rights, privileges, and powers as a corporation, and monetary penalties, until the required statement is filed. It is unclear what penalties attach when an unincorporated association fails to file. See Civil Code § 5405.

VI. FINANCES

A. ACCOUNTING – PERIODIC BOARD REVIEW

Unless the governing documents impose more stringent requirements, the board must review the following on at least a monthly basis:

(1) A current reconciliation of the association's operating accounts.

(2) A current reconciliation of the association's reserve accounts.

(3) The current year's actual operating revenue and expenses compared to the current year's budget.

(4) The latest account statements of the financial institutions where the association has its operating and reserve accounts.

(5) An income and expense statement for the association operating and reserve accounts.

(6) The check register, monthly general ledger, and delinquent assessment receivable reports.

See Civil Code § 5500.

B. RESERVE FUNDS

1. Definition of Reserve Funds

Reserve funds are assessments the association has collected to defray the expense of ongoing maintenance and replacement of major components the association is required to maintain. Reserve funds are also funds received from a compensatory damage award or settlement for construction defects, and must be separately itemized from the reserve funds described in the prior sentence.

2. Handling and Withdrawal of Reserve Funds

An association must set up a reserve account separate from its operating account in which to deposit reserve funds collected through assessments.

The law requires the signatures of at least two directors, or of one officer and one director, for withdrawals from the association reserve account(s). See Civil Code § 5510(a).

C. USE OF RESERVE FUNDS

1. Use of Reserve Funds for Reserve Expenses

Reserve funds cannot be spent for any purpose other than the maintenance and replacement of components for which the association is responsible. Reserve funds set aside for a particular line item in a reserve study need not be restricted to expenditures on that line item alone, but rather the aggregate of all reserve funds may be used for the aggregate of all reserve expenses without reference to a particular component. If major components not in the reserve study are in need of repair or replacement, the reserve study should be updated to include those components with an adjustment to the funding plan. See Civil Code § 5510(b).

2. Use of Reserve Funds for Operating Expenses

The board may authorize the temporary transfer of reserve funds to the operating account to meet short-term cash-flow requirements or other expenses – a liberal exception. However, before the board may transfer reserve funds, it must fulfill certain procedural requirements. It must notify the owners of the intent to consider a transfer at an open meeting of the board, and must identify the reasons for the transfer, the options for repayment, and whether a special assessment may be considered. If the board authorizes the transfer at an open meeting, it must prepare written findings, included in the minutes, explaining the reasons for the transfer, and describing when and how the funds will be repaid to the reserve account. See Civil Code § 5515.

Funds transferred from the reserve account must be restored to the reserve account within one year of the date of the initial transfer with one more liberal exception. The board may delay repayment upon making a written finding that temporary delay would be in the best interest of the association. A decision to delay repayment must also be made at an open meeting of the board. See Civil Code § 5515.

3. Use of Reserve Funds for Litigation Purposes

When reserve funds are transferred for litigation purposes, the association must notify the owners of that decision and the availability of an accounting in the next mailing to the owners. The association is then required to make an accounting of expenses related to litigation available to the owners on at least a quarterly basis. The accounting need not be sent to all owners, but must be available upon request by owners at the association's office. See Civil Code § 5520.

D. RESERVE PLANNING

1. Preparation of Reserve Study

An association is required to prepare a reserve study at least once every three years based on a diligent visual inspection of the accessible areas of components for which the Association is responsible to maintain, repair and replace. Components with an estimated service life of less than 30 years are included in the reserve study. See Civil Code § 5550.

A reserve study at a minimum must include: (1) an identification of the major components with a remaining service life of 30 years or less; (2) a determination of the remaining service life of those major components; (3) the cost of maintaining or replacing those major components over the next 30 years; (4) an estimate of the annual contribution necessary to meet the cost of maintaining or replacing those major components over the next 30 years; and (5) a reserve funding plan that indicates how the association plans to fund the reserves. See Civil Code § 5550. The board is required to review the reserve study annually and determine whether intervening events over the past year warrant adjustment of the reserve funding.

Associations must also incorporate into the reserve study any written reports regarding exterior elevated elements (such as balconies and decks) prepared pursuant to Civil Code § 5551.

2. Summary of Association Reserves

The law requires an association to prepare a summary of association reserves for distribution with the annual budget report. It must be based on the most recent reserve study or interim review and take into account only assets held in cash or cash equivalents. The summary must be printed in boldface type and contain all of the following:

(1) The current estimated replacement cost, remaining life and the useful life of each major component.

(2) As of the end of the fiscal year for which the study or review is prepared: (i) the estimated cash reserves necessary for the association's maintenance and repair obligations; (ii) the amount of accumulated cash reserves; (iii) the amount of funds received from a damage award or settlement for construction defects; and (iv) the expenditures for repair of such defects reported as a separate line item under cash reserves.

(3) The percentage that the accumulated cash reserves bears to the current estimate of cash reserves necessary to meet the association's maintenance and repair obligations of major components.

(4) The current deficiency in reserve funding expressed on a per unit basis, except that if assessments vary by size or type of ownership interest, the deficiency must be calculated in a manner that reflects the variation.

See Civil Code § 5565.

3. Assessment and Reserve Funding Disclosure

Commencing January 1, 2009, an assessment and reserve funding disclosure summary must be provided to the members with the annual budget report and must include a notice that the full reserve funding study plan is available upon request of a member.

Reserve funding disclosures are now in a form prescribed by statute. Civil Code § 5570 sets forth the statutory form which includes all of the following:

(1) Current assessments per unit/lot.

(2) Additional assessments that have been scheduled to be imposed.

(3) Whether current reserve balances will be sufficient to meet the requirements of the current funding goals.

(4) If not, what is the plan to meet the requirements of the current funding goals.

(5) Identification of the major components included in the existing reserve study but not included in the reserve funding program.

(6) The current balance of reserve funds in cash or cash equivalent on deposit.

VII. ASSESSMENTS AND ASSESSMENT COLLECTION

A. ESTABLISHMENT AND IMPOSITION OF ASSESSMENTS

1. Power to Levy Assessments

An association is required to levy regular and special assessments sufficient to perform its obligations under the governing documents. It may also impose usage and service fees, separate from regular or other types of assessments, as long as the amount of the fee does not exceed the amount necessary to defray the cost for which it is imposed. See Civil Code § 5600.

2. Budgeting: Definition, Creation and Review

As part of the annual budget report, association must maintain a pro forma operating budget showing the estimated revenue and expenses on an accrual basis. See Civil Code § 5300(b)(1).

3. Determination of Each Owner's Share of Assessments

The governing documents specify how assessments are allocated among the members. The allocation is established by the developer at the time the governing documents are prepared, and is reviewed for fairness by the California Department of Real Estate for projects consisting of five or more units or lots.

4. Regular and Special Assessments – Limitations

Regular assessments must be based upon the funding needs projected in the budget. Regardless of any restrictions in the governing documents, the board may increase regular assessments up to 20% greater than the previous fiscal year without the approval of the members, except in emergency situations. See Civil Code § 5605.

A special assessment is an assessment for an association expense that was under-budgeted or not budgeted. Regardless of the restrictions in the governing documents, a board may levy a special assessment of not more than 5% of the budgeted gross expenses for the current fiscal year without the approval of the members and a special assessment in excess of 5% of the budgeted gross expenses for the fiscal year must be approved by a majority of a quorum of the member. See Civil Code § 5605.

5. Emergency Assessments

Emergency assessments, either by an increase in regular assessments or the levy of a special assessment, may be imposed without prior member approval in the following three circumstances:

(1) An extraordinary expense which is required by a court order.

(2) An extraordinary expense necessary to repair or maintain the common interest development or any part of it for which the association is responsible where a threat to personal safety on the property is discovered.

(3) An extraordinary expense necessary to repair or maintain the common interest development or any part of it for which the association is responsible that could not have been reasonably foreseen by the board when it prepared and distributed the annual budget report, provided that the board passes a written resolution which contains findings as to the necessity of the expense and why it could not be reasonably foreseen and the notice is distributed to the members with the notice of assessment. See Civil Code § 5610.

6. Reimbursement Assessments

A reimbursement assessment is an assessment against only one member. The authority to levy a reimbursement assessment is prescribed in the governing documents. If permitted by the governing documents, an association may levy a reimbursement assessment against a member to reimburse the association for costs incurred repairing common area damage or correcting governing document violations caused by the member or his or her guests, or to reimburse the association for costs incurred collecting delinquent assessments. A reimbursement assessment may only be levied after providing the member with notice and a hearing, as required in the governing documents and Civil Code § 5855.

7. Notice of Assessment Increases

All members must be notified of an increase in regular assessments or the levy of a special assessment by "individual notice" between 30 and 60 days before the increase or the assessment is due. See Civil Code § 5615.

B. ASSESSMENT PAYMENT AND DELINQUENCY

1. Delinquent Assessments

An assessment becomes a debt of the member as of the date it is levied. An assessment is levied when a notice is sent to a member of the assessment's due date. Regular and special assessments become delinquent 15 days after the due date, unless the governing documents provide for a longer period. If an assessment is delinquent, the association may recover all of the following:

(1) Reasonable collection costs, including attorney fees.

(2) A late charge not exceeding 10% of the delinquent assessment or $10, whichever is greater, unless the CC&Rs specify a smaller amount.

(3) Interest on all of the above sums at an annual interest rate not to exceed 12% commencing 30 days after the assessment's due date. See Civil Code § 5650.

Any assessment payment must be applied first to the assessments owed until they are fully satisfied and then to collection costs, attorney fees, late charges and interest.

The association must have a written statement of its policies and practices for collecting delinquent assessments and must distribute it to all members as part of its annual policy statement. See Civil Code § 5310.

2. Disputed Charges

If a member disagrees with the amount of an assessment, he or she can challenge the assessment through a court action or internal dispute resolution. A member may, at his or her option, pay under protest any disputed charge or sum levied by the association, including an assessment, fine, penalty, late fee, collection cost, or monetary penalty, and by so doing, reserve the right to contest the disputed charge in court or otherwise. See Civil Code § 5658.

3. Notice of Intent to Lien

If a member is delinquent in paying assessments, the association can record a lien upon the member's unit or lot. Before a lien may be recorded, the association must first provide the member with a written notice sent by certified mail at least 30 days before recording the lien. The notice must contain the information required by statute, including all of the following:

(1) A general description of the association's collection and lien enforcement procedures and method of calculating the amount due.

(2) An itemized statement of the charges owed by the member, including delinquent assessments, late fees, collection costs, attorneys' fees, and interest.

(3) A statement that the member is not liable to pay the charges owed by the member, including delinquent assessments, late fees, collection costs, attorneys' fees, and interest, if it is determined the assessment was, in fact, paid on time.

(4) A statement that the member may request a meeting with the board regarding the delinquency if the member so requests.

(5) A statement that the member has the right to participate in non-binding internal dispute resolution ("meet and confer") or mediation with a neutral third party. See Civil Code § 5660.

4. Pre-Lien Payment Plan Option

A member may submit a written request to meet with the board and discuss a payment plan after receipt of a notice of intent to lien from the association. The board must meet with the member within 45 days of the postmark of the request, unless there is no regularly scheduled board meeting within that time, in which case the board may designate a committee of one or more directors to meet with the member. The board must provide the member with payment plan standards if they have been adopted. At no point is an association obligated to enter into a payment plant with a delinquent owner.

Payment plans may incorporate assessments that fall due during the payment plan period. Additional late fees do not accrue as long as the member is in compliance with the payment plan. The existence of a payment plan does not delay or otherwise restrict the association from recording an assessment lien. If the member falls out of compliance with a payment plan, the association may resume its collection efforts from the point that existed when the payment plan was commenced. See Civil Code § 5665.

5. Pre-Lien Dispute Resolution Option

Before recording an assessment lien, the association must offer the delinquent member the option of participating in dispute resolution under the association's internal dispute resolution or "meet and confer" program. See Civil Code § 5670 et seq.

6. Decision to Record an Assessment Lien

Only the board may decide to record an assessment lien and the decision must be made by a majority of directors at an open meeting and the vote must be recorded in the minutes of the meeting. See Civil Code § 5673.

7. Content of Notice of Delinquent Assessment

The Davis-Stirling Act uses the terminology "assessment lien" and "notice of delinquent assessment" synonymously but the proper title of the recorded document is "Notice of Delinquent Assessment." A notice of delinquent assessment is recorded in office of the county recorder in the county where the property is located and must contain all of the following:

(1) The amounts due for delinquent assessments, late fees, collection, attorneys' fees, and interest.

(2) A legal description of the member's lot or unit.

(3) The name of the record owner of the lot or unit.

(4) The itemized statement of charges sent to the member with the notice of intent to lien.

(5) If the lien is to be enforced by non-judicial foreclosure, the notice must state the name and address of the trustee authorized to enforce the lien by a sale of the property.

(6) The signature of the person designated in the CC&Rs for that purpose or, if no one is designated, the signature of the association president.

Once recorded and within 10 days of recording, a copy of the notice of delinquent assessment must be mailed by certified mail to each owner of the lot or unit shown on the association's records. See Civil Code § 5675.

8. Release of Lien

Within 21 days of payment of all amounts specified in a notice of delinquent assessment, the association must record a lien release indicating that the lien has been satisfied, and provide each owner of the subject property with a copy. If it is determined that a notice of delinquent assessment was improperly recorded, the association shall record a similar release, provide a copy to the owner(s), reverse all charges to the owner(s), and absorb all costs related to dispute resolution. See Civil Code § 5685.

9. Failure to Follow Lien Procedures

The failure to follow the statutory lien process will result in the association having to recommence the required notice process from the beginning. Any cost associated with recommencing the notice process must be borne by the association and not the delinquent member. See Civil Code § 5690.

10. Restrictions on Foreclosure

An association may not enforce an assessment delinquency by judicial foreclosure or non-judicial foreclosure unless the delinquent assessment amount (exclusive of accelerated assessments, interest and collection costs) exceeds $1,800 or the assessment secured by a lien is more than 12 months delinquent. If an association seeks to enforce an assessment delinquency that is less than $1,800, it may pursue an action in Small Claims Court for a debt of up to $5,000 or in Superior Court for any amount. An association may not pursue more than two actions in Small Claims Court per calendar year that seek to recover more than $2,500. See Civil Code § 5720 and Code of Civil Procedure §§ 116.220 and 116.231.

If the association secures a judgment in Small Claims Court or Superior Court, it may record an abstract of judgment that automatically results in a judgment lien against all real property of the judgment debtor in the county where the abstract is recorded. While the judgment lien will remain of record until it is satisfied, it cannot be foreclosed by judicial or non-judicial foreclosure until assessment delinquency (exclusive of accelerated assessments, interest and collection costs) exceeds $1,800 or the assessment secured by a lien is more than 12 months delinquent.

11. Right of Redemption

If a member's lot or unit is sold by non-judicial foreclosure for delinquent assessments, there is a 90-day redemption period after the sale during which the member may redeem the property by paying all arrears and related costs. The association must notify the member of this right of redemption with the notice of foreclosure sale. See Civil Code § 5715.

12. Assignment of Delinquent Assessments

An association may not assign or pledge the association's right to collect delinquent assessments or enforce lien rights to a third party, except when the assignment or pledge is to a financial institution licensed under state or federal law as security for a loan to the association. See Civil Code § 5735.

VIII. INSURANCE AND LIABILITY

A. DIRECTORS' AND OFFICERS' LIABILITY INSURANCE

The law provides that a volunteer director or officer may not be held liable for damages resulting from his or her service to the association if he or she performs his or her duties: (1) in good faith; (2) in a manner which he or she believes to be in the best interests of the association; and (3) with such care, including reasonable inquiry, as an ordinarily prudent person in a similar position would exercise under similar circumstances Directors are entitled to rely on information and opinions provided by the association's officers, committees, and hired experts. See Corp. Code § 7231. To provide additional liability protection to directors and officers, most governing documents state that the association will indemnify them absent gross negligence, intentional misconduct, or fraud. Indemnity means that the association will pay for an attorney to defend the director or officer and will pay the damages if the defense fails. Most governing documents require the association to carry director and officer ("D&O") liability insurance for these costs, and such insurance is always recommended.

The law states that if the D&O insurance meets statutory minimums, the director or officer cannot be held personally liable even if the damages exceed the insurance coverage. The statutory minimum is $500,000 if the project consists of 100 or fewer units or lots, and $1,000,000 if the project consists of more than 100 units or lots. This limited immunity does not apply to a member who owns more than two lots or units in the development where he or she serves as an officer or director, and it does not apply to the liability of an association itself for the actions of its officers and directors. See Corp. Code §§ 7231.5 and 7237, and Civil Code § 5800.

B. ASSOCIATION LIABILITY INSURANCE

General liability insurance covers the association and sometimes its members for personal injuries, bodily injury and property damage to third parties. The policy may also cover liability for defamation, advertising injury, non-owned automobile accidents, employment practices, and similar additional coverages. All general liability policies contain a number of important exclusions that must be considered in assessing the validity of a claim. The law does not require a minimum amount of liability insurance, but most governing documents specify minimum policy limits. The law does state that if certain minimum statutory policy limits are met, the individual owners cannot be held responsible if damages exceed the coverage. The statutory minimum is $2,000,000 if the project consists of 100 or fewer units or lots, and $3,000,000 if the project consists of more than 100 units or lots. See Civil Code § 5805.

C. ASSOCIATION PROPERTY/CASUALTY INSURANCE

1. Property/Casualty Insurance

Governing documents contain detailed property insurance requirements. In condominium projects, these typically require that the association obtain property damage insurance (sometimes called casualty insurance) for everything located on the property except the contents of the units. These policies usually cover damage to interior walls, floors and ceilings within units, but may not cover damage to cabinets, plumbing and electrical fixtures, appliances, wall and floor coverings, and built-in furniture. The individual members are typically responsible for insuring the contents of their units against damage.

In planned developments, the governing documents usually require the association to insure all portions of the property which it is obligated to maintain. In some cases, however, the individual members are required to insure everything on their lots even though the exterior surfaces of the homes are maintained by the association.

2. Earthquake Insurance

Earthquake insurance is not typically part of the property/casualty policy. It is obtained by an additional policy or endorsement at additional expense.

D. DISCLOSURE OF INSURANCE COVERAGE TO OWNERS

Associations are required to provide a summary of the terms of certain insurance policies to the members each year as part of the annual budget report. The summary must include the name of the insurer, the type of insurance, the limits of the policy or policies, the amount of deductibles, and a notice to members the language of which is specified in Civil Code § 5300(b)(9). Associations are also required to notify each member as soon as reasonably practical whenever a policy has lapsed, been canceled, not renewed or replaced, or when the limits have been decreased or the deductibles increased. Associations must provide complete copies of the policies to a member upon request. See Civil Code § 5810.

E. MEMBER LIABILITY AND ASSOCIATION DEBTS

If the association is incorporated, an individual member cannot be held responsible for personal injuries or property damage that occur in another member's unit or lot or in the common area simply by reason of being a member of the association. If the association is unincorporated, an individual member can be held responsible only if the association is responsible and unable to satisfy the claim, and then only if the association does not carry liability insurance meeting the statutory minimums. See Civil Code § 5805.

If the association is incorporated, an individual member cannot be held responsible for the association's debts. If the association is unincorporated, an individual member can be held responsible only if the member: (1) expressly assumes responsibility for the obligation in writing; (2) expressly authorizes the obligation; (3) receives the benefit of the obligation; or (4) executes a contract authorizing the obligation without authority to do so. See Corp. Code § 18610.

IX. DISPUTE RESOLUTION AND ENFORCEMENT

A. TYPES OF DISCIPLINE THAT MAY BE IMPOSED

An association has a wide range of possible disciplinary measures it can impose upon a member who violates the governing documents, which typically includes monetary fines, suspension of voting rights, and suspension of privileges (such as use of portions of the common area).

An association may not discipline a member for a violation unless the governing documents provide that the conduct at issue is impermissible and subject to specified disciplinary action by the association. See Civil Code § 5850(a).

B. DISCIPLINE AND COST REIMBURSEMENT

1. Schedule of Monetary Penalties

In order to assess monetary penalties, the association must adopt and distribute to the members with the annual policy statement a schedule of fines that may be assessed for governing document violations. A new or revised schedule of monetary penalties can be distributed between annual policy statements by "individual delivery" to the members. The amount of the monetary penalty may not exceed the amount shown in the schedule. The association must provide a copy of the schedule to a member upon request. See Civil Code § 5850.

2. Disciplinary Hearings

When the board is to meet to consider imposing discipline upon a member, or to impose property reimbursement assessment, the board at a minimum must do all of the following:

(1) Notify the member in writing, either by personal delivery or "individual delivery," at least 10 days before the hearing, unless the governing documents require a longer period of notice.

(2) The notice must state the date, time, and place of the hearing, the nature of the alleged violation or the nature of the damage to the common area or facilities for which a monetary charge may be imposed, and a statement that the member has a right to attend, may address the board at the hearing and has a right to have the hearing held in executive session.

(3) If the board decides to impose discipline or a charge, it must notify the member in writing, either by personal delivery or "individual delivery," within 15 days following the action. See Civil Code § 5855.

C. INTERNAL DISPUTE RESOLUTION

1. Association-Established Internal Dispute Resolution

An association is required by law to provide a fair, reasonable and expeditious procedure for resolving a dispute between an association and a member involving their rights under the Davis-Stirling Act, the Corporations Code or the association's governing documents. The law specifies the minimum requirements of a fair, reasonable and expeditious procedure for an internal dispute resolution process adopted by the board. The procedure must:

(1) Allow for either party to a dispute to invoke the process.

(2) Be invoked in writing.

(3) Provide for prompt deadlines.

(4) Be used if invoked by a member.

(5) Allow a member to decline to participate in the process.

(6) Allow a dissatisfied member to appeal to the full board.

(7) Allow a member to explain his or her position.

(8) Provide that a resolution of the dispute (without an agreement) binds the association and is judicially enforceable, provided it is not in conflict with the governing documents or the law.

(9) Provide that a resolution of the dispute by an agreement binds all parties and is judicially enforceable, provided it is not in conflict with the governing documents or the law.

(10) Provide that a member may not be charged a fee to participate in the process. See Civil Code § 5910.

2. Statutory Default Procedure

If the association fails to establish such a procedure for internal dispute resolution, the law specifies a "meet and confer" procedure to be followed. The statutory requirements are:

(1) Either party may request an opportunity to meet and confer to resolve a dispute.

(2) The request must be in writing.

(3) A member may refuse an association's request to meet and confer.

(4) An association may not refuse a member's request to meet and confer.

(5) The board must designate at least one director to meet and confer.

(6) The parties must meet and confer at a mutually convenient time and place.

(7) The parties may be assisted by an attorney or another person at their own cost when conferring

(8) The parties must have an opportunity to explain their positions.

(9) The parties must confer in good faith in an effort to resolve the dispute.

(10) A resolution agreed to by the parties must be in writing and signed by the parties.

(11) A written agreement signed by both parties to resolve a dispute binds all parties and is judicially enforceable, provided it is not in conflict with the governing documents or the law and, provided further, it is consistent with the director designee's authority or is subsequently ratified by the board.

(12) A member may not be charged a fee to participate in the process.

See Civil Code § 5915.

D. ALTERNATIVE DISPUTE RESOLUTION

Alternative dispute resolution ("ADR") means mediation, arbitration or other non-judicial procedure that involves a neutral party in the decision-making process. Its purpose is to save time and money by resolving disputes without going to court. Mediation involves a neutral person who attempts to help the parties resolve their dispute through discussion and compromise. A mediator does not make rulings or decisions. Consequently, mediation is always informal and non-binding. Arbitration involves a neutral person who acts as a surrogate judge. An arbitrator considers the position of each side, the applicable law, and then makes a ruling. The parties decide in advance whether the arbitration ruling will be binding or non-binding.

Most governing documents require some form of ADR, but there is wide variation regarding the type of ADR required and the situations where the requirement applies. Regardless of what the governing documents say about ADR, the law requires that when a party is seeking declaratory relief (i.e., a judicial pronouncement on some issue), injunctive relief (i.e., a judicial order prohibiting some action), or either of those types of relief in connection with a damage claim of less than $5,000, the party must send a "Request for Resolution" to the opposing party offering to participate in some form of alternative dispute resolution before filing suit. Failing to send a Request for Resolution may impact a party's ability to file of a lawsuit. A party receiving a Request for Resolution can decline to participate in ADR unless ADR is mandatory under the governing documents, but by doing so the party may adversely affect his or her ability to recover attorney fees in the subsequent litigation even if he or she prevails.

If the recipient of a Request for Resolution accepts the invitation, the parties must complete the ADR within 90 days of the acceptance, although they can extend the deadline by a written stipulation signed by both parties. The cost of the third party neutral must be shared equally by the parties to ADR unless otherwise agreed by the parties. Aside from payment of the third party neutral, each party participating in ADR bears its own legal expenses. See Civil Code § 5940.

ADR as a prerequisite to litigation does not apply to an action in Small Claims Court or to an assessment dispute. The pendency of ADR tolls or suspends the running of any statute of limitations on claims arising out of the dispute. See Civil Code §§ 5930 and 5945.

2

DAVIS-STIRLING
COMMON INTEREST DEVELOPMENT ACT

CHAPTER 1.

GENERAL PROVISIONS

Article 1.

Preliminary Provisions

Civ. Code § 4000. Citation.

This part shall be known and may be cited as the Davis-Stirling Common Interest Development Act. In a provision of this part, the part may be referred to as the act.

Civ. Code § 4005. Headings.

Division, part, title, chapter, and article, and section headings do not in any manner affect the scope, meaning, or intent of this act.

Civ. Code § 4010. Effect of Act on Documents or Actions Before January 1, 2014.

Nothing in the act that added this part shall be construed to invalidate a document prepared or action taken before January 1, 2014, if the document or action was proper under the law governing common interest developments at the time that the document was prepared or the action was taken. For the purposes of this section, "document" does not include a governing document.

Civ. Code § 4020. Local Zoning Ordinances.

Unless a contrary intent is clearly expressed, a local zoning ordinance is construed to treat like structures, lots, parcels, areas, or spaces in like manner regardless of the form of the common interest development.

Civ. Code § 4035. Delivery of Documents to Association.

(a) If a provision of this act requires that a document be delivered to an association, the document shall be delivered to the person designated in the annual policy statement, prepared pursuant to Section 5310, to receive documents on behalf of the association. If no person has been designated to receive documents, the document shall be delivered to the president or secretary of the association.

(b) A document delivered pursuant to this section may be delivered by any of the following methods:

(1) By email, facsimile, or other electronic means, if the association has assented to that method of delivery.

(2) By personal delivery, if the association has assented to that method of delivery. If the association accepts a document by personal delivery it shall provide a written receipt acknowledging delivery of the document.

(3) By first-class mail, postage prepaid, registered or certified mail, express mail, or overnight delivery by an express service center.

Civ. Code § 4040. Individual Delivery / Individual Notice. [Effective Until January 1, 2023]

(a) If a provision of this act requires that an association deliver a document by "individual delivery" or "individual notice," the document shall be delivered by one of the following methods:

(1) First-class mail, postage prepaid, registered or certified mail, express mail, or overnight delivery by an express service carrier. The document shall be addressed to the recipient at the address last shown on the books of the association.

(2) Email, facsimile, or other electronic means, if the recipient has consented, in writing or by email, to that method of delivery. The consent may be revoked, in writing or by email, by the recipient.

(b) Upon receipt of a request by a member, pursuant to Section 5260, identifying a secondary address for delivery of notices of the following types, the association shall deliver an additional copy of those notices to the secondary address identified in the request:

(1) The documents to be delivered to the member pursuant to Article 7 (commencing with Section 5300) of Chapter 6.

(2) The documents to be delivered to the member pursuant to Article 2 (commencing with Section 5650) of Chapter 8, and Section 5710.

(c) For the purposes of this section, an unrecorded provision of the governing documents providing for a particular method of delivery does not constitute agreement by a member to that method of delivery.

(d) This section shall remain in effect only until January 1, 2023, and as of that date is repealed.

Civ. Code § 4040. Individual Delivery / Individual Notice. [Effective January 1, 2023]

(a) (1) If a provision of this act requires an association to deliver a document by "individual delivery" or "individual notice," the association shall deliver that document in accordance with the preferred delivery method specified by the member pursuant to Section 4041.

(2) If the member has not provided a valid delivery method pursuant to Section 4041, the association shall deliver the document by first-class mail, registered or certified mail, express mail, or overnight delivery by an express service carrier addressed to the recipient at the address last shown on the books of the association.

(b) Upon receipt of a request by a member identifying a secondary email or mailing address for delivery of notices, pursuant to Section 5260, the association shall deliver an additional copy of both of the following to the secondary address identified in that request:

(1) The documents to be delivered to the member pursuant to Article 7 (commencing with Section 5300) of Chapter 6.

(2) The documents to be delivered to the member pursuant to Article 2 (commencing with Section 5650) of Chapter 8 and Section 5710.

(c) For the purposes of this section, an unrecorded provision of the governing documents providing for a particular method of delivery does not constitute agreement by a member to that method of delivery.

(d) This section shall become operative on January 1, 2023.

Civ. Code § 4041. Process for Updating Owner Addresses.

(a) A member shall, on an annual basis, provide written notice to the association of all of the following:

(1) The member's preferred delivery method for receiving notices from the association, which shall include the option of receiving notices at one or both of the following:

(A) A mailing address.

(B) A valid email address.

(2) An alternate or secondary delivery method for receiving notices from the association, which shall include the option to receive notices at one or both of the following:

(A) A mailing address.

(B) A valid email address.

(3) The name, mailing address, and, if available, valid email address of the owner's legal representative, if any, including any person with power of attorney or other person who can be contacted in the event of the member's extended absence from the separate interest.

(4) Whether the separate interest is owner-occupied, is rented out, if the parcel is developed but vacant, or if the parcel is undeveloped land.

(b) (1) The association shall solicit the annual notices described in subdivision (a) of each owner and, at least 30 days before making its own required disclosure under Section 5300, shall enter the data into its books and records.

(2) The association shall include in the solicitation required by paragraph (1) both of the following:

(A) Notification that the member does not have to provide an email address to the association.

(B) A simple method for the member to inform the association in writing that the member wishes to change their preferred delivery method for receiving notices from the association.

(c) If a member fails to provide the notices set forth in subdivision (a), the last mailing address provided in writing by the member or, if none, the property address shall be deemed to be the address to which notices are to be delivered.

(d) (1) To the extent that interests regulated in Chapter 2 (commencing with Section 11210) of Part 2 of Division 4 of the Business and Professions Code are part of a mixed-use project where those interests comprise a portion of a common interest development, the association, as defined in Section 4080, shall be deemed compliant with this section if, at least once annually, it obtains from the time-share plan association a copy of the list described in subdivision (e) of Section 11273 of the Business and Professions Code, and enters the data into its books and records.

(2) Notwithstanding subdivision (e) of Section 11273 of the Business and Professions Code, the time-share plan association shall provide the list required by paragraph (1) to the association at least annually for this purpose.

(e) For the purposes of this section, a valid email address is one that, after a notice is sent, does not result in a bounce or other error notification indicating failure of the message. If the association delivers a notice to a member's email address and finds that the email address provided is no longer valid, the association shall resend the notice to a mailing or email address identified by the member pursuant to Section 4040.

Civ. Code § 4045. General Delivery / General Notice.

(a) If a provision of this act requires "general delivery" or "general notice," the document shall be provided by one or more of the following methods:

(1) Any method provided for delivery of an individual notice pursuant to Section 4040.

(2) Inclusion in a billing statement, newsletter, or other document that is delivered by one of the methods provided in this section.

(3) Posting the printed document in a prominent location that is accessible to all members, if the location has been designated for the posting of general notices by the association in the annual policy statement prepared pursuant to Section 5310.

(4) If the association broadcasts television programming for the purpose of distributing information on association business to its members, by inclusion in the programming.

(5) If the association maintains an internet website for the purpose of distributing information on association business to its members, by posting the notice on the association's internet website in a prominent location that is accessible to all members if designated as a location for posting general notices in the annual policy statement prepared pursuant to Section 5310.

(b) Notwithstanding subdivision (a), if a member requests to receive general notices by individual delivery, all general notices to that member, given under this section, shall be delivered pursuant to Section 4040. The option provided in this subdivision shall be described in the annual policy statement, prepared pursuant to Section 5310.

Civ. Code § 4050. Effective Date of Delivery.

(a) This section governs the delivery of a document pursuant to this act.

(b) If a document is delivered by mail, delivery is deemed to be complete on deposit into the United States mail.

(c) If a document is delivered by electronic means, delivery is complete at the time of transmission.

Civ. Code § 4055. Electronic Delivery.

If the association or a member receives information by electronic delivery pursuant to Section 4040, and a provision of this act requires that the information be in writing, that requirement is satisfied if the information is provided in an electronic record capable of retention by the recipient at the time of receipt. An electronic record is not capable of retention by the recipient if the sender or its information processing system inhibits the ability of the recipient to print or store the electronic record.

Civ. Code § 4065. Approval by Majority Vote.

If a provision of this act requires that an action be approved by a majority of all members, the action shall be approved or ratified by an affirmative vote of a majority of the votes entitled to be cast.

Civ. Code § 4070. Approval by Majority of a Quorum.

If a provision of this act requires that an action be approved by a majority of a quorum of the members, the action shall be approved or ratified by an affirmative vote of a majority of the votes represented and voting in a duly held election in which a quorum is represented, which affirmative votes also constitute a majority of the required quorum.

Article 2.
Definitions

Civ. Code § 4075. Application of Definitions.

The definitions in this article govern the construction of this act.

Civ. Code § 4076. "Annual Budget Report."

"Annual budget report" means the report described in Section 5300.

Civ. Code § 4078. "Annual Policy Statement."

"Annual policy statement" means the statement described in Section 5310.

Civ. Code § 4080. "Association."

"Association" means a nonprofit corporation or unincorporated association created for the purpose of managing a common interest development.

Civ. Code § 4085. "Board."

"Board" means the board of directors of the association.

Civ. Code § 4090. "Board Meeting."

"Board meeting" means either of the following:

(a) A congregation, at the same time and place, of a sufficient number of directors to establish a quorum of the board, to hear, discuss, or deliberate upon any item of business that is within the authority of the board.

(b) A teleconference, where a sufficient number of directors to establish a quorum of the board, in different locations, are connected by electronic means, through audio or video, or both. A teleconference meeting shall be conducted in a manner that protects the rights of members of the association and otherwise complies with the requirements of this act. Except for a meeting that will be held solely in executive session or conducted under Section 5450, the notice of the teleconference meeting shall identify at least one physical location so that members of the association may attend, and at least one director or a person designated by the board shall be present at that location. Participation by directors in a teleconference meeting constitutes presence at that meeting as long as all directors participating are able to hear one another, as well as members of the association speaking on matters before the board.

Civ. Code § 4095. "Common Area."

(a) "Common area" means the entire common interest development except the separate interests therein. The estate in the common area may be a fee, a life estate, an estate for years, or any combination of the foregoing.

(b) Notwithstanding subdivision (a), in a planned development described in subdivision (b) of Section 4175, the common area may consist of mutual or reciprocal easement rights appurtenant to the separate interests.

Civ. Code § 4100. "Common Interest Development."

"Common interest development" means any of the following:

(a) A community apartment project.

(b) A condominium project.

(c) A planned development.

(d) A stock cooperative.

Civ. Code § 4105. "Community Apartment Project."

"Community apartment project" means a development in which an undivided interest in land is coupled with the right of exclusive occupancy of any apartment located thereon.

Civ. Code § 4110. "Community Service Organization."

(a) "Community service organization or similar entity" means a nonprofit entity, other than an association, that is organized to provide services to residents of the common interest development or to the public in addition to the residents, to the extent community common area or facilities are available to the public.

(b) "Community service organization or similar entity" does not include an entity that has been organized solely to raise moneys and contribute to other nonprofit organizations that are qualified as tax exempt under Section 501(c)(3) of the Internal Revenue Code and that provide housing or housing assistance.

Civ. Code § 4120. "Condominium Plan."

"Condominium plan" means a plan described in Section 4285.

Civ. Code § 4125. "Condominium Project."

(a) A "condominium project" means a real property development consisting of condominiums.

(b) A condominium consists of an undivided interest in common in a portion of real property coupled with a separate interest in space called a unit, the boundaries of which are described on a recorded final map, parcel map, or condominium plan in sufficient detail to locate all boundaries thereof. The area within these boundaries may be filled with air, earth, water, or fixtures, or any combination thereof, and need not be physically attached to land except by easements for access and, if necessary, support. The description of the unit may refer to (1) boundaries described in the recorded final map, parcel map, or condominium plan, (2) physical boundaries, either in existence, or to be constructed, such as walls, floors, and ceilings of a structure or any portion thereof, (3) an entire structure containing one or more units, or (4) any combination thereof.

(c) The portion or portions of the real property held in undivided interest may be all of the real property, except for the separate interests, or may include a particular three-dimensional portion thereof, the boundaries of which are described on a recorded final map, parcel map, or condominium plan. The area within these boundaries may be filled with air, earth, water, or fixtures, or any combination thereof, and need not be physically attached to land except by easements for access and, if necessary, support.

(d) An individual condominium within a condominium project may include, in addition, a separate interest in other portions of the real property.

Civ. Code § 4130. "Declarant."

"Declarant" means the person or group of persons designated in the declaration as declarant, or if no declarant is designated, the person or group of persons who sign the original declaration or who succeed to special rights, preferences, or privileges designated in the declaration as belonging to the signator of the original declaration.

Civ. Code § 4135. "Declaration."

"Declaration" means the document, however denominated, that contains the information required by Sections 4250 and 4255.

Civ. Code § 4140. "Director."

"Director" means a natural person who serves on the board.

Civ. Code § 4145. "Exclusive Use Common Area."

(a) "Exclusive use common area" means a portion of the common area designated by the declaration for the exclusive use of one or more, but fewer than all, of the owners of the separate interests and which is or will be appurtenant to the separate interest or interests.

(b) Unless the declaration otherwise provides, any shutters, awnings, window boxes, doorsteps, stoops, porches, balconies, patios, exterior doors, doorframes, and hardware incident thereto, screens and windows or other fixtures designed to serve a single separate interest, but located outside the boundaries of the separate interest, are exclusive use common area allocated exclusively to that separate interest.

(c) Notwithstanding the provisions of the declaration, internal and external telephone wiring designed to serve a single separate interest, but located outside the boundaries of the separate interest, is exclusive use common area allocated exclusively to that separate interest.

Civ. Code § 4148. "General Notice."

"General notice" means the delivery of a document pursuant to Section 4045.

Civ. Code § 4150. "Governing Documents."

"Governing documents" means the declaration and any other documents, such as bylaws, operating rules of the association, articles of incorporation, or articles of association, which govern the operation of the common interest development or association.

Civ. Code § 4153. "Individual Notice."

"Individual notice" means the delivery of a document pursuant to Section 4040.

Civ. Code § 4155. "Item of Business."

"Item of business" means any action within the authority of the board, except those actions that the board has validly delegated to any other person or persons, managing agent, officer of the association, or committee of the board comprising less than a quorum of the board.

Civ. Code § 4158. "Managing Agent."

(a) A "managing agent" is a person who, for compensation or in expectation of compensation, exercises control over the assets of a common interest development.

(b) A "managing agent" does not include any of the following:

(1) A regulated financial institution operating within the normal course of its regulated business practice.

(2) An attorney at law acting within the scope of the attorney's license.

Civ. Code § 4160. "Member."

"Member" means an owner of a separate interest.

Civ. Code § 4170. "Person."

"Person" means a natural person, corporation, government or governmental subdivision or agency, business trust, estate, trust, partnership, limited liability company, association, or other entity.

Civ. Code § 4175. "Planned Development."

"Planned development" means a real property development other than a community apartment project, a condominium project, or a stock cooperative, having either or both of the following features:

(a) Common area that is owned either by an association or in common by the owners of the separate interests who possess appurtenant rights to the beneficial use and enjoyment of the common area.

(b) Common area and an association that maintains the common area with the power to levy assessments that may become a lien upon the separate interests in accordance with Article 2 (commencing with Section 5650) of Chapter 8.

Civ. Code § 4177. "Reserve Accounts."

"Reserve accounts" means both of the following:

(a) Moneys that the board has identified for use to defray the future repair or replacement of, or additions to, those major components that the association is obligated to maintain.

(b) The funds received, and not yet expended or disposed of, from either a compensatory damage award or settlement to an association from any person for injuries to property, real or personal, arising from any construction or design defects. These funds shall be separately itemized from funds described in subdivision (a).

Civ. Code § 4178. "Reserve Account Requirements."

"Reserve account requirements" means the estimated funds that the board has determined are required to be available at a specified point in time to repair, replace, or restore those major components that the association is obligated to maintain.

Civ. Code § 4185. "Separate Interest."

(a) "Separate interest" has the following meanings:

(1) In a community apartment project, "separate interest" means the exclusive right to occupy an apartment, as specified in Section 4105.

(2) In a condominium project, "separate interest" means a separately owned unit, as specified in Section 4125.

(3) In a planned development, "separate interest" means a separately owned lot, parcel, area, or space.

(4) In a stock cooperative, "separate interest" means the exclusive right to occupy a portion of the real property, as specified in Section 4190.

(b) Unless the declaration or condominium plan, if any exists, otherwise provides, if walls, floors, or ceilings are designated as boundaries of a separate interest, the interior surfaces of the perimeter walls, floors, ceilings, windows, doors, and outlets located within the separate interest are part of the separate interest and any other portions of the walls, floors, or ceilings are part of the common area.

(c) The estate in a separate interest may be a fee, a life estate, an estate for years, or any combination of the foregoing.

Civ. Code § 4190. "Stock Cooperative."

(a) "Stock cooperative" means a development in which a corporation is formed or availed of, primarily for the purpose of holding title to, either in fee simple or for a term of years, improved real property, and all or substantially all of the shareholders of the corporation receive a right of exclusive occupancy in a portion of the real property, title to which is held by the corporation. The owners' interest in the corporation, whether evidenced by a share of stock, a certificate of membership, or otherwise, shall be deemed to be an interest in a common interest development and a real estate development for purposes of subdivision (f) of Section 25100 of the Corporations Code.

(b) A "stock cooperative" includes a limited equity housing cooperative which is a stock cooperative that meets the criteria of Section 817.

CHAPTER 2.
APPLICATION OF ACT

Civ. Code § 4200. Requirements for Creation of a Common Interest Development.

This act applies and a common interest development is created whenever a separate interest coupled with an interest in the common area or membership in the association is, or has been, conveyed, provided all of the following are recorded:

(a) A declaration.

(b) A condominium plan, if any exists.

(c) A final map or parcel map, if Division 2 (commencing with Section 66410) of Title 7 of the Government Code requires the recording of either a final map or parcel map for the common interest development.

Civ. Code § 4201. Requirement of Common Area.

Nothing in this act may be construed to apply to a real property development that does not contain common area. This section is declaratory of existing law.

Civ. Code § 4202. Nonapplicable Provisions for Commercial and Industrial CIDS.

This part does not apply to a commercial or industrial common interest development, as defined in Section 6531.

CHAPTER 3.
GOVERNING DOCUMENTS

Article 1.
General Provisions

Civ. Code § 4205. Controlling Authority.

(a) To the extent of any conflict between the governing documents and the law, the law shall prevail.

(b) To the extent of any conflict between the articles of incorporation and the declaration, the declaration shall prevail.

(c) To the extent of any conflict between the bylaws and the articles of incorporation or declaration, the articles of incorporation or declaration shall prevail.

(d) To the extent of any conflict between the operating rules and the bylaws, articles of incorporation, or declaration, the bylaws, articles of incorporation, or declaration shall prevail.

Civ. Code § 4210. Association Information Statement.

In order to facilitate the collection of regular assessments, special assessments, transfer fees as authorized by Sections 4530, 4575, and 4580, and similar charges, the board is authorized to record a statement or amended statement identifying relevant information for the association. This statement may include any or all of the following information:

(a) The name of the association as shown in the declaration or the current name of the association, if different.

(b) The name and address of a managing agent or treasurer of the association or other individual or entity authorized to receive assessments and fees imposed by the association.

(c) A daytime telephone number of the authorized party identified in subdivision (b) if a telephone number is available.

(d) A list of separate interests subject to assessment by the association, showing the assessor's parcel number or legal description, or both, of the separate interests.

(e) The recording information identifying the declaration governing the association.

(f) If an amended statement is being recorded, the recording information identifying the prior statement or statements which the amendment is superseding.

Civ. Code § 4215. Liberal Construction of Documents.

Any deed, declaration, or condominium plan for a common interest development shall be liberally construed to facilitate the operation of the common interest development, and its provisions shall be presumed to be independent and severable. Nothing in Article 3 (commencing with Section 715) of Chapter 2 of Title 2 of Part 1 of Division 2 shall operate to invalidate any provisions of the governing documents.

Civ. Code § 4220. Existing Physical Boundaries.

In interpreting deeds and condominium plans, the existing physical boundaries of a unit in a condominium project, when the boundaries of the unit are contained within a building, or of a unit reconstructed in substantial accordance with the original plans thereof, shall be conclusively presumed to be its boundaries rather than the metes and bounds expressed in the deed or condominium plan, if any exists, regardless of settling or lateral movement of the building and regardless of minor variance between boundaries shown on the plan or in the deed and those of the building.

Civ. Code § 4225. Discriminatory Restrictive Covenants.

(a) No declaration or other governing document shall include a restrictive covenant in violation of Section 12955 of the Government Code.

(b) Notwithstanding any other provision of law or provision of the governing documents, the board, without approval of the members, shall amend any declaration or other governing document that includes a restrictive covenant prohibited by this section to delete the restrictive covenant, and shall restate the declaration or other governing document without the restrictive covenant but with no other change to the declaration or governing document.

(c) If the declaration is amended under this section, the board shall record the restated declaration in each county in which the common interest development is located. If the articles of incorporation are amended under this section, the board shall file a certificate of amendment with the Secretary of State pursuant to Section 7814 of the Corporations Code.

(d) If after providing written notice to an association, pursuant to Section 4035, requesting that the association delete a restrictive covenant that violates subdivision (a), and the association fails to delete the restrictive covenant within 30 days of receiving the notice, the Department of Fair Employment and Housing, a city or county in which a common interest development is located, or any person may bring an action against the association for injunctive relief to enforce subdivision (a). The court may award attorney's fees to the prevailing party.

Civ. Code § 4230. Amendment to Delete Certain Declarant Provisions.

(a) Notwithstanding any provision of the governing documents to the contrary, the board may, after the developer has completed construction of the development, has terminated construction activities, and has terminated marketing activities for the sale, lease, or other disposition of separate interests within the development, adopt an amendment deleting from any of the governing documents any provision which is unequivocally designed and intended, or which by its nature can only have been designed or intended, to facilitate the developer in completing the construction or marketing of the development. However, provisions of the governing documents relative to a particular construction or marketing phase of the development may not be deleted under the authorization of this subdivision until that construction or marketing phase has been completed.

(b) The provisions which may be deleted by action of the board shall be limited to those which provide for access by the developer over or across the common area for the purposes of (1) completion of construction of the development, and (2) the erection, construction, or maintenance of structures or other facilities designed to facilitate the completion of construction or marketing of separate interests.

(c) At least 30 days prior to taking action pursuant to subdivision (a), the board shall deliver to all members, by individual delivery, pursuant to Section 4040, (1) a copy of all amendments to the governing documents proposed to be adopted under subdivision (a), and (2) a notice of the time, date, and place the board will consider adoption of the amendments. The board may consider adoption of amendments to the governing documents pursuant to subdivision (a) only at a meeting that is open to all members, who shall be given opportunity to make comments thereon. All deliberations of the board on any action proposed under subdivision (a) shall only be conducted in an open meeting.

(d) The board may not amend the governing documents pursuant to this section without the approval of a majority of a quorum of the members, pursuant to Section 4070. For the purposes of this section, "quorum" means more than 50 percent of the members who own no more than two separate interests in the development.

Civ. Code § 4235. Amendment of Governing Documents to Reflect Changes in the Davis-Stirling Common Interest Development Act.

(a) Notwithstanding any other provision of law or provision of the governing documents, if the governing documents include a reference to a provision of the Davis-Stirling Common Interest Development Act that was repealed and continued in a new provision by the act that added this section, the board may amend the governing documents, solely to correct the cross-reference, by adopting a board resolution that shows the correction. Member approval is not required in order to adopt a resolution pursuant to this section.

(b) A declaration that is corrected under this section may be restated in corrected form and recorded, provided that a copy of the board resolution authorizing the corrections is recorded along with the restated declaration.

Article 2.

Declaration

Civ. Code § 4250. Required Elements of Declaration.

(a) A declaration, recorded on or after January 1, 1986, shall contain a legal description of the common interest development, and a statement that the common interest development is a community apartment project, condominium project, planned development, stock cooperative, or combination thereof. The declaration shall additionally set forth the name of the association and the restrictions on the use or enjoyment of any portion of the common interest development that are intended to be enforceable equitable servitudes.

(b) The declaration may contain any other matters the declarant or the members consider appropriate.

Civ. Code § 4255. Notice of Airport in Vicinity; Notice of San Francisco Bay Conservation and Development Commission Jurisdiction.

(a) If a common interest development is located within an airport influence area, a declaration, recorded after January 1, 2004, shall contain the following statement:

"NOTICE OF AIRPORT IN VICINITY

This property is presently located in the vicinity of an airport, within what is known as an airport influence area. For that reason, the property may be subject to some of the annoyances or inconveniences associated with proximity to airport operations (for example: noise, vibration, or odors). Individual sensitivities to those annoyances can vary from person to person. You may wish to consider what airport annoyances, if any, are associated with the property before you complete your purchase and determine whether they are acceptable to you."

(b) For purposes of this section, an "airport influence area," also known as an "airport referral area," is the area in which current or future airport-related noise, overflight, safety, or airspace protection factors may significantly affect land uses or necessitate restrictions on those uses as determined by an airport land use commission.

(c) If a common interest development is within the San Francisco Bay Conservation and Development Commission jurisdiction, as described in Section 66610 of the Government Code, a declaration recorded on or after January 1, 2006, shall contain the following notice:

"NOTICE OF SAN FRANCISCO BAY CONSERVATION AND DEVELOPMENT COMMISSION JURISDICTION

This property is located within the jurisdiction of the San Francisco Bay Conservation and Development Commission. Use and development of property within the commission's jurisdiction may be subject to special regulations, restrictions, and permit requirements. You may wish to investigate and determine whether they are acceptable to you and your intended use of the property before you complete your transaction."

(d) The statement in a declaration acknowledging that a property is located in an airport influence area or within the jurisdiction of the San Francisco Bay Conservation and Development Commission does not constitute a title defect, lien, or encumbrance.

Civ. Code § 4260. Permissible Amendment of Declaration.

Except to the extent that a declaration provides by its express terms that it is not amendable, in whole or in part, a declaration that fails to include provisions permitting its amendment at all times during its existence may be amended at any time.

Civ. Code § 4265. Extension of Declaration Termination Date.

(a) The Legislature finds that there are common interest developments that have been created with deed restrictions that do not provide a means for the members to extend the term of the declaration. The Legislature further finds that covenants and restrictions contained in the declaration, are an appropriate method for protecting the common plan of developments and to provide for a mechanism for financial support for the upkeep of common area including, but not limited to, roofs, roads, heating systems, and recreational facilities. If declarations terminate prematurely, common interest developments may deteriorate and the housing supply of affordable units could be impacted adversely. The Legislature further finds and declares that it is in the public interest to provide a vehicle for extending the term of the declaration if the extension is approved by a majority of all members, pursuant to Section 4065.

(b) A declaration that specifies a termination date, but that contains no provision for extension of the termination date, may be extended, before its termination date, by the approval of members pursuant to Section 4270.

(c) No single extension of the terms of the declaration made pursuant to this section shall exceed the initial term of the declaration or 20 years, whichever is less. However, more than one extension may occur pursuant to this section.

Civ. Code § 4270. Effective Amendment of Declaration.

(a) A declaration may be amended pursuant to the declaration or this act. Except where an alternative process for approving, certifying, or recording an amendment is provided in Section 4225, 4230, 4235, or 4275, an amendment is effective after all of the following requirements have been met:

(1) The amendment has been approved by the percentage of members required by the declaration and any other person whose approval is required by the declaration.

(2) That fact has been certified in a writing executed and acknowledged by the officer designated in the declaration or by the association for that purpose, or if no one is designated, by the president of the association.

(3) The amendment has been recorded in each county in which a portion of the common interest development is located.

(b) If the declaration does not specify the percentage of members who must approve an amendment of the declaration, an amendment may be approved by a majority of all members, pursuant to Section 4065.

Civ. Code § 4275. Court Approval of Amendment of Declaration.

(a) If in order to amend a declaration, the declaration requires members having more than 50 percent of the votes in the association, in a single class voting structure, or members having more than 50 percent of the votes in more than one class in a voting structure with more than one class, to vote in favor of the amendment, the association, or any member, may petition the superior court of the county in which the common interest development is located for an order reducing the percentage of the affirmative votes necessary for such an amendment. The petition shall describe the effort that has been made to solicit approval of the association members in the manner provided in the declaration, the number of affirmative and negative votes actually received, the number or percentage of affirmative votes required to effect the amendment in accordance with the existing declaration, and other matters the petitioner considers relevant to the court's determination. The petition shall also contain, as exhibits thereto, copies of all of the following:

(1) The governing documents.

(2) A complete text of the amendment.

(3) Copies of any notice and solicitation materials utilized in the solicitation of member approvals.

(4) A short explanation of the reason for the amendment.

(5) Any other documentation relevant to the court's determination.

(b) Upon filing the petition, the court shall set the matter for hearing and issue an ex parte order setting forth the manner in which notice shall be given.

(c) The court may, but shall not be required to, grant the petition if it finds all of the following:

(1) The petitioner has given not less than 15 days written notice of the court hearing to all members of the association, to any mortgagee of a mortgage or beneficiary of a deed of trust who is entitled to notice under the terms of the declaration, and to the city, county, or city and county in which the common interest development is located that is entitled to notice under the terms of the declaration.

(2) Balloting on the proposed amendment was conducted in accordance with the governing documents, this act, and any other applicable law.

(3) A reasonably diligent effort was made to permit all eligible members to vote on the proposed amendment.

(4) Members having more than 50 percent of the votes, in a single class voting structure, voted in favor of the amendment. In a voting structure with more than one class, where the declaration requires a majority of more than one class to vote in favor of the amendment, members having more than 50 percent of the votes of each class required by the declaration to vote in favor of the amendment voted in favor of the amendment.

(5) The amendment is reasonable.

(6) Granting the petition is not improper for any reason stated in subdivision (e).

(d) If the court makes the findings required by subdivision (c), any order issued pursuant to this section may confirm the amendment as being validly approved on the basis of the affirmative votes actually received during the balloting period or the order may dispense with any requirement relating to quorums or to the number or percentage of votes needed for approval of the amendment that would otherwise exist under the governing documents.

(e) Subdivisions (a) to (d), inclusive, notwithstanding, the court shall not be empowered by this section to approve any amendment to the declaration that:

Civil

(1) Would change provisions in the declaration requiring the approval of members having more than 50 percent of the votes in more than one class to vote in favor of an amendment, unless members having more than 50 percent of the votes in each affected class approved the amendment.

(2) Would eliminate any special rights, preferences, or privileges designated in the declaration as belonging to the declarant, without the consent of the declarant.

(3) Would impair the security interest of a mortgagee of a mortgage or the beneficiary of a deed of trust without the approval of the percentage of the mortgagees and beneficiaries specified in the declaration, if the declaration requires the approval of a specified percentage of the mortgagees and beneficiaries.

(f) An amendment is not effective pursuant to this section until the court order and amendment have been recorded in every county in which a portion of the common interest development is located. The amendment may be acknowledged by, and the court order and amendment may be recorded by, any person designated in the declaration or by the association for that purpose, or if no one is designated for that purpose, by the president of the association. Upon recordation of the amendment and court order, the declaration, as amended in accordance with this section, shall have the same force and effect as if the amendment were adopted in compliance with every requirement imposed by the governing documents.

(g) Within a reasonable time after the amendment is recorded the association shall deliver to each member, by individual delivery, pursuant to Section 4040, a copy of the amendment, together with a statement that the amendment has been recorded.

Article 3.

Articles of Incorporation

Civ. Code § 4280. Required Elements of Articles of Incorporation.

(a) The articles of incorporation of an association filed with the Secretary of State shall include a statement, which shall be in addition to the statement of purposes of the corporation, that does all of the following:

(1) Identifies the corporation as an association formed to manage a common interest development under the Davis-Stirling Common Interest Development Act.

(2) States the business or corporate office of the association, if any, and, if the office is not on the site of the common interest development, states the front street and nearest cross street for the physical location of the common interest development.

(3) States the name and address of the association's managing agent, if any.

(b) The statement filed by an incorporated association with the Secretary of State pursuant to Section 8210 of the Corporations Code shall also contain a statement identifying the corporation as an association formed to manage a common interest development under the Davis-Stirling Common Interest Development Act.

(c) Documents filed prior to January 1, 2014, in compliance with former Section 1363.5, as it read on January 1, 2013, are deemed to be in compliance with this section.

Article 4.
Condominium Plan

Civ. Code § 4285. Required Elements of Condominium Plan.

A condominium plan shall contain all of the following:

(a) A description or survey map of a condominium project, which shall refer to or show monumentation on the ground.

(b) A three-dimensional description of a condominium project, one or more dimensions of which may extend for an indefinite distance upwards or downwards, in sufficient detail to identify the common area and each separate interest.

(c) A certificate consenting to the recordation of the condominium plan pursuant to this act that is signed and acknowledged as provided in Section 4290.

Civ. Code § 4290. Certificate Consenting to Recordation of Condominium Plan.

(a) The certificate consenting to the recordation of a condominium plan that is required by subdivision (c) of Section 4285 shall be signed and acknowledged by all of the following persons:

(1) The record owner of fee title to that property included in the condominium project.

(2) In the case of a condominium project that will terminate upon the termination of an estate for years, by all lessors and lessees of the estate for years.

(3) In the case of a condominium project subject to a life estate, by all life tenants and remainder interests.

(4) The trustee or the beneficiary of each recorded deed of trust, and the mortgagee of each recorded mortgage encumbering the property.

(b) Owners of mineral rights, easements, rights-of-way, and other nonpossessory interests do not need to sign the certificate.

(c) In the event a conversion to condominiums of a community apartment project or stock cooperative has been approved by the required number of owners, trustees, beneficiaries, and mortgagees pursuant to Section 66452.10 of the Government Code, the certificate need only be signed by those owners, trustees, beneficiaries, and mortgagees approving the conversion.

Civ. Code § 4295. Amendment or Revocation of Condominium Plan.

A condominium plan may be amended or revoked by a recorded instrument that is acknowledged and signed by all the persons who, at the time of amendment or revocation, are persons whose signatures are required under Section 4290.

Article 5.
Operating Rules

Civ. Code § 4340. "Operating Rule" And "Rule Change" Defined.

For the purposes of this article:

(a) "Operating rule" means a regulation adopted by the board that applies generally to the management and operation of the common interest development or the conduct of the business and affairs of the association.

(b) "Rule change" means the adoption, amendment, or repeal of an operating rule by the board.

Civ. Code § 4350. Required Elements of an Operating Rule.

An operating rule is valid and enforceable only if all of the following requirements are satisfied:

(a) The rule is in writing.

(b) The rule is within the authority of the board conferred by law or by the declaration, articles of incorporation or association, or bylaws of the association.

(c) The rule is not in conflict with governing law and the declaration, articles of incorporation or association, or bylaws of the association.

(d) The rule is adopted, amended, or repealed in good faith and in substantial compliance with the requirements of this article.

(e) The rule is reasonable.

Civ. Code § 4355. Application of Member Review and Comment Requirement.

(a) Sections 4360 and 4365 only apply to an operating rule that relates to one or more of the following subjects:

(1) Use of the common area or of an exclusive use common area.

(2) Use of a separate interest, including any aesthetic or architectural standards that govern alteration of a separate interest.

(3) Member discipline, including any schedule of monetary penalties for violation of the governing documents and any procedure for the imposition of penalties.

(4) Any standards for delinquent assessment payment plans.

(5) Any procedures adopted by the association for resolution of disputes.

(6) Any procedures for reviewing and approving or disapproving a proposed physical change to a member's separate interest or to the common area.

(7) Procedures for elections.

(b) Sections 4360 and 4365 do not apply to the following actions by the board:

(1) A decision regarding maintenance of the common area.

(2) A decision on a specific matter that is not intended to apply generally.

(3) A decision setting the amount of a regular or special assessment.

(4) A rule change that is required by law, if the board has no discretion as to the substantive effect of the rule change.

(5) Issuance of a document that merely repeats existing law or the governing documents.

Civ. Code § 4360. Notice of Rule Change.

(a) The board shall provide general notice pursuant to Section 4045 of a proposed rule change at least 28 days before making the rule change. The notice shall include the text of the proposed rule change and a description of the purpose and effect of the proposed rule change. Notice is not required under this subdivision if the board determines that an immediate rule change is necessary to address an imminent threat to public health or safety or imminent risk of substantial economic loss to the association.

(b) A decision on a proposed rule change shall be made at a board meeting, after consideration of any comments made by association members.

(c) As soon as possible after making a rule change, but not more than 15 days after making the rule change, the board shall deliver general notice pursuant to Section 4045 of the rule change. If the rule change was an emergency rule change made under subdivision (d), the notice shall include the text of the rule change, a description of the purpose and effect of the rule change, and the date that the rule change expires.

(d) If the board determines that an immediate rule change is required to address an imminent threat to public health or safety, or an imminent risk of substantial economic loss to the association, it may make an emergency rule change, and no notice is required, as specified in subdivision (a). An emergency rule change is effective for 120 days, unless the rule change provides for a shorter effective period. A rule change made under this subdivision may not be readopted under this subdivision.

Civ. Code § 4365. Reversal of Rule Change.

(a) Members of an association owning 5 percent or more of the separate interests may call a special vote of the members to reverse a rule change.

(b) A special vote of the members may be called by delivering a written request to the association. Not less than 35 days nor more than 90 days after receipt of a proper request, the association shall hold a vote of the members on whether to reverse the rule change, pursuant to Article 4 (commencing with Section 5100) of Chapter 6. The written request may not be delivered more than 30 days after the association gives general notice of the rule change, pursuant to Section 4045.

(c) For the purposes of Section 5225 of this code and Section 8330 of the Corporations Code, collection of signatures to call a special vote under this section is a purpose reasonably related to the interests of the members of the association. A member request to copy or inspect the membership list solely for that purpose may not be denied on the grounds that the purpose is not reasonably related to the member's interests as a member.

(d) The rule change may be reversed by the affirmative vote of a majority of a quorum of the members, pursuant to Section 4070, or if the declaration or bylaws require a greater percentage, by the affirmative vote of the percentage required.

(e) Unless otherwise provided in the declaration or bylaws, for the purposes of this section, a member may cast one vote per separate interest owned.

(f) A rule change reversed under this section may not be readopted for one year after the date of the vote reversing the rule change. Nothing in this section precludes the board from adopting a different rule on the same subject as the rule change that has been reversed.

(g) As soon as possible after the close of voting, but not more than 15 days after the close of voting, the board shall provide general notice pursuant to Section 4045 of the results of the member vote.

(h) This section does not apply to an emergency rule change made under subdivision (d) of Section 4360.

Civ. Code § 4370. Application of Article to Rule Changes after January 1, 2004.

(a) This article applies to a rule change commenced on or after January 1, 2004.

(b) Nothing in this article affects the validity of a rule change commenced before January 1, 2004.

(c) For the purposes of this section, a rule change is commenced when the board takes its first official action leading to adoption of the rule change.

CHAPTER 4.
OWNERSHIP RIGHTS AND TRANSFER OF INTERESTS

Article 1.
Ownership Rights and Interests

Civ. Code § 4500. Ownership of Common Area.

Unless the declaration otherwise provides, in a condominium project, or in a planned development in which the common area is owned by the owners of the separate interests, the common area is owned as tenants in common, in equal shares, one for each separate interest.

Civ. Code § 4505. Common Area Rights and Easements.

Unless the declaration otherwise provides:

(a) In a community apartment project and condominium project, and in those planned developments with common area owned in common by the owners of the separate interests, there are appurtenant to each separate interest nonexclusive rights of ingress, egress, and support, if necessary, through the common area. The common area is subject to these rights.

(b) In a stock cooperative, and in a planned development with common area owned by the association, there is an easement for ingress, egress, and support, if necessary, appurtenant to each separate interest. The common area is subject to these easements.

Civ. Code § 4510. Access to Owners' Separate Interest.

Except as otherwise provided in law, an order of the court, or an order pursuant to a final and binding arbitration decision, an association may not deny a member or occupant physical access to the member's or occupant's separate interest, either by restricting access through the common area to the separate interest, or by restricting access solely to the separate interest.

Civ. Code § 4515. Peaceful Assembly.

(a) It is the intent of the Legislature to ensure that members and residents of common interest developments have the ability to exercise their rights under law to peacefully assemble and freely communicate with one another and with others with respect to common interest development living or for social, political, or educational purposes.

(b) The governing documents, including bylaws and operating rules, shall not prohibit a member or resident of a common interest development from doing any of the following:

(1) Peacefully assembling or meeting with members, residents, and their invitees or guests during reasonable hours and in a reasonable manner for purposes relating to common interest development living, association elections, legislation, election to public office, or the initiative, referendum, or recall processes.

(2) Inviting public officials, candidates for public office, or representatives of homeowner organizations to meet with members, residents, and their invitees or guests and speak on matters of public interest.

(3) Using the common area, including the community or recreation hall or clubhouse, or, with the consent of the member, the area of a separate interest, for an assembly or meeting described in paragraph (1) or (2) when that facility or separate interest is not otherwise in use.

(4) Canvassing and petitioning the members, the association board, and residents for the activities described in paragraphs (1) and (2) at reasonable hours and in a reasonable manner.

(5) Distributing or circulating, without prior permission, information about common interest development living, association elections, legislation, election to public office, or the initiative, referendum, or recall processes, or other issues of concern to members and residents at reasonable hours and in a reasonable manner.

(6) (A) Using social media or other online resources to discuss any of the following, even if the content is critical of the association or its governance:

(i) Development living.

(ii) Association elections.

(iii) Legislation.

(iv) Election to public office.

(v) The initiative, referendum, or recall processes.

(vi) Any other issues of concern to members and residents.

(B) This paragraph does not require an association to provide social media or other online resources to members.

(C) This paragraph does not require an association to allow members to post content on the association's internet website.

(c) A member or resident of a common interest development shall not be required to pay a fee, make a deposit, obtain liability insurance, or pay the premium or deductible on the association's insurance policy, in order to use a common area for the activities described in paragraphs (1), (2), and (3) of subdivision (b).

(d) A member or resident of a common interest development who is prevented by the association or its agents from engaging in any of the activities described in this section may bring a civil or small claims court action to enjoin the enforcement of a governing document, including a bylaw and operating rule that violates this section. The court may assess a civil penalty of not more than five hundred dollars ($500) for each violation.

(e) An association shall not retaliate against a member or a resident for exercising any of the rights contained in this section.

Article 2.

Transfer Disclosure

Civ. Code § 4525. Owner Disclosure of Specified Items to Prospective Purchasers.

(a) The owner of a separate interest shall provide the following documents to a prospective purchaser of the separate interest, as soon as practicable before the transfer of title or the execution of a real property sales contract, as defined in Section 2985:

(1) A copy of all governing documents. If the association is not incorporated, this shall include a statement in writing from an authorized representative of the association that the association is not incorporated.

(2) If there is a restriction in the governing documents limiting the occupancy, residency, or use of a separate interest on the basis of age in a manner different from that provided in Section 51.3, a statement that the restriction is only enforceable to the extent permitted by Section 51.3 and a statement specifying the applicable provisions of Section 51.3.

(3) A copy of the most recent documents distributed pursuant to Article 7 (commencing with Section 5300) of Chapter 6.

(4) A true statement in writing obtained from an authorized representative of the association as to the amount of the association's current regular and special assessments and fees, any assessments levied upon the owner's interest in the common interest development that are unpaid on the date of the statement, and any monetary fines or penalties levied upon the owner's interest and unpaid on the date of the statement. The statement obtained from an authorized representative shall also include true information on late charges, interest, and costs of collection which, as of the date of the statement, are or may be made a lien upon the owner's interest in a common interest development pursuant to Article 2 (commencing with Section 5650) of Chapter 8.

(5) A copy or a summary of any notice previously sent to the owner pursuant to Section 5855 that sets forth any alleged violation of the governing documents that remains unresolved at the time of the request. The notice shall not be deemed a waiver of the association's right to enforce the governing documents against the owner or the prospective purchaser of the separate interest with respect to any violation. This paragraph shall not be construed to require an association to inspect an owner's separate interest.

(6) A copy of the initial list of defects provided to each member pursuant to Section 6000, unless the association and the builder subsequently enter into a settlement agreement or otherwise resolve the matter and the association complies with Section 6100. Disclosure of the initial list of defects pursuant to this paragraph does not waive any privilege attached to the document. The initial list of defects shall also include a statement that a final determination as to whether the list of defects is accurate and complete has not been made.

(7) A copy of the latest information provided for in Section 6100.

(8) Any change in the association's current regular and special assessments and fees which have been approved by the board, but have not become due and payable as of the date disclosure is provided pursuant to this subdivision.

(9) If there is a provision in the governing documents that prohibits the rental or leasing of any of the separate interests in the common interest development to a renter, lessee, or tenant, a statement describing the prohibition and its applicability.

(10) If requested by the prospective purchaser, a copy of the minutes of board meetings, excluding meetings held in executive session, conducted over the previous 12 months, that were approved by the board.

(b) This section does not apply to an owner that is subject to the requirements of Section 11018.6 of the Business and Professions Code.

Civ. Code § 4528. Statutory Disclosure Form.

The form for billing disclosures required by Section 4530 shall be in at least 10-point type and substantially the following form:

CHARGES FOR DOCUMENTS PROVIDED AS REQUIRED BY SECTION 4525*

The seller may, in accordance with Section 4530 of the Civil Code, provide to the prospective purchaser, at no cost, current copies of any documents specified by Section 4525 that are in the possession of the seller.

A seller may request to purchase some or all of these documents, but shall not be required to purchase ALL of the documents listed on this form.

Property Address ______________________________

Owner of Property ______________________________

Owner's Mailing Address ______________________________

(If known or different from property address.)

Provider of the Section 4525 Items:

____

Print Name   Position or Title   Association or Agent   Date Form Completed

Check or Complete Applicable Column or Columns Below

Document	Civil Code Section	Fee for Document	Not Available (N/A) or Not Applicable (N/App), or Directly Provided (DP) by Seller and confirmed in writing by Seller as a current document
Articles of Incorporation or statement that not incorporated	Section 4525(a)(1)		
CC&Rs	Section 4525(a)(1)		
Bylaws	Section 4525(a)(1)		
Operating Rules	Section 4525(a)(1)		
Age restrictions, if any	Section 4525(a)(2)		
Rental restrictions, if any	Section 4525(a)(9)		
Annual budget report or summary, including reserve study	Sections 5300 and 4525(a)(3)		
Assessment and reserve funding disclosure summary	Sections 5300 and 4525(a)(4)		
Financial statement review	Sections5305 and 4525(a)(3)		
Assessment enforcement policy	Sections 5310 and 4525(a)(4)		
Insurance summary	Sections 5300 and 4525(a)(3)		
Regular assessment	Section 4525(a)(4)		
Special assessment	Section 4525(a)(4)		
Emergency assessment	Section 4525(a)(4)		
Other unpaid obligations of seller	Sections 5675 and 4525(a)(4)		
Approved changes to assessments	Sections 5300 and 4525(a)(4), (8)		
Settlement notice regarding common area defects	Sections 4525(a)(6),(7) and 6100		
Preliminary list of defects	Sections 4525(a)(6), 6000, and 6100		
Notice(s) of violation	Sections 5855 and 4525(a)(5)		
Required statement of fees	Section 4525		
Minutes of regular meetings of the board of directors conducted over the previous 12 months, if requested	Section 4525(a)(10)		
Total fees for these documents:			

* The information provided by this form may not include all fees that may be imposed before the close of escrow. Additional fees that are not related to the requirements of Section 4525 may be charged separately.

Civ. Code § 4530. Copies of Escrow Documents to Owners.

(a) (1) Upon written request, the association shall, within 10 days of the mailing or delivery of the request, provide the owner of a separate interest, or any other recipient authorized by the owner, with a copy of all of the requested documents specified in Section 4525.

(2) The documents required to be made available pursuant to this section may be maintained in electronic form, and may be posted on the association's Internet Web site. Requesting parties shall have the option of receiving the documents by electronic transmission if the association maintains the documents in electronic form.

(3) Delivery of the documents required by this section shall not be withheld for any reason nor subject to any condition except the payment of the fee authorized pursuant to subdivision (b).

(b) (1) The association may collect a reasonable fee from the seller based upon the association's actual cost for the procurement, preparation, reproduction, and delivery of the documents requested pursuant to this section. An additional fee shall not be charged for the electronic delivery in lieu of a hard copy delivery of the documents requested.

(2) Upon receipt of a written request, the association shall provide, on the form described in Section 4528, a written or electronic estimate of the fees that will be assessed for providing the requested documents prior to processing the request in paragraph (1) of subdivision (a).

(3) (A) A cancellation fee for documents specified in subdivision (a) shall not be collected if either of the following applies:

(i) The request was canceled in writing by the same party that placed the order and work had not yet been performed on the order.

(ii) The request was canceled in writing and any work that had been performed on the order was compensated.

(B) The association shall refund all fees collected pursuant to paragraph (1) if the request was canceled in writing and work had not yet been performed on the order.

(C) If the request was canceled in writing, the association shall refund the share of fees collected pursuant to paragraph (1) that represents the portion of the work not performed on the order.

(4) Fees for any documents required by this section shall be distinguished from, separately stated, and separately billed from, all other fees, fines, or assessments billed as part of the transfer or sales transaction.

(5) Any documents not expressly required by Section 4525 to be provided to a prospective purchaser by the seller shall not be included in the document disclosure required by this section. Bundling of documents required to be provided pursuant to this section with other documents relating to the transaction is prohibited.

(6) A seller shall provide to the prospective purchaser, at no cost, current copies of any documents specified by Section 4525 that are in the possession of the seller.

(7) The fee for each document provided to the seller for the purpose of transmission to the prospective purchaser shall be individually itemized in the statement required to be provided by the seller to the prospective purchaser.

(8) It is the responsibility of the seller to compensate the association, person, or entity that provides the documents required to be provided by Section 4525 to the prospective purchaser.

(c) An association may contract with any person or entity to facilitate compliance with this section on behalf of the association.

(d) The association shall also provide a recipient authorized by the owner of a separate interest with a copy of the completed form specified in Section 4528 at the time the required documents are delivered. A seller may request to purchase some or all of these documents, but shall not be required to purchase all of the documents listed on the form specified in Section 4528.

Civ. Code § 4535. Additional Transfer Requirements.

In addition to the requirements of this article, an owner transferring title to a separate interest shall comply with applicable requirements of Sections 1133 and 1134.

Civ. Code § 4540. Penalty for Violations of this Article.

Any person who willfully violates this article is liable to the purchaser of a separate interest that is subject to this section for actual damages occasioned thereby and, in addition, shall pay a civil penalty in an amount not to exceed five hundred dollars ($500). In an action to enforce this liability, the prevailing party shall be awarded reasonable attorney's fees.

Civ. Code § 4545. Validity of Title Transfer in Violation.

Nothing in this article affects the validity of title to real property transferred in violation of this article.

Article 3.
Transfer Fees

Civ. Code § 4575. Prohibition of Transfer Fees.

Except as provided in Section 4580, neither an association nor a community service organization or similar entity may impose or collect any assessment, penalty, or fee in connection with a transfer of title or any other interest except for the following:

(a) An amount not to exceed the association's actual costs to change its records.

(b) An amount authorized by Section 4530.

Civ. Code § 4580. Exceptions to the Prohibition of Transfer Fees.

The prohibition in Section 4575 does not apply to a community service organization or similar entity, or to a nonprofit entity that provides services to a common interest development under a declaration of trust, of either of the following types:

(a) An organization or entity that satisfies both of the following conditions:

(1) It was established before February 20, 2003.

(2) It exists and operates, in whole or in part, to fund or perform environmental mitigation or to restore or maintain wetlands or native habitat, as required by the state or local government as an express written condition of development.

(b) An organization or entity that satisfies all of the following conditions:

(1) It is not an organization or entity described by subdivision (a).

(2) It was established and received a transfer fee before January 1, 2004.

(3) On and after January 1, 2006, it offers a purchaser the following payment options for the fee or charge it collects at time of transfer:

(A) Paying the fee or charge at the time of transfer.

(B) Paying the fee or charge pursuant to an installment payment plan for a period of not less than seven years. If the purchaser elects to pay the fee or charge in installment payments, the organization or entity may also collect additional amounts that do not exceed the actual costs for billing and financing on the amount owed. If the purchaser sells the separate interest before the end of the installment payment plan period, the purchaser shall pay the remaining balance before the transfer.

Article 4.

Restrictions on Transfer

Civ. Code § 4600. Grant of Exclusive Use Common Area.

(a) Unless the governing documents specify a different percentage, the affirmative vote of members owning at least 67 percent of the separate interests in the common interest development shall be required before the board may grant exclusive use of any portion of the common area to a member.

(b) Subdivision (a) does not apply to the following actions:

(1) A reconveyance of all or any portion of that common area to the subdivider to enable the continuation of development that is in substantial conformance with a detailed plan of phased development submitted to the Real Estate Commissioner with the application for a public report.

(2) Any grant of exclusive use that is in substantial conformance with a detailed plan of phased development submitted to the Real Estate Commissioner with the application for a public report or in accordance with the governing documents approved by the Real Estate Commissioner.

(3) Any grant of exclusive use that is for any of the following reasons:

(A) To eliminate or correct engineering errors in documents recorded with the county recorder or on file with a public agency or utility company.

(B) To eliminate or correct encroachments due to errors in construction of any improvements.

(C) To permit changes in the plan of development submitted to the Real Estate Commissioner in circumstances where the changes are the result of topography, obstruction, hardship, aesthetic considerations, or environmental conditions.

(D) To fulfill the requirement of a public agency.

(E) To transfer the burden of management and maintenance of any common area that is generally inaccessible and not of general use to the membership at large of the association.

(F) To accommodate a disability.

(G) To assign a parking space, storage unit, or other amenity, that is designated in the declaration for assignment, but is not assigned by the declaration to a specific separate interest.

(H) To install and use an electric vehicle charging station in an owner's garage or a designated parking space that meets the requirements of Section 4745, where the installation or use of the charging station requires reasonable access through, or across, the common area for utility lines or meters.

(I) To install and use an electric vehicle charging station through a license granted by an association under Section 4745.

(J) To install and use a solar energy system on the common area roof of a residence that meets the requirements of Sections 714, 714.1, and, if applicable, Section 4746.

(K) To comply with governing law.

(c) Any measure placed before the members requesting that the board grant exclusive use of any portion of the common area shall specify whether the association will receive any monetary consideration for the grant and whether the association or the transferee will be responsible for providing any insurance coverage for exclusive use of the common area.

Civ. Code § 4605. Remedies for Violation of Section 4600.

(a) A member of an association may bring a civil action for declaratory or equitable relief for a violation of Section 4600 by the association, including, but not limited to, injunctive relief, restitution, or a combination thereof, within one year of the date the cause of action accrues.

(b) A member who prevails in a civil action to enforce the member's rights pursuant to Section 4600 shall be entitled to reasonable attorney's fees and court costs, and the court may impose a civil penalty of up to five hundred dollars ($500) for each violation, except that each identical violation shall be subject to only one penalty if the violation affects each member equally. A prevailing association shall not recover any costs, unless the court finds the action to be frivolous, unreasonable, or without foundation.

Civ. Code § 4610. Restrictions on Partition of Common Areas.

(a) Except as provided in this section, the common area in a condominium project shall remain undivided, and there shall be no judicial partition thereof. Nothing in this section shall be deemed to prohibit partition of a cotenancy in a condominium.

(b) The owner of a separate interest in a condominium project may maintain a partition action as to the entire project as if the owners of all of the separate interests in the project were tenants in common in the entire project in the same proportion as their interests in the common area. The court shall order partition under this subdivision only by sale of the entire condominium project and only upon a showing of one of the following:

(1) More than three years before the filing of the action, the condominium project was damaged or destroyed, so that a material part was rendered unfit for its prior use, and the condominium project has not been rebuilt or repaired substantially to its state prior to the damage or destruction.

(2) Three-fourths or more of the project is destroyed or substantially damaged and owners of separate interests holding in the aggregate more than a 50-percent interest in the common area oppose repair or restoration of the project.

(3) The project has been in existence more than 50 years, is obsolete and uneconomic, and owners of separate interests holding in the aggregate more than a 50-percent interest in the common area oppose repair or restoration of the project.

(4) Any conditions in the declaration for sale under the circumstances described in this subdivision have been met.

Civ. Code § 4615. Liens for Labor and Materials.

(a) In a common interest development, no labor performed or services or materials furnished with the consent of, or at the request of, an owner in the common interest development or the owners' agent or contractor shall be the basis for the filing of a lien against any other property of another owner in the common interest development unless that ot7her owner has expressly consented to or requested the performance of the labor or furnishing of the materials or services. However, express consent is deemed to have been given by the owner of any separate interest in the case of emergency repairs thereto.

(b) Labor performed or services or materials furnished for the common area, if duly authorized by the association, are deemed to be performed or furnished with the express consent of each separate interest owner.

(c) The owner of any separate interest may remove that owner's separate interest from a lien against two or more separate interests or any part thereof by doing either of the following:

(1) Pay to the holder of the lien the fraction of the total sum secured by the lien that is attributable to the owner's separate interest.

(2) Record a lien release bond, pursuant to Section 8424, in an amount equal to 125 percent of the sum secured by the lien that is attributable to the owner's separate interest.

Civ. Code § 4620. Notice of Lien.

If the association is served with a claim of lien pursuant to Part 6 (commencing with Section 8000) for a work of improvement on a common area, the association shall, within 60 days of service, give individual notice to the members, pursuant to Section 4040.

Article 5.
Transfer of Separate Interest

Civ. Code § 4625. Transfer of Separate Interest in Community Apartment Project.

In a community apartment project, any conveyance, judicial sale, or other voluntary or involuntary transfer of the separate interest includes the undivided interest in the community apartment project. Any conveyance, judicial sale, or other voluntary or involuntary transfer of the owner's entire estate also includes the owner's membership interest in the association.

Civ. Code § 4630. Transfer of Separate Interest in Condominium Project.

In a condominium project the common area is not subject to partition, except as provided in Section 4610. Any conveyance, judicial sale, or other voluntary or involuntary transfer of the separate interest includes the undivided interest in the common area. Any conveyance, judicial sale, or other voluntary or involuntary transfer of the owner's entire estate also includes the owner's membership interest in the association.

Civ. Code § 4635. Transfer of Separate Interest in Planned Development.

In a planned development, any conveyance, judicial sale, or other voluntary or involuntary transfer of the separate interest includes the undivided interest in the common area, if any exists. Any conveyance, judicial sale, or other voluntary or involuntary transfer of the owner's entire estate also includes the owner's membership interest in the association.

Civ. Code § 4640. Transfer of Separate Interest in Stock Cooperative.

In a stock cooperative, any conveyance, judicial sale, or other voluntary or involuntary transfer of the separate interest includes the ownership interest in the corporation, however evidenced. Any conveyance, judicial sale, or other voluntary or involuntary transfer of the owner's entire estate also includes the owner's membership interest in the association.

Civ. Code § 4645. Transfer of Exclusive Use Areas.

Nothing in this article prohibits the transfer of exclusive use areas, independent of any other interest in a common interest subdivision, if authorization to separately transfer exclusive use areas is expressly stated in the declaration and the transfer occurs in accordance with the terms of the declaration.

Civ. Code § 4650. Restrictions on Partition.

Any restrictions upon the severability of the component interests in real property which are contained in the declaration shall not be deemed conditions repugnant to the interest created within the meaning of Section 711. However, these restrictions shall not extend beyond the period in which the right to partition a project is suspended under Section 4610.

CHAPTER 5.
PROPERTY USE AND MAINTENANCE

Article 1.
Protected Uses

Civ. Code § 4700. Limitations of Regulation of Separate Interest.

This article includes provisions that limit the authority of an association or the governing documents to regulate the use of a member's separate interest. Nothing in this article is intended to affect the application of any other provision that limits the authority of an association to regulate the use of a member's separate interest, including, but not limited to, the following provisions:

(a) Sections 712 and 713, relating to the display of signs.

(b) Sections 714 and 714.1, relating to solar energy systems.

(c) Section 714.5, relating to structures that are constructed offsite and moved to the property in sections or modules.

(d) Sections 782, 782.5, and 6150 of this code and Section 12956.1 of the Government Code, relating to racial restrictions.

(e) Section 12927 of the Government Code, relating to the modification of property to accommodate a disability.

(f) Section 1597.40 of the Health and Safety Code, relating to the operation of a family day care home.

Civ. Code § 4705. Display of United States Flag.

(a) Except as required for the protection of the public health or safety, no governing document shall limit or prohibit, or be construed to limit or prohibit, the display of the flag of the United States by a member on or in the member's separate interest or within the member's exclusive use common area.

(b) For purposes of this section, "display of the flag of the United States" means a flag of the United States made of fabric, cloth, or paper displayed from a staff or pole or in a window, and does not mean a depiction or emblem of the flag of the United States made of lights, paint, roofing, siding, paving materials, flora, or balloons, or any other similar building, landscaping, or decorative component.

(c) In any action to enforce this section, the prevailing party shall be awarded reasonable attorney's fees and costs.

Civ. Code § 4706. Display of Religious Items.

(a) Except as restricted in Section 1940.5, no governing document shall limit or prohibit the display of one or more religious items on the entry door or entry door frame of the member's separate interest.

(b) If an association is performing maintenance, repair, or replacement of an entry door or door frame that serves a member's separate interest, the member may be required to remove a religious item during the time the work is being performed. After completion of the association's work, the member may again display or affix the religious item. The association shall provide individual notice to the member regarding the temporary removal of the religious item.

Civ. Code § 4710. Display of Noncommercial Signs Or Flags.

(a) The governing documents may not prohibit posting or displaying of noncommercial signs, posters, flags, or banners on or in a member's separate interest, except as required for the protection of public health or safety or if the posting or display would violate a local, state, or federal law.

(b) For purposes of this section, a noncommercial sign, poster, flag, or banner may be made of paper, cardboard, cloth, plastic, or fabric, and may be posted or displayed from the yard, window, door, balcony, or outside wall of the separate interest, but may not be made of lights, roofing, siding, paving materials, flora, or balloons, or any other similar building, landscaping, or decorative component, or include the painting of architectural surfaces.

(c) An association may prohibit noncommercial signs and posters that are more than nine square feet in size and noncommercial flags or banners that are more than 15 square feet in size.

Civ. Code § 4715. Pet Restrictions.

(a) No governing documents shall prohibit the owner of a separate interest within a common interest development from keeping at least one pet within the common interest development, subject to reasonable rules and regulations of the association. This section may not be construed to affect any other rights provided by law to an owner of a separate interest to keep a pet within the development.

(b) For purposes of this section, "pet" means any domesticated bird, cat, dog, aquatic animal kept within an aquarium, or other animal as agreed to between the association and the homeowner.

(c) If the association implements a rule or regulation restricting the number of pets an owner may keep, the new rule or regulation shall not apply to prohibit an owner from continuing to keep any pet that the owner currently keeps in the owner's separate interest if the pet otherwise conforms with the previous rules or regulations relating to pets.

(d) For the purposes of this section, "governing documents" shall include, but are not limited to, the conditions, covenants, and restrictions of the common interest development, and the bylaws, rules, and regulations of the association.

(e) This section shall become operative on January 1, 2001, and shall only apply to governing documents entered into, amended, or otherwise modified on or after that date.

Civ. Code § 4720. Fire Retardant Roofs.

(a) No association may require a homeowner to install or repair a roof in a manner that is in violation of Section 13132.7 of the Health and Safety Code.

(b) Governing documents of a common interest development located within a very high fire severity zone, as designated by the Director of Forestry and Fire Protection pursuant to Article 9 (commencing with Section 4201) of Chapter 1 of Part 2 of Division 4 of the Public Resources Code or by a local agency pursuant to Chapter 6.8 (commencing with Section 51175) of Part 1 of Division 1 of Title 5 of the Government Code, shall allow for at least one type of fire retardant roof covering material that meets the requirements of Section 13132.7 of the Health and Safety Code.

Civ. Code § 4725. Antenna and Satellite Restrictions.

(a) Any covenant, condition, or restriction contained in any deed, contract, security instrument, or other instrument affecting the transfer or sale of, or any interest in, a common interest development that effectively prohibits or restricts the installation or use of a video or television antenna, including a satellite dish, or that effectively prohibits or restricts the attachment of that antenna to a structure within that development where the antenna is not visible from any street or common area, except as otherwise prohibited or restricted by law, is void and unenforceable as to its application to the installation or use of a video or television antenna that has a diameter or diagonal measurement of 36 inches or less.

(b) This section shall not apply to any covenant, condition, or restriction, as described in subdivision (a), that imposes reasonable restrictions on the installation or use of a video or television antenna, including a satellite dish, that has a diameter or diagonal measurement of 36 inches or less. For purposes of this section, "reasonable restrictions" means those restrictions that do not significantly increase the cost of the video or television antenna system, including all related equipment, or significantly decrease its efficiency or performance and include all of the following:

(1) Requirements for application and notice to the association prior to the installation.

(2) Requirement of a member to obtain the approval of the association for the installation of a video or television antenna that has a diameter or diagonal measurement of 36 inches or less on a separate interest owned by another.

(3) Provision for the maintenance, repair, or replacement of roofs or other building components.

(4) Requirements for installers of a video or television antenna to indemnify or reimburse the association or its members for loss or damage caused by the installation, maintenance, or use of a video or television antenna that has a diameter or diagonal measurement of 36 inches or less.

(c) Whenever approval is required for the installation or use of a video or television antenna, including a satellite dish, the application for approval shall be processed by the appropriate approving entity for the common interest development in the same manner as an application for approval of an architectural modification to the property, and the issuance of a decision on the application shall not be willfully delayed.

(d) In any action to enforce compliance with this section, the prevailing party shall be awarded reasonable attorney's fees.

Civ. Code § 4730. Marketing Restrictions.

(a) Any provision of a governing document that arbitrarily or unreasonably restricts an owner's ability to market the owner's interest in a common interest development is void.

(b) No association may adopt, enforce, or otherwise impose any governing document that does either of the following:

(1) Imposes an assessment or fee in connection with the marketing of an owner's interest in an amount that exceeds the association's actual or direct costs. That assessment or fee shall be deemed to violate the limitation set forth in subdivision (b) of Section 5600.

(2) Establishes an exclusive relationship with a real estate broker through which the sale or marketing of interests in the development is required

to occur. The limitation set forth in this paragraph does not apply to the sale or marketing of separate interests owned by the association or to the sale or marketing of common area by the association.

(c) For purposes of this section, "market" and "marketing" mean listing, advertising, or obtaining or providing access to show the owner's interest in the development.

(d) This section does not apply to rules or regulations made pursuant to Section 712 or 713 regarding real estate signs.

Civ. Code § 4735. Low Water-Using Plants and Landscaping Restrictions.

(a) Notwithstanding any other law, a provision of the governing documents or architectural or landscaping guidelines or policies shall be void and unenforceable if it does any of the following:

(1) Prohibits, or includes conditions that have the effect of prohibiting, the use of low water-using plants as a group or as a replacement of existing turf.

(2) Prohibits, or includes conditions that have the effect of prohibiting, the use of artificial turf or any other synthetic surface that resembles grass.

(3) Has the effect of prohibiting or restricting compliance with either of the following:

(A) A water-efficient landscape ordinance adopted or in effect pursuant to subdivision (c) of Section 65595 of the Government Code.

(B) Any regulation or restriction on the use of water adopted pursuant to Section 353 or 375 of the Water Code.

(b) This section shall not prohibit an association from applying landscaping rules established in the governing documents, to the extent the rules fully conform with subdivision (a).

(c) Notwithstanding any other provision of this part, except as provided in subdivision (d), an association shall not impose a fine or assessment against an owner of a separate interest for reducing or eliminating the watering of vegetation or lawns during any period for which either of the following have occurred:

(1) The Governor has declared a state of emergency due to drought pursuant to subdivision (b) of Section 8558 of the Government Code.

(2) A local government has declared a local emergency due to drought pursuant to subdivision (c) of Section 8558 of the Government Code.

(d) Subdivision (c) shall not apply to an owner of a separate interest that, prior to the imposition of a fine or assessment described in subdivision (c), receives recycled water, as defined in Section 13050 of the Water Code, from a retail water supplier, as defined in Section 13575 of the Water Code, and fails to use that recycled water for landscaping irrigation.

(e) An owner of a separate interest upon which water-efficient landscaping measures have been installed in response to a declaration of a state of emergency described in subdivision (c) shall not be required to reverse or remove the water-efficient landscaping measures upon the conclusion of the state of emergency.

Civ. Code § 4736. Pressure Washing Restrictions.

(a) A provision of the governing documents shall be void and unenforceable if it requires pressure washing the exterior of a separate interest and any exclusive use common area appurtenant to the separate interest during a state or local government declared drought emergency.

(b) For the purposes of this section, "pressure washing" means the use of a high-pressure sprayer or hose and potable water to remove loose paint, mold, grime, dust, mud, and dirt from surfaces and objects, including buildings, vehicles, and concrete surfaces.

Civ. Code § 4739. Rental Restrictions.

(a) Notwithstanding Section 4740, an owner of a separate interest in a common interest development shall not be subject to a provision in a governing document, or amendments thereto, that prohibits the rental or leasing of a portion of the owner-occupied separate interest in that common interest development to a renter, lessee, or tenant for a period of more than 30 days.

(b) Nothing in this section shall permit an owner of a separate interest or a resident renting or leasing a portion of the owner-occupied separate

interest to violate any provision of the association governing documents that govern conduct in the separate interest or common areas, or that govern membership rights or privileges, including, but not limited to, parking restrictions and guest access to common facilities.

Civ. Code § 4740. Rental Restrictions.

(a) An owner of a separate interest in a common interest development shall not be subject to a provision in a governing document or an amendment to a governing document that prohibits the rental or leasing of any of the separate interests in that common interest development to a renter, lessee, or tenant unless that governing document, or amendment thereto, was effective prior to the date the owner acquired title to their separate interest.

(b) For purposes of this section, the right to rent or lease the separate interest of an owner shall not be deemed to have terminated if the transfer by the owner of all or part of the separate interest meets at least one of the following conditions:

(1) Pursuant to Section 62 or 480.3 of the Revenue and Taxation Code, the transfer is exempt, for purposes of reassessment by the county tax assessor.

(2) Pursuant to subdivision (b) of, solely with respect to probate transfers, or subdivision (e), (f), or (g) of, Section 1102.2, the transfer is exempt from the requirements to prepare and deliver a Real Estate Transfer Disclosure Statement, as set forth in Section 1102.6.

(c) Prior to renting or leasing their separate interest as provided by this section, an owner shall provide the association verification of the date the owner acquired title to the separate interest and the name and contact information of the prospective tenant or lessee or the prospective tenant's or lessee's representative.

(d) Nothing in this section shall be deemed to revise, alter, or otherwise affect the voting process by which a common interest development adopts or amends its governing documents.

Civil Code § 4741. Limitations on Rental Restrictions.

(a) An owner of a separate interest in a common interest development shall not be subject to a provision in a governing document or an amendment to a governing document that prohibits, has the effect of prohibiting, or unreasonably restricts the rental or leasing of any of the separate interests, accessory dwelling units, or junior accessory dwelling units in that common interest development to a renter, lessee, or tenant.

(b) A common interest development shall not adopt or enforce a provision in a governing document or amendment to a governing document that restricts the rental or lease of separate interests within a common interest to less than 25 percent of the separate interests. Nothing in this subdivision prohibits a common interest development from adopting or enforcing a provision authorizing a higher percentage of separate interests to be rented or leased.

(c) This section does not prohibit a common interest development from adopting and enforcing a provision in a governing document that prohibits transient or short-term rental of a separate property interest for a period of 30 days or less.

(d) For purposes of this section, an accessory dwelling unit or junior accessory dwelling unit shall not be construed as a separate interest.

(e) For purposes of this section, a separate interest shall not be counted as occupied by a renter if the separate interest, or the accessory dwelling unit or junior accessory dwelling unit of the separate interest, is occupied by the owner.

(f) A common interest development shall comply with the prohibition on rental restrictions specified in this section on and after January 1, 2021, regardless of whether the common interest development has revised their governing documents to comply with this section. Notwithstanding any other provision of law or provision of the governing documents, the board, without approval of the members, shall amend any declaration or other governing document no later than July 1, 2022, that includes a restrictive covenant prohibited by this section by either deleting or restating the restrictive covenant to be compliant with this section, and shall restate the declaration or other governing document without the restrictive covenant but with no other change to the declaration or governing document. A board shall provide general notice pursuant to Section 4045 of the amendment at least 28 days before approving the amendment. The notice shall include the text of the amendment and a description of the purpose and effect of the amendment. The decision on the amendment shall be made at a board meeting, after consideration of any comments made by association members.

(g) A common interest development that willfully violates this section shall be liable to the applicant or other party for actual damages, and shall pay a civil penalty to the applicant or other party in an amount not to exceed one thousand dollars ($1,000).

(h) In accordance with Section 4740, this section does not change the right of an owner of a separate interest who acquired title to their separate interest before the effective date of this section to rent or lease their property.

Civ. Code § 4745. Electric Vehicle Charging Stations.

(a) Any covenant, restriction, or condition contained in any deed, contract, security instrument, or other instrument affecting the transfer or sale of any interest in a common interest development, and any provision of a governing document, as defined in Section 4150, that either effectively prohibits or unreasonably restricts the installation or use of an electric vehicle charging station within an owner's unit or in a designated parking space, including, but not limited to, a deeded parking space, a parking space in an owner's exclusive use common area, or a parking space that is specifically designated for use by a particular owner, or is in conflict with the provisions of this section is void and unenforceable.

(b) (1) This section does not apply to provisions that impose reasonable restrictions on electric vehicle charging stations. However, it is the policy of the state to promote, encourage, and remove obstacles to the use of electric vehicle charging stations.

(2) For purposes of this section, "reasonable restrictions" are restrictions that do not significantly increase the cost of the station or significantly decrease its efficiency or specified performance.

(c) An electric vehicle charging station shall meet applicable health and safety standards and requirements imposed by state and local authorities, and all other applicable zoning, land use, or other ordinances, or land use permits.

(d) For purposes of this section, "electric vehicle charging station" means a station that is designed in compliance with the California Building Standards Code and delivers electricity from a source outside an electric vehicle into one or more electric vehicles. An electric vehicle charging station may include several charge points simultaneously connecting several electric vehicles to the station and any related equipment needed to facilitate charging plug-in electric vehicles.

(e) If approval is required for the installation or use of an electric vehicle charging station, the application for approval shall be processed and approved by the association in the same manner as an application for approval of an architectural modification to the property, and shall not be willfully avoided or delayed. The approval or denial of an application shall be in writing. If an application is not denied in writing within 60 days from the date of receipt of the application, the application shall be deemed approved, unless that delay is the result of a reasonable request for additional information.

(f) If the electric vehicle charging station is to be placed in a common area or an exclusive use common area, as designated in the common interest development's declaration, the following provisions apply:

(1) The owner first shall obtain approval from the association to install the electric vehicle charging station and the association shall approve the installation if the owner agrees in writing to do all of the following:

(A) Comply with the association's architectural standards for the installation of the charging station.

(B) Engage a licensed contractor to install the charging station.

(C) Within 14 days of approval, provide a certificate of insurance that names the association as an additional insured under the owner' s insurance policy in the amount set forth in paragraph (3).

(D) Pay for both the costs associated with the installation of and the electricity usage associated with the charging station.

(2) The owner and each successive owner of the charging station shall be responsible for all of the following:

(A) Costs for damage to the charging station, common area, exclusive use common area, or separate interests resulting from the installation, maintenance, repair, removal, or replacement of the charging station.

(B) Costs for the maintenance, repair, and replacement of the charging station until it has been removed and for the restoration of the common area after removal.

(C) The cost of electricity associated with the charging station.

(D) Disclosing to prospective buyers the existence of any charging station of the owner and the related responsibilities of the owner under this section.

(3) The owner of the charging station, whether located within a separate unit or within the common area or exclusive use common area, shall, at all times, maintain a liability coverage policy. The owner that submitted the application to install the charging station shall provide the association with the corresponding certificate of insurance within 14 days of approval of the application. That owner and each successor owner shall provide the association with the certificate of insurance annually thereafter.

(4) A homeowner shall not be required to maintain a homeowner liability coverage policy for an existing National Electrical Manufacturers Association standard alternating current power plug.

(g) Except as provided in subdivision (h), installation of an electric vehicle charging station for the exclusive use of an owner in a common area, that is not an exclusive use common area, shall be authorized by the association only if installation in the owner's designated parking space is impossible or unreasonably expensive. In such cases, the association shall enter into a license agreement with the owner for the use of the space in a common area, and the owner shall comply with all of the requirements in subdivision (f).

(h) The association or owners may install an electric vehicle charging station in the common area for the use of all members of the association and, in that case, the association shall develop appropriate terms of use for the charging station.

(i) An association may create a new parking space where one did not previously exist to facilitate the installation of an electric vehicle charging station.

(j) An association that willfully violates this section shall be liable to the applicant or other party for actual damages, and shall pay a civil penalty to the applicant or other party in an amount not to exceed one thousand dollars ($1,000).

(k) In any action by a homeowner requesting to have an electric vehicle charging station installed and seeking to enforce compliance with this section, the prevailing plaintiff shall be awarded reasonable attorney's fees.

Civ. Code § 4745.1. Electric Vehicle-Dedicated TOU Meters.

(a) Any covenant, restriction, or condition contained in any deed, contract, security instrument, or other instrument affecting the transfer or sale of any interest in a common interest development, and any provision of a governing document, as defined in Section 4150, that either effectively prohibits or unreasonably restricts the installation or use of an EV-dedicated TOU meter or is in conflict with this section is void and unenforceable.

(b) (1) This section does not apply to provisions that impose reasonable restrictions on the installation of an EV-dedicated TOU meter. However, it is the policy of the state to promote, encourage, and remove obstacles to the effective installation of EV-dedicated TOU meters.

(2) For purposes of this section, "reasonable restrictions" are restrictions based upon space, aesthetics, structural integrity, and equal access to these services for all homeowners, but an association shall attempt to find a reasonable way to accommodate the installation request, unless the association would need to incur an expense.

(c) An EV-dedicated TOU meter shall meet applicable health and safety standards and requirements imposed by state and local authorities, and all other applicable zoning, land use, or other ordinances, or land use permits.

(d) For purposes of this section, an "EV-dedicated TOU meter" means an electric meter supplied and installed by an electric utility, that is separate from, and in addition to, any other electric meter and is devoted exclusively to the charging of electric vehicles, and that tracks the time of use (TOU) when charging occurs. An "EV-dedicated TOU meter" includes any wiring or conduit necessary to connect the electric meter to an electric vehicle charging station, as defined in Section 4745, regardless of whether it is supplied or installed by an electric utility.

(e) If approval is required for the installation or use of an EV-dedicated TOU meter, the application for approval shall be processed and approved by the association in the same manner as an application for approval of an architectural modification to the property, and shall not be willfully avoided or delayed. The approval or denial of an application shall be in writing. If an application is not denied in writing within 60 days from the date of receipt of the application, the application shall be deemed approved, unless that delay is the result of a reasonable request for additional information.

(f) If the EV-dedicated TOU meter is to be placed in a common area or an exclusive use common area, as designated in the common interest development's declaration, the following provisions apply:

(1) The owner first shall obtain approval from the association to install the EV-dedicated TOU meter and the association shall approve the installation if the owner agrees in writing to do both of the following:

(A) Comply with the association's architectural standards for the installation of the EV-dedicated TOU meter.

(B) Engage the relevant electric utility to install the EV-dedicated TOU meter and, if necessary, a licensed contractor to install wiring or conduit necessary to connect the electric meter to an EV charging station.

(2) The owner and each successive owner of an EV-dedicated TOU meter shall be responsible for all of the following:

(A) Costs for damage to the EV-dedicated TOU meter, common area, exclusive use common area, or separate interests resulting from the installation, maintenance, repair, removal, or replacement of the EV-dedicated TOU meter.

(B) Costs for the maintenance, repair, and replacement of the EV-dedicated TOU meter until it has been removed and for the restoration of the common area after removal.

(C) Disclosing to prospective buyers the existence of any EV-dedicated TOU meter of the owner and the related responsibilities of the owner under this section.

(g) The association or owners may install an EV-dedicated TOU meter in the common area for the use of all members of the association and, in that case, the association shall develop appropriate terms of use for the EV-dedicated TOU meter.

(h) An association that willfully violates this section shall be liable to the applicant or other party for actual damages, and shall pay a civil penalty to the applicant or other party in an amount not to exceed one thousand dollars ($1,000).

(i) In any action by a homeowner requesting to have an EV-dedicated TOU meter installed and seeking to enforce compliance with this section, the prevailing plaintiff shall be awarded reasonable attorney's fees.

It is the intent of the Legislature, in enacting this act, to take important initial steps to protect the owners in a common interest development from fraudulent activity by those entrusted with the management of the association's finances, recognizing that still further action may be necessary to achieve that goal.

Civ. Code § 4746. Solar Energy Systems.

(a) When reviewing a request to install a solar energy system on a multifamily common area roof shared by more than one homeowner pursuant to Sections 714 and 714.1, an association shall require both of the following:

(1) An applicant to notify each owner of a unit in the building on which the installation will be located of the application to install a solar energy system.

(2) The owner and each successive owner to maintain a homeowner liability coverage policy at all times and provide the association with the corresponding certificate of insurance within 14 days of approval of the application and annually thereafter.

(b) When reviewing a request to install a solar energy system on a multifamily common area roof shared by more than one homeowner pursuant to Sections 714 and 714.1, an association may impose additional reasonable provisions that:

(1) (A) Require the applicant to submit a solar site survey showing the placement of the solar energy system prepared by a licensed contractor or the contractor's registered salesperson knowledgeable in the installation of solar energy systems to determine usable solar roof area. This survey or the costs to determine useable space shall not be deemed as part of the cost of the system as used in Section 714.

(B) The solar site survey shall also include a determination of an equitable allocation of the usable solar roof area among all owners sharing the same roof, garage, or carport.

(2) Require the owner and each successive owner of the solar energy system to be responsible for all of the following:

(A) Costs for damage to the common area, exclusive use common area, or separate interests resulting from the installation, maintenance, repair, removal, or replacement of the solar energy system.

(B) Costs for the maintenance, repair, and replacement of solar energy system until it has been removed and for the restoration of the common area, exclusive use common area, or separate interests after removal.

(C) Disclosing to prospective buyers the existence of any solar energy system of the owner and the related responsibilities of the owner under this section.

(c) For purposes of this section:

(1) "Association" has the same meaning as defined in Section 4080 or 6528.

(2) "Common area" has the same meaning as defined in Section 4095 or 6532.

(3) "Separate interest" has the same meaning as defined in Section 4185 or 6564.

(d) This section imposes additional requirements for any proposed installation of a solar energy system on a multifamily common area roof shared by more than one homeowner.

(e) This section does not diminish the authority of an association to impose reasonable provisions pursuant to Section 714.1.

Civ. Code § 4747. Floor Area Standards.

(a) Any covenant, restriction, or condition contained in any deed, contract, security instrument, or other instrument affecting the transfer or sale of any interest in a planned development, and any provision of a governing document, is void and unenforceable if it effectively prohibits or unreasonably restricts an eligible housing development project from using the floor area ratio standards authorized under Section 65913.11 of the Government Code.

(b) This section does not apply to provisions that impose reasonable restrictions on an eligible housing development that do not make the implementation of the floor area standards authorized in Section 65913.11 of the Government Code infeasible.

(c) For purposes of this section:

(1) "Eligible housing development project" means a housing development project that meets the requirements of subdivision (b) of Section 65913.11 of the Government Code.

(2) "Reasonable restrictions" means restrictions that do not unreasonably increase the cost to construct, effectively prohibit the construction of, or extinguish the ability to otherwise construct an eligible housing development project using the floor area ratio standards in a manner authorized by Section 65913.11 of the Government Code.

(d) The Legislature finds and declares that the provision of adequate housing, in light of the severe shortage of housing at all income levels in this state, is a matter of statewide concern and that this section serves a significant and legitimate public purpose by eliminating potential restrictions that could inhibit the production of adequate housing.

Civ. Code § 4750. Personal Agriculture.

(a) For the purposes of this section, "personal agriculture" has the same definition as in Section 1940.10.

(b) Any provision of a governing document, as defined in Section 4150, shall be void and unenforceable if it effectively prohibits or unreasonably restricts the use of a homeowner's backyard for personal agriculture.

(c) (1) This section does not apply to provisions that impose reasonable restrictions on the use of a homeowner's yard for personal agriculture.

(2) For the purposes of this section, "reasonable restrictions" are restrictions that do not significantly increase the cost of engaging in personal agriculture or significantly decreases its efficiency.

(d) This section applies only to yards that are designated for the exclusive use of the homeowner.

(e) This section shall not prohibit a homeowners' association from applying rules and regulations requiring that dead plant material and weeds, with the exception of straw, mulch, compost, and other organic materials intended to encourage vegetation and retention of moisture in the soil, are regularly cleared from the backyard.

Civ. Code § 4751. Accessory Dwelling Units.

(a) Any covenant, restriction, or condition contained in any deed, contract, security instrument, or other instrument affecting the transfer or sale of any interest in a planned development, and any provision of a governing document, that either effectively prohibits or unreasonably restricts the construction or use of an accessory dwelling unit or junior accessory dwelling unit on a lot zoned for single-family residential use that meets the requirements of Section 65852.2 or 65852.22 of the Government Code, is void and unenforceable.

(b) This section does not apply to provisions that impose reasonable restrictions on accessory dwelling units or junior accessory dwelling units. For purposes of this subdivision, "reasonable restrictions" means restrictions that do not unreasonably increase the cost to construct, effectively prohibit the construction of, or extinguish the ability to otherwise construct, an accessory dwelling unit or junior accessory dwelling unit consistent with the provisions of Section 65852.2 or 65852.22 of the Government Code.

Civ. Code § 4753. Clotheslines.

(a) For purposes of this section, "clothesline" includes a cord, rope, or wire from which laundered items may be hung to dry or air. A balcony, railing, awning, or other part of a structure or building shall not qualify as a clothesline.

(b) For purposes of this section, "drying rack" means an apparatus from which laundered items may be hung to dry or air. A balcony, railing, awning, or other part of a structure or building shall not qualify as a drying rack.

(c) Any provision of a governing document, as defined in Section 4150, shall be void and unenforceable if it effectively prohibits or unreasonably restricts an owner's ability to use a clothesline or drying rack in the owner's backyard.

(d) (1) This section does not apply to provisions that impose reasonable restrictions on an owner's backyard for the use of a clothesline or drying rack.

(2) For purposes of this section, "reasonable restrictions" are restrictions that do not significantly increase the cost of using a clothesline or drying rack.

(3) This section applies only to backyards that are designated for the exclusive use of the owner.

(e) Nothing in this section shall prohibit an association from establishing and enforcing reasonable rules governing clotheslines or drying racks.

Article 2.
Modification of Separate Interest

Civ. Code § 4760. Modification of Separate Interest.

(a) Subject to the governing documents and applicable law, a member may do the following:

(1) Make any improvement or alteration within the boundaries of the member's separate interest that does not impair the structural integrity or mechanical systems or lessen the support of any portions of the common interest development.

(2) Modify the member's separate interest, at the member's expense, to facilitate access for persons who are blind, visually handicapped, deaf, or physically disabled, or to alter conditions which could be hazardous to these persons. These modifications may also include modifications of the route from the public way to the door of the separate interest for the purposes of this paragraph if the separate interest is on the ground floor or already accessible by an existing ramp or elevator. The right granted by this paragraph is subject to the following conditions:

(A) The modifications shall be consistent with applicable building code requirements.

(B) The modifications shall be consistent with the intent of otherwise applicable provisions of the governing documents pertaining to safety or aesthetics.

(C) Modifications external to the dwelling shall not prevent reasonable passage by other residents, and shall be removed by the member when the separate interest is no longer occupied by persons requiring those modifications who are blind, visually handicapped, deaf, or physically disabled.

(D) Any member who intends to modify a separate interest pursuant to this paragraph shall submit plans and specifications to the association for review to determine whether the modifications will comply with the provisions of this paragraph. The association shall not deny approval of the proposed modifications under this paragraph without good cause.

(b) Any change in the exterior appearance of a separate interest shall be in accordance with the governing documents and applicable provisions of law.

Civ. Code § 4765. Architectural Review and Procedure for Approval.

(a) This section applies if the governing documents require association approval before a member may make a physical change to the member's separate interest or to the common area. In reviewing and approving or disapproving a proposed change, the association shall satisfy the following requirements:

(1) The association shall provide a fair, reasonable, and expeditious procedure for making its decision. The procedure shall be included in the association's governing documents. The procedure shall provide for prompt deadlines. The procedure shall state the maximum time for response to an application or a request for reconsideration by the board.

(2) A decision on a proposed change shall be made in good faith and may not be unreasonable, arbitrary, or capricious.

(3) Notwithstanding a contrary provision of the governing documents, a decision on a proposed change may not violate any governing provision of law, including, but not limited to, the Fair Employment and Housing Act (Part 2.8 (commencing with Section 12900) of Division 3 of Title 2 of the Government Code), or a building code or other applicable law governing land use or public safety.

(4) A decision on a proposed change shall be in writing. If a proposed change is disapproved, the written decision shall include both an explanation

of why the proposed change is disapproved and a description of the procedure for reconsideration of the decision by the board.

(5) If a proposed change is disapproved, the applicant is entitled to reconsideration by the board, at an open meeting of the board. This paragraph does not require reconsideration of a decision that is made by the board or a body that has the same membership as the board, at a meeting that satisfies the requirements of Article 2 (commencing with Section 4900) of Chapter 6. Reconsideration by the board does not constitute dispute resolution within the meaning of Section 5905.

(b) Nothing in this section authorizes a physical change to the common area in a manner that is inconsistent with an association's governing documents, unless the change is required by law.

(c) An association shall annually provide its members with notice of any requirements for association approval of physical changes to property. The notice shall describe the types of changes that require association approval and shall include a copy of the procedure used to review and approve or disapprove a proposed change.

Article 3.
Maintenance

Civ. Code § 4775. Common Area Maintenance Effective 1/1/2017.

(a) (1) Except as provided in paragraph (3), unless otherwise provided in the declaration of a common interest development, the association is responsible for repairing, replacing, and maintaining the common area.

(2) Unless otherwise provided in the declaration of a common interest development, the owner of each separate interest is responsible for repairing, replacing, and maintaining that separate interest.

(3) Unless otherwise provided in the declaration of a common interest development, the owner of each separate interest is responsible for maintaining the exclusive use common area appurtenant to that separate interest and the association is responsible for repairing and replacing the exclusive use common area.

(b) The costs of temporary relocation during the repair and maintenance of the areas within the responsibility of the association shall be borne by the owner of the separate interest affected.

(c) This section shall become operative on January 1, 2017.

Civ. Code § 4777. Application of Pesticides by Non-Licensed Persons.

(a) For the purposes of this section:

(1) "Adjacent separate interest" means a separate interest that is directly beside, above, or below a particular separate interest or the common area.

(2) "Authorized agent" means an individual, organization, or other entity that has entered into an agreement with the association to act on the association's behalf.

(3) "Broadcast application" means spreading pesticide over an area greater than two square feet.

(4) "Electronic delivery" means delivery of a document by electronic means to the electronic address at, or through which, an owner of a separate interest has authorized electronic delivery.

(5) "Licensed pest control operator" means anyone licensed by the state to apply pesticides.

(6) "Pest" means a living organism that causes damage to property or economic loss, or transmits or produces diseases.

(7) "Pesticide" means any substance, or mixture of substances, that is intended to be used for controlling, destroying, repelling, or mitigating any pest or organism, excluding antimicrobial pesticides as defined by the Federal Insecticide, Fungicide, and Rodenticide Act (7 U.S.C. Sec. 136(mm)).

(b) (1) An association or its authorized agent that applies any pesticide to a separate interest or to the common area without a licensed pest control operator shall provide the owner and, if applicable, the tenant of an affected separate interest and, if making broadcast applications, or using total release foggers or aerosol sprays, the owner and, if applicable, the tenant in an adjacent separate interest that could reasonably be impacted by the pesticide use with written notice that contains the following statements and information using words with common and everyday meaning:

(A) The pest or pests to be controlled.

(B) The name and brand of the pesticide product proposed to be used.

(C) "State law requires that you be given the following information:

CAUTION – PESTICIDES ARE TOXIC CHEMICALS.

The California Department of Pesticide Regulation and the United States Environmental Protection Agency allow the unlicensed use of certain pesticides based on existing scientific evidence that there are no appreciable risks if proper use conditions are followed or that the risks are outweighed by the benefits. The degree of risk depends upon the degree of exposure, so exposure should be minimized.

If within 24 hours following application of a pesticide, a person experiences symptoms similar to common seasonal illness comparable to influenza, the person should contact a physician, appropriate licensed health care provider, or the California Poison Control System (1-800-222-1222).

For further information, contact any of the following: for Health Questions – the County Health Department (telephone number) and for Regulatory Information – the Department of Pesticide Regulation (916-324-4100)."

(D) The approximate date, time, and frequency with which the pesticide will be applied.

(E) The following notification:

"The approximate date, time, and frequency of this pesticide application is subject to change."

(2) At least 48 hours prior to application of the pesticide to a separate interest, the association or its authorized agent shall provide individual notice to the owner and, if applicable, the tenant of the separate interest and notice to an owner and, if applicable, the tenant occupying any adjacent separate interest that is required to be notified pursuant to paragraph (1).

(3) (A) At least 48 hours prior to application of the pesticide to a common area, the association or its authorized agent shall, if practicable, post the written notice described in paragraph (1) in a conspicuous place in or around the common area in which the pesticide is to be applied. Otherwise, if not practicable, the association or its authorized agent shall provide individual notice to the owner and, if applicable, the tenant of the separate interest that is adjacent to the common area.

(B) If the pest poses an immediate threat to health and safety, thereby making compliance with notification prior to the pesticide application unreasonable, the association or its authorized agent shall post the written notice as soon as practicable, but not later than one hour after the pesticide is applied.

(4) Notice to tenants of separate interests shall be provided, in at least one of the following ways:

(A) First-class mail.

(B) Personal delivery to a tenant 18 years of age or older.

(C) Electronic delivery, if an electronic mailing address has been provided by the tenant.

(5) (A) Upon receipt of written notification, the owner of the separate interest or the tenant may agree in writing or, if notification was delivered electronically, the tenant may agree through electronic delivery, to allow the association or authorized agent to apply a pesticide immediately or at an agreed upon time.

(B) (i) Prior to receipt of written notification, the association or authorized agent may agree orally to an immediate pesticide application if the owner or, if applicable, the tenant requests that the pesticide be applied before the 48-hour notice of the pesticide product proposed to be used.

(ii) With respect to an owner or, if applicable, a tenant entering into an oral agreement for immediate pesticide application, the association or authorized agent, no later than the time of pesticide application, shall leave the written notice specified in paragraph (1) in a conspicuous place in the separate interest or at the entrance of the separate interest in a manner in which a reasonable person would discover the notice.

(iii) If any owner or, if applicable, any tenant of a separate interest or an owner or, if applicable, a tenant of an adjacent separate interest is also required to be notified pursuant to this subparagraph, the association or authorized agent shall provide that person with this notice as soon as practicable after the oral agreement is made authorizing immediate pesticide application, but in no case later than commencement of application of the pesticide.

(6) A copy of a written notice provided pursuant to paragraph (1) shall be attached to the minutes of the board meeting immediately subsequent the application of the pesticide.

Civ. Code § 4780. Damage by Wood-Destroying Pests or Organisms.

(a) In a community apartment project, condominium project, or stock cooperative, unless otherwise provided in the declaration, the association is responsible for the repair and maintenance of the common area occasioned by the presence of wood-destroying pests or organisms.

(b) In a planned development, unless a different maintenance scheme is provided in the declaration, each owner of a separate interest is responsible for the repair and maintenance of that separate interest as may be occasioned by the presence of wood-destroying pests or organisms. Upon approval of the majority of all members of the association, pursuant to Section 4065, that responsibility may be delegated to the association, which shall be entitled to recover the cost thereof as a special assessment.

Civ. Code § 4785. Relocation During Treatment For Pests.

(a) The association may cause the temporary, summary removal of any occupant of a common interest development for such periods and at such times as may be necessary for prompt, effective treatment of wood-destroying pests or organisms.

(b) The association shall give notice of the need to temporarily vacate a separate interest to the occupants and to the owners, not less than 15 days nor more than 30 days prior to the date of the temporary relocation. The notice shall state the reason for the temporary relocation, the date and time of the beginning of treatment, the anticipated date and time of termination of treatment, and that the occupants will be responsible for their own accommodations during the temporary relocation.

(c) Notice by the association shall be deemed complete upon either:

(1) Personal delivery of a copy of the notice to the occupants, and if an occupant is not the owner, individual delivery pursuant to Section 4040, of a copy of the notice to the owner.

(2) Individual delivery pursuant to Section 4040 to the occupant at the address of the separate interest, and if the occupant is not the owner, individual delivery pursuant to Section 4040, of a copy of the notice to the owner.

(d) For purposes of this section, "occupant" means an owner, resident, guest, invitee, tenant, lessee, sublessee, or other person in possession of the separate interest.

Civ. Code § 4790. Access for Maintenance of Telephone Wiring.

Notwithstanding the provisions of the declaration, a member is entitled to reasonable access to the common area for the purpose of maintaining the internal and external telephone wiring made part of the exclusive use common area of the member's separate interest pursuant to subdivision (c) of Section 4145. The access shall be subject to the consent of the association, whose approval shall not be unreasonably withheld, and which may include the association's approval of telephone wiring upon the exterior of the common area, and other conditions as the association determines reasonable.

CHAPTER 6.
ASSOCIATION GOVERNANCE

Article 1.
Association Existence and Powers

Civ. Code § 4800. CID to be Managed by Association.

A common interest development shall be managed by an association that may be incorporated or unincorporated. The association may be referred to as an owner's association or a community association.

Civ. Code § 4805. Exercise of Powers of Nonprofit Mutual Benefit Corporation.

(a) Unless the governing documents provide otherwise, and regardless of whether the association is incorporated or unincorporated, the association may exercise the powers granted to a nonprofit mutual benefit corporation, as enumerated in Section 7140 of the Corporations Code, except that an unincorporated association may not adopt or use a corporate seal or issue membership certificates in accordance with Section 7313 of the Corporations Code.

(b) The association, whether incorporated or unincorporated, may exercise the powers granted to an association in this act.

Civ. Code § 4820. Membership Rights in Joint Neighborhood Associations.

Whenever two or more associations have consolidated any of their functions under a joint neighborhood association or similar organization, members of each participating association shall be (a) entitled to attend all meetings of the joint association other than executive sessions, (b) given reasonable opportunity for participation in those meetings, and (c) entitled to the same access to the joint association's records as they are to the participating association's records.

Article 2.
Board Meeting

Civ. Code § 4900. Open Meeting Act.

This article shall be known and may be cited as the Common Interest Development Open Meeting Act.

Civ. Code § 4910. No Action on Business Outside of Board Meeting; Limitation on Electronic Transmission.

(a) The board shall not take action on any item of business outside of a board meeting.

(b) (1) Notwithstanding Section 7211 of the Corporations Code, the board shall not conduct a meeting via a series of electronic transmissions, including, but not limited to, electronic mail, except as specified in paragraph (2).

(2) Electronic transmissions may be used as a method of conducting an emergency board meeting if all directors, individually or collectively, consent in writing to that action, and if the written consent or consents are filed with the minutes of the board meeting. These written consents may be transmitted electronically.

Civ. Code § 4920. Notice of Board Meeting.

(a) Except as provided in subdivision (b), the association shall give notice of the time and place of a board meeting at least four days before the meeting.

(b) (1) If a board meeting is an emergency meeting held pursuant to Section 4923, the association is not required to give notice of the time and place of the meeting.

(2) If a nonemergency board meeting is held solely in executive session, the association shall give notice of the time and place of the meeting at least two days prior to the meeting.

(3) If the association's governing documents require a longer period of notice than is required by this section, the association shall comply with

the period stated in its governing documents. For the purposes of this paragraph, a governing document provision does not apply to a notice of an emergency meeting or a meeting held solely in executive session unless it specifically states that it applies to those types of meetings.

(c) Notice of a board meeting shall be given by general delivery pursuant to Section 4045.

(d) Notice of a board meeting shall contain the agenda for the meeting.

Civ. Code § 4923. Emergency Board Meeting.

An emergency board meeting may be called by the president of the association, or by any two directors other than the president, if there are circumstances that could not have been reasonably foreseen which require immediate attention and possible action by the board, and which of necessity make it impracticable to provide notice as required by Section 4920.

Civ. Code § 4925. Member Attendance at Board Meeting.

(a) Any member may attend board meetings, except when the board adjourns to, or meets solely in, executive session. As specified in subdivision (b) of Section 4090, a member of the association shall be entitled to attend a teleconference meeting or the portion of a teleconference meeting that is open to members, and that meeting or portion of the meeting shall be audible to the members in a location specified in the notice of the meeting.

(b) The board shall permit any member to speak at any meeting of the association or the board, except for meetings of the board held in executive session. A reasonable time limit for all members of the association to speak to the board or before a meeting of the association shall be established by the board.

Civ. Code § 4930. Requirement for Action by Board.

(a) Except as described in subdivisions (b) to (e), inclusive, the board may not discuss or take action on any item at a nonemergency meeting unless the item was placed on the agenda included in the notice that was distributed pursuant to subdivision (a) of Section 4920. This subdivision does not prohibit a member or resident who is not a director from speaking on issues not on the agenda.

(b) Notwithstanding subdivision (a), a director, a managing agent or other agent of the board, or a member of the staff of the board, may do any of the following:

(1) Briefly respond to statements made or questions posed by a person speaking at a meeting as described in subdivision (b) of Section 4925.

(2) Ask a question for clarification, make a brief announcement, or make a brief report on the person's own activities, whether in response to questions posed by a member or based upon the person's own initiative.

(c) Notwithstanding subdivision (a), the board or a director, subject to rules or procedures of the board, may do any of the following:

(1) Provide a reference to, or provide other resources for factual information to, its managing agent or other agents or staff.

(2) Request its managing agent or other agents or staff to report back to the board at a subsequent meeting concerning any matter, or take action to direct its managing agent or other agents or staff to place a matter of business on a future agenda.

(3) Direct its managing agent or other agents or staff to perform administrative tasks that are necessary to carry out this section.

(d) Notwithstanding subdivision (a), the board may take action on any item of business not appearing on the agenda distributed pursuant to subdivision (a) of Section 4920 under any of the following conditions:

(1) Upon a determination made by a majority of the board present at the meeting that an emergency situation exists. An emergency situation exists if there are circumstances that could not have been reasonably foreseen by the board, that require immediate attention and possible action by the board, and that, of necessity, make it impracticable to provide notice.

(2) Upon a determination made by the board by a vote of two-thirds of the directors present at the meeting, or, if less than two-thirds of total membership of the board is present at the meeting, by a unanimous vote of the directors present, that there is a need to take immediate action

and that the need for action came to the attention of the board after the agenda was distributed pursuant to subdivision (a) of Section 4920.

(3) The item appeared on an agenda that was distributed pursuant to subdivision (a) of Section 4920 for a prior meeting of the board that occurred not more than 30 calendar days before the date that action is taken on the item and, at the prior meeting, action on the item was continued to the meeting at which the action is taken.

(e) Before discussing any item pursuant to subdivision (d), the board shall openly identify the item to the members in attendance at the meeting.

Civ. Code § 4935. Executive Session Board Meeting.

(a) The board may adjourn to, or meet solely in, executive session to consider litigation, matters relating to the formation of contracts with third parties, member discipline, personnel matters, or to meet with a member, upon the member's request, regarding the member's payment of assessments, as specified in Section 5665.

(b) The board shall adjourn to, or meet solely in, executive session to discuss member discipline, if requested by the member who is the subject of the discussion. That member shall be entitled to attend the executive session.

(c) The board shall adjourn to, or meet solely in, executive session to discuss a payment plan pursuant to Section 5665.

(d) The board shall adjourn to, or meet solely in, executive session to decide whether to foreclose on a lien pursuant to subdivision (b) of Section 5705.

(e) Any matter discussed in executive session shall be generally noted in the minutes of the immediately following meeting that is open to the entire membership.

Civ. Code § 4950. Minutes of Meeting.

(a) The minutes, minutes proposed for adoption that are marked to indicate draft status, or a summary of the minutes, of any board meeting, other than an executive session, shall be available to members within 30 days of the meeting. The minutes, proposed minutes, or summary minutes shall be distributed to any member upon request and upon reimbursement of the association's costs for making that distribution.

(b) The annual policy statement, prepared pursuant to Section 5310, shall inform the members of their right to obtain copies of board meeting minutes and of how and where to do so.

Civ. Code § 4955. Remedies for Violation of Open Meeting Act.

(a) A member of an association may bring a civil action for declaratory or equitable relief for a violation of this article by the association, including, but not limited to, injunctive relief, restitution, or a combination thereof, within one year of the date the cause of action accrues.

(b) A member who prevails in a civil action to enforce the member's rights pursuant to this article shall be entitled to reasonable attorney's fees and court costs, and the court may impose a civil penalty of up to five hundred dollars ($500) for each violation, except that each identical violation shall be subject to only one penalty if the violation affects each member equally. A prevailing association shall not recover any costs, unless the court finds the action to be frivolous, unreasonable, or without foundation.

Article 3.
Member Meeting

Civ. Code § 5000. Member Meetings.

(a) Meetings of the membership of the association shall be conducted in accordance with a recognized system of parliamentary procedure or any parliamentary procedures the association may adopt.

(b) The board shall permit any member to speak at any meeting of the membership of the association. A reasonable time limit for all members to speak at a meeting of the association shall be established by the board.

Article 4.
Member Election

Civ. Code § 5100. Secret Ballot Election.

(a) (1) Notwithstanding any other law or provision of the governing documents, elections regarding assessments legally requiring a vote, election and removal of directors, amendments to the governing documents, or the grant of exclusive use of common area pursuant to Section 4600 shall be held by secret ballot in accordance with the procedures set forth in this article.

(2) An association shall hold an election for a seat on the board of directors in accordance with the procedures set forth in this article at the expiration of the corresponding director's term and at least once every four years.

(b) This article also governs an election on any topic that is expressly identified in the operating rules as being governed by this article.

(c) The provisions of this article apply to both incorporated and unincorporated associations, notwithstanding any contrary provision of the governing documents.

(d) The procedures set forth in this article shall apply to votes cast directly by the membership, but do not apply to votes cast by delegates or other elected representatives.

(e) In the event of a conflict between this article and the provisions of the Nonprofit Mutual Benefit Corporation Law (Part 3 (commencing with Section 7110) of Division 2 of Title 1 of the Corporations Code) relating to elections, the provisions of this article shall prevail.

(f) Directors shall not be required to be elected pursuant to this article if the governing documents provide that one member from each separate interest is a director.

Civ. Code § 5103. Elections by Acclamation.

Notwithstanding the secret balloting requirement in Section 5100, or any contrary provision in the governing documents, when, as of the deadline for submitting nominations provided for in subdivision (a) of Section 5115, the number of qualified candidates is not more than the number of vacancies to be elected, as determined by the inspector or inspectors of the elections, the association may, but is not required to, consider the qualified candidates elected by acclamation if all of the following conditions have been met:

(a) The association has held a regular election for the directors in the last three years. The three-year time period shall be calculated from the date ballots were due in the last full election to the start of voting for the proposed election.

(b) The association provided individual notice of the election and the procedure for nominating candidates as follows:

(1) Initial notice at least 90 days before the deadline for submitting nominations provided for in subdivision (a) of Section 5115. The initial notice shall include all of the following:

(A) The number of board positions that will be filled at the election.

(B) The deadline for submitting nominations.

(C) The manner in which nominations can be submitted.

(D) A statement informing members that if, at the close of the time period for making nominations, there are the same number or fewer qualified candidates as there are board positions to be filled, then the board of directors may, after voting to do so, seat the qualified candidates by acclamation without balloting.

(2) A reminder notice between 7 and 30 days before the deadline for submitting nominations provided for in subdivision (a) of Section 5115. The reminder notice shall include all of the following:

(A) The number of board positions that will be filled at the election.

(B) The deadline for submitting nominations.

(C) The manner in which nominations can be submitted.

(D) A list of the names of all of the qualified candidates to fill the board positions as of the date of the reminder notice.

(E) A statement reminding members that if, at the close of the time period for making nominations, there are the same number or fewer qualified candidates as there are board positions to be filled, then the board of directors may, after voting to do so, seat the qualified candidates by acclamation without balloting. This statement is not required if, at the time the reminder notice will be delivered, the number of qualified candidates already exceeds the number of board positions to be filled.

(c) (1) The association provides, within seven business days of receiving a nomination, a written or electronic communication acknowledging the nomination to the member who submitted the nomination.

(2) The association provides, within seven business days of receiving a nomination, a written or electronic communication to the nominee, indicating either of the following:

(A) The nominee is a qualified candidate for the board of directors.

(B) The nominee is not a qualified candidate for the board of directors, the basis for the disqualification, and the procedure, which shall comply with Article 2 (commencing with Section 5900) of Chapter 10, by which the nominee may appeal the disqualification.

(3) The association may combine the written or electronic communication described in paragraphs (1) and (2) into a single written or electronic communication if the nominee and the nominator are the same person.

(d) (1) The association permits all candidates to run if nominated, except for nominees disqualified for running as allowed or required pursuant to subdivisions (b) to (e), inclusive, of Section 5105.

(2) Notwithstanding paragraph (1), an association may disqualify a nominee if the person has served the maximum number of terms or sequential terms allowed by the association.

(3) If an association disqualifies a nominee pursuant to this subdivision, an association in its election rules shall also require a director to comply with the same requirements.

(e) The association board votes to consider the qualified candidates elected by acclamation at a meeting pursuant to Article 2 (commencing with Section 4900) for which the agenda item reflects the name of each qualified candidate that will be seated by acclamation if the item is approved.

Civ. Code § 5105. Election Rules.

(a) An association shall adopt operating rules in accordance with the procedures prescribed by Article 5 (commencing with Section 4340) of Chapter 3, that do all of the following:

(1) Ensure that if any candidate or member advocating a point of view is provided access to association media, newsletters, or internet websites during a campaign, for purposes that are reasonably related to that election, equal access shall be provided to all candidates and members advocating a point of view, including those not endorsed by the board, for purposes that are reasonably related to the election. The association shall not edit or redact any content from these communications, but may include a statement specifying that the candidate or member, and not the association, is responsible for that content.

(2) Ensure access to the common area meeting space, if any exists, during a campaign, at no cost, to all candidates, including those who are not incumbents, and to all members advocating a point of view, including those not endorsed by the board, for purposes reasonably related to the election.

(3) Specify the qualifications for candidates for the board and any other elected position, subject to subdivision (b), and procedures for the nomination of candidates, consistent with the governing documents. A nomination or election procedure shall not be deemed reasonable if it disallows any member from nominating themself for election to the board.

(4) Specify the voting power of each membership, the authenticity, validity, and effect of proxies, and the voting period for elections, including the times at which polls will open and close, consistent with the governing documents.

(5) Specify a method of selecting one or three independent third parties as inspector or inspectors of elections utilizing one of the following methods:

(A) Appointment of the inspector or inspectors by the board.

(B) Election of the inspector or inspectors by the members of the association.

(C) Any other method for selecting the inspector or inspectors.

(6) Allow the inspector or inspectors to appoint and oversee additional persons to verify signatures and to count and tabulate votes as the inspector or inspectors deem appropriate, provided that the persons are independent third parties who meet the requirements in subdivision (b) of Section 5110.

(7) Require retention of, as association election materials, both a candidate registration list and a voter list. The candidate list shall include name and address of individuals nominated as a candidate for election to the board of directors. The voter list shall include name, voting power, and either the physical address of the voter's separate interest, the parcel number, or both. The mailing address for the ballot shall be listed on the voter list if it differs from the physical address of the voter's separate interest or if only the parcel number is used. The association shall permit members to verify the accuracy of their individual information on both lists at least 30 days before the ballots are distributed. The association or member shall report any errors or omissions to either list to the inspector or inspectors who shall make the corrections within two business days.

(b) An association shall disqualify a person from a nomination as a candidate for not being a member of the association at the time of the nomination.

(1) This subdivision does not restrict a developer from making a nomination of a nonmember candidate consistent with the voting power of the developer as set forth in the regulations of the Department of Real Estate and the association's governing documents.

(2) If title to a separate interest parcel is held by a legal entity that is not a natural person, the governing authority of that legal entity shall have the power to appoint a natural person to be a member for purposes of this article.

(c) Through its bylaws or election operating rules adopted pursuant to subdivision (a) of Section 5105 only, an association may disqualify a person from nomination as a candidate pursuant to any of the following:

(1) Subject to paragraph (2) of subdivision (d), an association may require a nominee for a board seat, and a director during their board tenure, to be current in the payment of regular and special assessments, which are consumer debts subject to validation. If an association requires a nominee to be current in the payment of regular and special assessments, it shall also require a director to be current in the payment of regular and special assessments.

(2) An association may disqualify a person from nomination as a candidate if the person, if elected, would be serving on the board at the same time as another person who holds a joint ownership interest in the same separate interest parcel as the person and the other person is either properly nominated for the current election or an incumbent director.

(3) An association may disqualify a nominee if that person has been a member of the association for less than one year.

(4) An association may disqualify a nominee if that person discloses, or if the association is aware or becomes aware of, a past criminal conviction that would, if the person was elected, either prevent the association from purchasing the insurance required by Section 5806 or terminate the association's existing insurance coverage required by Section 5806 as to that person should the person be elected.

(d) An association may disqualify a person from nomination for nonpayment of regular and special assessments, but may not disqualify a nominee for nonpayment of fines, fines renamed as assessments, collection charges, late charges, or costs levied by a third party. The person shall not be disqualified for failure to be current in payment of regular and special assessments if either of the following circumstances is true:

(1) The person has paid the regular or special assessment under protest pursuant to Section 5658.

(2) The person has entered into and is in compliance with a payment plan pursuant to Section 5665.

(e) An association shall not disqualify a person from nomination if the person has not been provided the opportunity to engage in internal dispute resolution pursuant to Article 2 (commencing with Section 5900) of Chapter 10.

(f) Notwithstanding any other law, the rules adopted pursuant to this section may provide for the nomination of candidates from the floor of membership meetings or nomination by any other manner. Those rules may permit write-in candidates for ballots.

(g) Notwithstanding any other law, the rules adopted pursuant to this section shall do all of the following:

(1) Prohibit the denial of a ballot to a member for any reason other than not being a member at the time when ballots are distributed.

(2) Prohibit the denial of a ballot to a person with general power of attorney for a member.

(3) Require the ballot of a person with general power of attorney for a member to be counted if returned in a timely manner.

(4) Require the inspector or inspectors of elections to deliver, or cause to be delivered, at least 30 days before an election, to each member both of the following documents:

(A) The ballot or ballots.

(B) A copy of the election operating rules. Delivery of the election operating rules may be accomplished by either of the following methods:

(i) Posting the election operating rules to an internet website and including the corresponding internet website address on the ballot together with the phrase, in at least 12-point font: "The rules governing this election may be found here:"

(ii) Individual delivery.

(h) Election operating rules adopted pursuant to this section shall not be amended less than 90 days prior to an election.

Civ. Code § 5110. Inspectors of Elections.

(a) The association shall select an independent third party or parties as an inspector of elections. The number of inspectors of elections shall be one or three.

(b) For the purposes of this section, an independent third party includes, but is not limited to, a volunteer poll worker with the county registrar of voters, a licensee of the California Board of Accountancy, or a notary public. An independent third party may be a member, but may not be a director or a candidate for director or be related to a director or to a candidate for director. An independent third party may not be a person, business entity, or subdivision of a business entity who is currently employed or under contract to the association for any compensable services other than serving as an inspector of elections.

(c) The inspector or inspectors of elections shall do all of the following:

(1) Determine the number of memberships entitled to vote and the voting power of each.

(2) Determine the authenticity, validity, and effect of proxies, if any.

(3) Receive ballots.

(4) Hear and determine all challenges and questions in any way arising out of or in connection with the right to vote.

(5) Count and tabulate all votes.

(6) Determine when the polls shall close, consistent with the governing documents.

(7) Determine the tabulated results of the election.

(8) Perform any acts as may be proper to conduct the election with fairness to all members in accordance with this article, the Corporations Code, and all applicable rules of the association regarding the conduct of the election that are not in conflict with this article.

(d) An inspector of elections shall perform all duties impartially, in good faith, to the best of the inspector of election's ability, as expeditiously as is practical, and in a manner that protects the interest of all members of the association. If there are three inspectors of elections, the decision or act of a majority shall be effective in all respects as the decision or act of all. Any report made by the inspector or inspectors of elections is prima facie evidence of the facts stated in the report.

Civ. Code § 5115. Secret Ballot Procedures.

(a) An association shall provide general notice of the procedure and deadline for submitting a nomination at least 30 days before any deadline for submitting a nomination. Individual notice shall be delivered pursuant to Section 4040 if individual notice is requested by a member. This subdivision shall only apply to elections of directors and to recall elections.

(b) For elections of directors and for recall elections, an association shall provide general notice of all of the following at least 30 days before the ballots are distributed:

(1) The date and time by which, and the physical address where, ballots are to be returned by mail or handed to the inspector or inspectors of elections.

(2) The date, time, and location of the meeting at which ballots will be counted.

(3) The list of all candidates' names that will appear on the ballot.

(4) Individual notice of the above paragraphs shall be delivered pursuant to Section 4040 if individual notice is requested by a member.

(c) Ballots and two preaddressed envelopes with instructions on how to return ballots shall be mailed by first-class mail or delivered by the association to every member not less than 30 days prior to the deadline for voting. In order to preserve confidentiality, a voter may not be identified by name, address, or lot, parcel, or unit number on the ballot. The association shall use as a model those procedures used by California counties for ensuring confidentiality of vote by mail ballots, including all of the following:

(1) The ballot itself is not signed by the voter, but is inserted into an envelope that is sealed. This envelope is inserted into a second envelope that is sealed. In the upper left-hand corner of the second envelope, the voter shall sign the voter's name, indicate the voter's name, and indicate the address or separate interest identifier that entitles the voter to vote.

(2) The second envelope is addressed to the inspector or inspectors of elections, who will be tallying the votes. The envelope may be mailed or delivered by hand to a location specified by the inspector or inspectors of elections. The member may request a receipt for delivery.

(d) A quorum shall be required only if so stated in the governing documents or other provisions of law. If a quorum is required by the governing documents, each ballot received by the inspector of elections shall be treated as a member present at a meeting for purposes of establishing a quorum.

(e) An association shall allow for cumulative voting using the secret ballot procedures provided in this section, if cumulative voting is provided for in the governing documents.

(f) Except for the meeting to count the votes required in subdivision (a) of Section 5120, an election may be conducted entirely by mail unless otherwise specified in the governing documents.

(g) In an election to approve an amendment of the governing documents, the text of the proposed amendment shall be delivered to the members with the ballot.

Civ. Code § 5120. Counting Ballots.

(a) All votes shall be counted and tabulated by the inspector or inspectors of elections, or the designee of the inspector of elections, in public at a properly noticed open meeting of the board or members. Any candidate or other member of the association may witness the counting and tabulation of the votes. No person, including a member of the association or an employee of the management company, shall open or otherwise review any ballot prior to the time and place at which the ballots are counted and tabulated. The inspector of elections, or the designee of the inspector of elections, may verify the member's information and signature on the outer envelope prior to the meeting at which ballots are tabulated. Once a secret ballot is received by the inspector of elections, it shall be irrevocable.

(b) The tabulated results of the election shall be promptly reported to the board and shall be recorded in the minutes of the next meeting of the board and shall be available for review by members of the association. Within 15 days of the election, the board shall give general notice pursuant to Section 4045 of the tabulated results of the election.

Civ. Code § 5125. Custody of Ballots.

The sealed ballots, signed voter envelopes, voter list, proxies, and candidate registration list shall at all times be in the custody of the inspector or inspectors of elections or at a location designated by the inspector or inspectors until after the tabulation of the vote, and until the time allowed by Section 5145 for challenging the election has expired, at which time custody shall be transferred to the association. If there is a recount or other challenge to the election process, the inspector or inspectors of elections shall, upon written request, make the ballots available for inspection and review by an association member or the member's authorized representative. Any recount shall be conducted in a manner that preserves the confidentiality of the vote.

Civ. Code § 5130. Proxies.

(a) For purposes of this article, the following definitions shall apply:

(1) "Proxy" means a written authorization signed by a member or the authorized representative of the member that gives another member or members the power to vote on behalf of that member.

(2) "Signed" means the placing of the member's name on the proxy (whether by manual signature, typewriting, telegraphic transmission, or otherwise) by the member or authorized representative of the member.

(b) Proxies shall not be construed or used in lieu of a ballot. An association may use proxies if permitted or required by the bylaws of the association and if those proxies meet the requirements of this article, other laws, and the governing documents, but the association shall not be required to prepare or distribute proxies pursuant to this article.

(c) Any instruction given in a proxy issued for an election that directs the manner in which the proxyholder is to cast the vote shall be set forth on a separate page of the proxy that can be detached and given to the proxyholder to retain. The proxyholder shall cast the member's vote by secret ballot.

The proxy may be revoked by the member prior to the receipt of the ballot by the inspector of elections as described in Section 7613 of the Corporations Code.

Civ. Code § 5135. Prohibition of Association Funds for Campaign Purposes.

(a) Association funds shall not be used for campaign purposes in connection with any association board election. Funds of the association shall not be used for campaign purposes in connection with any other association election except to the extent necessary to comply with duties of the association imposed by law.

(b) For the purposes of this section, "campaign purposes" includes, but is not limited to, the following:

(1) Expressly advocating the election or defeat of any candidate that is on the association election ballot.

(2) Including the photograph or prominently featuring the name of any candidate on a communication from the association or its board, excepting the ballot, ballot materials, or a communication that is legally required, within 30 days of an election. This is not a campaign purpose if the communication is one for which subdivision (a) of Section 5105 requires that equal access be provided to another candidate or advocate.

Civ. Code § 5145. Remedies Violation of Ballot Election Statutes.

(a) A member of an association may bring a civil action for declaratory or equitable relief for a violation of this article by the association, including, but not limited to, injunctive relief, restitution, or a combination thereof, within one year of the date that the inspector or inspectors of elections notifies the board and membership of the election results or the cause of action accrues, whichever is later. If a member establishes, by a preponderance of the evidence, that the election procedures of this article, or the adoption of and adherence to rules provided by Article 5 (commencing with Section 4340) of Chapter 3, were not followed, a court shall void any results of the election unless the association establishes, by a preponderance of the evidence, that the association's noncompliance with this article or the election operating rules did not affect the results of the election. The findings of the court shall be stated in writing as part of the record.

(b) A member who prevails in a civil action to enforce the member's rights pursuant to this article shall be entitled to reasonable attorney's fees and court costs, and the court may impose a civil penalty of up to five hundred dollars ($500) for each violation, except that each identical violation shall be subject to only one penalty if the violation affects each member of the association equally. A prevailing association shall not recover any costs, unless the court finds the action to be frivolous, unreasonable, or without foundation. If a member prevails in a civil action brought in small claims court, the member shall be awarded court costs and reasonable attorney's fees incurred for consulting an attorney in connection with this civil action.

(c) A cause of action under subdivision (a) may be brought in either the superior court or, if the amount of the demand does not exceed the jurisdictional amount of the small claims court, in small claims court.

Article 5.
Record Inspection

Civ. Code § 5200. Records Inspection Definitions.

For the purposes of this article, the following definitions shall apply:

(a) "Association records" means all of the following:

(1) Any financial document required to be provided to a member in Article 7 (commencing with Section 5300) or in Sections 5565 and 5810.

(2) Any financial document or statement required to be provided in Article 2 (commencing with Section 4525) of Chapter 4.

(3) Interim financial statements, periodic or as compiled, containing any of the following:

(A) Balance sheet.

(B) Income and expense statement.

(C) Budget comparison.

(D) General ledger. A "general ledger" is a report that shows all transactions that occurred in an association account over a specified period of time.

The records described in this paragraph shall be prepared in accordance with an accrual or modified accrual basis of accounting.

(4) Executed contracts not otherwise privileged under law.

(5) Written board approval of vendor or contractor proposals or invoices.

(6) State and federal tax returns.

(7) Reserve account balances and records of payments made from reserve accounts.

(8) Agendas and minutes of meetings of the members, the board, and any committees appointed by the board pursuant to Section 7212 of the Corporations Code; excluding, however, minutes and other information from executive sessions of the board as described in Article 2 (commencing with Section 4900).

(9) Membership lists, including name, property address, mailing address, email address, as collected by the association in accordance with Section 4041 where applicable, but not including information for members who have opted out pursuant to Section 5220.

(10) Check registers.

(11) The governing documents.

(12) An accounting prepared pursuant to subdivision (b) of Section 5520.

(13) An "enhanced association record" as defined in subdivision (b).

(14) "Association election materials" as defined in subdivision (c).

(b) "Enhanced association records" means invoices, receipts and canceled checks for payments made by the association, purchase orders approved by the association, bank account statements for bank accounts in which assessments are deposited or withdrawn, credit card statements for credit cards issued in the name of the association, statements for services rendered, and reimbursement requests submitted to the association.

(c) "Association election materials" means returned ballots, signed voter envelopes, the voter list of names, parcel numbers, and voters to whom ballots were to be sent, proxies, and the candidate registration list. Signed voter envelopes may be inspected but may not be copied. An association shall maintain association election materials for one year after the date of the election.

Civ. Code § 5205. Inspection and Copying of Association Records.

(a) The association shall make available association records for the time periods and within the timeframes provided in Section 5210 for inspection and copying by a member of the association, or the member's designated representative.

(b) A member of the association may designate another person to inspect and copy the specified association records on the member's behalf. The member shall make this designation in writing.

(c) The association shall make the specified association records available for inspection and copying in the association's business office within the common interest development.

(d) If the association does not have a business office within the development, the association shall make the specified association records available for inspection and copying at a place agreed to by the requesting member and the association.

(e) If the association and the requesting member cannot agree upon a place for inspection and copying pursuant to subdivision (d) or if the requesting member submits a written request directly to the association for copies of specifically identified records, the association may satisfy the requirement to make the association records available for inspection and copying by delivering copies of the specifically identified records to the member by individual delivery pursuant to Section 4040 within the timeframes set forth in subdivision (b) of Section 5210.

(f) The association may bill the requesting member for the direct and actual cost of copying and mailing requested documents. The association shall inform the member of the amount of the copying and mailing costs, and the member shall agree to pay those costs, before copying and sending the requested documents.

(g) In addition to the direct and actual costs of copying and mailing, the association may bill the requesting member an amount not in excess of ten dollars ($10) per hour, and not to exceed two hundred dollars ($200) total per written request, for the time actually and reasonably involved in redacting an enhanced association record. If the enhanced association record includes a reimbursement request, the person submitting the reimbursement request shall be solely responsible for removing all personal identification information from the request. The association shall inform the member of the estimated costs, and the member shall agree to pay those costs, before retrieving the requested documents.

(h) Requesting parties shall have the option of receiving specifically identified records by electronic transmission or machine-readable storage media as long as those records can be transmitted in a redacted format that does not allow the records to be altered. The cost of duplication shall be limited to the direct cost of producing the copy of a record in that electronic format. The association may deliver specifically identified records by electronic transmission or machine-readable storage media as long as those records can be transmitted in a redacted format that prevents the records from being altered.

Civ. Code § 5210. Time Periods for Access to Records.

(a) Association records are subject to member inspection for the following time periods:

(1) For the current fiscal year and for each of the previous two fiscal years.

(2) Notwithstanding paragraph (1), minutes of member and board meetings are subject to inspection permanently. If a committee has decision making authority, minutes of the meetings of that committee shall be made available commencing January 1, 2007, and shall thereafter be permanently subject to inspection.

(b) When a member properly requests access to association records, access to the requested records shall be granted within the following time periods:

(1) Association records prepared during the current fiscal year, within 10 business days following the association's receipt of the request.

(2) Association records prepared during the previous two fiscal years, within 30 calendar days following the association's receipt of the request.

(3) Any record or statement available pursuant to Article 2 (commencing with Section 4525) of Chapter 4, Article 7 (commencing with Section 5300), Section 5565, or Section 5810, within the timeframe specified therein.

(4) Minutes of member and board meetings, within the timeframe specified in subdivision (a) of Section 4950.

(5) Minutes of meetings of committees with decision making authority for meetings commencing on or after January 1, 2007, within 15 calendar days following approval.

(6) Membership list, within the timeframe specified in Section 8330 of the Corporations Code.

(c) There shall be no liability pursuant to this article for an association that fails to retain records for the periods specified in subdivision (a) that were created prior to January 1, 2006.

Civ. Code § 5215. Permissible Redaction in Records.

(a) Except as provided in subdivision (b), the association may withhold or redact information from the association records if any of the following are true:

(1) The release of the information is reasonably likely to lead to identity theft. For the purposes of this section, "identity theft" means the unauthorized use of another person's personal identifying information to obtain credit, goods, services, money, or property. Examples of information that may be withheld or redacted pursuant to this paragraph include bank account numbers of members or vendors, social security or tax identification numbers, and check, stock, and credit card numbers.

(2) The release of the information is reasonably likely to lead to fraud in connection with the association.

(3) The information is privileged under law. Examples include documents subject to attorney-client privilege or relating to litigation in which the association is or may become involved, and confidential settlement agreements.

(4) The release of the information is reasonably likely to compromise the privacy of an individual member of the association.

(5) The information contains any of the following:

(A) Records of goods or services provided a la carte to individual members of the association for which the association received monetary consideration other than assessments.

(B) Records of disciplinary actions, collection activities, or payment plans of members other than the member requesting the records.

(C) Any person's personal identification information, including, without limitation, social security number, tax identification number, driver's license number, credit card account numbers, bank account number, and bank routing number.

(D) Minutes and other information from executive sessions of the board as described in Article 2 (commencing with Section 4900), except for executed contracts not otherwise privileged. Privileged contracts shall not include contracts for maintenance, management, or legal services.

(E) Personnel records other than the payroll records required to be provided under subdivision (b).

(F) Interior architectural plans, including security features, for individual homes.

(b) Except as provided by the attorney-client privilege, the association may not withhold or redact information concerning the compensation paid to employees, vendors, or contractors. Compensation information for individual employees shall be set forth by job classification or title, not by the employee's name, social security number, or other personal information.

(c) No association, officer, director, employee, agent, or volunteer of an association shall be liable for damages to a member of the association or any third party as the result of identity theft or other breach of privacy because of the failure to withhold or redact that member's information under this section unless the failure to withhold or redact the information was intentional, willful, or negligent.

(d) If requested by the requesting member, an association that denies or redacts records shall provide a written explanation specifying the legal basis for withholding or redacting the requested records.

Civ. Code § 5216. Safe at Home Participants.

(a) Notwithstanding any other law, upon request of a member of an association who is an active participant in the Safe at Home program, the association shall do both of the following:

(1) Accept and use the address designated by the Secretary of State as the Safe at Home participant's substitute address under the Safe at Home program for all association communications.

(2) Withhold or redact information that would reveal the name, community property address, or email address of the Safe at Home participant from both of the following:

(A) All resident community membership lists, including mailbox bank listings, resident directories, electronic keypads, unit property numbers, and internet web portal accounts.

(B) Any membership list that will be shared with other members of the association.

(b) An association shall keep member participation in the Safe at Home program confidential.

(c) For purposes of this section:

(1) "Community property address" means the address of the member's property within the community governed by the association.

(2) "Safe at Home participant" means a person certified as a program participant in the Safe at Home program.

(3) "Safe at Home program" means the address confidentiality program established pursuant to Chapter 3.1 (commencing with Section 6205) of Division 7 of Title 1 of the Government Code.

Civ. Code § 5220. Member Opt Out.

A member of the association may opt out of the sharing of that member's name, property address, email address, and mailing address by notifying the association in writing that the member prefers to be contacted via the alternative process described in subdivision (c) of Section 8330 of the Corporations Code. This opt-out shall remain in effect until changed by the member.

Civ. Code § 5225. Reason for Request of Membership List.

A member requesting the membership list shall state the purpose for which the list is requested which purpose shall be reasonably related to the requester's interest as a member. If the association reasonably believes that the information in the list will be used for another purpose, it may deny the member access to the list. If the request is denied, in any subsequent action brought by the member under Section 5235, the association shall have the burden to prove that the member would have allowed use of the information for purposes unrelated to the member's interest as a member.

Civ. Code § 5230. Restriction on Use of Association Records.

(a) The association records, and any information from them, may not be sold, used for a commercial purpose, or used for any other purpose not reasonably related to a member's interest as a member. An association may bring an action against any person who violates this article for injunctive relief and for actual damages to the association caused by the violation.

(b) This article may not be construed to limit the right of an association to damages for misuse of information obtained from the association records pursuant to this article or to limit the right of an association to injunctive relief to stop the misuse of this information.

(c) (1) An association or its managing agent shall not do either of the following:

(A) Sell a member's personal information for any purpose without the consent of the member.

(B) Transmit a member's personal information to a third party without the consent of the member unless required to do so by law, including, but not limited to, Article 5 (commencing with Section 5200).

(2) A member may bring an action against an association that violates this subdivision for injunctive relief and actual damages caused by the violation. A member shall be entitled to recover reasonable costs and expenses, including reasonable attorney's fees, in a successful action to enforce the member's rights under this subdivision.

(d) An association shall be entitled to recover reasonable costs and expenses, including reasonable attorney's fees, in a successful action to enforce its rights under this article.

Civ. Code § 5235. Remedy to Enforce Access to Records.

(a) A member may bring an action to enforce that member's right to inspect and copy the association records. If a court finds that the association unreasonably withheld access to the association records, the court shall award the member reasonable costs and expenses, including reasonable attorney's fees, and may assess a civil penalty of up to five hundred dollars ($500) for the denial of each separate written request.

(b) A cause of action under this section may be brought in small claims court if the amount of the demand does not exceed the jurisdiction of that court.

(c) A prevailing association may recover any costs if the court finds the action to be frivolous, unreasonable, or without foundation.

Civ. Code § 5240. Applicability of the Corporations Code to Article.

(a) As applied to an association and its members, the provisions of this article are intended to supersede the provisions of Sections 8330 and 8333 of the Corporations Code to the extent those sections are inconsistent.

(b) Except as provided in subdivision (a), members of the association shall have access to association records, including accounting books and records and membership lists, in accordance with Article 3 (commencing with Section 8330) of Chapter 13 of Part 3 of Division 2 of Title 1 of the Corporations Code.

(c) This article applies to any community service organization or similar entity that is related to the association, and to any nonprofit entity that provides services to a common interest development under a declaration of trust. This article shall operate to give a member of the organization or entity a right to inspect and copy the records of that organization or entity equivalent to that granted to association members by this article.

(d) This article shall not apply to any common interest development in which separate interests are being offered for sale by a subdivider under the authority of a public report issued by the Bureau of Real Estate so long as the subdivider or all subdividers offering those separate interests for sale, or any employees of those subdividers or any other person who receives direct or indirect compensation from any of those subdividers, comprise a majority of the directors. Notwithstanding the foregoing, this article shall apply to that common interest development no later than 10 years after the close of escrow for the first sale of a separate interest to a member of the general public pursuant to the public report issued for the first phase of the development.

Article 6.
Recordkeeping

Civ. Code § 5260. Written Requests.

To be effective, any of the following requests shall be delivered in writing to the association, pursuant to Section 4035:

(a) A request to change the member's information in the association membership list.

(b) A request to add or remove a second email or mailing address for delivery of individual notices to the member, pursuant to Section 4040.

(c) A request for individual delivery of general notices to the member, pursuant to subdivision (b) of Section 4045, or a request to cancel a prior request for individual delivery of general notices.

(d) A request to opt out of the membership list pursuant to Section 5220, or a request to cancel a prior request to opt out of the membership list.

(e) A request to receive a full copy of a specified annual budget report or annual policy statement pursuant to Section 5320.

(f) A request to receive all reports in full, pursuant to subdivision (b) of Section 5320, or a request to cancel a prior request to receive all reports in full.

Article 7.
Annual Reports

Civ. Code § 5300. Annual Budget Report.

(a) Notwithstanding a contrary provision in the governing documents, an association shall distribute an annual budget report 30 to 90 days before the end of its fiscal year.

(b) Unless the governing documents impose more stringent standards, the annual budget report shall include all of the following information:

(1) A pro forma operating budget, showing the estimated revenue and expenses on an accrual basis.

(2) A summary of the association's reserves, prepared pursuant to Section 5565.

(3) A summary of the reserve funding plan adopted by the board, as specified in paragraph (5) of subdivision (b) of Section 5550. The summary shall include notice to members that the full reserve study plan is available upon request, and the association shall provide the full reserve plan to any member upon request.

(4) A statement as to whether the board has determined to defer or not undertake repairs or replacement of any major component with a remaining life of 30 years or less, including a justification for the deferral or decision not to undertake the repairs or replacement.

(5) A statement as to whether the board, consistent with the reserve funding plan adopted pursuant to Section 5560, has determined or anticipates that the levy of one or more special assessments will be required to repair, replace, or restore any major component or to provide adequate reserves therefor. If so, the statement shall also set out the estimated amount, commencement date, and duration of the assessment.

(6) A statement as to the mechanism or mechanisms by which the board will fund reserves to repair or replace major components, including assessments, borrowing, use of other assets, deferral of selected replacements or repairs, or alternative mechanisms.

(7) A general statement addressing the procedures used for the calculation and establishment of those reserves to defray the future repair, replacement, or additions to those major components that the association is obligated to maintain. The statement shall include, but need not be limited to, reserve calculations made using the formula described in paragraph (4) of subdivision (b) of Section 5570, and may not assume a rate of return on cash reserves in excess of 2 percent above the discount rate published by the Federal Reserve Bank of San Francisco at the time the calculation was made.

(8) A statement as to whether the association has any outstanding loans with an original term of more than one year, including the payee, interest rate, amount outstanding, annual payment, and when the loan is scheduled to be retired.

(9) A summary of the association's property, general liability, earthquake, flood, and fidelity insurance policies. For each policy, the summary shall include the name of the insurer, the type of insurance, the policy limit, and the amount of the deductible, if any. To the extent that any of the required information is specified in the insurance policy declaration page, the association may meet its obligation to disclose that information by making copies of that page and distributing it with the annual budget report. The summary distributed pursuant to this paragraph shall contain, in at least 10-point boldface type, the following statement:

"This summary of the association's policies of insurance provides only certain information, as required by Section 5300 of the Civil Code, and should not be considered a substitute for the complete policy terms and conditions contained in the actual policies of insurance. Any association member may, upon request and provision of reasonable notice, review the association's insurance policies and, upon request and payment of reasonable duplication charges, obtain copies of those policies. Although the association maintains the policies of insurance specified in this summary, the association's policies of insurance may not cover your property, including personal property or real property improvements to or around your dwelling, or personal injuries or other losses that occur within or around your dwelling. Even if a loss is covered, you may nevertheless be responsible for paying all or a portion of any deductible that applies. Association members should consult with their individual insurance broker or agent for appropriate additional coverage."

(10) When the common interest development is a condominium project, a statement describing the status of the common interest development as a Federal Housing Administration (FHA)-approved condominium project pursuant to FHA guidelines, including whether the common interest development is an FHA-approved condominium project. The statement shall be in at least 10-point font on a separate piece of paper and in the following form:

"Certification by the Federal Housing Administration may provide benefits to members of an association, including an improvement in an owner's ability to refinance a mortgage or obtain secondary financing and an increase in the pool of potential buyers of the separate interest.

This common interest development [is/is not (circle one)] a condominium project. The association of this common interest development [is/is not (circle one)] certified by the Federal Housing Administration."

(11) When the common interest development is a condominium project, a statement describing the status of the common interest development as a federal Department of Veterans Affairs (VA)-approved condominium project pursuant to VA guidelines, including whether the common interest development is a VA-approved condominium project. The statement shall be in at least 10-point font on a separate piece of paper and in the following form:

"Certification by the federal Department of Veterans Affairs may provide benefits to members of an association, including an improvement in an owner's ability to refinance a mortgage or obtain secondary financing and an increase in the pool of potential buyers of the separate interest.

This common interest development [is/is not (circle one)] a condominium project. The association of this common interest development [is/is not (circle one)] certified by the federal Department of Veterans Affairs."

(12) A copy of the completed "Charges For Documents Provided" disclosure identified in Section 4528. For purposes of this section, "completed" means that the "Fee for Document" section of the form individually identifies the costs associated with providing each document listed on the form.

(c) The annual budget report shall be made available to the members pursuant to Section 5320.

(d) The summary of the association's reserves disclosed pursuant to paragraph (2) of subdivision (b) shall not be admissible in evidence to show improper financial management of an association, provided that other relevant and competent evidence of the financial condition of the association is not made inadmissible by this provision.

(e) The Assessment and Reserve Funding Disclosure Summary form, prepared pursuant to Section 5570, shall accompany each annual budget report or summary of the annual budget report that is delivered pursuant to this article.

Civ. Code § 5305. Review of Financial Statement.

Unless the governing documents impose more stringent standards, a review of the financial statement of the association shall be prepared in accordance with generally accepted accounting principles by a licensee of the California Board of Accountancy for any fiscal year in which the gross income to the association exceeds seventy-five thousand dollars ($75,000). A copy of the review of the financial statement shall be distributed to the members within 120 days after the close of each fiscal year, by individual delivery pursuant to Section 4040.

Civ. Code § 5310. Annual Policy Statement.

(a) Within 30 to 90 days before the end of its fiscal year, the board shall distribute an annual policy statement that provides the members with information about association policies. The annual policy statement shall include all of the following information:

(1) The name and address of the person designated to receive official communications to the association, pursuant to Section 4035.

(2) A statement explaining that a member may submit a request to have notices sent to up to two different specified addresses, pursuant to Section 4040.

(3) The location, if any, designated for posting of a general notice, pursuant to subdivision (a) of Section 4045.

(4) Notice of a member's option to receive general notices by individual delivery, pursuant to subdivision (b) of Section 4045.

(5) Notice of a member's right to receive copies of meeting minutes, pursuant to subdivision (b) of Section 4950.

(6) The statement of assessment collection policies required by Section 5730.

(7) A statement describing the association's policies and practices in enforcing lien rights or other legal remedies for default in the payment of assessments.

(8) A statement describing the association's discipline policy, if any, including any schedule of penalties for violations of the governing documents pursuant to Section 5850.

(9) A summary of dispute resolution procedures, pursuant to Sections 5920 and 5965.

(10) A summary of any requirements for association approval of a physical change to property, pursuant to Section 4765.

(11) The mailing address for overnight payment of assessments, pursuant to Section 5655.

(12) Any other information that is required by law or the governing documents or that the board determines to be appropriate for inclusion.

(b) The annual policy statement shall be made available to the members pursuant to Section 5320.

Civ. Code § 5320. Delivery of Full Report or Summary of Annual Disclosures.

(a) When a report is prepared pursuant to Section 5300 or 5310, the association shall deliver one of the following documents to all members by individual delivery pursuant to Section 4040:

(1) The full report.

(2) A summary of the report that includes, on the first page, a general description of the content of the report and instructions, printed in at least 10-point boldface type, regarding how to request a complete copy of the report at no cost to the member.

(b) Notwithstanding subdivision (a), if a member has requested to receive all reports in full, the association shall deliver the full report to that member, rather than a summary of the report.

Article 8.

Conflict of Interest

Civ. Code § 5350. Director Conflict of Interest.

(a) Notwithstanding any other law, and regardless of whether an association is incorporated or unincorporated, the provisions of Sections 7233 and 7234 of the Corporations Code shall apply to any contract or other transaction authorized, approved, or ratified by the board or a committee of the board.

(b) A director or member of a committee shall not vote on any of the following matters:

(1) Discipline of the director or committee member.

(2) An assessment against the director or committee member for damage to the common area or facilities.

(3) A request, by the director or committee member, for a payment plan for overdue assessments.

(4) A decision whether to foreclose on a lien on the separate interest of the director or committee member.

(5) Review of a proposed physical change to the separate interest of the director or committee member.

(6) A grant of exclusive use common area to the director or committee member.

(c) Nothing in this section limits any other provision of law or the governing documents that govern a decision in which a director may have an interest.

Article 9.

Managing Agent

Civ. Code § 5375. Prospective Managing Agent.

A prospective managing agent of a common interest development shall provide a written statement to the board as soon as practicable, but in no event more than 90 days, before entering into a management agreement which shall contain all of the following information concerning the managing agent:

(a) The names and business addresses of the owners or general partners of the managing agent. If the managing agent is a corporation, the written statement shall include the names and business addresses of the directors and officers and shareholders holding greater than 10 percent of the shares of the corporation.

(b) Whether or not any relevant licenses such as architectural design, construction, engineering, real estate, or accounting have been issued by this state and are currently held by the persons specified in subdivision (a). If a license is currently held by any of those persons, the statement shall contain the following information:

(1) What license is held.

(2) The dates the license is valid.

(3) The name of the licensee appearing on that license.

(c) Whether or not any relevant professional certifications or designations such as architectural design, construction, engineering, real property management, or accounting are currently held by any of the persons specified in subdivision (a), including, but not limited to, a professional common interest development manager. If any certification or designation is held, the statement shall include the following information:

(1) What the certification or designation is and what entity issued it.

(2) The dates the certification or designation is valid.

(3) The names in which the certification or designation is held.

(d) Disclose any business or company in which the common interest development manager or common interest development management firm has any ownership interests, profit-sharing arrangements, or other monetary incentives provided to the management firm or managing agent.

(e) Whether or not the common interest development manager or common interest development management firm receives a referral fee or other monetary benefit from a third-party provider distributing documents pursuant to Sections 4528 and 4530.

Civ. Code § 5375.5. Managing Agent Disclosures.

A common interest development manager or common interest development management firm shall disclose, in writing, any potential conflict of interest when presenting a bid for service to an association's board of directors. "Conflict of interest," for purposes of this section, means:

(a) Any referral fee or other monetary benefit that could be derived from a business or company providing products or services to the association.

(b) Any ownership interests or profit-sharing arrangements with service providers recommended to, or used by, the association.

Civ. Code § 5376. Managing Agent Facilitation of Disclosures.

The common interest development manager, common interest development management firm, or its contracted third-party agent shall facilitate the delivery of disclosures required pursuant to paragraph (1) of subdivision (a), paragraph (2) of subdivision (b), and subdivision (d), of Section 4530 if the common interest development manager, or common interest development management firm, is contractually responsible for delivering those documents.

Civ. Code § 5380. Management of Association Funds.

(a) A managing agent of a common interest development who accepts or receives funds belonging to the association shall deposit those funds that are not placed into an escrow account with a bank, savings association, or credit union or into an account under the control of the association, into a trust fund account maintained by the managing agent in a bank, savings association, or credit union in this state. All funds deposited by the managing agent in the trust fund account shall be kept in this state in a financial institution, as defined in Section 31041 of the Financial Code, which is insured by the federal government, or is a guaranty corporation subject to Section 14858 of the Financial Code, and shall be maintained there until disbursed in accordance with written instructions from the association entitled to the funds.

(b) At the written request of the board, the funds the managing agent accepts or receives on behalf of the association shall be deposited into an account in a bank, savings association, or credit union in this state that is insured by the Federal Deposit Insurance Corporation, National Credit Union Administration Insurance Fund, or a guaranty corporation subject to Section 14858 of the Financial Code, provided all of the following requirements are met:

(1) The account is in the name of the managing agent as trustee for the association or in the name of the association.

(2) All of the funds in the account are covered by insurance provided by an agency of the federal government or a guaranty corporation subject to Section 14858 of the Financial Code. Those funds may only be deposited in accounts that protect the principal. In no event may those funds be invested in stocks or high-risk investment options.

(3) The funds in the account are kept separate, distinct, and apart from the funds belonging to the managing agent or to any other person for whom the managing agent holds funds in trust.

(4) The managing agent discloses to the board the nature of the account, how interest will be calculated and paid, whether service charges will be paid to the depository and by whom, and any notice requirements or penalties for withdrawal of funds from the account.

(5) No interest earned on funds in the account shall inure directly or indirectly to the benefit of the managing agent or the managing agent's employees.

(6) Transfers of funds out of the association's reserve or operating accounts shall not be authorized without prior written approval from the board of the association unless the amount of the transfer is less than the following:

(A) The lesser of five thousand dollars ($5,000) or 5 percent of the estimated income in the annual operating budget, for associations with 50 or less separate interests.

(B) The lesser of ten thousand dollars ($10,000) or 5 percent of estimated income in the annual operating budget, for associations with 51 or more separate interests.

(c) The managing agent shall maintain a separate record of the receipt and disposition of all funds described in this section, including any interest earned on the funds.

(d) The managing agent shall not commingle the funds of the association with the managing agent's own money or with the money of others that the managing agent receives or accepts.

(e) The prevailing party in an action to enforce this section shall be entitled to recover reasonable legal fees and court costs.

(f) As used in this section, "completed payment" means funds received that clearly identify the account to which the funds are to be credited.

Civ. Code § 5385. Meaning of Managing Agent.

For the purposes of this article, "managing agent" does not include a full-time employee of the association.

Article 10.

Government Assistance

Civ. Code § 5400. Online Education for Directors.

To the extent existing funds are available, the Department of Consumer Affairs and the Department of Real Estate shall develop an online education course for the board regarding the role, duties, laws, and responsibilities of directors and prospective directors, and the nonjudicial foreclosure process.

Civ. Code § 5405. Identification and Regulation of Community Associations.

(a) To assist with the identification of common interest developments, each association, whether incorporated or unincorporated, shall submit to the Secretary of State, on a form and for a fee not to exceed thirty dollars ($30) that the Secretary of State shall prescribe, the following information concerning the association and the development that it manages:

(1) A statement that the association is formed to manage a common interest development under the Davis-Stirling Common Interest Development Act.

(2) The name of the association.

(3) The street address of the business or corporate office of the association, if any.

(4) The street address of the association's onsite office, if different from the street address of the business or corporate office, or if there is no onsite office, the street address of the responsible officer or managing agent of the association.

(5) The name, address, and either the daytime telephone number or email address of the president of the association, other than the address, telephone number, or email address of the association's onsite office or managing agent.

(6) The name, street address, and daytime telephone number of the association's managing agent, if any.

(7) The county, and, if in an incorporated area, the city in which the development is physically located. If the boundaries of the development are physically located in more than one county, each of the counties in which it is located.

(8) If the development is in an unincorporated area, the city closest in proximity to the development.

(9) The front street and nearest cross street of the physical location of the development.

(10) The type of common interest development managed by the association.

(11) The number of separate interests in the development.

(b) The association shall submit the information required by this section as follows:

(1) By incorporated associations, within 90 days after the filing of its original articles of incorporation, and thereafter at the time the association files its statement of principal business activity with the Secretary of State pursuant to Section 8210 of the Corporations Code.

(2) By unincorporated associations, in July 2003, and in that same month biennially thereafter. Upon changing its status to that of a corporation, the association shall comply with the filing deadlines in paragraph (1).

(c) The association shall notify the Secretary of State of any change in the street address of the association's onsite office or of the responsible officer or managing agent of the association in the form and for a fee prescribed by the Secretary of State, within 60 days of the change.

(d) The penalty for an incorporated association's noncompliance with the initial or biennial filing requirements of this section shall be suspension of the association's rights, privileges, and powers as a corporation and monetary penalties, to the same extent and in the same manner as suspension and monetary penalties imposed pursuant to Section 8810 of the Corporations Code.

(e) The statement required by this section may be filed, notwithstanding suspension of the corporate powers, rights, and privileges under this section or under provisions of the Revenue and Taxation Code. Upon the filing of a statement under this section by a corporation that has suffered suspension under this section, the Secretary of State shall certify that fact to the Franchise Tax Board and the corporation may thereupon be relieved from suspension, unless the corporation is held in suspension by the Franchise Tax Board by reason of Section 23301, 23301.5, or 23775 of the Revenue and Taxation Code.

(f) The Secretary of State shall make the information submitted pursuant to paragraph (5) of subdivision (a) available only for governmental purposes and only to Members of the Legislature and the Business, Consumer Services, and Housing Agency, upon written request. All other information submitted pursuant to this section shall be subject to public inspection pursuant to the California Public Records Act (Division 10 (commencing with Section 7920.000) of Title 1 of the Government Code). The information submitted pursuant to this section shall be made available for governmental or public inspection.

(g) Whenever any form is filed pursuant to this section, it supersedes any previously filed form.

(h) The Secretary of State may destroy or otherwise dispose of any form filed pursuant to this section after it has been superseded by the filing of a new form.

Civ. Code § 5450. Remote Meeting Requirements.

(a) This section only applies to a common interest development if gathering in person is unsafe or impossible because the common interest development is in an area affected by one or more of the following conditions:

(1) A state of disaster or emergency declared by the federal government.

(2) A state of emergency proclaimed by the Governor under Section 8625 of the Government Code.

(3) A local emergency proclaimed by a local governing body or official under Section 8630 of the Government Code.

(b) Notwithstanding any other law or the association's governing documents, and except as provided in subdivision (d), a board meeting or meeting of the members may be conducted entirely by teleconference, without any physical location being held open for the attendance of any director or member, if all of the following conditions are satisfied:

(1) Notice of the first meeting that is conducted under this section for a particular disaster or emergency affecting the association is delivered to members by individual delivery.

(2) The notice for each meeting conducted under this section includes, in addition to other required content for meeting notices, all of the following:

(A) Clear technical instructions on how to participate by teleconference.

(B) The telephone number and electronic mail address of a person who can provide technical assistance with the teleconference process, both before and during the meeting.

(C) A reminder that a member may request individual delivery of meeting notices, with instructions on how to do so.

(3) Every director and member has the same ability to participate in the meeting that would exist if the meeting were held in person.

(4) Any vote of the directors shall be conducted by a roll call vote.

(5) Any person who is entitled to participate in the meeting shall be given the option of participating by telephone.

(c) If, as a result of the disaster or emergency, mail delivery or retrieval is not possible at any association onsite address and the address on file with the association for that member is the same association onsite address, then the association shall send the notice of the first meeting referenced in paragraph (1) of subdivision (b) to any email address provided to the association by that member, in writing, pursuant to paragraph (2) of subdivision (a) of Section 4040 or subdivision (b) of Section 4041.

(d) Subdivision (b) does not apply to a meeting at which ballots are counted and tabulated pursuant to Section 5120, unless both of the following conditions are met:

(1) The meeting at which ballots are to be counted and tabulated is conducted by video conference.

(2) The camera is placed in a location such that members can witness the inspector of elections counting and tabulating the votes.

(e) The remedies available pursuant to Section 4955 shall also be available to address violations of this section.

CHAPTER 7.
FINANCES

Article 1.
Accounting

Civ. Code § 5500. Monthly Financial Review by Board.

Unless the governing documents impose more stringent standards, the board shall do all of the following:

(a) Review, on a monthly basis, a current reconciliation of the association's operating accounts.

(b) Review, on a monthly basis, a current reconciliation of the association's reserve accounts.

(c) Review, on a monthly basis, the current year's actual operating revenues and expenses compared to the current year's budget.

(d) Review, on a monthly basis, the latest account statements prepared by the financial institutions where the association has its operating and reserve accounts.

(e) Review, on a monthly basis, an income and expense statement for the association's operating and reserve accounts.

(f) Review, on a monthly basis, the check register, monthly general ledger, and delinquent assessment receivable reports.

Civ. Code § 5501. Financial Review Outside of Meeting.

The review requirements of Section 5500 may be met when every individual member of the board, or a subcommittee of the board consisting of the treasurer and at least one other board member, reviews the documents and statements described in Section 5500 independent of a board meeting, so long as the review is ratified at the board meeting subsequent to the review and that ratification is reflected in the minutes of that meeting.

Civ. Code § 5502. Board Authorization of Financial Transfers.

(a) Notwithstanding any other law, transfers shall not be authorized from the association's reserve or operating accounts without prior written approval from the board of the association unless the amount of the transfer is less than the following:

(1) The lesser of five thousand dollars ($5,000) or 5 percent of the estimated income in the annual operating budget, for associations with 50 or less separate interests.

(2) The lesser of ten thousand dollars ($10,000) or 5 percent of the estimated income in the annual operating budget, for associations with 51 or more separate interests.

(b) This section applies in addition to any other applicable requirements of this part.

Article 2.

Use of Reserve Funds

Civ. Code § 5510. Expenditure of Reserve Accounts.

(a) The signatures of at least two persons, who shall be directors, or one officer who is not a director and one who is a director, shall be required for the withdrawal of moneys from the association's reserve accounts.

(b) The board shall not expend funds designated as reserve funds for any purpose other than the repair, restoration, replacement, or maintenance of, or litigation involving the repair, restoration, replacement, or maintenance of, major components that the association is obligated to repair, restore, replace, or maintain and for which the reserve fund was established.

Civ. Code § 5515. Borrowing from Reserve Account.

(a) Notwithstanding Section 5510, the board may authorize the temporary transfer of moneys from a reserve fund to the association's general operating fund to meet short-term cashflow requirements or other expenses, if the board has provided notice of the intent to consider the transfer in a board meeting notice provided pursuant to Section 4920.

(b) The notice shall include the reasons the transfer is needed, some of the options for repayment, and whether a special assessment may be considered.

(c) If the board authorizes the transfer, the board shall issue a written finding, recorded in the board's minutes, explaining the reasons that the transfer is needed, and describing when and how the moneys will be repaid to the reserve fund.

(d) The transferred funds shall be restored to the reserve fund within one year of the date of the initial transfer, except that the board may, after giving the same notice required for considering a transfer, and, upon making a finding supported by documentation that a temporary delay would be in the best interests of the common interest development, temporarily delay the restoration.

(e) The board shall exercise prudent fiscal management in maintaining the integrity of the reserve account, and shall, if necessary, levy a special assessment to recover the full amount of the expended funds within the time limits required by this section. This special assessment is subject to the limitation imposed by Section 5605. The board may, at its discretion, extend the date the payment on the special assessment is due. Any extension shall not prevent the board from pursuing any legal remedy to enforce the collection of an unpaid special assessment.

Civ. Code § 5520. Use of Reserve Accounts; Notice to Members.

(a) When the decision is made to use reserve funds or to temporarily transfer moneys from the reserve fund to pay for litigation pursuant to subdivision (b) of Section 5510, the association shall provide general notice pursuant to Section 4045 of that decision, and of the availability of an accounting of those expenses.

(b) Unless the governing documents impose more stringent standards, the association shall make an accounting of expenses related to the litigation on at least a quarterly basis. The accounting shall be made available for inspection by members of the association at the association's office.

Article 3.

Reserve Planning

Civ. Code § 5550. Reserve Study Requirements.

(a) At least once every three years, the board shall cause to be conducted a reasonably competent and diligent visual inspection of the accessible areas of the major components that the association is obligated to repair, replace, restore, or maintain as part of a study of the reserve account requirements of the common interest development, if the current replacement value of the major components is equal to or greater than one-half of the gross budget of the association, excluding the association's reserve account for that period. The board shall review this study, or cause it to be reviewed, annually and shall consider and implement necessary adjustments to the board's analysis of the reserve account requirements as a result of that review.

(b) The study required by this section shall at a minimum include:

(1) Identification of the major components that the association is obligated to repair, replace, restore, or maintain that, as of the date of the study, have a remaining useful life of less than 30 years.

(2) Identification of the probable remaining useful life of the components identified in paragraph (1) as of the date of the study.

(3) An estimate of the cost of repair, replacement, restoration, or maintenance of the components identified in paragraph (1).

(4) An estimate of the total annual contribution necessary to defray the cost to repair, replace, restore, or maintain the components identified in paragraph (1) during and at the end of their useful life, after subtracting total reserve funds as of the date of the study.

(5) A reserve funding plan that indicates how the association plans to fund the contribution identified in paragraph (4) to meet the association's obligation for the repair and replacement of all major components with an expected remaining life of 30 years or less, not including those components that the board has determined will not be replaced or repaired.

Civ. Code § 5551. Balcony, Deck, and Elevated Elements Inspections.

(a) For purposes of this section, the following definitions apply:

(1) "Associated waterproofing systems" include flashings, membranes, coatings, and sealants that protect the load-bearing components of exterior elevated elements from exposure to water.

(2) "Exterior elevated elements" mean the load-bearing components together with their associated waterproofing system.

(3) "Load-bearing components" means those components that extend beyond the exterior walls of the building to deliver structural loads to the building from decks, balconies, stairways, walkways, and their railings, that have a walking surface elevated more than six feet above ground level, that are designed for human occupancy or use, and that are supported in whole or in substantial part by wood or wood-based products.

(4) "Statistically significant sample" means a sufficient number of units inspected to provide 95 percent confidence that the results from the sample are reflective of the whole, with a margin of error of no greater than plus or minus 5 percent.

(5) "Visual inspection" means inspection through the least intrusive method necessary to inspect load-bearing components, including visual observation only or visual observation in conjunction with, for example, the use of moisture meters, borescopes, or infrared technology.

(b) (1) At least once every nine years, the board of an association of a condominium project shall cause a reasonably competent and diligent visual inspection to be conducted by a licensed structural engineer or architect of a random and statistically significant sample of exterior elevated elements for which the association has maintenance or repair responsibility.

(2) The inspection shall determine whether the exterior elevated elements are in a generally safe condition and performing in accordance with applicable standards.

(c) Prior to conducting the first visual inspection, the inspector shall generate a random list of the locations of each type of exterior elevated element. The list shall include all exterior elevated elements for which the association has maintenance or repair responsibility. The list shall be provided to the association for future use.

(d) The inspector shall perform the visual inspections in accordance with the random list generated pursuant to subdivision (c). If during the visual inspection the inspector observes building conditions indicating that unintended water or water vapor has passed into the associated waterproofing system, thereby creating the potential for damage to the load-bearing components, then the inspector may conduct a further inspection. The inspector shall exercise their best professional judgment in determining the necessity, scope, and breadth of any further inspection.

(e) Based upon the inspector's visual inspections, further inspection, and construction and materials expertise, the inspector shall issue a written report containing the following information:

(1) The identification of the building components comprising the load-bearing components and associated waterproofing system.

(2) The current physical condition of the load-bearing components and associated waterproofing system, including whether the condition presents an immediate threat to the health and safety of the residents.

(3) The expected future performance and remaining useful life of the load-bearing components and associated waterproofing system.

(4) Recommendations for any necessary repair or replacement of the load-bearing components and associated waterproofing system.

(f) The report issued pursuant to subdivision (e) shall be stamped or signed by the inspector, presented to the board, and incorporated into the study required by Section 5550.

(g) (1) If, after inspection of any exterior elevated element, the inspector advises that the exterior elevated element poses an immediate threat to the safety of the occupants, the inspector shall provide a copy of the inspection report to the association immediately upon completion of the report, and to the local code enforcement agency within 15 days of completion of the report. Upon receiving the report, the association shall take preventive measures immediately, including preventing occupant access to the exterior elevated element until repairs have been inspected and approved by the local enforcement agency.

(2) Local enforcement agencies shall have the ability to recover enforcement costs associated with the requirements of this section from the association.

(h) Each subsequent visual inspection conducted under this section shall commence with the next exterior elevated element identified on the random list and shall proceed in order through the list.

(i) The first inspection shall be completed by January 1, 2025, and then every nine years thereafter in coordination with the reserve study inspection pursuant to Section 5550. All written reports shall be maintained for two inspection cycles as records of the association.

(j) (1) The association shall be responsible for complying with the requirements of this section.

(2) The continued and ongoing maintenance and repair of the load-bearing components and associated waterproofing systems in a safe, functional, and sanitary condition shall be the responsibility of the association as required by the association's governing documents.

(k) The inspection of buildings for which a building permit application has been submitted on or after January 1, 2020, shall occur no later than six years following the issuance of a certificate of occupancy. The inspection shall otherwise comply with the provisions of this section.

(l) This section shall only apply to buildings containing three or more multifamily dwelling units.

(m) The association board may enact rules or bylaws imposing requirements greater than those imposed by this section.

(n) A local government or local enforcement agency may enact an ordinance or other rule imposing requirements greater than those imposed by this section

Civ. Code § 5560. Reserve Funding Plan.

(a) The reserve funding plan required by Section 5550 shall include a schedule of the date and amount of any change in regular or special assessments that would be needed to sufficiently fund the reserve funding plan.

(b) The plan shall be adopted by the board at an open meeting before the membership of the association as described in Article 2 (commencing with Section 4900) of Chapter 6.

(c) If the board determines that an assessment increase is necessary to fund the reserve funding plan, any increase shall be approved in a separate action of the board that is consistent with the procedure described in Section 5605.

Civ. Code § 5565. Summary of Reserves.

The summary of the association's reserves required by paragraph (2) of subdivision (b) of Section 5300 shall be based on the most recent review or study conducted pursuant to Section 5550, shall be based only on assets held in cash or cash equivalents, shall be printed in boldface type, and shall include all of the following:

(a) The current estimated replacement cost, estimated remaining life, and estimated useful life of each major component.

(b) As of the end of the fiscal year for which the study is prepared:

(1) The current estimate of the amount of cash reserves necessary to repair, replace, restore, or maintain the major components.

(2) The current amount of accumulated cash reserves actually set aside to repair, replace, restore, or maintain major components.

(3) If applicable, the amount of funds received from either a compensatory damage award or settlement to an association from any person for injuries to property, real or personal, arising out of any construction or design defects, and the expenditure or disposition of funds, including the amounts expended for the direct and indirect costs of repair of construction or design defects. These amounts shall be reported at the end of the fiscal year for which the study is prepared as separate line items under cash reserves pursuant to paragraph (2). Instead of complying with the requirements set forth in this paragraph, an association that is obligated to issue a review of its financial statement pursuant to Section 5305 may include in the review a statement containing all of the information required by this paragraph.

(c) The percentage that the amount determined for purposes of paragraph (2) of subdivision (b) equals the amount determined for purposes of paragraph (1) of subdivision (b).

(d) The current deficiency in reserve funding expressed on a per unit basis. The figure shall be calculated by subtracting the amount determined for purposes of paragraph (2) of subdivision (b) from the amount determined for purposes of paragraph (1) of subdivision (b) and then dividing the result by the number of separate interests within the association, except that if assessments vary by the size or type of ownership interest, then the association shall calculate the current deficiency in a manner that reflects the variation.

Civ. Code § 5570. Reserve Funding Disclosure Form.

(a) The disclosures required by this article with regard to an association or a property shall be summarized on the following form:

Assessment and Reserve Funding Disclosure Summary For the Fiscal Year Ending ___

(1) The regular assessment per ownership interest is $______ per _______.

Note: If assessments vary by the size or type of ownership interest, the assessment applicable to this ownership interest may be found on page _____ of the attached summary.

(2) Additional regular or special assessments that have already been scheduled to be imposed or charged, regardless of the purpose, if they have been approved by the board and/or members:

Date assessment will be due:	Amount per ownership interest per month or year (If assessments are variable, see note immediately below):	Purpose of the assessment:
	Total:	

Note: If assessments vary by the size or type of ownership interest, the assessment applicable to this ownership interest may be found on page _____ of the attached report.

(3) Based upon the most recent reserve study and other information available to the board of directors, will currently projected reserve account balances be sufficient at the end of each year to meet the association's obligation for repair and/or replacement of major components during the next 30 years?

Yes ______ No _______

(4) If the answer to (3) is no, what additional assessments or other contributions to reserves would be necessary to ensure that sufficient reserve funds will be available each year during the next 30 years that have not yet been approved by the board or the members?

Approximate date assessment will be due:	Amount per ownership interest per month or year:
	Total:

(5) All major components are included in the reserve study and are included in its calculations.

(6) Based on the method of calculation in paragraph (4) of subdivision (b) of Section 5570, the estimated amount required in the reserve fund at the end of the current fiscal year is $_______, based in whole or in part on the last reserve study or update prepared by ____________ as of _______ (month), ______ (year). The projected reserve fund cash balance at the end of the current fiscal year is $_________, resulting in reserves being ____ percent funded at this date. If an alternate, but generally accepted, method of calculation is also used, the required reserve amount is $_______. (See attached explanation)

(7) Based on the method of calculation in paragraph (4) of subdivision (b) of Section 5570 of the Civil Code, the estimated amount required in the reserve fund at the end of each of the next five budget years is $_____, and the projected reserve fund cash balance in each of those years, taking into account only assessments already approved and other known reserves, is $_____, leaving the reserve at ___ percent funded. If the reserve funding plan approved by the association is implemented, the projected reserve fund cash balance in each of those years will be $______, leaving the reserve at ___ percent funded.

Note: The financial representations set forth in this summary are based on the best estimates of the preparer at that time. The estimates are subject to change. At the time this summary was prepared, the assumed long-term before-tax interest rate earned on reserve funds was ____ percent per year, and the assumed long-term inflation rate to be applied to major component repair and replacement costs was ____ percent per year.

(b) For the purposes of preparing a summary pursuant to this section:

(1) "Estimated remaining useful life" means the time reasonably calculated to remain before a major component will require replacement.

(2) "Major component" has the meaning used in Section 5550. Components with an estimated remaining useful life of more than 30 years may be included in a study as a capital asset or disregarded from the reserve calculation, so long as the decision is revealed in the reserve study report and reported in the Assessment and Reserve Funding Disclosure Summary.

(3) The form set out in subdivision (a) shall accompany each annual budget report or summary thereof that is delivered pursuant Section 5300. The form may be supplemented or modified to clarify the information delivered, so long as the minimum information set out in subdivision (a) is provided.

(4) For the purpose of the report and summary, the amount of reserves needed to be accumulated for a component at a given time shall be computed as the current cost of replacement or repair multiplied by the number of years the component has been in service divided by the useful life of the component. This shall not be construed to require the board to fund reserves in accordance with this calculation.

Civ. Code § 5580. Community Service Organization Financial Disclosures.

(a) Unless the governing documents impose more stringent standards, any community service organization whose funding from the association or its members exceeds 10 percent of the organization's annual budget shall prepare and distribute to the association a report that meets the requirements of Section 5012 of the Corporations Code, and that describes in detail administrative costs and identifies the payees of those costs in a manner consistent with the provisions of Article 5 (commencing with Section 5200) of Chapter 6.

(b) If the community service organization does not comply with the standards, the report shall disclose the noncompliance in detail. If a community service organization is responsible for the maintenance of major components for which an association would otherwise be responsible, the community service organization shall supply to the association the information regarding those components that the association would use to complete disclosures and reserve reports required under this article and Section 5300. An association may rely upon information received from a community service organization, and shall provide access to the information pursuant to the provisions of Article 5 (commencing with Section 5200) of Chapter 6.

CHAPTER 8.
ASSESSMENTS AND ASSESSMENT COLLECTION

Article 1.
Establishment and Imposition of Assessments

Civ. Code § 5600. Levy of Assessments.

(a) Except as provided in Section 5605, the association shall levy regular and special assessments sufficient to perform its obligations under the governing documents and this act.

(b) An association shall not impose or collect an assessment or fee that exceeds the amount necessary to defray the costs for which it is levied.

Civ. Code § 5605. Limit on Increases in Assessments.

(a) Annual increases in regular assessments for any fiscal year shall not be imposed unless the board has complied with paragraphs (1), (2), (4), (5), (6), (7), and (8) of subdivision (b) of Section 5300 with respect to that fiscal year, or has obtained the approval of a majority of a quorum of members, pursuant to Section 4070, at a member meeting or election.

(b) Notwithstanding more restrictive limitations placed on the board by the governing documents, the board may not impose a regular assessment that is more than 20 percent greater than the regular assessment for the association's preceding fiscal year or impose special assessments which in the aggregate exceed 5 percent of the budgeted gross expenses of the association for that fiscal year without the approval of a majority of a quorum of members, pursuant to Section 4070, at a member meeting or election.

(c) For the purposes of this section, "quorum" means more than 50 percent of the members.

Civ. Code § 5610. Emergency Assessment.

Section 5605 does not limit assessment increases necessary for emergency situations. For purposes of this section, an emergency situation is any one of the following:

(a) An extraordinary expense required by an order of a court.

(b) An extraordinary expense necessary to repair or maintain the common interest development or any part of it for which the association is responsible where a threat to personal safety on the property is discovered.

(c) An extraordinary expense necessary to repair or maintain the common interest development or any part of it for which the association is responsible that could not have been reasonably foreseen by the board in preparing and distributing the annual budget report under Section 5300. However, prior to the imposition or collection of an assessment under this subdivision, the board shall pass a resolution containing written findings as to the necessity of the extraordinary expense involved and why the expense was not or could not have been reasonably foreseen in the budgeting process, and the resolution shall be distributed to the members with the notice of assessment.

Civ. Code § 5615. Notice of Increased or Special Assessment.

The association shall provide individual notice pursuant to Section 4040 to the members of any increase in the regular or special assessments of the association, not less than 30 nor more than 60 days prior to the increased assessment becoming due.

Civ. Code § 5620. Assessments Exempt from Judgment Creditors.

(a) Regular assessments imposed or collected to perform the obligations of an association under the governing documents or this act shall be exempt from execution by a judgment creditor of the association only to the extent necessary for the association to perform essential services, such as paying for utilities and insurance. In determining the appropriateness of an exemption, a court shall ensure that only essential services are protected under this subdivision.

(b) This exemption shall not apply to any consensual pledges, liens, or encumbrances that have been approved by a majority of a quorum of members, pursuant to Section 4070, at a member meeting or election, or to any state tax lien, or to any lien for labor or materials supplied to the common area.

Civ. Code § 5625. Assessment not Based on Taxable Value.

(a) Except as provided in subdivision (b), notwithstanding any provision of this act or the governing documents to the contrary, an association shall not levy assessments on separate interests within the common interest development based on the taxable value of the separate interests unless the association, on or before December 31, 2009, in accordance with its governing documents, levied assessments on those separate interests based on their taxable value, as determined by the tax assessor of the county in which the separate interests are located.

(b) An association that is responsible for paying taxes on the separate interests within the common interest development may levy that portion of assessments on separate interests that is related to the payment of taxes based on the taxable value of the separate interest, as determined by the tax assessor.

Article 2.

Assessment Payment and Delinquency

Civ. Code § 5650. Delinquent Assessments; Fees, Costs, and Interest.

(a) A regular or special assessment and any late charges, reasonable fees and costs of collection, reasonable attorney's fees, if any, and interest, if any, as determined in accordance with subdivision (b), shall be a debt of the owner of the separate interest at the time the assessment or other sums are levied.

(b) Regular and special assessments levied pursuant to the governing documents are delinquent 15 days after they become due, unless the declaration provides a longer time period, in which case the longer time period shall apply. If an assessment is delinquent, the association may recover all of the following:

(1) Reasonable costs incurred in collecting the delinquent assessment, including reasonable attorney's fees.

(2) A late charge not exceeding 10 percent of the delinquent assessment or ten dollars ($10), whichever is greater, unless the declaration specifies a late charge in a smaller amount, in which case any late charge imposed shall not exceed the amount specified in the declaration.

(3) Interest on all sums imposed in accordance with this section, including the delinquent assessments, reasonable fees and costs of collection, and reasonable attorney's fees, at an annual interest rate not to exceed 12 percent, commencing 30 days after the assessment becomes due, unless the declaration specifies the recovery of interest at a rate of a lesser amount, in which case the lesser rate of interest shall apply.

(c) Associations are hereby exempted from interest-rate limitations imposed by Article XV of the California Constitution, subject to the limitations of this section.

Civ. Code § 5655. Payments of Delinquent Assessments.

(a) Any payments made by the owner of a separate interest toward a debt described in subdivision (a) of Section 5650 shall first be applied to the assessments owed, and, only after the assessments owed are paid in full shall the payments be applied to the fees and costs of collection, attorney's fees, late charges, or interest.

(b) When an owner makes a payment, the owner may request a receipt and the association shall provide it. The receipt shall indicate the date of payment and the person who received it.

(c) The association shall provide a mailing address for overnight payment of assessments. The address shall be provided in the annual policy statement.

Civ. Code § 5658. Payment Under Protest.

(a) If a dispute exists between the owner of a separate interest and the association regarding any disputed charge or sum levied by the association, including, but not limited to, an assessment, fine, penalty, late fee, collection cost, or monetary penalty imposed as a disciplinary measure, and the amount in dispute does not exceed the jurisdictional limits of the small claims court stated in Sections 116.220 and 116.221 of the Code of Civil Procedure, the owner of the separate interest may, in addition to pursuing dispute resolution pursuant to Article 3 (commencing with Section 5925) of Chapter 10, pay under protest the disputed amount and all other amounts levied, including any fees and reasonable costs of collection, reasonable attorney's fees, late charges, and interest, if any, pursuant to subdivision (b) of Section 5650, and commence an action in small claims court pursuant to Chapter 5.5 (commencing with Section 116.110) of Title 1 of the Code of Civil Procedure.

(b) Nothing in this section shall impede an association's ability to collect delinquent assessments as provided in this article or Article 3 (commencing with Section 5700).

Civ. Code § 5660. Notice of Intent to Lien.

At least 30 days prior to recording a lien upon the separate interest of the owner of record to collect a debt that is past due under Section 5650, the association shall notify the owner of record in writing by certified mail of the following:

(a) A general description of the collection and lien enforcement procedures of the association and the method of calculation of the amount, a statement that the owner of the separate interest has the right to inspect the association records pursuant to Section 5205, and the following statement in 14-point boldface type, if printed, or in capital letters, if typed:

> "IMPORTANT NOTICE: IF YOUR SEPARATE INTEREST IS PLACED IN FORECLOSURE BECAUSE YOU ARE BEHIND IN YOUR ASSESSMENTS, IT MAY BE SOLD WITHOUT COURT ACTION."

(b) An itemized statement of the charges owed by the owner, including items on the statement which indicate the amount of any delinquent assessments, the fees and reasonable costs of collection, reasonable attorney's fees, any late charges, and interest, if any.

(c) A statement that the owner shall not be liable to pay the charges, interest, and costs of collection, if it is determined the assessment was paid on time to the association.

(d) The right to request a meeting with the board as provided in Section 5665.

(e) The right to dispute the assessment debt by submitting a written request for dispute resolution to the association pursuant to the association's "meet and confer" program required in Article 2 (commencing with Section 5900) of Chapter 10.

(f) The right to request alternative dispute resolution with a neutral third party pursuant to Article 3 (commencing with Section 5925) of Chapter 10 before the association may initiate foreclosure against the owner's separate interest, except that binding arbitration shall not be available if the association intends to initiate a judicial foreclosure.

Civ. Code § 5665. Payment Plans.

(a) An owner, other than an owner of any interest that is described in Section 11212 of the Business and Professions Code that is not otherwise exempt from this section pursuant to subdivision (a) of Section 11211.7 of the Business and Professions Code, may submit a written request to meet with the board to discuss a payment plan for the debt noticed pursuant to Section 5660. The association shall provide the owners the standards for payment plans, if any exists.

(b) The board shall meet with the owner in executive session within 45 days of the postmark of the request, if the request is mailed within 15 days of the date of the postmark of the notice, unless there is no regularly scheduled board meeting within that period, in which case the board may designate a committee of one or more directors to meet with the owner.

(c) Payment plans may incorporate any assessments that accrue during the payment plan period. Additional late fees shall not accrue during the payment plan period if the owner is in compliance with the terms of the payment plan.

(d) Payment plans shall not impede an association's ability to record a lien on the owner's separate interest to secure payment of delinquent assessments.

(e) In the event of a default on any payment plan, the association may resume its efforts to collect the delinquent assessments from the time prior to entering into the payment plan.

Civ. Code § 5670. Dispute Resolution Offer Prior to Recording Lien.

Prior to recording a lien for delinquent assessments, an association shall offer the owner and, if so requested by the owner, participate in dispute resolution pursuant to the association's "meet and confer" program required in Article 2 (commencing with Section 5900) of Chapter 10.

Civ. Code § 5673. Board Approval Required to Record Lien.

For liens recorded on or after January 1, 2006, the decision to record a lien for delinquent assessments shall be made only by the board and may not be delegated to an agent of the association. The board shall approve the decision by a majority vote of the directors in an open meeting. The board shall record the vote in the minutes of that meeting.

Civ. Code § 5675. Lien; Notice of Delinquent Assessment.

(a) The amount of the assessment, plus any costs of collection, late charges, and interest assessed in accordance with subdivision (b) of Section 5650, shall be a lien on the owner's separate interest in the common interest development from and after the time the association causes to be recorded with the county recorder of the county in which the separate interest is located, a notice of delinquent assessment, which shall state the amount of the assessment and other sums imposed in accordance with subdivision (b) of Section 5650, a legal description of the owner's separate interest in the common interest development against which the assessment and other sums are levied, and the name of the record owner of the separate interest in the common interest development against which the lien is imposed.

(b) The itemized statement of the charges owed by the owner described in subdivision (b) of Section 5660 shall be recorded together with the notice of delinquent assessment.

(c) In order for the lien to be enforced by nonjudicial foreclosure as provided in Sections 5700 to 5710, inclusive, the notice of delinquent assessment shall state the name and address of the trustee authorized by the association to enforce the lien by sale.

(d) The notice of delinquent assessment shall be signed by the person designated in the declaration or by the association for that purpose, or if no one is designated, by the president of the association.

(e) A copy of the recorded notice of delinquent assessment shall be mailed by certified mail to every person whose name is shown as an owner of the separate interest in the association's records, and the notice shall be mailed no later than 10 calendar days after recordation.

Civ. Code § 5680. Priority of Lien.

A lien created pursuant to Section 5675 shall be prior to all other liens recorded subsequent to the notice of delinquent assessment, except that the declaration may provide for the subordination thereof to any other liens and encumbrances.

Civ. Code § 5685. Recording of Lien; Release of Lien; Notice of Rescission.

(a) Within 21 days of the payment of the sums specified in the notice of delinquent assessment, the association shall record or cause to be recorded in the office of the county recorder in which the notice of delinquent assessment is recorded a lien release or notice of rescission and provide the owner of the separate interest a copy of the lien release or notice that the delinquent assessment has been satisfied.

(b) If it is determined that a lien previously recorded against the separate interest was recorded in error, the party who recorded the lien shall, within 21 calendar days, record or cause to be recorded in the office of the county recorder in which the notice of delinquent assessment is recorded a lien release or notice of rescission and provide the owner of the separate interest with a declaration that the lien filing or recording was in error and a copy of the lien release or notice of rescission.

(c) If it is determined that an association has recorded a lien for a delinquent assessment in error, the association shall promptly reverse all late charges, fees, interest, attorney's fees, costs of collection, costs imposed for the notice prescribed in Section 5660, and costs of recordation and release of the lien authorized under subdivision (b) of Section 5720, and pay all costs related to any related dispute resolution or alternative dispute resolution.

Civ. Code § 5690. Failure to Comply with Article.

An association that fails to comply with the procedures set forth in this article shall, prior to recording a lien, recommence the required notice process. Any costs associated with recommencing the notice process shall be borne by the association and not by the owner of a separate interest.

Article 3.
Assessment Collection

Civ. Code § 5700. Enforcement of Lien.

(a) Except as otherwise provided in this article, after the expiration of 30 days following the recording of a lien created pursuant to Section 5675, the lien may be enforced in any manner permitted by law, including sale by the court, sale by the trustee designated in the notice of delinquent assessment, or sale by a trustee substituted pursuant to Section 2934a.

(b) Nothing in Article 2 (commencing with Section 5650) or in subdivision (a) of Section 726 of the Code of Civil Procedure prohibits actions against the owner of a separate interest to recover sums for which a lien is created pursuant to Article 2 (commencing with Section 5650) or prohibits an association from taking a deed in lieu of foreclosure.

Civ. Code § 5705. Prior to Foreclosure of Liens; Offer to Meet and Confer; Approval by Board.

(a) Notwithstanding any law or any provisions of the governing documents to the contrary, this section shall apply to debts for assessments that arise on and after January 1, 2006.

(b) Prior to initiating a foreclosure on an owner's separate interest, the association shall offer the owner and, if so requested by the owner, participate in dispute resolution pursuant to the association's "meet and confer" program required in Article 2 (commencing with Section 5900) of Chapter 10 or alternative dispute resolution as set forth in Article 3 (commencing with Section 5925) of Chapter 10. The decision to pursue dispute resolution or a particular type of alternative dispute resolution shall be the choice of the owner, except that binding arbitration shall not be available if the association intends to initiate a judicial foreclosure.

(c) The decision to initiate foreclosure of a lien for delinquent assessments that has been validly recorded shall be made only by the board and may not be delegated to an agent of the association. The board shall approve the decision by a majority vote of the directors in an executive session. The board shall record the vote in the minutes of the next meeting of the board open to all members. The board shall maintain the confidentiality of the owner or owners of the separate interest by identifying the matter in the minutes by the parcel number of the property, rather than the name of the owner or owners. A board vote to approve foreclosure of a lien shall take place at least 30 days prior to any public sale.

(d) The board shall provide notice by personal service in accordance with the manner of service of summons in Article 3 (commencing with Section 415.10) of Chapter 4 of Title 5 of Part 2 of the Code of Civil Procedure to an owner of a separate interest who occupies the separate interest or to the owner's legal representative, if the board votes to foreclose upon the separate interest. The board shall provide written notice to an owner of a separate interest who does not occupy the separate interest by first-class mail, postage prepaid, at the most current address shown on the books of the association. In the absence of written notification by the owner to the association, the address of the owner's separate interest may be treated as the owner's mailing address.

Civ. Code § 5710. Sale by Trustee.

(a) Any sale by the trustee shall be conducted in accordance with Sections 2924, 2924b, and 2924c applicable to the exercise of powers of sale in mortgages and deeds of trust.

(b) In addition to the requirements of Section 2924, the association shall serve a notice of default on the person named as the owner of the separate interest in the association's records or, if that person has designated a legal representative pursuant to this subdivision, on that legal representative. Service shall be in accordance with the manner of service of summons in Article 3 (commencing with Section 415.10) of Chapter 4 of Title 5 of Part 2 of the Code of Civil Procedure. An owner may designate a legal representative in a writing that is mailed to the association in a manner that indicates that the association has received it.

(c) The fees of a trustee may not exceed the amounts prescribed in Sections 2924c and 2924d, plus the cost of service for either of the following:

(1) The notice of default pursuant to subdivision (b).

(2) The decision of the board to foreclose upon the separate interest of an owner as described in subdivision (d) of Section 5705.

Civ. Code § 5715. Right of Redemption.

(a) Notwithstanding any law or any provisions of the governing documents to the contrary, this section shall apply to debts for assessments that arise on and after January 1, 2006.

(b) A nonjudicial foreclosure by an association to collect upon a debt for delinquent assessments shall be subject to a right of redemption. The redemption period within which the separate interest may be redeemed from a foreclosure sale under this paragraph ends 90 days after the sale. In addition to the requirements of Section 2924f, a notice of sale in connection with an association's foreclosure of a separate interest in a common interest development shall include a statement that the property is being sold subject to the right of redemption created in this section.

Civ. Code § 5720. Assessment Collection Through Foreclosure.

(a) Notwithstanding any law or any provisions of the governing documents to the contrary, this section shall apply to debts for assessments that arise on and after January 1, 2006.

(b) An association that seeks to collect delinquent regular or special assessments of an amount less than one thousand eight hundred dollars ($1,800), not including any accelerated assessments, late charges, fees and costs of collection, attorney's fees, or interest, may not collect that debt through judicial or nonjudicial foreclosure, but may attempt to collect or secure that debt in any of the following ways:

(1) By a civil action in small claims court, pursuant to Chapter 5.5 (commencing with Section 116.110) of Title 1 of Part 1 of the Code of Civil Procedure. An association that chooses to proceed by an action in small claims court, and prevails, may enforce the judgment as permitted under Article 8 (commencing with Section 116.810) of Chapter 5.5 of Title 1 of Part 1 of the Code of Civil Procedure. The amount that may be recovered in small claims court to collect upon a debt for delinquent assessments may not exceed the jurisdictional limits of the small claims court and shall be the sum of the following:

(A) The amount owed as of the date of filing the complaint in the small claims court proceeding.

(B) In the discretion of the court, an additional amount to that described in subparagraph (A) equal to the amount owed for the period from the date the complaint is filed until satisfaction of the judgment, which total amount may include accruing unpaid assessments and any reasonable late charges, fees and costs of collection, attorney's fees, and interest, up to the jurisdictional limits of the small claims court.

(2) By recording a lien on the owner's separate interest upon which the association may not foreclose until the amount of the delinquent assessments secured by the lien, exclusive of any accelerated assessments, late charges, fees and costs of collection, attorney's fees, or interest, equals or exceeds one thousand eight hundred dollars ($1,800) or the assessments secured by the lien are more than 12 months delinquent. An association that chooses to record a lien under these provisions, prior to recording the lien, shall offer the owner and, if so requested by the owner, participate in dispute resolution as set forth in Article 2 (commencing with Section 5900) of Chapter 10.

(3) Any other manner provided by law, except for judicial or nonjudicial foreclosure.

(c) The limitation on foreclosure of assessment liens for amounts under the stated minimum in this section does not apply to any of the following:

(1) Assessments secured by a lien that are more than 12 months delinquent.

(2) Assessments owed by owners of separate interests in time-share estates, as defined in subdivision (x) of Section 11212 of the Business and Professions Code.

(3) Assessments owed by the developer.

Civ. Code § 5725. Distinction Between Monetary Charge and Monetary Penalty.

(a) A monetary charge imposed by the association as a means of reimbursing the association for costs incurred by the association in the repair of damage to common area and facilities caused by a member or the member's guest or tenant may become a lien against the member's separate interest enforceable by the sale of the interest under Sections 2924, 2924b, and 2924c, provided the authority to impose a lien is set forth in the governing documents. It is the intent of the Legislature not to contravene Section 2792.26 of Title 10 of the California Code of Regulations, as that section appeared on January 1, 1996, for associations of subdivisions that are being sold under authority of a subdivision public report, pursuant to Part 2 (commencing with Section 11000) of Division 4 of the Business and Professions Code.

(b) A monetary penalty imposed by the association as a disciplinary measure for failure of a member to comply with the governing documents, except for the late payments, may not be characterized nor treated in the governing documents as an assessment that may become a lien against the member's separate interest enforceable by the sale of the interest under Sections 2924, 2924b, and 2924c.

Civ. Code § 5730. Annual Policy Statement; Form Notice.

(a) The annual policy statement, prepared pursuant to Section 5310, shall include the following notice, in at least 12-point type:

"NOTICE ASSESSMENTS AND FORECLOSURE

This notice outlines some of the rights and responsibilities of owners of property in common interest developments and the associations that manage them. Please refer to the sections of the Civil Code indicated for further information. A portion of the information in this notice applies only to liens recorded on or after January 1, 2003. You may wish to consult a lawyer if you dispute an assessment.

ASSESSMENTS AND FORECLOSURE

Assessments become delinquent 15 days after they are due, unless the governing documents provide for a longer time. The failure to pay association assessments may result in the loss of an owner's property through foreclosure. Foreclosure may occur either as a result of a court action, known as judicial foreclosure, or without court action, often referred to as nonjudicial foreclosure. For liens recorded on and after January 1, 2006, an association may not use judicial or nonjudicial foreclosure to enforce that lien if the amount of the delinquent assessments or dues, exclusive of any accelerated assessments, late charges, fees, attorney's fees, interest, and costs of collection, is less than one thousand eight hundred dollars ($1,800). For delinquent assessments or dues in excess of one thousand eight hundred dollars ($1,800) or more than 12 months delinquent, an association may use judicial or nonjudicial foreclosure subject to the conditions set forth in Article 3 (commencing with Section 5700) of Chapter 8 of Part 5 of Division 4 of the Civil Code. When using judicial or nonjudicial foreclosure, the association records a lien on the owner's property. The owner's property may be sold to satisfy the lien if the amounts secured by the lien are not paid. (Sections 5700 through 5720 of the Civil Code, inclusive)

In a judicial or nonjudicial foreclosure, the association may recover assessments, reasonable costs of collection, reasonable attorney's fees, late charges, and interest. The association may not use nonjudicial foreclosure to collect fines or penalties, except for costs to repair common area damaged by a member or a member's guests, if the governing documents provide for this. (Section 5725 of the Civil Code)

The association must comply with the requirements of Article 2 (commencing with Section 5650) of Chapter 8 of Part 5 of Division 4 of the Civil Code when collecting delinquent assessments. If the association fails to follow these requirements, it may not record a lien on the owner's property until it has satisfied those requirements. Any additional costs that result from satisfying the requirements are the responsibility of the association. (Section 5675 of the Civil Code)

At least 30 days prior to recording a lien on an owner's separate interest, the association must provide the owner of record with certain documents by certified mail, including a description of its collection and lien enforcement procedures and the method of calculating the amount. It must also provide an itemized statement of the charges owed by the owner. An owner has a right to review the association's records to verify the debt. (Section 5660 of the Civil Code)

If a lien is recorded against an owner's property in error, the person who recorded the lien is required to record a lien release within 21 days, and to provide an owner certain documents in this regard. (Section 5685 of the Civil Code)

The collection practices of the association may be governed by state and federal laws regarding fair debt collection. Penalties can be imposed for debt collection practices that violate these laws.

PAYMENTS

When an owner makes a payment, the owner may request a receipt, and the association is required to provide it. On the receipt, the association must indicate the date of payment and the person who received it. The association must inform owners of a mailing address for overnight payments. (Section 5655 of the Civil Code)

An owner may, but is not obligated to, pay under protest any disputed charge or sum levied by the association, including, but not limited to, an assessment, fine, penalty, late fee, collection cost, or monetary penalty imposed as a disciplinary measure, and by so doing, specifically reserve the right to contest the disputed charge or sum in court or otherwise.

An owner may dispute an assessment debt by submitting a written request for dispute resolution to the association as set forth in Article 2 (commencing with Section 5900) of Chapter 10 of Part 5 of Division 4 of the Civil Code. In addition, an association may not initiate a foreclosure without participating in alternative dispute resolution with a neutral third party as set forth in Article 3 (commencing with Section 5925) of Chapter 10 of Part 5 of Division 4 of the Civil Code, if so requested by the owner. Binding arbitration shall not be available if the association intends to initiate a judicial foreclosure.

An owner is not liable for charges, interest, and costs of collection, if it is established that the assessment was paid properly on time. (Section 5685 of the Civil Code)

MEETINGS AND PAYMENT PLANS

An owner of a separate interest that is not a time-share interest may request the association to consider a payment plan to satisfy a delinquent assessment. The association must inform owners of the standards for payment plans, if any exists. (Section 5665 of the Civil Code)

The board must meet with an owner who makes a proper written request for a meeting to discuss a payment plan when the owner has received a notice of a delinquent assessment. These payment plans must conform with the payment plan standards of the association, if they exist. (Section 5665 of the Civil Code)"

(b) An association distributing the notice required by this section to an owner of an interest that is described in Section 11212 of the Business and Professions Code that is not otherwise exempt from this section pursuant to subdivision (a) of Section 11211.7 of the Business and Professions Code may delete from the notice described in subdivision (a) the portion regarding meetings and payment plans.

Civ. Code § 5735. Limitation on Assignment of Right to Collect.

(a) An association may not voluntarily assign or pledge the association's right to collect payments or assessments, or to enforce or foreclose a lien to a third party, except when the assignment or pledge is made to a financial institution or lender chartered or licensed under federal or state law, when acting within the scope of that charter or license, as security for a loan obtained by the association.

(b) Nothing in subdivision (a) restricts the right or ability of an association to assign any unpaid obligations of a former member to a third party for purposes of collection.

Civ. Code § 5740. Applicability to Liens Created on or After January 1, 2003.

(a) Except as otherwise provided, this article applies to a lien created on or after January 1, 2003.

(b) A lien created before January 1, 2003, is governed by the law in existence at the time the lien was created.

CHAPTER 9.
INSURANCE AND LIABILITY

Civ. Code § 5800. Limited Liability of Volunteer Officer or Director.

(a) A volunteer officer or volunteer director described in subdivision (e) of an association that manages a common interest development that is residential or mixed use shall not be personally liable in excess of the coverage of insurance specified in paragraph (4) to any person who suffers injury, including, but not limited to, bodily injury, emotional distress, wrongful death, or property damage or loss as a result of the tortious act or omission of the volunteer officer or volunteer director if all of the following criteria are met:

(1) The act or omission was performed within the scope of the officer's or director's association duties.

(2) The act or omission was performed in good faith.

(3) The act or omission was not willful, wanton, or grossly negligent.

(4) The association maintained and had in effect at the time the act or omission occurred and at the time a claim is made one or more policies of insurance that shall include coverage for (A) general liability of the association and (B) individual liability of officers and directors of the association for negligent acts or omissions in that capacity; provided that both types of coverage are in the following minimum amounts:

(A) At least five hundred thousand dollars ($500,000) if the common interest development consists of 100 or fewer separate interests.

(B) At least one million dollars ($1,000,000) if the common interest development consists of more than 100 separate interests.

(b) The payment of actual expenses incurred by a director or officer in the execution of the duties of that position does not affect the director's or officer's status as a volunteer within the meaning of this section.

(c) An officer or director who at the time of the act or omission was a declarant, or who received either direct or indirect compensation as an employee from the declarant, or from a financial institution that purchased a separate interest at a judicial or nonjudicial foreclosure of a mortgage or deed of trust on real property, is not a volunteer for the purposes of this section.

(d) Nothing in this section shall be construed to limit the liability of the association for its negligent act or omission or for any negligent act or omission of an officer or director of the association.

(e) This section shall only apply to a volunteer officer or director who is a tenant of a residential separate interest in the common interest development or is an owner of no more than two separate interests and whose ownership in the common interest development consists exclusively of residential separate interests.

(f) (1) For purposes of paragraph (1) of subdivision (a), the scope of the officer's or director's association duties shall include, but shall not be limited to, both of the following decisions:

(A) Whether to conduct an investigation of the common interest development for latent deficiencies prior to the expiration of the applicable statute of limitations.

(B) Whether to commence a civil action against the builder for defects in design or construction.

(2) It is the intent of the Legislature that this section clarify the scope of association duties to which the protections against personal liability in this section apply. It is not the intent of the Legislature that these clarifications be construed to expand, or limit, the fiduciary duties owed by the directors or officers.

Civ. Code § 5805. Liability of Owner in Tenancy-In-Common Common Area.

(a) It is the intent of the Legislature to offer civil liability protection to owners of the separate interests in a common interest development that have common area owned in tenancy-in-common if the association carries a certain level of prescribed insurance that covers a cause of action in tort.

(b) Any cause of action in tort against any owner of a separate interest arising solely by reason of an ownership interest as a tenant-in-common in the common area of a common interest development shall be brought only against the association and not against the individual owners of the separate interests, if both of the insurance requirements in paragraphs (1) and (2) are met:

(1) The association maintained and has in effect for this cause of action, one or more policies of insurance that include coverage for general liability of the association.

(2) The coverage described in paragraph (1) is in the following minimum amounts:

(A) At least two million dollars ($2,000,000) if the common interest development consists of 100 or fewer separate interests.

(B) At least three million dollars ($3,000,000) if the common interest development consists of more than 100 separate interests.

Civ. Code § 5806. Fidelity Bond Coverage.

Unless the governing documents require greater coverage amounts, the association shall maintain crime insurance, employee dishonesty coverage, fidelity bond coverage, or their equivalent, for its directors, officers, and employees in an amount that is equal to or more than the combined amount of the reserves of the association and total assessments for three months. The coverage maintained by the association shall also include protection in an equal amount against computer fraud and funds transfer fraud. If the association uses a managing agent or management company, the association's crime insurance, employee dishonesty coverage, fidelity bond coverage, or their equivalent shall additionally include coverage for, or otherwise be endorsed to provide coverage for, dishonest acts by that person or entity and its employees. Self-insurance does not meet the requirements of this section.

Civ. Code § 5810. Notice of Insurance Policies.

The association shall, as soon as reasonably practicable, provide individual notice pursuant to Section 4040 to all members if any of the policies described in the annual budget report pursuant to Section 5300 have lapsed, been canceled, and are not immediately renewed, restored, or replaced, or if there is a significant change, such as a reduction in coverage or limits or an increase in the deductible, as to any of those policies. If the association receives any notice of nonrenewal of a policy described in the annual budget report pursuant to Section 5300, the association shall immediately notify its members if replacement coverage will not be in effect by the date the existing coverage will lapse.

CHAPTER 10.
DISPUTE RESOLUTION AND ENFORCEMENT

Article 1.
Discipline and Cost Reimbursement

Civ. Code § 5850. Schedule of Monetary Penalties.

(a) If an association adopts or has adopted a policy imposing any monetary penalty, including any fee, on any association member for a violation of the governing documents, including any monetary penalty relating to the activities of a guest or tenant of the member, the board shall adopt and distribute to each member, in the annual policy statement prepared pursuant to Section 5310, a schedule of the monetary penalties that may be assessed for those violations, which shall be in accordance with authorization for member discipline contained in the governing documents.

(b) Any new or revised monetary penalty that is adopted after complying with subdivision (a) may be included in a supplement that is delivered to the members individually, pursuant to Section 4040.

(c) A monetary penalty for a violation of the governing documents shall not exceed the monetary penalty stated in the schedule of monetary penalties or supplement that is in effect at the time of the violation.

(d) An association shall provide a copy of the most recently distributed schedule of monetary penalties, along with any applicable supplements to that schedule, to any member upon request.

Civ. Code § 5855. Requirements for Disciplinary Action by Board.

(a) When the board is to meet to consider or impose discipline upon a member, or to impose a monetary charge as a means of reimbursing the association for costs incurred by the association in the repair of damage to common area and facilities caused by a member or the member's guest or tenant, the board shall notify the member in writing, by either personal delivery or individual delivery pursuant to Section 4040, at least 10 days prior to the meeting.

(b) The notification shall contain, at a minimum, the date, time, and place of the meeting, the nature of the alleged violation for which a member may be disciplined or the nature of the damage to the common area and facilities for which a monetary charge may be imposed, and a statement that the member has a right to attend and may address the board at the meeting. The board shall meet in executive session if requested by the member.

(c) If the board imposes discipline on a member or imposes a monetary charge on the member for damage to the common area and facilities, the board shall provide the member a written notification of the decision, by either personal delivery or individual delivery pursuant to Section 4040, within 15 days following the action.

(d) A disciplinary action or the imposition of a monetary charge for damage to the common area shall not be effective against a member unless the board fulfills the requirements of this section.

Civ. Code § 5865. Board Authority to Impose Monetary Penalties.

Nothing in Section 5850 or 5855 shall be construed to create, expand, or reduce the authority of the board to impose monetary penalties on a member for a violation of the governing documents.

Civ. Code § 5875. Enforcement Actions During State of Emergency.

An association shall not pursue any enforcement actions for a violation of the governing documents, except those actions relating to the homeowner's nonpayment of assessments, during a declared state or local emergency if the nature of the emergency giving rise to the declaration makes it unsafe or impossible for the homeowner to either prevent or fix the violation.

Article 2.

Internal Dispute Resolution

Civ. Code § 5900. Internal Dispute Resolution.

(a) This article applies to a dispute between an association and a member involving their rights, duties, or liabilities under this act, under the Nonprofit Mutual Benefit Corporation Law (Part 3 (commencing with Section 7110) of Division 2 of Title 1 of the Corporations Code), or under the governing documents of the common interest development or association.

(b) This article supplements, and does not replace, Article 3 (commencing with Section 5925), relating to alternative dispute resolution as a prerequisite to an enforcement action.

Civ. Code § 5905. Fair, Reasonable, and Expeditious Procedure.

(a) An association shall provide a fair, reasonable, and expeditious procedure for resolving a dispute within the scope of this article.

(b) In developing a procedure pursuant to this article, an association shall make maximum, reasonable use of available local dispute resolution programs involving a neutral third party, including low-cost mediation programs such as those listed on the Internet Web sites of the Department of Consumer Affairs and the United States Department of Housing and Urban Development.

(c) If an association does not provide a fair, reasonable, and expeditious procedure for resolving a dispute within the scope of this article, the procedure provided in Section 5915 applies and satisfies the requirement of subdivision (a).

Civ. Code § 5910. Minimum Requirements of Dispute Resolution Procedure.

A fair, reasonable, and expeditious dispute resolution procedure shall at a minimum satisfy all of the following requirements:

(a) The procedure may be invoked by either party to the dispute. A request invoking the procedure shall be in writing.

(b) The procedure shall provide for prompt deadlines. The procedure shall state the maximum time for the association to act on a request invoking the procedure.

(c) If the procedure is invoked by a member, the association shall participate in the procedure.

(d) If the procedure is invoked by the association, the member may elect not to participate in the procedure. If the member participates but the dispute is resolved other than by agreement of the member, the member shall have a right of appeal to the board.

(e) A written resolution, signed by both parties, of a dispute pursuant to the procedure, that is not in conflict with the law or the governing documents, binds the association and is judicially enforceable. A written agreement, signed by both parties, reached pursuant to the procedure, that is not in conflict with the law or the governing documents binds the parties and is judicially enforceable.

(f) The procedure shall provide a means by which the member and the association may explain their positions. The member and association may be assisted by an attorney or another person in explaining their positions at their own cost.

(g) A member of the association shall not be charged a fee to participate in the process.

Civ. Code § 5910.1. Prelitigation Good Faith Participation in IDR.

An association may not file a civil action regarding a dispute in which the member has requested dispute resolution unless the association has complied with Section 5910 by engaging in good faith in the internal dispute resolution procedures after a member invokes those procedures.

Civ. Code § 5915. Statutory Default Procedure.

(a) This section applies to an association that does not otherwise provide a fair, reasonable, and expeditious dispute resolution procedure. The procedure provided in this section is fair, reasonable, and expeditious, within the meaning of this article.

(b) Either party to a dispute within the scope of this article may invoke the following procedure:

(1) The party may request the other party to meet and confer in an effort to resolve the dispute. The request shall be in writing.

(2) A member of an association may refuse a request to meet and confer. The association may not refuse a request to meet and confer.

(3) The board shall designate a director to meet and confer.

(4) The parties shall meet promptly at a mutually convenient time and place, explain their positions to each other, and confer in good faith in an effort to resolve the dispute. The parties may be assisted by an attorney or another person at their own cost when conferring.

(5) A resolution of the dispute agreed to by the parties shall be memorialized in writing and signed by the parties, including the board designee on behalf of the association.

(c) A written agreement reached under this section binds the parties and is judicially enforceable if it is signed by both parties and both of the following conditions are satisfied:

(1) The agreement is not in conflict with law or the governing documents of the common interest development or association.

(2) The agreement is either consistent with the authority granted by the board to its designee or the agreement is ratified by the board.

(d) A member may not be charged a fee to participate in the process.

Civ. Code § 5920. Inclusion in Annual Policy Statement.

The annual policy statement prepared pursuant to Section 5310 shall include a description of the internal dispute resolution process provided pursuant to this article.

Article 3.

Alternative Dispute Resolution As Prerequisite To Civil Action

Civ. Code § 5925. Alternative Dispute Resolution Definitions.

As used in this article:

(a) "Alternative dispute resolution" means mediation, arbitration, conciliation, or other nonjudicial procedure that involves a neutral party in the decisionmaking process. The form of alternative dispute resolution chosen pursuant to this article may be binding or nonbinding, with the voluntary consent of the parties.

(b) "Enforcement action" means a civil action or proceeding, other than a cross-complaint, for any of the following purposes:

(1) Enforcement of this act.

(2) Enforcement of the Nonprofit Mutual Benefit Corporation Law (Part 3 (commencing with Section 7110) of Division 2 of Title 1 of the Corporations Code).

(3) Enforcement of the governing documents.

Civ. Code § 5930. Litigation Pre-Filing Requirements.

(a) An association or a member may not file an enforcement action in the superior court unless the parties have endeavored to submit their dispute to alternative dispute resolution pursuant to this article.

(b) This section applies only to an enforcement action that is solely for declaratory, injunctive, or writ relief, or for that relief in conjunction with a claim for monetary damages not in excess of the jurisdictional limits stated in Sections 116.220 and 116.221 of the Code of Civil Procedure.

(c) This section does not apply to a small claims action.

(d) Except as otherwise provided by law, this section does not apply to an assessment dispute.

Civ. Code § 5935. Request for Resolution.

(a) Any party to a dispute may initiate the process required by Section 5930 by serving on all other parties to the dispute a Request for Resolution. The Request for Resolution shall include all of the following:

(1) A brief description of the dispute between the parties.

(2) A request for alternative dispute resolution.

(3) A notice that the party receiving the Request for Resolution is required to respond within 30 days of receipt or the request will be deemed rejected.

(4) If the party on whom the request is served is the member, a copy of this article.

(b) Service of the Request for Resolution shall be by personal delivery, first-class mail, express mail, facsimile transmission, or other means reasonably calculated to provide the party on whom the request is served actual notice of the request.

(c) A party on whom a Request for Resolution is served has 30 days following service to accept or reject the request. If a party does not accept the request within that period, the request is deemed rejected by the party.

Civ. Code § 5940. Completing the Process.

(a) If the party on whom a Request for Resolution is served accepts the request, the parties shall complete the alternative dispute resolution within 90 days after the party initiating the request receives the acceptance, unless this period is extended by written stipulation signed by both parties.

(b) Chapter 2 (commencing with Section 1115) of Division 9 of the Evidence Code applies to any form of alternative dispute resolution initiated by a Request for Resolution under this article, other than arbitration.

(c) The costs of the alternative dispute resolution shall be borne by the parties.

Civ. Code § 5945. Statute of Limitiations.

If a Request for Resolution is served before the end of the applicable time limitation for commencing an enforcement action, the time limitation is tolled during the following periods:

(a) The period provided in Section 5935 for response to a Request for Resolution.

(b) If the Request for Resolution is accepted, the period provided by Section 5940 for completion of alternative dispute resolution, including any extension of time stipulated to by the parties pursuant to Section 5940.

Civ. Code § 5950. Certificate Of Compliance.

(a) At the time of commencement of an enforcement action, the party commencing the action shall file with the initial pleading a certificate stating that one or more of the following conditions are satisfied:

(1) Alternative dispute resolution has been completed in compliance with this article.

(2) One of the other parties to the dispute did not accept the terms offered for alternative dispute resolution.

(3) Preliminary or temporary injunctive relief is necessary.

(b) Failure to file a certificate pursuant to subdivision (a) is grounds for a demurrer or a motion to strike unless the court finds that dismissal of the action for failure to comply with this article would result in substantial prejudice to one of the parties.

Civ. Code § 5955. Stay of Action During Alternative Dispute Resolution.

(a) After an enforcement action is commenced, on written stipulation of the parties, the matter may be referred to alternative dispute resolution. The referred action is stayed. During the stay, the action is not subject to the rules implementing subdivision (c) of Section 68603 of the Government Code.

(b) The costs of the alternative dispute resolution shall be borne by the parties.

Civ. Code § 5960. Consideration of Refusal to Participate in Alternative Dispute Resolution.

In an enforcement action in which attorney's fees and costs may be awarded, the court, in determining the amount of the award, may consider whether a party's refusal to participate in alternative dispute resolution before commencement of the action was reasonable.

Civ. Code § 5965. Summary of Alternative Dispute Resolution in Annual Policy Statement.

(a) An association shall annually provide its members a summary of the provisions of this article that specifically references this article. The summary shall include the following language:

> "Failure of a member of the association to comply with the alternative dispute resolution requirements of Section 5930 of the Civil Code may result in the loss of the member's right to sue the association or another member of the association regarding enforcement of the governing documents or the applicable law."

(b) The summary shall be included in the annual policy statement prepared pursuant to Section 5310.

Article 4.
Civil Action

Civ. Code § 5975. Enforcement of Governing Documents.

(a) The covenants and restrictions in the declaration shall be enforceable equitable servitudes, unless unreasonable, and shall inure to the benefit of and bind all owners of separate interests in the development. Unless the declaration states otherwise, these servitudes may be enforced by any owner of a separate interest or by the association, or by both.

(b) A governing document other than the declaration may be enforced by the association against an owner of a separate interest or by an owner of a separate interest against the association.

(c) In an action to enforce the governing documents, the prevailing party shall be awarded reasonable attorney's fees and costs.

Civ. Code § 5980. Association Standing.

An association has standing to institute, defend, settle, or intervene in litigation, arbitration, mediation, or administrative proceedings in its own name as the real party in interest and without joining with it the members, in matters pertaining to the following:

(a) Enforcement of the governing documents.

(b) Damage to the common area.

(c) Damage to a separate interest that the association is obligated to maintain or repair.

(d) Damage to a separate interest that arises out of, or is integrally related to, damage to the common area or a separate interest that the association is obligated to maintain or repair.

Civ. Code § 5985. Allocation of Damages.

(a) In an action maintained by an association pursuant to subdivision (b), (c), or (d) of Section 5980, the amount of damages recovered by the association shall be reduced by the amount of damages allocated to the association or its managing agents in direct proportion to their percentage of fault based upon principles of comparative fault. The comparative fault of the association or its managing agents may be raised by way of defense, but shall not be the basis for a cross-action or separate action against the association or its managing agents for contribution or implied indemnity, where the only damage was sustained by the association or its members. It is the intent of the Legislature in enacting this subdivision to require that comparative fault be pleaded as an affirmative defense, rather than a separate cause of action, where the only damage was sustained by the association or its members.

(b) In an action involving damages described in subdivision (b), (c), or (d) of Section 5980, the defendant or cross-defendant may allege and prove the comparative fault of the association or its managing agents as a setoff to the liability of the defendant or cross-defendant even if the association is not a party to the litigation or is no longer a party whether by reason of settlement, dismissal, or otherwise.

(c) Subdivisions (a) and (b) apply to actions commenced on or after January 1, 1993.

(d) Nothing in this section affects a person's liability under Section 1431, or the liability of the association or its managing agent for an act or omission that causes damages to another.

Civ. Code § 5986. Construction Defect Voting Requirements Deemed "Void".

(a) Subject to compliance with Section 6150, which requires the board to provide notice of a meeting with the members to discuss, among other things, problems that may lead to the filing of a civil action, before the board files a civil action against a declarant or other developer, or within 30 days after it files the action, if the association has reason to believe that the applicable statute of limitations will expire, and notwithstanding any provision to the contrary in the governing documents, the board shall have the authority to commence and pursue a claim, civil action, arbitration, prelitigation process pursuant to Section 6000 or Title 7 (commencing with Section 895) of Part 2 of Division 2, or other legal proceeding against a declarant, developer, or builder of a common interest development. If the board includes members appointed by, or affiliated with, the declarant, developer, or builder, the decision and authority to commence and pursue legal proceedings shall be vested solely in the nonaffiliated board members.

(b) The governing documents shall not impose any preconditions or limitations on the board's authority to commence and pursue any claim, civil action, arbitration, prelitigation process pursuant to Section 6000 or Title 7 (commencing with Section 895) of Part 2 of Division 2, or other legal proceeding against a declarant, developer, or builder of a common interest development. Any limitation or precondition, including, but not limited to, requiring a membership vote as a prerequisite to, or otherwise providing the declarant, developer, or builder with veto authority over, the board's commencement and pursuit of a claim, civil action, arbitration, prelitigation process, or legal proceeding against the declarant, developer, or builder, or any incidental decision of the board, including, but not limited to, retaining legal counsel or incurring costs or expenses, is unenforceable, null, and void. The failure to comply with those limitations or preconditions, if only, shall not be asserted as a defense to any claim or action described in this section.

(c) Notwithstanding subdivision (a) or (b), any provision in the governing documents imposing limitations or preconditions on the board's authority to commence and pursue claims shall be valid and enforceable if the provision is adopted solely by the nondeclarant affiliated members of the association and the provision is adopted in accordance with the requirements necessary to amend the governing documents of the association.

(d) This section applies to all governing documents, whether recorded before or after the effective date of this section, and applies retroactively to claims initiated before the effective date of this section, except if those claims have been resolved through an executed settlement, a final arbitration decision, or a final judicial decision on the merits.

(e) Nothing in this section extends any applicable statute of limitation or repose to file or initiate any claim, civil action, arbitration, prelitigation process, or other legal proceeding. Nothing in this section shall affect any other obligations of an association contained in Title 7 (commencing with Section 895) of Part 2 of Division 2, or any other provision in the covenants, conditions, and restrictions of the association related to arbitration or other alternative dispute resolution procedures.

CHAPTER 11.
CONSTRUCTION DEFECT LITIGATION

Civ. Code § 6000. Filing a Claim for Construction Defects.

(a) Before an association files a complaint for damages against a builder, developer, or general contractor (respondent) of a common interest development based upon a claim for defects in the design or construction of the common interest development, all of the requirements of this section shall be satisfied with respect to the builder, developer, or general contractor.

(b) The association shall serve upon the respondent a "Notice of Commencement of Legal Proceedings." The notice shall be served by certified mail to the registered agent of the respondent, or if there is no registered agent, then to any officer of the respondent. If there are no current officers of the respondent, service shall be upon the person or entity otherwise authorized by law to receive service of process. Service upon the general contractor shall be sufficient to initiate the process set forth in this section with regard to any builder or developer, if the builder or developer is not amenable to service of process by the foregoing methods. This notice shall toll all applicable statutes of limitation and repose, whether contractual or statutory, by and against all potentially responsible parties, regardless of whether they were named in the notice, including claims for indemnity applicable to the claim for the period set forth in subdivision (c). The notice shall include all of the following:

(1) The name and location of the project.

(2) An initial list of defects sufficient to apprise the respondent of the general nature of the defects at issue.

(3) A description of the results of the defects, if known.

(4) A summary of the results of a survey or questionnaire distributed to homeowners to determine the nature and extent of defects, if a survey has been conducted or a questionnaire has been distributed.

(5) Either a summary of the results of testing conducted to determine the nature and extent of defects or the actual test results, if that testing has been conducted.

(c) Service of the notice shall commence a period, not to exceed 180 days, during which the association, the respondent, and all other participating parties shall try to resolve the dispute through the processes set forth in this section. This 180-day period may be extended for one additional period, not to exceed 180 days, only upon the mutual agreement of the association, the respondent, and any parties not deemed peripheral pursuant to paragraph (3) of subdivision (e). Any extensions beyond the first extension shall require the agreement of all participating parties. Unless extended, the dispute resolution process prescribed by this section shall be deemed completed. All extensions shall continue the tolling period described in subdivision (b).

(d) Within 25 days of the date the association serves the Notice of Commencement of Legal Proceedings, the respondent may request in writing to meet and confer with the board. Unless the respondent and the association otherwise agree, there shall be not more than one meeting, which shall take place no later than 10 days from the date of the respondent's written request, at a mutually agreeable time and place. The meeting shall be subject to subdivision (a) of Section 4925 and subdivisions (a) and (b) of Section 4935. The discussions at the meeting are privileged communications and are not admissible in evidence in any civil action, unless the association and the respondent consent in writing to their admission.

(e) Upon receipt of the notice, the respondent shall, within 60 days, comply with the following:

(1) The respondent shall provide the association with access to, for inspection and copying of, all plans and specifications, subcontracts, and other construction files for the project that are reasonably calculated to lead to the discovery of admissible evidence regarding the defects claimed. The association shall provide the respondent with access to, for inspection and copying of, all files reasonably calculated to lead to the discovery of admissible evidence regarding the defects claimed, including all reserve studies, maintenance records and any survey questionnaires, or results of testing to determine the nature and extent of defects. To the extent any of the above documents are withheld based on privilege, a privilege log shall be prepared and submitted to all other parties. All other potentially responsible parties shall have the same rights as the respondent regarding the production of documents upon receipt of written notice of the claim, and shall produce all relevant documents within 60 days of receipt of the notice of the claim.

(2) The respondent shall provide written notice by certified mail to all subcontractors, design professionals, their insurers, and the insurers of any additional insured whose identities are known to the respondent or readily ascertainable by review of the project files or other similar sources and whose potential responsibility appears on the face of the notice. This notice to subcontractors, design professionals, and insurers shall include a copy of the Notice of Commencement of Legal Proceedings, and shall specify the date and manner by which the parties shall meet and confer to select a dispute resolution facilitator pursuant to paragraph (1) of subdivision (f), advise the recipient of its obligation to participate in the meet and confer or serve a written acknowledgment of receipt regarding this notice, advise the recipient that it will waive any challenge to selection of the dispute resolution facilitator if it elects not to participate in the meet and confer, advise the recipient that it may seek the assistance of an attorney, and advise the recipient that it should contact its insurer, if any. Any subcontractor or design professional, or insurer for that subcontractor, design professional, or additional insured, who receives written notice from the respondent regarding the meet and confer shall, prior to the meet and confer, serve on the respondent a written acknowledgment of receipt. That subcontractor or design professional shall, within 10 days of service of the written acknowledgment of receipt, provide to the association and the respondent a Statement of Insurance that includes both of the following:

(A) The names, addresses, and contact persons, if known, of all insurance carriers, whether primary or excess and regardless of whether a deductible or self-insured retention applies, whose policies were in effect from the commencement of construction of the subject project to the present and which potentially cover the subject claims.

(B) The applicable policy numbers for each policy of insurance provided.

(3) Any subcontractor or design professional, or insurer for that subcontractor, design professional, or additional insured, who so chooses, may, at any time, make a written request to the dispute resolution facilitator for designation as a peripheral party. That request shall be served contemporaneously on the association and the respondent. If no objection to that designation is received within 15 days, or upon rejection of that objection, the dispute resolution facilitator shall

designate that subcontractor or design professional as a peripheral party, and shall thereafter seek to limit the attendance of that subcontractor or design professional only to those dispute resolution sessions deemed peripheral party sessions or to those sessions during which the dispute resolution facilitator believes settlement as to peripheral parties may be finalized. Nothing in this subdivision shall preclude a party who has been designated a peripheral party from being reclassified as a nonperipheral party, nor shall this subdivision preclude a party designated as a nonperipheral party from being reclassified as a peripheral party after notice to all parties and an opportunity to object. For purposes of this subdivision, a peripheral party is a party having total claimed exposure of less than twenty-five thousand dollars ($25,000).

(f) (1) Within 20 days of sending the notice set forth in paragraph (2) of subdivision (e), the association, respondent, subcontractors, design professionals, and their insurers who have been sent a notice as described in paragraph (2) of subdivision (e) shall meet and confer in an effort to select a dispute resolution facilitator to preside over the mandatory dispute resolution process prescribed by this section. Any subcontractor or design professional who has been given timely notice of this meeting but who does not participate, waives any challenge he or she may have as to the selection of the dispute resolution facilitator. The role of the dispute resolution facilitator is to attempt to resolve the conflict in a fair manner. The dispute resolution facilitator shall be sufficiently knowledgeable in the subject matter and be able to devote sufficient time to the case. The dispute resolution facilitator shall not be required to reside in or have an office in the county in which the project is located. The dispute resolution facilitator and the participating parties shall agree to a date, time, and location to hold a case management meeting of all parties and the dispute resolution facilitator, to discuss the claims being asserted and the scheduling of events under this section. The case management meeting with the dispute resolution facilitator shall be held within 100 days of service of the Notice of Commencement of Legal Proceedings at a location in the county where the project is located. Written notice of the case management meeting with the dispute resolution facilitator shall be sent by the respondent to the association, subcontractors and design professionals, and their insurers who are known to the respondent to be on notice of the claim, no later than 10 days prior to the case management meeting, and shall specify its date, time, and location. The dispute resolution facilitator in consultation with the respondent shall maintain a contact list of the participating parties.

(2) No later than 10 days prior to the case management meeting, the dispute resolution facilitator shall disclose to the parties all matters that could cause a person aware of the facts to reasonably entertain a doubt that the proposed dispute resolution facilitator would be able to resolve the conflict in a fair manner. The facilitator's disclosure shall include the existence of any ground specified in Section 170.1 of the Code of Civil Procedure for disqualification of a judge, any attorney-client relationship the facilitator has or had with any party or lawyer for a party to the dispute resolution process, and any professional or significant personal relationship the facilitator or his or her spouse or minor child living in the household has or had with any party to the dispute resolution process. The disclosure shall also be provided to any subsequently noticed subcontractor or design professional within 10 days of the notice.

(3) A dispute resolution facilitator shall be disqualified by the court if he or she fails to comply with this subdivision and any party to the dispute resolution process serves a notice of disqualification prior to the case management meeting. If the dispute resolution facilitator complies with this subdivision, he or she shall be disqualified by the court on the basis of the disclosure if any party to the dispute resolution process serves a notice of disqualification prior to the case management meeting.

(4) If the parties cannot mutually agree to a dispute resolution facilitator, then each party shall submit a list of three dispute resolution facilitators. Each party may then strike one nominee from the other parties' list, and petition the court, pursuant to the procedure described in subdivisions (n) and (o), for final selection of the dispute resolution facilitator. The court may issue an order for final selection of the dispute resolution facilitator pursuant to this paragraph.

(5) Any subcontractor or design professional who receives notice of the association's claim without having previously received timely notice of the meet and confer to select the dispute resolution facilitator shall be notified by the respondent regarding the name, address, and telephone number of the dispute resolution facilitator. Any such subcontractor or design professional may serve upon the parties and the dispute resolution facilitator a written objection to the dispute resolution facilitator within 15 days of receiving notice of the claim. Within seven days after service of this objection, the subcontractor or design professional may petition the superior court to replace the dispute resolution facilitator. The court

may replace the dispute resolution facilitator only upon a showing of good cause, liberally construed. Failure to satisfy the deadlines set forth in this subdivision shall constitute a waiver of the right to challenge the dispute resolution facilitator.

(6) The costs of the dispute resolution facilitator shall be apportioned in the following manner: one-third to be paid by the association; one-third to be paid by the respondent; and one-third to be paid by the subcontractors and design professionals, as allocated among them by the dispute resolution facilitator. The costs of the dispute resolution facilitator shall be recoverable by the prevailing party in any subsequent litigation pursuant to Section 1032 of the Code of Civil Procedure, provided however that any nonsettling party may, prior to the filing of the complaint, petition the facilitator to reallocate the costs of the dispute resolution facilitator as they apply to any nonsettling party. The determination of the dispute resolution facilitator with respect to the allocation of these costs shall be binding in any subsequent litigation. The dispute resolution facilitator shall take into account all relevant factors and equities between all parties in the dispute resolution process when reallocating costs.

(7) In the event the dispute resolution facilitator is replaced at any time, the case management statement created pursuant to subdivision (h) shall remain in full force and effect.

(8) The dispute resolution facilitator shall be empowered to enforce all provisions of this section.

(g) (1) No later than the case management meeting, the parties shall begin to generate a data compilation showing the following information regarding the alleged defects at issue:

(A) The scope of the work performed by each potentially responsible subcontractor.

(B) The tract or phase number in which each subcontractor provided goods or services, or both.

(C) The units, either by address, unit number, or lot number, at which each subcontractor provided goods or services, or both.

(2) This data compilation shall be updated as needed to reflect additional information. Each party attending the case management meeting, and any subsequent meeting pursuant to this section, shall provide all information available to that party relevant to this data compilation.

(h) At the case management meeting, the parties shall, with the assistance of the dispute resolution facilitator, reach agreement on a case management statement, which shall set forth all of the elements set forth in paragraphs (1) to (8), inclusive, except that the parties may dispense with one or more of these elements if they agree that it is appropriate to do so. The case management statement shall provide that the following elements shall take place in the following order:

(1) Establishment of a document depository, located in the county where the project is located, for deposit of documents, defect lists, demands, and other information provided for under this section. All documents exchanged by the parties and all documents created pursuant to this subdivision shall be deposited in the document depository, which shall be available to all parties throughout the prefiling dispute resolution process and in any subsequent litigation. When any document is deposited in the document depository, the party depositing the document shall provide written notice identifying the document to all other parties. The costs of maintaining the document depository shall be apportioned among the parties in the same manner as the costs of the dispute resolution facilitator.

(2) Provision of a more detailed list of defects by the association to the respondent after the association completes a visual inspection of the project. This list of defects shall provide sufficient detail for the respondent to ensure that all potentially responsible subcontractors and design professionals are provided with notice of the dispute resolution process. If not already completed prior to the case management meeting, the Notice of Commencement of Legal Proceedings shall be served by the respondent on all additional subcontractors and design professionals whose potential responsibility appears on the face of the more detailed list of defects within seven days of receipt of the more detailed list. The respondent shall serve a copy of the case management statement, including the name, address, and telephone number of the dispute resolution facilitator, to all the potentially responsible subcontractors and design professionals at the same time.

(3) Nonintrusive visual inspection of the project by the respondent, subcontractors, and design professionals.

(4) Invasive testing conducted by the association, if the association deems appropriate. All parties may observe and photograph any testing conducted by the association pursuant to this paragraph, but may not take samples or direct testing unless, by mutual agreement, costs of testing are shared by the parties.

(5) Provision by the association of a comprehensive demand which provides sufficient detail for the parties to engage in meaningful dispute resolution as contemplated under this section.

(6) Invasive testing conducted by the respondent, subcontractors, and design professionals, if they deem appropriate.

(7) Allowance for modification of the demand by the association if new issues arise during the testing conducted by the respondent, subcontractor, or design professionals.

(8) Facilitated dispute resolution of the claim, with all parties, including peripheral parties, as appropriate, and insurers, if any, present and having settlement authority. The dispute resolution facilitators shall endeavor to set specific times for the attendance of specific parties at dispute resolution sessions. If the dispute resolution facilitator does not set specific times for the attendance of parties at dispute resolution sessions, the dispute resolution facilitator shall permit those parties to participate in dispute resolution sessions by telephone.

(i) In addition to the foregoing elements of the case management statement described in subdivision (h), upon mutual agreement of the parties, the dispute resolution facilitator may include any or all of the following elements in a case management statement: the exchange of consultant or expert photographs; expert presentations; expert meetings; or any other mechanism deemed appropriate by the parties in the interest of resolving the dispute.

(j) The dispute resolution facilitator, with the guidance of the parties, shall at the time the case management statement is established, set deadlines for the occurrence of each event set forth in the case management statement, taking into account such factors as the size and complexity of the case, and the requirement of this section that this dispute resolution process not exceed 180 days absent agreement of the parties to an extension of time.

(k) (1) (A) At a time to be determined by the dispute resolution facilitator, the respondent may submit to the association all of the following:

(i) A request to meet with the board to discuss a written settlement offer.

(ii) A written settlement offer, and a concise explanation of the reasons for the terms of the offer.

(iii) A statement that the respondent has access to sufficient funds to satisfy the conditions of the settlement offer.

(iv) A summary of the results of testing conducted for the purposes of determining the nature and extent of defects, if this testing has been conducted, unless the association provided the respondent with actual test results.

(B) If the respondent does not timely submit the items required by this subdivision, the association shall be relieved of any further obligation to satisfy the requirements of this subdivision only.

(C) No less than 10 days after the respondent submits the items required by this paragraph, the respondent and the board shall meet and confer about the respondent's settlement offer.

(D) If the board rejects a settlement offer presented at the meeting held pursuant to this subdivision, the board shall hold a meeting open to each member of the association. The meeting shall be held no less than 15 days before the association commences an action for damages against the respondent.

(E) No less than 15 days before this meeting is held, a written notice shall be sent to each member of the association specifying all of the following:

(i) That a meeting will take place to discuss problems that may lead to the filing of a civil action, and the time and place of this meeting.

(ii) The options that are available to address the problems, including the filing of a civil action and a statement of the various alternatives that are reasonably foreseeable by the association to pay for those options and whether these payments are expected to be made from the use of reserve account funds or the imposition of regular or special assessments, or emergency assessment increases.

(iii) The complete text of any written settlement offer, and a concise explanation of the specific reasons for the terms of the offer submitted to the board at the meeting held pursuant to subdivision (d) that was received from the respondent.

(F) The respondent shall pay all expenses attributable to sending the settlement offer to all members of the association. The respondent shall also pay the expense of holding the meeting, not to exceed three dollars ($3) per association member.

(G) The discussions at the meeting and the contents of the notice and the items required to be specified in the notice pursuant to subparagraph (E) are privileged communications and are not admissible in evidence in any civil action, unless the association consents to their admission.

(H) No more than one request to meet and discuss a written settlement offer may be made by the respondent pursuant to this subdivision.

(l) All defect lists and demands, communications, negotiations, and settlement offers made in the course of the prelitigation dispute resolution process provided by this section shall be inadmissible pursuant to Sections 1119 to 1124, inclusive, of the Evidence Code and all applicable decisional law. This inadmissibility shall not be extended to any other documents or communications which would not otherwise be deemed inadmissible.

(m) Any subcontractor or design professional may, at any time, petition the dispute resolution facilitator to release that party from the dispute resolution process upon a showing that the subcontractor or design professional is not potentially responsible for the defect claims at issue. The petition shall be served contemporaneously on all other parties, who shall have 15 days from the date of service to object. If a subcontractor or design professional is released, and it later appears to the dispute resolution facilitator that it may be a responsible party in light of the current defect list or demand, the respondent shall renotice the party as provided by paragraph (2) of subdivision (e), provide a copy of the current defect list or demand, and direct the party to attend a dispute resolution session at a stated time and location. A party who subsequently appears after having been released by the dispute resolution facilitator shall not be prejudiced by its absence from the dispute resolution process as the result of having been previously released by the dispute resolution facilitator.

(n) Any party may, at any time, petition the superior court in the county where the project is located, upon a showing of good cause, and the court may issue an order, for any of the following, or for appointment of a referee to resolve a dispute regarding any of the following:

(1) To take a deposition of any party to the process, or subpoena a third party for deposition or production of documents, which is necessary to further prelitigation resolution of the dispute.

(2) To resolve any disputes concerning inspection, testing, production of documents, or exchange of information provided for under this section.

(3) To resolve any disagreements relative to the timing or contents of the case management statement.

(4) To authorize internal extensions of timeframes set forth in the case management statement.

(5) To seek a determination that a settlement is a good faith settlement pursuant to Section 877.6 of the Code of Civil Procedure and all related authorities. The page limitations and meet and confer requirements specified in this section shall not apply to these motions, which may be made on shortened notice. Instead, these motions shall be subject to other applicable state law, rules of court, and local rules. A determination made by the court pursuant to this motion shall have the same force and effect as the determination of a postfiling application or motion for good faith settlement.

(6) To ensure compliance, on shortened notice, with the obligation to provide a Statement of Insurance pursuant to paragraph (2) of subdivision (c).

(7) For any other relief appropriate to the enforcement of the provisions of this section, including the ordering of parties, and insurers, if any, to the dispute resolution process with settlement authority.

(o) (1) A petition filed pursuant to subdivision (n) shall be filed in the superior court in the county in which the project is located. The court shall hear and decide the petition within 10 days after filing. The petitioning party shall serve the petition on all parties, including the date, time, and location of the hearing no later than five business days prior to the hearing. Any responsive papers shall be filed and served no later than three business days prior to the hearing. Any petition or response filed under this section shall be no more than three pages in length.

(2) All parties shall meet with the dispute resolution facilitator, if one has been appointed and confer in person or by telephone prior to the filing of that petition to attempt to resolve the matter without requiring court intervention.

(p) As used in this section:

(1) "Association" shall have the same meaning as defined in Section 4080.

(2) "Builder" means the declarant, as defined in Section 4130.

(3) "Common interest development" shall have the same meaning as in Section 4100, except that it shall not include developments or projects with less than 20 units.

(q) The alternative dispute resolution process and procedures described in this section shall have no application or legal effect other than as described in this section.

(r) This section shall become operative on July 1, 2002, however it shall not apply to any pending suit or claim for which notice has previously been given.

(s) This section shall become inoperative on July 1, 2024, and, as of January 1, 2025, is repealed, unless a later enacted statute, that becomes operative on or before January 1, 2025, deletes or extends the dates on which it becomes inoperative and is repealed.

Civ. Code § 6100. Disclosure of Settlement of Construction Defect Claim.

(a) As soon as is reasonably practicable after the association and the builder have entered into a settlement agreement or the matter has otherwise been resolved regarding alleged defects in the common areas, alleged defects in the separate interests that the association is obligated to maintain or repair, or alleged defects in the separate interests that arise out of, or are integrally related to, defects in the common areas or separate interests that the association is obligated to maintain or repair, where the defects giving rise to the dispute have not been corrected, the association shall, in writing, inform only the members of the association whose names appear on the records of the association that the matter has been resolved, by settlement agreement or other means, and disclose all of the following:

(1) A general description of the defects that the association reasonably believes, as of the date of the disclosure, will be corrected or replaced.

(2) A good faith estimate, as of the date of the disclosure, of when the association believes that the defects identified in paragraph (1) will be corrected or replaced. The association may state that the estimate may be modified.

(3) The status of the claims for defects in the design or construction of the common interest development that were not identified in paragraph (1) whether expressed in a preliminary list of defects sent to each member of the association or otherwise claimed and disclosed to the members of the association.

(b) Nothing in this section shall preclude an association from amending the disclosures required pursuant to subdivision (a), and any amendments shall supersede any prior conflicting information disclosed to the members of the association and shall retain any privilege attached to the original disclosures.

(c) Disclosure of the information required pursuant to subdivision (a) or authorized by subdivision (b) shall not waive any privilege attached to the information.

(d) For the purposes of the disclosures required pursuant to this section, the term "defects" shall be defined to include any damage resulting from defects.

Civ. Code § 6150. Pre-Filing Notice to Members.

(a) Not later than 30 days before filing of any civil action by the association against the declarant or other developer of a common interest development for alleged damage to the common areas, alleged damage to the separate interests that the association is obligated to maintain or repair, or alleged damage to the separate interests that arises out of, or is integrally related to, damage to the common areas or separate interests that the association is obligated to maintain or repair, the board shall provide a written notice to each member of the association who appears on the records of the association when the notice is provided. This notice shall specify all of the following:

(1) That a meeting will take place to discuss problems that may lead to the filing of a civil action, in addition to the potential impacts thereof to the association and its members, including any financial impacts.

(2) The options, including civil actions, that are available to address the problems.

(3) The time and place of the meeting.

(b) Notwithstanding subdivision (a), if the association has reason to believe that the applicable statute of limitations will expire before the association files the civil action, the association may give the notice, as described above, within 30 days after the filing of the action.

3

SELECTED CORPORATIONS CODE PROVISIONS AFFECTING COMMON INTEREST DEVELOPMENTS

Definitions

Corp. Code § 8. "Writing."

Writing includes any form of recorded message capable of comprehension by ordinary visual means; and when used to describe communications between a corporation, partnership, or limited liability company and its shareholders, members, partners, directors, or managers, writing shall include electronic transmissions by and to a corporation (Sections 20 and 21), electronic transmissions by and to a partnership (subdivisions (4) and (5) of Section 16101), and electronic transmissions by and to a limited liability company (paragraphs (1) and (2) of subdivision (o) of Section 17001). Whenever any notice, report, statement, or record is required or authorized by this code, it shall be made in writing in the English language.

Whenever any notice or other communication is required by this code to be mailed by registered mail by or to any person or corporation, the mailing of such notice or other communication by certified mail shall be deemed to be a sufficient compliance with the requirements of law.

Corp. Code § 20. "Electronic Transmission by the Corporation."

"Electronic transmission by the corporation" means a communication (a) delivered by (1) facsimile telecommunication or electronic mail when directed to the facsimile number or electronic mail address, respectively, for that recipient on record with the corporation, (2) posting on an electronic message board or network which the corporation has designated for those communications, together with a separate notice to the recipient of the posting, which transmission shall be validly delivered upon the later of the posting or delivery of the separate notice thereof, or (3) other means of electronic communication, (b) to a recipient who has provided an unrevoked consent to the use of those means of transmission for communications under or pursuant to this code, and (c) that creates a record that is capable of retention, retrieval, and review, and that may thereafter be rendered into clearly legible tangible form. However, an electronic transmission under this code by a corporation to an individual shareholder or member of the corporation who is a natural person, and if an officer or director of the corporation, only if communicated to the recipient in that person's capacity as a shareholder or member, is not authorized unless, in addition to satisfying the requirements of this section, the consent to the transmission has been preceded by or includes a clear written statement to the recipient as to (a) any right of the recipient to have the record provided or made available on paper or in nonelectronic form, (b) whether the consent applies only to that transmission, to specified categories of communications, or to all communications from the corporation, and (c) the procedures the recipient must use to withdraw consent.

Corp. Code § 21. "Electronic Transmission to the Corporation."

"Electronic transmission to the corporation" means a communication (a) delivered by (1) facsimile telecommunication or electronic mail when directed to the facsimile number or electronic mail address, respectively, which the corporation has provided from time to time to shareholders or members and directors for sending communications to the corporation, (2) posting on an electronic message board or network which the corporation has designated for those communications, and which transmission shall be validly delivered upon the posting, or (3) other means of electronic communication, (b) as to which the corporation has placed in effect reasonable measures to verify that the sender is the shareholder or member (in person or by proxy) or director purporting to send the transmission, and (c) that creates a record that is capable of retention, retrieval, and review, and that may thereafter be rendered into clearly legible tangible form.

Corp. Code § 5009. "Mailing."

Except as otherwise required, any reference in this part, Part 2, Part 3, Part 4 or Part 5 to mailing means first-, second-, or third-class mail, postage prepaid, unless registered mail is specified. Registered mail includes certified mail.

Notices in Newsletters

Corp. Code § 5016. Notices or Reports Mailed or Delivered as Part of a Newsletter or Magazine.

A notice or report mailed or delivered as part of a newsletter, magazine or other organ regularly sent to members shall constitute written notice or report pursuant to this division when addressed and mailed or delivered to the member, or in the case of members who are residents of the same household and who have the same address on the books of the corporation, when addressed and mailed or delivered to one of such members, at the address appearing on the books of the corporation.

Corporate Operations

Corp. Code § 5032. Approval by the Board.

"Approved by the board" means approved or ratified by the vote of the board or by the vote of a committee authorized to exercise the powers of the board, except as to matters not within the competence of the committee under Section 5212, Section 7212, or Section 92121.

Corp. Code § 5033. Approval by or Approval of a Majority of All Members.

"Approval by (or approval of) a majority of all members" means approval by an affirmative vote (or written ballot in conformity with Section 5513, Section 7513, or Section 9413) of a majority of the votes entitled to be cast. Such approval shall include the affirmative vote of a majority of the outstanding memberships of each class, unit, or grouping of members entitled, by any provision of the articles or bylaws or of Part 2, Part 3, Part 4 or Part 5 to vote as a class, unit, or grouping of members on the subject matter being voted upon and shall also include the affirmative vote of such greater proportion, including all, of the votes of the memberships of any class, unit, or grouping of members if such greater proportion is required by the bylaws (subdivision (e) of Section 5151, subdivision (e) of Section 7151, or subdivision (e) of Section 9151) or Part 2, Part 3, Part 4 or Part 5.

Corp. Code § 5034. Approval By or Approval of the Members.

"Approval by (or approval of) the members" means approved or ratified by the affirmative vote of a majority of the votes represented and voting at a duly held meeting at which a quorum is present (which affirmative votes also constitute a majority of the required quorum) or written ballot in conformity with Section 5513, 7513, or 9413 or by the affirmative vote or written ballot of such greater proportion, including all of the votes of the memberships of any class, unit, or grouping of members as may be provided in the bylaws (subdivision (e) of Section 5151, subdivision (e) of Section 7151, or subdivision (e) of Section 9151) or in Part 2, Part 3, Part 4 or Part 5 for all or any specified member action.

Corp. Code § 5069. Proxy.

"Proxy" means a written authorization signed by a member or the member's attorney in fact giving another person or persons power to vote on behalf of such member. "Signed" for the purpose of this section means the placing of the member's name on the proxy (whether by manual signature, typewriting, telegraphic transmission or otherwise) by the member or such member's attorney in fact.

Corp. Code § 5079. "Written" or "In Writing."

"Written" or "in writing" includes facsimile, telegraphic, and other electronic communication as authorized by this code, including an electronic transmission by a corporation that satisfies the requirements of Section 20.

Corp. Code § 7210. Board of Directors; Exercise of Powers; Delegation of Management.

Each corporation shall have a board of directors. Subject to the provisions of this part and any limitations in the articles or bylaws relating to action required to be approved by the members (Section 5034), or by a majority of all members (Section 5033), the activities and affairs of a corporation shall be conducted and all corporate powers shall be exercised by or under the direction of the board. The board may delegate the management of the activities of the corporation to any person or persons, management company, or committee however composed, provided that the activities and affairs of the corporation shall be managed and all corporate powers shall be exercised under the ultimate direction of the board.

Corp. Code § 7211. Meetings.

(a) Unless otherwise provided in the articles or in the bylaws, all of the following apply:

(1) Meetings of the board may be called by the chair of the board or the president or any vice president or the secretary or any two directors.

(2) Regular meetings of the board may be held without notice if the time and place of the meetings are fixed by the bylaws or the board. Special meetings of the board shall be held upon four days' notice by first-class mail or 48 hours' notice delivered personally or by telephone, including a voice messaging system or by electronic transmission by the corporation (Section 20). The articles or bylaws may not dispense with notice of a special meeting. A notice, or waiver of notice, need not specify the purpose of any regular or special meeting of the board.

(3) Notice of a meeting need not be given to a director who provided a waiver of notice or consent to holding the meeting or an approval of the minutes thereof in writing, whether before or after the meeting, or who attends the meeting without protesting, prior thereto or at its commencement, the lack of notice to that director. These waivers, consents and approvals shall be filed with the corporate records or made a part of the minutes of the meetings.

(4) A majority of the directors present, whether or not a quorum is present, may adjourn any meeting to another time and place. If the meeting is adjourned for more than 24 hours, notice of an adjournment to another time or place shall be given prior to the time of the adjourned meeting to the directors who were not present at the time of the adjournment.

(5) Meetings of the board may be held at a place within or without the state that has been designated in the notice of the meeting or, if not stated in the notice or if there is no notice, designated in the bylaws or by resolution of the board.

(6) Directors may participate in a meeting through use of conference telephone, electronic video screen communication, or electronic transmission by and to the corporation (Sections 20 and 21). Participation in a meeting through use of conference telephone or electronic video screen communication pursuant to this subdivision constitutes presence in person at that meeting as long as all directors participating in the meeting are able to hear one another. Participation in a meeting through use of electronic transmission by and to the corporation, other than conference telephone and electronic video screen communication, pursuant to this subdivision constitutes presence in person at that meeting if both of the following apply:

(A) Each director participating in the meeting can communicate with all of the other directors concurrently.

(B) Each director is provided the means of participating in all matters before the board, including, without limitation, the capacity to propose, or to interpose an objection to, a specific action to be taken by the corporation.

(7) A majority of the number of directors authorized in or pursuant to the articles or bylaws constitutes a quorum of the board for the transaction of business. The articles or bylaws may require the presence of one or more specified directors in order to constitute a quorum of the board to transact business, as long as the death or nonexistence of a specified director or the death or nonexistence of the person or persons otherwise authorized to appoint or designate that director does not prevent the corporation from transacting business in the normal course of events. The articles or bylaws may not provide that a quorum shall be less than one-fifth the number of directors authorized in or pursuant to the articles or bylaws, or less than two, whichever is larger, unless the number of directors authorized in or pursuant to the articles or bylaws is one, in which case one director constitutes a quorum.

(8) Subject to the provisions of Sections 7212, 7233, 7234, and subdivision (e) of Section 7237 and Section 5233, insofar as it is made applicable pursuant to Section 7238, an act or decision done or made by a majority of the directors present at a meeting duly held at which a quorum is present is the act of the board. The articles or bylaws may not provide that a lesser vote than a majority of the directors present at a meeting is the act of the board. A meeting at which a quorum is initially present may continue to transact business notwithstanding the withdrawal of directors, if any action taken is approved by at least a majority of the required quorum for that meeting, or a greater number required by this division, the articles or the bylaws.

(b) An action required or permitted to be taken by the board may be taken without a meeting if all directors individually or collectively consent in writing to that action and if, subject to subdivision (a) of Section 7224, the number of directors then in office constitutes a quorum. The written consent or consents shall be filed with the minutes of the proceedings of the board. The action by written consent shall have the same force and effect as a unanimous vote of the directors. For purposes of this subdivision only, "all directors" does not include an "interested director" as defined in subdivision (a) of Section 5233, insofar as it is made applicable pursuant to Section 7238 or described in subdivision (a) of Section 7233, or a "common director"

Corporations

as described in subdivision (b) of Section 7233 who abstains in writing from providing consent, where (1) the facts described in paragraph (2) or (3) of subdivision (d) of Section 5233 are established or the provisions of paragraph (1) or (2) of subdivision (a) of Section 7233 or in paragraph (1) or (2) of subdivision (b) of Section 7233 are satisfied, as appropriate, at or prior to execution of the written consent or consents; (2) the establishment of those facts or satisfaction of those provisions, as applicable, is included in the written consent or consents executed by the noninterested directors or noncommon directors or in other records of the corporation; and (3) the noninterested directors or noncommon directors, as applicable, approve the action by a vote that is sufficient without counting the votes of the interested directors or common directors.

(c) Each director shall have one vote on each matter presented to the board of directors for action. A director shall not vote by proxy.

(d) This section applies also to incorporators, to committees of the board, and to action by those incorporators or committees mutatis mutandis.

Corp. Code § 7212. Committees.

(a) The board may, by resolution adopted by a majority of the number of directors then in office, provided that a quorum is present, create one or more committees, each consisting of two or more directors, to serve at the pleasure of the board. Appointments to such committees shall be by a majority vote of the directors then in office, unless the articles or bylaws require a majority vote of the number of directors authorized in or pursuant to the articles or bylaws. The bylaws may authorize one or more such committees, each consisting of two or more directors, and may provide that a specified officer or officers who are also directors of the corporation shall be a member or members of such committee or committees. The board may appoint one or more directors as alternate members of such committee, who may replace any absent member at any meeting of the committee. Such committee, to the extent provided in the resolution of the board or in the bylaws, shall have all the authority of the board, except with respect to:

(1) The approval of any action for which this part also requires approval of the members (Section 5034) or approval of a majority of all members (Section 5033), regardless of whether the corporation has members.

(2) The filling of vacancies on the board or in any committee which has the authority of the board.

(3) The fixing of compensation of the directors for serving on the board or on any committee.

(4) The amendment or repeal of bylaws or the adoption of new bylaws.

(5) The amendment or repeal of any resolution of the board which by its express terms is not so amendable or repealable.

(6) The appointment of committees of the board or the members thereof.

(7) The expenditure of corporate funds to support a nominee for director after there are more people nominated for director than can be elected.

(8) With respect to any assets held in charitable trust, the approval of any self-dealing transaction except as provided in paragraph (3) of subdivision (d) of Section 5233.

(b) A committee exercising the authority of the board shall not include as members persons who are not directors. However, the board may create other committees that do not exercise the authority of the board and these other committees may include persons regardless of whether they are directors.

(c) Unless the bylaws otherwise provide, the board may delegate to any committee, appointed pursuant to paragraph (4) of subdivision (c) of Section 7151 or otherwise, powers as authorized by Section 7210, but may not delegate the powers set forth in paragraphs (1) to (8), inclusive, of subdivision (a).

Corp. Code § 7213. Officers.

(a) A corporation shall have a chair of the board, who may be given the title chair of the board, chairperson of the board, chairman of the board, or chairwoman of the board, or a president or both, a secretary, a treasurer or a chief financial officer or both, and any other officers with any titles and duties as shall be stated in the bylaws or determined by the board and as may be necessary to enable it to sign instruments. The president, or if there is no president the chair of the board, is the general manager and chief executive officer of the corporation, unless otherwise provided in the articles or bylaws. Unless otherwise specified in the articles or the bylaws, if there is no chief financial officer, the treasurer is the chief financial officer of the corporation. Any number of offices may be held by the same person unless the articles or bylaws provide otherwise. Where a corporation holds assets in charitable trust, any compensation of the president or chief executive officer and the chief financial officer or treasurer shall be determined in accordance with subdivision (g) of Section 12586 of the Government Code, if applicable.

(b) Except as otherwise provided by the articles or bylaws, officers shall be chosen by the board and serve at the pleasure of the board, subject to the rights, if any, of an officer under any contract of employment. Any officer may resign at any time upon written notice to the corporation without prejudice to the rights, if any, of the corporation under any contract to which the officer is a party.

Directors and Officers

Corp. Code § 7220. Terms of Office; Designators.

(a) Except as provided in subdivision (d), directors shall be elected for such terms, not longer than four years, as are fixed in the articles or bylaws. However, the terms of directors of a corporation without members may be up to six years. In the absence of any provision in the articles or bylaws, the term shall be one year. The articles or bylaws may provide for staggering the terms of directors by dividing the total number of directors into groups of one or more directors. The terms of office of several groups and the number of directors in each group need not be uniform. No amendment of the articles or bylaws may extend the term of a director beyond that for which the director was elected, nor may any bylaw provision increasing the terms of directors be adopted without approval of the members (Section 5034).

(b) Unless the articles or bylaws otherwise provide, each director, including a director elected to fill a vacancy, shall hold office until the expiration of the term for which elected and until a successor has been elected and qualified, unless the director has been removed from office.

(c) The articles or bylaws may provide for the election of one or more directors by the members of any class voting as a class.

(d) For the purposes of this subdivision, "designator" means one or more designators. Subdivisions (a) through (c) notwithstanding, all or any portion of the directors authorized in the articles or bylaws of a corporation may hold office by virtue of designation or selection by a specified designator as provided by the articles or bylaws rather than by election. Such directors shall continue in office for the term prescribed by the governing article or bylaw provision, or, if there is no term prescribed, until the governing article or bylaw provision is duly amended or repealed, except as provided in subdivision (e) of Section 7222. A bylaw provision authorized by this subdivision may be adopted, amended, or repealed only by approval of the members (Section 5034), except as provided in subdivision (d) of Section 7150. Unless otherwise provided in the articles or bylaws, the entitlement to designate or select a director or directors shall cease if any of the following circumstances exist:

(1) The specified designator of that director or directors has died or ceased to exist.

(2) If the entitlement of the specified designator of that director or directors to designate is in the capacity of an officer, trustee, or other status and the office, trust, or status has ceased to exist.

(e) If a corporation has not issued memberships and (1) all the directors resign, die, or become incompetent, or (2) a corporation's initial directors have not been named in the articles and all incorporators resign, die, or become incompetent before the election of the initial directors, the superior court of any county may appoint directors of the corporation upon application by any party in interest.

Corp. Code § 7221. Declaration of Vacancy; Grounds; Director Qualifications.

(a) The board may declare vacant the office of a director who has been declared of unsound mind by a final order of court, or convicted of a felony, or, in the case of a corporation holding assets in charitable trust, has been found by a final order or judgment of any court to have breached any duty arising as a result of Section 7238, or, if at the time a director is elected, the bylaws provide that a director may be removed for missing a specified number of board meetings, fails to attend the specified number of meetings.

(b) As provided in paragraph (3) of subdivision (c) of Section 7151, the articles or bylaws may prescribe the qualifications of the directors. The board, by a majority vote of the directors who meet all of the required qualifications to be a director, may declare vacant the office of any director who fails or ceases to meet any required qualification that was in effect at the beginning of that director's current term of office.

Corp. Code § 7222. Removal; Reduction in Number.

(a) Subject to subdivisions (b) and (f), any or all directors may be removed without cause if:

(1) In a corporation with fewer than 50 members, the removal is approved by a majority of all members (Section 5033).

(2) In a corporation with 50 or more members, the removal is approved by the members (Section 5034).

(3) In a corporation with no members, the removal is approved by a majority of the directors then in office.

(b) Except for a corporation having no members, pursuant to Section 7310:

(1) In a corporation in which the articles or bylaws authorize members to cumulate their votes pursuant to subdivision (a) of Section 7615, no director may be removed (unless the entire board is removed) when the votes cast against removal, or not consenting in writing to the removal, would be sufficient to elect the director if voted cumulatively at an election at which the same total number of votes were cast (or, if the action is taken by written ballot, all memberships entitled to vote were voted) and the entire number of directors authorized at the time of the director's most recent election were then being elected.

(2) When by the provisions of the articles or bylaws the members of any class, voting as a class, are entitled to elect one or more directors, any director so elected may be removed only by the applicable vote of the members of that class.

(3) When by the provisions of the articles or bylaws the members within a chapter or other organizational unit, or region or other geographic grouping, voting as such, are entitled to elect one or more directors, any director so elected may be removed only by the applicable vote of the members within the organizational unit or geographic grouping.

(c) Any reduction of the authorized number of directors or any amendment reducing the number of classes of directors does not remove any director prior to the expiration of the director's term of office unless the reduction or amendment also provides for the removal of one or more specified directors.

(d) Except as provided in this section and Sections 7221 and 7223, a director may not be removed prior to the expiration of the director's term of office.

(e) Where a director removed under this section or Section 7221 or 7223 was chosen by designation pursuant to subdivision (d) of Section 7220, then:

(1) Where a different person may be designated pursuant to the governing article or bylaw provision, the new designation shall be made.

(2) Where the governing article or bylaw provision contains no provision under which a different person may be designated, the governing article or bylaw provision shall be deemed repealed.

(f) For the purposes of this subdivision, "designator" means one or more designators. If by the provisions of the articles or bylaws a designator is entitled to designate one or more directors, then:

(1) Unless otherwise provided in the articles or bylaws at the time of designation, any director so designated may be removed without cause by the designator of that director.

(2) Any director so designated may only be removed under subdivision (a) with the written consent of the designator of that director.

(3) Unless otherwise provided in the articles or bylaws, the right to remove shall not apply if any of the following circumstances exist:

(A) The designator entitled to that right has died or ceased to exist.

(B) If that right is in the capacity of an officer, trustee, or other status, and the office, trust, or status has ceased to exist.

Corp. Code § 7224. Filling Vacancies; Resignation; Successor to Take Office At Effective Date of Resignation.

(a) Unless otherwise provided in the articles or bylaws and except for a vacancy created by the removal of a director, vacancies on the board may be filled by approval of the board (Section 5032) or, if the number of directors then in office is less than a quorum, by (1) the unanimous written consent of the directors then in office, (2) the affirmative vote of a majority of the directors then in office at a meeting held pursuant to notice or waivers of notice complying with Section 7211, or (3) a sole remaining director. Unless the articles or a bylaw approved by the members (Section 5034) provide that the board may fill vacancies occurring in the board by reason of the removal of directors, or unless the corporation has no members pursuant to Section 7310, such vacancies may be filled only by the approval of the members (Section 5034).

(b) The members may elect a director at any time to fill any vacancy not filled by the directors.

(c) Any director may resign effective upon giving written notice to the chairman of the board, the president, the secretary or the board of directors of the corporation, unless the notice specifies a later time for the effectiveness of such resignation. If the resignation is effective at a future time, a successor may be elected to take office when the resignation becomes effective.

Corp. Code § 7231. Performance of Duties; Degree of Care; Reliance on Reports; Good Faith; Exemption from Liability.

(a) A director shall perform the duties of a director, including duties as a member of any committee of the board upon which the director may serve, in good faith, in a manner such director believes to be in the best interests of the corporation and with such care, including reasonable inquiry, as an ordinarily prudent person in a like position would use under similar circumstances.

(b) In performing the duties of a director, a director shall be entitled to rely on information, opinions, reports or statements, including financial statements and other financial data, in each case prepared or presented by:

(1) One or more officers or employees of the corporation whom the director believes to be reliable and competent in the matters presented;

(2) Counsel, independent accountants or other persons as to matters which the director believes to be within such person's professional or expert competence; or

(3) A committee upon which the director does not serve that is composed exclusively of any or any combination of directors, persons described in paragraph (1), or persons described in paragraph (2), as to matters within the committee's designated authority, which committee the director believes to merit confidence, so long as, in any case, the director

acts in good faith, after reasonable inquiry when the need therefor is indicated by the circumstances and without knowledge that would cause such reliance to be unwarranted.

(c) A person who performs the duties of a director in accordance with subdivisions (a) and (b) shall have no liability based upon any alleged failure to discharge the person's obligations as a director, including, without limiting the generality of the foregoing, any actions or omissions which exceed or defeat a public or charitable purpose to which assets held by a corporation are dedicated.

Corp. Code § 7233. Conflicts of Interest; Disclosure; Common Directorships; Just and Reasonable Contracts.

(a) No contract or other transaction between a corporation and one or more of its directors, or between a corporation and any domestic or foreign corporation, firm or association in which one or more of its directors has a material financial interest, is either void or voidable because such director or directors or such other corporation business corporation, firm or association are parties or because such director or directors are present at the meeting of the board or a committee thereof which authorizes, approves or ratifies the contract or transaction, if:

(1) The material facts as to the transaction and as to such director's interest are fully disclosed or known to the members and such contract or transaction is approved by the members (Section 5034) in good faith, with any membership owned by any interested director not being entitled to vote thereon;

(2) The material facts as to the transaction and as to such director's interest are fully disclosed or known to the board or committee, and the board or committee authorizes, approves or ratifies the contract or transaction in good faith by a vote sufficient without counting the vote of the interested director or directors and the contract or transaction is just and reasonable as to the corporation at the time it is authorized, approved or ratified; or

(3) As to contracts or transactions not approved as provided in paragraph (1) or (2) of this subdivision, the person asserting the validity of the contract or transaction sustains the burden of proving that the contract or transaction was just and reasonable as to the corporation at the time it was authorized, approved or ratified.

A mere common directorship does not constitute a material financial interest within the meaning of this subdivision. A director is not interested within the meaning of this subdivision in a resolution fixing the compensation of another director as a director, officer or employee of the corporation, notwithstanding the fact that the first director is also receiving compensation from the corporation.

(b) No contract or other transaction between a corporation and any corporation, business corporation or association of which one or more of its directors are directors is either void or voidable because such director or directors are present at the meeting of the board or a committee thereof which authorizes, approves or ratifies the contract or transaction, if:

(1) The material facts as to the transaction and as to such director's other directorship are fully disclosed or known to the board or committee, and the board or committee authorizes, approves or ratifies the contract or transaction in good faith by a vote sufficient without counting the vote of the common director or directors or the contract or transaction is approved by the members (Section 5034) in good faith; or

(2) As to contracts or transactions not approved as provided in paragraph (1) of this subdivision, the contract or transaction is just and reasonable as to the corporation at the time it is authorized, approved or ratified.

This subdivision does not apply to contracts or transactions covered by subdivision (a).

Member Discipline

Corp. Code § 7341. Expulsion, Suspension or Termination; Fairness and Reasonableness; Procedure.

(a) No member may be expelled or suspended, and no membership or memberships may be terminated or suspended, except according to procedures satisfying the requirements of this section. An expulsion, termination or suspension not in accord with this section shall be void and without effect.

(b) Any expulsion, suspension, or termination must be done in good faith and in a fair and reasonable manner. Any procedure which conforms to the requirements of subdivision (c) is fair and reasonable, but a court may also find other procedures to be fair and reasonable when the full circumstances of the suspension, termination, or expulsion are considered.

(c) A procedure is fair and reasonable when:

(1) The provisions of the procedure have been set forth in the articles or bylaws, or copies of such provisions are sent annually to all the members as required by the articles or bylaws;

(2) It provides the giving of 15 days' prior notice of the expulsion, suspension or termination and the reasons therefor; and

(3) It provides an opportunity for the member to be heard, orally or in writing, not less than five days before the effective date of the expulsion, suspension or termination by a person or body authorized to decide that the proposed expulsion, termination or suspension not take place.

(d) Any notice required under this section may be given by any method reasonably calculated to provide actual notice. Any notice given by mail must be given by first-class or registered mail sent to the last address of the members shown on the corporation's records.

(e) Any action challenging an expulsion, suspension or termination of membership, including any claim alleging defective notice, must be commenced within one year after the date of the expulsion, suspension or termination. In the event such an action is successful the court may order any relief, including reinstatement, it finds equitable under the circumstances, but no vote of the members or of the board may be set aside solely because a person was at the time of the vote wrongfully excluded by virtue of the challenged expulsion, suspension or termination, unless the court finds further that the wrongful expulsion, suspension or termination was in bad faith and for the purpose, and with the effect, of wrongfully excluding the member from the vote or from the meeting at which the vote took place, so as to affect the outcome of the vote.

(f) This section governs only the procedures for expulsion, suspension or termination and not the substantive grounds therefor. An expulsion, suspension or termination based upon substantive grounds which violate contractual or other rights of the member or are otherwise unlawful is not made valid by compliance with this section.

(g) A member who is expelled or suspended or whose membership is terminated shall be liable for any charges incurred, services or benefits actually rendered, dues, assessments or fees incurred before the expulsion, suspension or termination or arising from contract or otherwise.

Membership Meetings

Corp. Code § 7510. Annual Meetings; Place; Written Ballot; Court Order for Meeting; Special Meetings.

(a) Meetings of members may be held at a place within or without this state as may be stated in or fixed in accordance with the bylaws. If no other place is stated or so fixed, meetings of members shall be held at the principal executive office of the corporation. Subject to any limitations in the articles or bylaws of the corporation, if authorized by the board of directors in its sole discretion, and subject to those guidelines and procedures as the board of directors may adopt, members not physically present in person (or, if proxies are allowed, by proxy) at a meeting of members may, by electronic transmission by and to the corporation (Sections 20 and 21), electronic video screen communication, conference telephone, or other means of remote communication, participate in a meeting of members, be deemed present in person (or, if proxies are allowed, by proxy), and vote at a meeting of members, subject to subdivision (f).

(b) A regular meeting of members shall be held on a date and time, and with the frequency stated in or fixed in accordance with the bylaws, but in any event in each year in which directors are to be elected at that meeting for the purpose of conducting such election, and to transact any other proper business which may be brought before the meeting.

(c) If a corporation with members is required by subdivision (b) to hold a regular meeting and fails to hold the regular meeting for a period of 60 days after the date designated therefor or, if no date has been designated, for a period of 15 months after the formation of the corporation or after its last regular meeting, or if the corporation fails to hold a written ballot for a period of 60 days after the date designated therefor, then the superior court of the proper county may summarily order the meeting to be held or the ballot to be conducted upon the application of a member or the Attorney General, after notice to the corporation giving it an opportunity to be heard.

(d) The votes represented, either in person (or, if proxies are allowed, by proxy), at a meeting called or by written ballot ordered pursuant to subdivision (c) and entitled to be cast on the business to be transacted shall constitute a quorum, notwithstanding any provision of the articles or bylaws or in this part to the contrary. The court may issue such orders as may be appropriate including, without limitation, orders designating the time and place of the meeting, the record date for determination of members entitled to vote, and the form of notice of the meeting.

(e) Special meetings of members for any lawful purpose may be called by the board, the chair of the board, the president, or such other persons, if any, as are specified in the bylaws. In addition, special meetings of members for any lawful purpose may be called by 5 percent or more of the members.

(f) A meeting of the members may be conducted, in whole or in part, by electronic transmission by and to the corporation, electronic video screen communication, conference telephone, or other means of remote communication if the corporation implements reasonable measures: (1) to provide members and proxyholders, if proxies are allowed, a reasonable opportunity to participate in the meeting and to vote on matters submitted to the members, including an opportunity to read or hear the proceedings of the meeting substantially concurrently with those proceedings, (2) if any member or proxyholder, if proxies are allowed, votes or takes other action at the meeting by means of electronic transmission to the corporation, electronic video screen communication, conference telephone, or other means of remote communication, to maintain a record of that vote or action in its books and records, and (3) to verify that each person participating remotely is a member or proxyholder, if proxies are allowed. A corporation shall not conduct a meeting of members solely by electronic transmission by and to the corporation, electronic video screen communication, conference telephone, or other means of remote communication unless: (A) all of the members consent; or (B) the board determines it is necessary or appropriate because of an emergency, as defined in paragraph (5) of subdivision (m) of Section 7140.

Corp. Code § 7511. Notice of Meeting.

(a) Whenever members are required or permitted to take any action at a meeting, a written notice of the meeting shall be given not less than 10 nor more than 90 days before the date of the meeting to each member who, on the record date for notice of the meeting, is entitled to vote thereat; provided, however, that if notice is given by mail, and the notice is not mailed by first-class, registered, or certified mail, that notice shall be given not less than 20 days before the meeting. Subject to subdivision (f), and subdivision (b) of Section 7512, the notice shall state the place, date and time of the meeting, the means of electronic transmission by and to the corporation (Sections 20 and 21), electronic video screen communication, conference telephone, or other means of remote communication, if any, by which members may participate in that meeting, and (1) in the case of a special meeting, the general nature of the business to be transacted, and no other business may be transacted, or (2) in the case of the regular meeting, those matters which the board, at the time the notice is given, intends to present for action by the members, but, except as provided in subdivision (b) of Section 7512, any proper matter may be presented at the meeting for the action. The notice of any meeting at which directors are to be elected shall include the names of all those who are nominees at the time the notice is given to members.

(b) (1) Notice of a members' meeting or any report shall be given personally, by electronic transmission by a corporation, or by mail or other means of written communication, addressed to a member at the address of the member appearing on the books of the corporation or given by the member to the corporation for purpose of notice, or if no such address appears or is given, at the place where the principal office of the corporation is located or by publication at least once in a newspaper of general circulation in the county in which the principal office is located. Notwithstanding the foregoing, the notice of a members' meeting or any report may be sent by electronic communication or other means of remote communication if the board determines it is necessary or appropriate because of an emergency, as defined in paragraph (5) of subdivision (m) of Section 7140. An affidavit of giving of any notice or report as permitted because of an emergency or otherwise in accordance with the provisions of this part, executed by the secretary, assistant secretary, or any transfer agent, shall be prima facie evidence of the giving of the notice or report.

(2) If any notice or report addressed to the member at the address of the member appearing on the books of the corporation is returned to the corporation by the United States Postal Service marked to indicate that the United States Postal Service is unable to deliver the notice or report to the member at the address, all future notices or reports shall be deemed to have been duly given without further mailing if the same shall be available for the member upon written demand of the member

at the principal office of the corporation for a period of one year from the date of the giving of the notice or report to all other members.

(3) (A) Notice given by electronic transmission by the corporation under this subdivision shall be valid only if it complies with Section 20. Notwithstanding the foregoing, notice shall not be given by electronic transmission by the corporation under this subdivision after either of the following:

(i) The corporation is unable to deliver two consecutive notices to the member by that means.

(ii) The inability to so deliver the notices to the member becomes known to the secretary, any assistant secretary, the transfer agent, or other person responsible for the giving of the notice.

(B) This paragraph shall not apply if notices are provided by electronic communication or other means of remote communication as permitted because of an emergency.

(c) Upon request in writing to the corporation addressed to the attention of the chair of the board, president, vice president, or secretary by any person (other than the board) entitled to call a special meeting of members, the officer forthwith shall cause notice to be given to the members entitled to vote that a meeting will be held at a time fixed by the board not less than 35 nor more than 90 days after the receipt of the request. If the corporation is a common interest development, as defined in Section 4100 of the Civil Code, the corporation shall cause notice to be given to the members entitled to vote that a meeting will be held at a time fixed by the board not less than 35 nor more than 150 days after receipt of the request. If the notice is not given within 20 days after receipt of the request, the persons entitled to call the meeting may give the notice or the superior court of the proper county shall summarily order the giving of the notice, after notice to the corporation giving it an opportunity to be heard. The court may issue such orders as may be appropriate, including, without limitation, orders designating the time and place of the meeting, the record date for determination of members entitled to vote, and the form of notice.

(d) When a members' meeting is adjourned to another time or place, unless the bylaws otherwise require and except as provided in this subdivision, notice need not be given of the adjourned meeting if the time and place thereof (or the means of electronic transmission by and to the corporation or electronic video screen communication, conference telephone, or other means of remote communication, if any, by which members may participate) are announced at the meeting at which the adjournment is taken. No meeting may be adjourned for more than 45 days. At the adjourned meeting the corporation may transact any business which might have been transacted at the original meeting. If after the adjournment a new record date is fixed for notice or voting, a notice of the adjourned meeting shall be given to each member who, on the record date for notice of the meeting, is entitled to vote at the meeting.

(e) The transactions of any meeting of members however called and noticed, and wherever held, are as valid as though had at a meeting duly held after regular call and notice, if a quorum is present either in person or by proxy, and if, either before or after the meeting, each of the persons entitled to vote, not present in person (or, if proxies are allowed, by proxy), provides a waiver of notice or consent to the holding of the meeting or an approval of the minutes thereof in writing. All such waivers, consents, and approvals shall be filed with the corporate records or made a part of the minutes of the meeting. Attendance of a person at a meeting shall constitute a waiver of notice of and presence at the meeting, except when the person objects, at the beginning of the meeting, to the transaction of any business because the meeting is not lawfully called or convened and except that attendance at a meeting is not a waiver of any right to object to the consideration of matters required by this part to be included in the notice but not so included, if the objection is expressly made at the meeting. Neither the business to be transacted at nor the purpose of any regular or special meeting of members need be specified in any written waiver of notice, consent to the holding of the meeting or approval of the minutes thereof, unless otherwise provided in the articles or bylaws, except as provided in subdivision (f).

(f) Any approval of the members required under Section 7222, 7224, 7233, 7812, 8610, or 8719, other than unanimous approval by those entitled to vote, shall be valid only if the general nature of the proposal so approved was stated in the notice of meeting or in any written waiver of notice.

(g) A court may find that notice not given in conformity with this section is still valid, if it was given in a fair and reasonable manner.

Corp. Code § 7512. Quorum.

(a) One-third of the voting power, represented in person or by proxy, shall constitute a quorum at a meeting of members, but, subject to subdivisions (b) and (c), a bylaw may set a different quorum. Any bylaw amendment to increase the quorum may be adopted only by approval of the members (Section 5034). If a quorum is present, the affirmative vote of the majority of the voting power represented at the meeting, entitled to vote, and voting on any matter shall be the act of the members unless the vote of a greater number or voting by classes is required by this part or the articles or bylaws.

(b) Where a bylaw authorizes a corporation to conduct a meeting with a quorum of less than one-third of the voting power, then the only matters that may be voted upon at any regular meeting actually attended, in person or by proxy, by less than one-third of the voting power are matters notice of the general nature of which was given, pursuant to the first sentence of subdivision (a) of Section 7511.

(c) Subject to subdivision (b), the members present at a duly called or held meeting at which a quorum is present may continue to transact business until adjournment notwithstanding the withdrawal of enough members to leave less than a quorum, if any action taken (other than adjournment) is approved by at least a majority of the members required to constitute a quorum or, if required by this division, or by the articles or the bylaws, the vote of the greater number or voting by classes.

(d) In the absence of a quorum, any meeting of members may be adjourned from time to time by the vote of a majority of the votes represented either in person or by proxy, but no other business may be transacted, except as provided in subdivision (c).

Corp. Code § 7513. Acts Without Meeting; Written Ballot; Number of Ballots and Approvals; Solicitation; Revocation of Ballots; Election of Directors.

(a) Subject to subdivision (e), and unless prohibited in the articles or bylaws, any action which may be taken at any regular or special meeting of members may be taken without a meeting if the corporation distributes a written ballot to every member entitled to vote on the matter. Unless otherwise provided by the articles or bylaws and if approved by the board of directors, that ballot and any related material may be sent by electronic transmission by the corporation (Section 20) and responses may be returned to the corporation by electronic transmission to the corporation (Section 21). That ballot shall set forth the proposed action, provide an opportunity to specify approval or disapproval of any proposal, and provide a reasonable time within which to return the ballot to the corporation.

(b) Approval by written ballot pursuant to this section shall be valid only when the number of votes cast by ballot within the time period specified equals or exceeds the quorum required to be present at a meeting authorizing the action, and the number of approvals equals or exceeds the number of votes that would be required to approve at a meeting at which the total number of votes cast was the same as the number of votes cast by ballot.

(c) Ballots shall be solicited in a manner consistent with the requirements of subdivision (b) of Section 7511 and Section 7514. All such solicitations shall indicate the number of responses needed to meet the quorum requirement and, with respect to ballots other than for the election of directors, shall state the percentage of approvals necessary to pass the measure submitted. The solicitation must specify the time by which the ballot must be received in order to be counted.

(d) Unless otherwise provided in the articles or bylaws, a written ballot may not be revoked.

(e) Directors may be elected by written ballot under this section, where authorized by the articles or bylaws, except that election by written ballot may not be authorized where the directors are elected by cumulative voting pursuant to Section 7615.

(f) When directors are to be elected by written ballot and the articles or bylaws prescribe a nomination procedure, the procedure may provide for a date for the close of nominations prior to the printing and distributing of the written ballots.

Corp. Code § 7514. Form of Proxy or Written Ballot.

(a) Any form of proxy or written ballot distributed to 10 or more members of a corporation with 100 or more members shall afford an opportunity on the proxy or form of written ballot to specify a choice between approval and disapproval of each matter or group of related matters intended, at the time the written ballot or proxy is distributed, to be acted upon at the meeting for which the proxy is solicited or by such written ballot, and shall provide, subject to reasonable specified conditions, that where the person solicited specifies a choice with respect to any such matter the vote shall be cast in accordance therewith.

(b) In any election of directors, any form of proxy or written ballot in which the directors to be voted upon are named therein as candidates and which is marked by a member "withhold" or otherwise marked in a manner indicating that the authority to vote for the election of directors is withheld shall not be voted either for or against the election of a director.

(c) Failure to comply with this section shall not invalidate any corporate action taken, but may be the basis for challenging any proxy at a meeting or written ballot and the superior court may compel compliance therewith at the suit of any member.

Corp. Code § 7517. Ballots; Good Faith Acceptance or Rejection.

(a) If the name signed on a ballot, consent, waiver, or proxy appointment corresponds to the name of a member, the corporation if acting in good faith is entitled to accept the ballot, consent, waiver or proxy appointment and give it effect as the act of the member.

(b) If the name signed on a ballot, consent, waiver, or proxy appointment does not correspond to the record name of a member, the corporation if acting in good faith is nevertheless entitled to accept the ballot, consent, waiver, or proxy appointment and give it effect as the act of the member if any of the following occur:

(1) The member is an entity and the name signed purports to be that of an officer or agent of the entity.

(2) The name signed purports to be that of an attorney-in-fact of the member and if the corporation requests, evidence acceptable to the corporation of the signatory's authority to sign for the member has been presented with respect to the ballot, consent, waiver, or proxy appointment.

(3) Two or more persons hold the membership as cotenants or fiduciaries and the name signed purports to be the name of at least one of the coholders and the person signing appears to be acting on behalf of all the coholders.

(4) The name signed purports to be that of an administrator, executor, guardian, or conservator representing the member and, if the corporation requests, evidence of fiduciary status acceptable to the corporation has been presented with respect to the ballot, consent, waiver, or proxy appointment.

(5) The name signed purports to be that of a receiver or trustee in bankruptcy of the member, and, if the corporation requests, evidence of this status acceptable to the corporation has been presented with respect to the ballot, consent, waiver, or proxy appointment.

(c) The corporation is entitled to reject a ballot, consent, waiver, or proxy appointment if the secretary or other officer or agent authorized to tabulate votes, acting in good faith, has a reasonable basis for doubt concerning the validity of the signature or the signatory's authority to sign for the member.

(d) The corporation and any officer or agent thereof who accepts or rejects a ballot, consent, waiver, or proxy appointment in good faith and in accordance with the standards of this section shall not be liable in damages to the member for the consequences of the acceptance or rejection.

(e) Corporate action based on the acceptance or rejection of a ballot, consent, waiver, or proxy appointment under this section is valid unless a court of competent jurisdiction determines otherwise.

Corp. Code § 7527. Limitation of Actions; Validity of Election.

An action challenging the validity of any election, appointment or removal of a director or directors must be commenced within nine months after the election, appointment or removal. If no such action is commenced, in the absence of fraud, any election, appointment or removal of a director is conclusively presumed valid nine months thereafter.

Corp. Code § 7611. Record Date; Right to Vote; Notice; Adjournment.

(a) The bylaws may provide or, in the absence of such provision, the board may fix, in advance, a date as the record date for the purpose of determining the members entitled to notice of any meeting of members. Such record date shall not be more than 90 nor less than 10 days before the date of the meeting. If no record date is fixed, members at the close of business on the business day preceding the day on which notice is given or, if notice is waived, at the close of business on the business day preceding the day on which the meeting is held are entitled to notice of a meeting of members. A determination of members entitled to notice of a meeting of members shall apply to any adjournment of the meeting unless the board fixes a new record date for the adjourned meeting.

(b) The bylaws may provide or, in the absence of such provision, the board may fix, in advance, a date as the record date for the purpose of determining the members entitled to vote at a meeting of members. Such record date shall not be more than 60 days before the date of the meeting. Such record date shall also apply in the case of an adjournment of the meeting unless the board fixes a new record date for the adjourned meeting. If no record date is fixed, members on the day of the meeting who are otherwise eligible to vote are entitled to vote at the meeting of members or, in the case of an adjourned meeting, members on the day of the adjourned meeting who are otherwise eligible to vote are entitled to vote at the adjourned meeting of members.

(c) The bylaws may provide or, in the absence of such provision, the board may fix, in advance, a date as the record date for the purpose of determining the members entitled to cast written ballots (Section 7513). Such record date shall not be more than 60 days before the day on which the first written ballot is mailed or solicited. If no record date is fixed, members on the day the first written ballot is mailed or solicited who are otherwise eligible to vote are entitled to cast written ballots.

(d) The bylaws may provide or, in the absence of such provision, the board may fix, in advance, a date as the record date for the purpose of determining the members entitled to exercise any rights in respect of any other lawful action. Such record date shall not be more than 60 days prior to such other action. If no record date is fixed, members at the close of business on the day on which the board adopts the resolution relating thereto, or the 60th day prior to the date of such other action, whichever is later, are entitled to exercise such rights.

Corp. Code § 7612. Membership in Names of Two or More Persons.

If a membership stands of record in the names of two or more persons, whether fiduciaries, members of a partnership, joint tenants, tenants in common, spouses as community property, tenants by the entirety, persons entitled to vote under a voting agreement or otherwise, or if two or more persons (including proxyholders) have the same fiduciary relationship respecting the same membership, unless the secretary of the corporation is given written notice to the contrary and is furnished with a copy of the instrument or order appointing them or creating the relationship wherein it is so provided, their acts with respect to voting shall have the following effect:

(a) If only one votes, such act binds all; or

(b) If more than one vote, the act of the majority so voting binds all.

Corp. Code § 7613. Proxies.

(a) Any member may authorize another person or persons to act by proxy with respect to such membership except that this right may be limited or withdrawn by the articles or bylaws, subject to subdivision (f). Any proxy purported to be executed in accordance with the provisions of this part shall be presumptively valid.

(b) No proxy shall be valid after the expiration of 11 months from the date thereof unless otherwise provided in the proxy, except that the maximum term of any proxy shall be three years from the date of execution. Every proxy continues in full force and effect until revoked by the person executing it prior to the vote pursuant thereto, except as otherwise provided in this section. Such revocation may be effected by a writing delivered to the corporation stating that the proxy is revoked or by a subsequent proxy executed by the person executing the prior proxy and presented to the meeting, or as to any meeting by attendance at such meeting and voting in person by the person executing the proxy. The dates contained on the forms of proxy presumptively determine the order of execution, regardless of the postmark dates on the envelopes in which they are mailed.

(c) A proxy is not revoked by the death or incapacity of the maker or the termination of a membership as a result thereof unless, before the vote is counted, written notice of such death or incapacity is received by the corporation.

(d) Unless otherwise provided in the articles or bylaws, the proxy of a member which states that it is irrevocable is irrevocable for the period specified therein (notwithstanding subdivisions (b) and (c)) when it is held by any of the following or a nominee of any of the following:

(1) A person who has purchased or who has agreed to purchase the membership;

(2) A creditor or creditors of the corporation or the member who extended or continued credit to the corporation or the member in consideration of the proxy if the proxy states that it was given in consideration of such extension or continuation of credit and the name of the person extending or continuing the credit; or

(3) A person who has contracted to perform services as an employee of the corporation, if the proxy is required by the contract of employment and if the proxy states that it was given in consideration of such contract of employment, the name of the employee and the period of employment contracted for.

Notwithstanding the period of irrevocability specified, the proxy becomes revocable when the agreement to purchase is terminated; the debt of the corporation or the member is paid; or the period of employment provided for in the contract of employment has terminated. In addition to the foregoing paragraphs (1) through (3), a proxy of a member may be made irrevocable (notwithstanding subdivision (c)) if it is given to secure the performance of a duty or to protect a title, either legal or equitable, until the happening of events which, by its terms, discharge the obligations secured by it.

(e) A proxy may be revoked, notwithstanding a provision making it irrevocable, by a transferee of a membership without knowledge of the existence of the provision unless the existence of the proxy and its irrevocability appears on the certificate representing the membership.

(f) Subdivision (a) notwithstanding:

(1) No amendment of the articles or bylaws repealing, restricting, creating or expanding proxy rights may be adopted without approval by the members (Section 5034); and

(2) No amendment of the articles or bylaws restricting or limiting the use of proxies may affect the validity of a previously issued irrevocable proxy during the term of its irrevocability, so long as it complied with applicable provisions, if any, of the articles or bylaws at the time of its issuance, and is otherwise valid under this section.

(g) Anything to the contrary notwithstanding, any revocable proxy covering matters requiring a vote of the members pursuant to Section 7222; Section 7224; Section 7233; paragraph (1) of subdivision (f) of this section; Section 7812; paragraph (2) of subdivision (a) of Section 7911; Section 8012; subdivision (a) of Section 8015; Section 8610; or subdivision (a) of Section

8719 is not valid as to such matters unless it sets forth the general nature of the matter to be voted on.

Corp. Code § 7614. Inspectors of Election.

(a) In advance of any meeting of members, the board may appoint inspectors of election to act at the meeting and any adjournment thereof. If inspectors of election are not so appointed, or if any persons so appointed fail to appear or refuse to act, the chairman of any meeting of members may, and on the request of any member or a member's proxy shall, appoint inspectors of election (or persons to replace those who so fail or refuse) at the meeting. The number of inspectors shall be either one or three. If appointed at a meeting on the request of one or more members or proxies, the majority of members represented in person or by proxy shall determine whether one or three inspectors are to be appointed. In the case of any action by written ballot (Section 7513), the board may similarly appoint inspectors of election to act with powers and duties as set forth in this section.

(b) The inspectors of election shall determine the number of memberships outstanding and the voting power of each, the number represented at the meeting, the existence of a quorum, and the authenticity, validity and effect of proxies, receive votes, ballots or consents, hear and determine all challenges and questions in any way arising in connection with the right to vote, count and tabulate all votes or consents, determine when the polls shall close, determine the result and do such acts as may be proper to conduct the election or vote with fairness to all members.

(c) The inspectors of election shall perform their duties impartially, in good faith, to the best of their ability and as expeditiously as is practical. If there are three inspectors of election, the decision, act or certificate of a majority is effective in all respects as the decision, act or certificate of all. Any report or certificate made by the inspectors of election is prima facie evidence of the facts stated therein.

Corp. Code § 7615. Cumulative Voting.

(a) If the articles or bylaws authorize cumulative voting, but not otherwise, every member entitled to vote at any election of directors may cumulate the member's votes and give one candidate a number of votes equal to the number of directors to be elected multiplied by the number of votes to which the member is entitled, or distribute the member's votes on the same principle among as many candidates as the member thinks fit. An article or bylaw provision authorizing cumulative voting may be repealed or amended only by approval of the members (Section 5034), except that the governing article or bylaw provision may require the vote of a greater proportion of the members, or of the members of any class, for its repeal.

(b) No member shall be entitled to cumulate votes for a candidate or candidates unless the candidate's name or candidates' names have been placed in nomination prior to the voting and the member has given notice at the meeting prior to the voting of the member's intention to cumulate votes. If any one member has given this notice, all members may cumulate their votes for candidates in nomination.

(c) In any election of directors by cumulative voting, the candidates receiving the highest number of votes are elected, subject to any lawful provision specifying election by classes.

(d) In any election of directors not governed by subdivision (c), unless otherwise provided in the articles or bylaws, the candidates receiving the highest number of votes are elected.

(e) Elections for directors need not be by ballot unless a member demands election by ballot at the meeting and before the voting begins or unless the bylaws so require.

Annual Corporate Statement

Corp. Code § 8210. Statement of Names and Addresses of Officers and of Agent for Service of Process.

(a) Every corporation shall, within 90 days after the filing of its original articles and biennially thereafter during the applicable filing period, file, on a form prescribed by the Secretary of State, a statement containing: (1) the name of the corporation and the Secretary of State's file number; (2) the names and complete business or residence addresses of its chief executive officer, secretary, and chief financial officer; (3) the street address of its principal office in this state, if any; (4) the mailing address of the corporation, if different from the street address of its principal executive office or if the corporation has no principal office address in this state; and (5) if the corporation chooses to receive renewal notices and any other notifications from the Secretary of State by electronic mail instead of by United States mail, a valid electronic mail address for the corporation or for the corporation's designee to receive those notices.

(b) The statement required by subdivision (a) shall also designate, as the agent of the corporation for the purpose of service of process, a natural person residing in this state or any domestic or foreign or foreign business corporation that has complied with Section 1505 and whose capacity to act as an agent has not terminated. If a natural person is designated, the statement shall set forth the person's complete business or residence street address. If a corporate agent is designated, no address for it shall be set forth.

(c) For the purposes of this section, the applicable filing period for a corporation shall be the calendar month during which its original articles were filed and the immediately preceding five calendar months. The Secretary of State shall provide a notice to each corporation to comply with this section approximately three months prior to the close of the applicable filing period. The notice shall state the due date for compliance and shall be sent to the last address of the corporation according to the records of the Secretary of State or to the last electronic mail address according to the records of the Secretary of State if the corporation has elected to receive notices from the Secretary of State by electronic mail. Neither the failure of the Secretary of State to send the notice nor the failure of the corporation to receive it is an excuse for failure to comply with this section.

(d) Whenever any of the information required by subdivision (a) is changed, the corporation may file a current statement containing all the information required by subdivisions (a) and (b). In order to change its agent for service of process or the address of the agent, the corporation must file a current statement containing all the information required by subdivisions (a) and (b). Whenever any statement is filed pursuant to this section, it supersedes any previously filed statement and the statement in the articles as to the agent for service of process and the address of the agent.

(e) The Secretary of State may destroy or otherwise dispose of any statement filed pursuant to this section after it has been superseded by the filing of a new statement.

(f) This section shall not be construed to place any person dealing with the corporation on notice of, or under any duty to inquire about, the existence or content of a statement filed pursuant to this section.

Corporate Records

Corp. Code § 8311. Inspections; Persons Authorized; Copies.

Any inspection under this chapter may be made in person or by agent or attorney and the right of inspection includes the right to copy and make extracts.

Corp. Code § 8320. Books and Records.

(a) Each corporation shall keep:

(1) Adequate and correct books and records of account;

(2) Minutes of the proceedings of its members, board and committees of the board; and

(3) A record of its members giving their names and addresses and the class of membership held by each.

(b) Those minutes and other books and records shall be kept either in written form or in any other form capable of being converted into clearly legible tangible form or in any combination of the foregoing. When minutes and other books and records are kept in a form capable of being converted into clearly legible paper form, the clearly legible paper form into which those minutes and other books and records are converted shall be admissible in evidence, and accepted for all other purposes, to the same extent as an original paper record of the same information would have been, provided that the paper form accurately portrays the record.

Corp. Code § 8321. Annual Report.

(a) A corporation shall notify each member yearly of the member's right to receive a financial report pursuant to this subdivision. Except as provided in subdivision (c), upon written request of a member the board shall promptly cause the most recent annual report to be sent to the requesting member. An annual report shall be prepared not later than 120 days after the close of the corporation's fiscal year. Unless otherwise provided by the articles or bylaws and if approved by the board of directors, that report and any accompanying material may be sent by electronic transmission by the corporation (Section 20). That report shall contain in appropriate detail the following:

(1) A balance sheet as of the end of that fiscal year and an income statement and a statement of cashflows for that fiscal year.

(2) A statement of the place where the names and addresses of the current members are located.

(3) Any information required by Section 8322.

(b) The report required by subdivision (a) shall be accompanied by any report thereon of independent accountants, or, if there is no report, the certificate of an authorized officer of the corporation that the statements were prepared without audit from the books and records of the corporation.

(c) Subdivision (a) does not apply to any corporation that receives less than ten thousand dollars ($10,000) in gross revenues or receipts during the fiscal year.

Corp. Code § 8330. Demand; Persons Authorized; Reason; Alternative Proposal.

(a) Subject to Sections 8331 and 8332, and unless the corporation provides a reasonable alternative pursuant to subdivision (c), a member may do either or both of the following as permitted by subdivision (b):

(1) Inspect and copy the record of all the members' names, addresses and voting rights, at reasonable times, upon five business days' prior written demand upon the corporation which demand shall state the purpose for which the inspection rights are requested; or

(2) Obtain from the secretary of the corporation, upon written demand and tender of a reasonable charge, a list of the names, addresses and voting rights of those members entitled to vote for the election of directors, as of the most recent record date for which it has been compiled or as of a date specified by the member subsequent to the date of demand. The demand shall state the purpose for which the list is requested. The membership list shall be made available on or before the later of ten business days after the demand is received or after the date specified therein as the date as of which the list is to be compiled.

(b) The rights set forth in subdivision (a) may be exercised by:

(1) Any member, for a purpose reasonably related to such person's interest as a member. Where the corporation reasonably believes that the information will be used for another purpose, or where it provides a reasonable alternative pursuant to subdivision (c), it may deny the member access to the list. In any subsequent action brought by the member under Section 8336, the court shall enforce the rights set forth in subdivision (a) unless the corporation proves that the member will allow use of the information for purposes unrelated to the person's interest as a member or that the alternative method offered reasonably achieves the proper purpose set forth in the demand.

(2) The authorized number of members for a purpose reasonably related to the members' interest as members.

(c) The corporation may, within ten business days after receiving a demand under subdivision (a), deliver to the person or persons making the demand a written offer of an alternative method of achieving the purpose identified in said demand without providing access to or a copy of the membership list. An alternative method which reasonably and in a timely manner accomplishes the proper purpose set forth in a demand made under subdivision (a) shall be deemed a reasonable alternative, unless within a reasonable time after acceptance of the offer the corporation fails to do those things which it offered to do. Any rejection of the offer shall be in writing and shall indicate the reasons the alternative proposed by the corporation does not meet the proper purpose of the demand made pursuant to subdivision (a).

Corp. Code § 8333. Accounting Books; Minutes; Demand; Purpose.

The accounting books and records and minutes of proceedings of the members and the board and committees of the board shall be open to inspection upon the written demand on the corporation of any member at any reasonable time, for a purpose reasonably related to such person's interests as a member.

Corp. Code § 8334. Directors' Rights.

Every director shall have the absolute right at any reasonable time to inspect and copy all books, records and documents of every kind and to inspect the physical properties of the corporation of which such person is a director.

Corp. Code § 8338. Membership List; Authorized and Prohibited Uses; Damages; Injunction; Costs, Expenses and Attorney Fees.

(a) A membership list is a corporate asset. Without consent of the board a membership list or any part thereof may not be obtained or used by any person for any purpose not reasonably related to a member's interest as a member. Without limiting the generality of the foregoing, without the consent of the board a membership list or any part thereof may not be:

(1) Used to solicit money or property unless such money or property will be used solely to solicit the vote of the members in an election to be held by their corporation.

(2) Used for any purpose which the user does not reasonably and in good faith believe will benefit the corporation.

(3) Used for any commercial purpose or purpose in competition with the corporation.

(4) Sold to or purchased by any person.

(b) Any person who violates the provisions of subdivision (a) shall be liable for any damage such violation causes the corporation and shall account for and pay to the corporation any profit derived as a result of said violation. In addition, a court in its discretion may award exemplary damages for a fraudulent or malicious violation of subdivision (a).

(c) Nothing in this article shall be construed to limit the right of a corporation to obtain injunctive relief necessary to restrain misuse of a membership list or any part thereof.

(d) In any action or proceeding under this section, a court may award the corporation reasonable costs and expenses, including reasonable attorneys' fees, in connection with such action or proceeding.

(e) As used in this section, the term "membership list" means the record of the members' names and addresses.

4

SELECTED PROVISIONS OF THE BUSINESS AND PROFESSIONS CODE, CIVIL CODE, CODE OF CIVIL PROCEDURE, INTERNAL REVENUE CODE AND TAXATION CODE AFFECTING COMMON INTEREST DEVELOPMENTS

Certified Common Interest Development Managers

Bus. & Prof. Code § 11500. Definitions.

For purposes of this chapter, the following definitions apply:

(a) "Common interest development" means a residential development identified in Section 4100 of the Civil Code.

(b) "Association" has the same meaning as defined in Section 4080 of the Civil Code.

(c) "Financial services" means acts performed or offered to be performed, for compensation, for an association including, but not limited to, the preparation of internal unaudited financial statements, internal accounting and bookkeeping functions, billing of assessments, and related services.

(d) "Management services" means acts performed or offered to be performed in an advisory capacity for an association including, but not limited to, the following:

(1) Administering or supervising the collection, reporting, and archiving of the financial or common area assets of an association or common interest development, at the direction of the association's board of directors.

(2) Implementing resolutions and directives of the board of directors of the association elected to oversee the operation of a common interest development.

(3) Implementing provisions of governing documents, as defined in Section 4150 of the Civil Code, that govern the operation of the common interest development.

(4) Administering association contracts, including insurance contracts, within the scope of the association's duties or with other common interest development managers, vendors, contractors, and other third-party providers of goods and services to an association or common interest development.

(e) "Professional association for common interest development managers" means an organization that meets all of the following:

(1) Has at least 200 members or certificants who are common interest development managers in California.

(2) Has been in existence for at least five years.

(3) Operates pursuant to Section 501(c) of the Internal Revenue Code.

(4) Certifies that a common interest development manager has met the criteria set forth in Section 11502 without requiring membership in the association.

(5) Requires adherence to a code of professional ethics and standards of practice for certified common interest development managers.

Bus. & Prof. Code § 11501. "Common Interest Development Manager."

(a) "Common interest development manager" means an individual who for compensation, or in expectation of compensation, provides or contracts to provide management or financial services, or represents himself or herself to act in the capacity of providing management or financial services to an association. Notwithstanding any other provision of law, an individual may not be required to obtain a real estate or broker's license in order to perform the services of a common interest development manager to an association.

(b) "Common interest development manager" also means any of the following:

(1) An individual who is a partner in a partnership, a shareholder or officer in a corporation, or who, in any other business entity acts in a capacity

to advise, supervise, and direct the activity of a registrant or professional registrant, or who acts as a principal on behalf of a company that provides the services of a common interest development manager.

(2) An individual operating under a fictitious business name who provides the services of a common interest development manager.

This section may not be construed to require an association to hire for compensation a common interest development manager, unless required to do so by its governing documents. Nothing in this part shall be construed to supersede any law that requires a license, permit, or any other form of registration, to provide management or financial services. Nothing in this section shall preclude a licensee of the California Board of Accountancy from providing financial services to an association within the scope of his or her license in addition to the preparation of reviewed and audited financial statements and the preparation of the association's tax returns.

Bus. & Prof. Code § 11502. Certified Common Interest Development Manager; Criteria.

In order to be called a "certified common interest development manager," a person shall meet one of the following requirements:

(a) Prior to July 1, 2003, has passed a knowledge, skills, and aptitude examination as specified in Section 11502.5 or has been granted a certification or a designation by a professional association for common interest development managers, and who has, within five years prior to July 1, 2004, received instruction in California law pursuant to paragraph (1) of subdivision (b).

(b) On or after July 1, 2003, has successfully completed an educational curriculum that shall be no less than a combined 30 hours in coursework described in this subdivision and passed an examination or examinations that test competence in common interest development management in the following areas:

(1) The law that relates to the management of common interest developments, including, but not limited to, the following courses of study:

(A) Topics covered by the Davis-Stirling Common Interest Development Act, contained in Part 5 (commencing with section 4000) of Division 4 of the Civil Code, including, but not limited to, the types of California common interest developments, disclosure requirements pertaining to common interest developments, meeting requirements, financial reporting requirements, and member access to association records.

(B) Personnel issues, including, but not limited to, general matters related to independent contractor or employee status, the laws on harassment, the Unruh Civil Rights Act, the California Fair Employment and Housing Act, and the Americans with Disabilities Act.

(C) Risk management, including, but not limited to, insurance coverage, maintenance, operations, and emergency preparedness.

(D) Property protection for associations, including, but not limited to, pertinent matters relating to environmental hazards such as asbestos, radon gas, and lead-based paint, the Vehicle Code, local and municipal regulations, family day care facilities, energy conservation, Federal Communications Commission rules and regulations, and solar energy systems.

(E) Business affairs of associations, including, but not limited to, necessary compliance with federal, state, and local law.

(F) Basic understanding of governing documents, codes, and regulations relating to the activities and affairs of associations and common interest developments.

(2) Instruction in general management that is related to the managerial and business skills needed for management of a common interest development, including, but not limited to, the following:

(A) Finance issues, including, but not limited to, budget preparation; management; administration or supervision of the collection, reporting, and archiving of the financial or common area assets of an association or common interest development; bankruptcy laws; and assessment collection.

(B) Contract negotiation and administration.

(C) Supervision of employees and staff.

(D) Management of maintenance programs.

(E) Management and administration of rules, regulations, and parliamentary procedures.

(F) Management and administration of architectural standards.

(G) Management and administration of the association's recreational programs and facilities.

(H) Management and administration of owner and resident communications.

(I) Training and strategic planning for the association's board of directors and its committees.

(J) Implementation of association policies and procedures.

(K) Ethics, professional conduct, and standards of practice for common interest development managers.

(L) Current issues relating to common interest developments.

(M) Conflict avoidance and resolution mechanisms.

Bus. & Prof. Code § 11502.5. Competency Examination.

The course related competency examination or examinations and education provided to a certified common interest development manager pursuant to Section 11502 by any professional association for common interest development managers, or any postsecondary educational institution, shall be developed and administered in a manner consistent with standards and requirements set forth by the American Educational Research Association's "Standards for Educational and Psychological Testing," and the Equal Employment Opportunity Commission's "Uniform Guidelines for Employee Selection Procedures," the Unruh Civil Rights Act, the California Fair Employment and Housing Act, and the Americans with Disabilities Act of 1990, or the course or courses that have been approved as a continuing education course or an equivalent course of study pursuant to the regulations of the Real Estate Commissioner.

Bus. & Prof. Code § 11503. Exception.

A "certified common interest development manager" does not include a common interest development management firm.

Bus. & Prof. Code § 11504. Disclosures.

On or before September 1, 2003, and annually thereafter, a person who either provides or contemplates providing the services of a common interest development manager to an association shall disclose to the board of directors of the association the following information:

(a) Whether or not the common interest development manager has met the requirements of Section 11502 so he or she may be called a certified common interest development manager.

(b) The name, address, and telephone number of the professional association that certified the common interest development manager, the date the manager was certified, and the status of the certification.

(c) The location of his or her primary office.

(d) Prior to entering into or renewing a contract with an association, the common interest development manager shall disclose to the board of directors of the association or common interest development whether the fidelity insurance of the common interest development manager or his or her employer covers the current year's operating and reserve funds of the association. This requirement shall not be construed to compel an association to require a common interest development manager to obtain or maintain fidelity insurance.

(e) Whether the common interest development manager possesses an active real estate license.

(f) A common interest development manager or common interest development management firm shall disclose information required in Section 5375 of the Civil Code.

(g) Whether or not the common interest development manager receives a referral fee or other monetary benefit from a third-party provider distributing documents pursuant to Section 5300 of the Civil Code.

(h) An affirmative written acknowledgment that the disclosure provided to a member or potential member pursuant to Sections 4528 and 5300 of the Civil Code, and all documents provided thereunder, are the property of the association and not its managing agent or the agent's managing firm.

Bus. & Prof. Code § 11505. Unfair Business Practice.

It is an unfair business practice for a common interest development manager, a company that employs the common interest development manager, or a company that is controlled by a company that also has a financial interest in a company employing that manager, to do any of the following:

(a) On or after July 1, 2003, to hold oneself out or use the title of "certified common interest development manager" or any other term that implies or suggests that the person is certified as a common interest development manager without meeting the requirements of Section 11502.

(b) To state or advertise that he or she is certified, registered, or licensed by a governmental agency to perform the functions of a certified common interest development manager.

(c) To state or advertise a registration or license number, unless the license or registration is specified by a statute, regulation, or ordinance.

(d) To fail to comply with any item to be disclosed in Section 11504 of this code, or Section 5375 of the Civil Code.

Bus. & Prof. Code § 11506. Review.

This part shall be subject to review by the appropriate policy committees of the Legislature.

Signs Advertising Property for Sale

Civil Code § 712. Conditions Restraining Right to Display Sign Advertising Property for Sale.

(a) Every provision contained in or otherwise affecting a grant of a fee interest in, or purchase money security instrument upon, real property in this state heretofore or hereafter made, which purports to prohibit or restrict the right of the property owner or his or her agent to display or have displayed on the real property, or on real property owned by others with their consent, or both, signs which are reasonably located, in plain view of the public, are of reasonable dimensions and design, and do not adversely affect public safety, including traffic safety, and which advertise the property for sale, lease, or exchange, or advertise directions to the property, by the property owner or his or her agent is void as an unreasonable restraint upon the power of alienation.

(b) This section shall operate retrospectively, as well as prospectively, to the full extent that it may constitutionally operate retrospectively.

(c) A sign that conforms to the ordinance adopted in conformity with Section 713 shall be deemed to be of reasonable dimension and design pursuant to this section.

Civil Code § 713. Local Regulations; Signs Advertising Property for Sale, Lease or Exchange.

(a) Notwithstanding any provision of any ordinance, an owner of real property or his or her agent may display or have displayed on the owner's real property, or on real property owned by others with their consent, signs which are reasonably located, in plain view of the public, are of reasonable dimensions and design, and do not adversely affect public safety, including traffic safety, as determined by the city, county, or city and county, advertising the following:

(1) That the property is for sale, lease, or exchange by the owner or his or her agent.

(2) Directions to the property.

(3) The owner's or agent's name.

(4) The owner's or agent's address and telephone number.

Misc. Codes

(b) Nothing in this section limits any authority which a person or local governmental entity may have to limit or regulate the display or placement of a sign on a private or public right-of-way.

Solar Energy Systems

Civil Code § 714. Solar Energy System; Prohibition or Restriction of Installation or Use; Invalidity and Unenforceability of Instruments Affecting Real Property; Cost, Efficiency Defined; Exceptions.

(a) Any covenant, restriction, or condition contained in any deed, contract, security instrument, or other instrument affecting the transfer or sale of, or any interest in, real property, and any provision of a governing document, as defined in Section 4150 or 6552, that effectively prohibits or restricts the installation or use of a solar energy system is void and unenforceable.

(b) This section does not apply to provisions that impose reasonable restrictions on solar energy systems. However, it is the policy of the state to promote and encourage the use of solar energy systems and to remove obstacles thereto. Accordingly, reasonable restrictions on a solar energy system are those restrictions that do not significantly increase the cost of the system or significantly decrease its efficiency or specified performance, or that allow for an alternative system of comparable cost, efficiency, and energy conservation benefits.

(c) (1) A solar energy system shall meet applicable health and safety standards and requirements imposed by state and local permitting authorities, consistent with Section 65850.5 of the Government Code.

(2) Solar energy systems used for heating water in single family residences and solar collectors used for heating water in commercial or swimming pool applications shall be certified by an accredited listing agency as defined in the Plumbing and Mechanical Codes.

(3) A solar energy system for producing electricity shall also meet all applicable safety and performance standards established by the California Electrical Code, the Institute of Electrical and Electronics Engineers, and accredited testing laboratories such as Underwriters Laboratories and, where applicable, rules of the Public Utilities Commission regarding safety and reliability.

(d) For the purposes of this section:

(1) (A) For solar domestic water heating systems or solar swimming pool heating systems that comply with state and federal law, "significantly" means an amount exceeding 10 percent of the cost of the system, but in no case more than one thousand dollars ($1,000), or decreasing the efficiency of the solar energy system by an amount exceeding 10 percent, as originally specified and proposed.

(B) For photovoltaic systems that comply with state and federal law, "significantly" means an amount not to exceed one thousand dollars ($1,000) over the system cost as originally specified and proposed, or a decrease in system efficiency of an amount exceeding 10 percent as originally specified and proposed.

(2) "Solar energy system" has the same meaning as defined in paragraphs (1) and (2) of subdivision (a) of Section 801.5.

(e) (1) Whenever approval is required for the installation or use of a solar energy system, the application for approval shall be processed and approved by the appropriate approving entity in the same manner as an application for approval of an architectural modification to the property, and shall not be willfully avoided or delayed.

(2) For an approving entity that is an association, as defined in Section 4080 or 6528, and that is not a public entity, both of the following shall apply:

(A) The approval or denial of an application shall be in writing.

(B) If an application is not denied in writing within 45 days from the date of receipt of the application, the application shall be deemed approved, unless the delay is the result of a reasonable request for additional information.

(f) Any entity, other than a public entity, that willfully violates this section shall be liable to the applicant or other party for actual damages occasioned thereby, and shall pay a civil penalty to the applicant or other party in an amount not to exceed one thousand dollars ($1,000).

(g) In any action to enforce compliance with this section, the prevailing party shall be awarded reasonable attorney's fees.

(h) (1) A public entity that fails to comply with this section may not receive funds from a state-sponsored grant or loan program for solar energy.

A public entity shall certify its compliance with the requirements of this section when applying for funds from a state-sponsored grant or loan program.

(2) A local public entity may not exempt residents in its jurisdiction from the requirements of this section.

Civil Code § 714.1. Solar Energy System; Reasonable Restrictions in Community Associations.

(a) Notwithstanding Section 714, an association may impose reasonable provisions that:

(1) Restrict the installation of solar energy systems in common areas to those systems approved by the association.

(2) Require the owner of a separate interest to obtain the approval of the association for the installation of a solar energy system in a separate interest owned by another.

(3) Provide for the maintenance, repair, or replacement of roofs or other building components.

(4) Require installers of solar energy systems to indemnify or reimburse the association or its members for loss or damage caused by the installation, maintenance, or use of the solar energy system.

(b) An association shall not:

(1) Establish a general policy prohibiting the installation or use of a rooftop solar energy system for household purposes on the roof of the building in which the owner resides, or a garage or carport adjacent to the building that has been assigned to the owner for exclusive use.

(2) Require approval by a vote of members owning separate interests in the common interest development, including that specified by Section 4600, for installation of a solar energy system for household purposes on the roof of the building in which the owner resides, or a garage or carport adjacent to the building that has been assigned to the owner for exclusive use.

An action by an association that contravenes paragraph (1) or (2) shall be void and unenforceable.

(c) For purposes of this section:

(1) "Association" has the same meaning as defined in Section 4080 or 6528.

(2) "Common area" has the same meaning as defined in Section 4095 or 6532.

(3) "Separate interest" has the same meaning as defined in Section 4185 or 6564.

Civ. Code § 714.3. Accessory and Junior Accessory Dwelling Units.

(a) Any covenant, restriction, or condition contained in any deed, contract, security instrument, or other instrument affecting the transfer or sale of any interest in real property that either effectively prohibits or unreasonably restricts the construction or use of an accessory dwelling unit or junior accessory dwelling unit on a lot zoned for single-family residential use that meets the requirements of Section 65852.2 or 65852.22 of the Government Code is void and unenforceable.

(b) This section does not apply to provisions that impose reasonable restrictions on accessory dwelling units or junior accessory dwelling units. For purposes of this subdivision, "reasonable restrictions" means restrictions that do not unreasonably increase the cost to construct, effectively prohibit the construction of, or extinguish the ability to otherwise construct, an accessory dwelling unit or junior accessory dwelling unit consistent with the provisions of Section 65852.2 or 65852.22 of the Government Code.

Clotheslines

Civil Code § 1940.20. Clotheslines and Drying Racks.

(a) For purposes of this section, the following definitions shall apply:

(1) "Clothesline" includes a cord, rope, or wire from which laundered items may be hung to dry or air. A balcony, railing, awning, or other part of a structure or building shall not qualify as a clothesline.

(2) "Drying rack" means an apparatus from which laundered items may be hung to dry or air. A balcony, railing, awning, or other part of a structure or building shall not qualify as a drying rack.

(3) "Private area" means an outdoor area or an area in the tenant's premises enclosed by a wall or fence with access from a door of the premises.

(b) A tenant may utilize a clothesline or drying rack in the tenant's private area if all of the following conditions are met:

(1) The clothesline or drying rack will not interfere with the maintenance of the rental property.

(2) The clothesline or drying rack will not create a health or safety hazard, block doorways, or interfere with walkways or utility service equipment.

(3) The tenant seeks the landlord's consent before affixing a clothesline to a building.

(4) Use of the clothesline or drying rack does not violate reasonable time or location restrictions imposed by the landlord.

(5) The tenant has received approval of the clothesline or drying rack, or the type of clothesline or drying rack, from the landlord.

Display of Religious Items

Civ. Code § 1940.45. Display of Religious Items.

(a) Except as otherwise provided by this section, a property owner shall not enforce or adopt a restrictive covenant or any other restriction that prohibits one or more religious items from being displayed or affixed on any entry door or entry door frame of a dwelling.

(b) To the extent permitted by Article 1, Section 4, of the California Constitution and the First Amendment to the United States Constitution, this section does not prohibit the enforcement or adoption of a restrictive covenant or other restriction prohibiting the display or affixing of a religious item on any entry door or entry door frame to a dwelling that:

(1) Threatens the public health or safety.

(2) Hinders the opening or closing of any entry door.

(3) Violates any federal, state, or local law.

(4) Contains graphics, language or any display that is obscene or otherwise illegal.

(5) Individually or in combination with any other religious item displayed or affixed on any entry door or door frame that has a total size greater than 36 by 12 square inches, provided it does not exceed the size of the door.

(c) As used in this section, the following terms have the following meanings:

(1) "Property owner" means all of the following:

(A) An association, as that term is defined in Section 4080.

(B) A board, as that term is defined in Section 4085.

(C) A member, as that term is defined in Section 4160.

(D) A landlord, as that term is defined in Section 1940.8.5.

(E) A sublessor.

(2) "Religious item" means an item displayed because of sincerely held religious beliefs.

Non-judicial Foreclosure

Civil Code § 2924b. Procedures for Requesting Copies of Lender Notices of Default, Notices of Sale, and Trustee's Deeds Upon Sale.

(a) Any person desiring a copy of any notice of default and of any notice of sale under any deed of trust or mortgage with power of sale upon real property or an estate for years therein, as to which deed of trust or mortgage the power of sale cannot be exercised until these notices are given for the time and in the manner provided in Section 2924 may, at any time subsequent to recordation of the deed of trust or mortgage and prior to recordation of notice of default thereunder, cause to be filed for record in the office of the recorder of any county in which any part or parcel of the real property is situated, a duly acknowledged request for a copy of the notice of default and of sale. This request shall be signed and acknowledged by the person making the request, specifying the name and address of the person to whom the notice is to be mailed, shall identify the deed of trust or mortgage by stating the names of the parties thereto, the date of recordation thereof, and the book and page where the deed of trust or mortgage is recorded or the recorder's number, and shall be in substantially the following form:

"In accordance with Section 2924b, Civil Code, request is hereby made that a copy of any notice of default and a copy of any notice of sale under the deed of trust (or mortgage) recorded __________, ______, in Book ______ page ______ records of ______________ County, (or filed for record with recorder's serial number ________________, ______________ County), California, executed by ________________ as trustor (or mortgagor) in which ______________________ is named as beneficiary (or mortgagee) and ______________________ as trustee be mailed to ______________________ at ______________________.

Name Address

NOTICE: A copy of any notice of default and of any notice of sale will be sent only to the address contained in this recorded request. If your address changes, a new request must be recorded.

Signature ______________________"

Upon the filing for record of the request, the recorder shall index in the general index of grantors the names of the trustors (or mortgagors) recited therein and the names of the persons requesting copies.

[Intervening subdivisions omitted.]

(f) (1) Notwithstanding subdivision (a), with respect to separate interests governed by an association, as defined in Section 4080 or 6528, the association may cause to be filed in the office of the recorder in the county in which the separate interests are situated a request that a mortgagee, trustee, or other person authorized to record a notice of default regarding any of those separate interests mail to the association a copy of any trustee's deed upon sale concerning a separate interest. The request shall include a legal description or the assessor's parcel number of all the separate interests. A request recorded pursuant to this subdivision shall include the name and address of the association and a statement that it is an association as defined in Section 4080 or 6528. Subsequent requests of any association shall supersede prior requests. A request pursuant to this subdivision shall be recorded before the filing of a notice of default. The mortgagee, trustee, or other authorized person shall mail the requested information to the association within 15 business days following the date of the trustee's sale. Failure to mail the request, pursuant to this subdivision, shall not affect the title to real property.

(2) A request filed pursuant to paragraph (1) does not, for purposes of Section 27288.1 of the Government Code, constitute a document that either effects or evidences a transfer or encumbrance of an interest in real property or that releases or terminates any interest, right, or encumbrance of an interest in real property.

[Remainder of section omitted.]

Code of Civil Procedure § 729.035. Foreclosure of Delinquent Assessment Liens and Right of Redemption.

Notwithstanding any provision of law to the contrary, the sale of a separate interest in a common interest development is subject to the right of redemption within 90 days after the sale if the sale arises from a foreclosure by the association of a common interest development pursuant to Sections 5700, 5710, and 5735 of the Civil Code, subject to the conditions of Sections 5705, 5715, and 5720 of the Civil Code.

Taxation of Homeowners Associations

Internal Revenue Code § 528. Taxation of Homeowner Associations.

(a) General rule. A homeowners association [as defined in subsection (c)] shall be subject to taxation under this subtitle only to the extent provided in this section. A homeowners association shall be considered an organization exempt from income taxes for the purpose of any law which refers to organizations exempt from income taxes.

(b) Tax imposed. A tax is hereby imposed for each taxable year on the owners association taxable income of every homeowners association. Such tax shall be equal to 30 percent of the homeowners association taxable income.

(c) Homeowners association defined. For purposes of this section

(1) Homeowners association. The term "homeowners association" means: an organization which is a condominium management association or a residential real estate management association if

(A) such organization is organized and operated to provide for the acquisition, construction, management, maintenance, and care of association property,

(B) sixty percent or more of the gross income of such organization for the taxable year consists solely of amounts received as membership dues, fees, or assessments from (i) owners of residential units in the case of a condominium management association, or (ii) owners of residences or residential lots in the case of a residential real estate management association.

(C) ninety percent or more of the expenditures of the organization for the taxable year are expenditures for the acquisition, construction, management, maintenance, and care of association property,

(D) no part of the net earnings of such organization inures (other than by acquiring, constructing, or providing management, maintenance, and care of association property, and other than by a rebate of excess membership dues, fees, or assessments) to the benefit of any private shareholder or individual, and

(E) such organization elects (at such time and in such manner as the Secretary by regulations prescribes) to have this section apply for the taxable year.

(2) Condominium management association. The term "condominium management association" means any organization meeting the requirement of subparagraph (A) of paragraph (1) with respect to a condominium project substantially all of the units of which are used by individuals for residences.

(3) Residential real estate management association. The term "residential real estate management association" means any organization meeting the requirements of subparagraph (A) of paragraph (1) with respect to a subdivision, development, or similar area substantially all the lots or buildings of which may only be used by individuals for residences.

(4) Association property. The term "association property" means:

(A) property held by the organization

(B) property commonly held by the members of the organization

(C) property within the organization privately held by the members of the organization, and

(D) property owned by a governmental unit and used for the benefit of residents of such unit.

(d) Homeowners association taxable income defined.

(1) Taxable income defined. For purposes of this section, the homeowners association taxable income of any organization for any taxable year is an amount equal to the excess (if any) of

(A) the gross amount for the taxable year (excluding any exempt function income), over

(B) the deductions allowed by this chapter which are directly connected with the production of the gross income (excluding exempt function income), computed with the modifications provided in paragraph (2).

(2) Modifications. For purposes of this subsection

(A) there shall be allowed a specific deduction of $100,

(B) no net operating loss deduction shall be allowed under Section 172, and

(C) no deduction shall be allowed under part VIII of subchapter B (relating to special deductions for corporations).

(3) Exempt function income. For purposes of this subsection, the term "exempt function income" means any amount received as membership dues, fees, or assessments from

(A) owners of condominium housing units in the case of a condominium management association, or

(B) owners of real property in the case of a residential real estate management association.

IRS Revenue Ruling 70-604. Excess Assessments.

A condominium management corporation assesses its stockholder-owners for the purposes of managing, operating, maintaining, and replacing the common elements of the condominium property. This is the sole activity of the corporation and its by-laws do not authorize it to engage in any other activity.

A meeting is held each year by the stockholder-owners of the corporation, at which they decide what is to be done with any excess assessments not actually used for the purposes described above, i.e., they decide either to return the excess to themselves or to have the excess applied against the following year's assessments.

Held, the excess assessments for the taxable year over and above the actual expenses paid or incurred for the purposes described above are not taxable income to the corporation, since such excess, in effect, has been returned to the stockholder-owners.

Rev. & Tax. Code § 2188.3. Condominiums.

Whenever real property has been divided into condominiums, as defined in Section 783 of the Civil Code, (a) each condominium owned in fee shall be separately assessed to the owner thereof, and the tax on each such condominium shall constitute a lien solely thereon; (b) each condominium not owned in fee shall be separately assessed, as if it were owned in fee, to the owner of the condominium or the owner of the fee or both (and the tax on each such condominium shall be a lien solely on the interest of the owner of the fee in the real property included in such condominium and on such condominium), if so agreed by the assessor in a writing of record; such an agreement shall be binding upon such assessor and his successors in office with respect to such project so long as it continues to be divided into condominiums in the same manner as that in effect when the agreement was made.

Rev. & Tax. Code § 2188.5. Planned Developments; Assessment; Application of Amendment to Subd. (b).

(a) (1) Subject to the limitations set forth in subdivision (b), whenever real property has been divided into planned developments as defined in Section 11003 of the Business and Professions Code, the interests therein shall be presumed to be the value of each separately owned lot, parcel or area, and the assessment shall reflect this value which includes all of the following:

(A) The assessment attributable to the value of the separately owned lot, parcel or area and the improvements thereon.

(B) The assessment attributable to the share in the common area reserved as an appurtenance of the separately owned lot, parcel or area.

(C) The new base year value of the common area resulting from any change in ownership pursuant to Chapter 2 (commencing with Section 60) or new construction pursuant to Chapter 3 (commencing with Section 70) attributable to the share in the common area reserved as an appurtenance of the separately owned lot, parcel or area.

(2) For the purpose of this section, "common area" shall mean the land and improvements within a lot, parcel or area, the beneficial use and enjoyment of which is reserved in whole or in part as an appurtenance to the separately owned lots, parcels or area, whether this common area is held in common or through ownership of share of stock or membership in an owners' association. The tax on each separately owned lot, parcel or area shall constitute a lien solely thereon and upon the proportionate interest in the common area appurtenant thereto.

(b) Assessment in accordance with the provisions of subdivision (a) shall only be required with respect to those planned developments which satisfy both of the following conditions:

(1) The development is located entirely within a single tax code area.

(2) The entire beneficial ownership of the common area is reserved as an appurtenance to the separately owned lots, parcels or areas.

(c) The amendment to subdivision (b) made by the act Chapter 407 of the Statutes of 1984 shall apply to real property which has been divided into planned developments as defined in Sections 11003 and 11003.1 of the Business and Professions Code, on and after the effective date of Chapter 407 of the Statutes of 1984.

Rev. & Tax. Code § 2188.6. Separate Unit Assessment and Tax Bill; Lien On Unit Only.

(a) Unless a request for exemption has been recorded pursuant to subdivision (d), prior to the creation of a condominium as defined in Section 783 of the Civil Code, the county assessor may separately assess each individual unit which is shown on the condominium plan of a proposed condominium project when all of the following documents have been recorded as required by law:

(1) A subdivision final map or parcel map, as described in Sections 66434 and 66445, respectively, of the Government Code.

(2) A condominium plan, as defined in Section 4120 or 6540 of the Civil Code.

(3) A declaration, as defined in Section 4135 or 6546 of the Civil Code.

(b) The tax due on each individual unit shall constitute a lien solely on that unit.

(c) The lien created pursuant to this section shall be a lien on an undivided interest in a portion of real property coupled with a separate interest in space called a unit as described in Section 4125 or 6542 of the Civil Code.

(d) The record owner of the real property may record with the condominium plan a request that the real property be exempt from separate assessment pursuant to this section. If a request for exemption is recorded, separate assessment of a condominium unit shall be made only in accordance with Section 2188.3.

(e) This section shall become operative on January 1, 1990, and shall apply to condominium projects for which a condominium plan is recorded after that date.

Rev. & Tax. Code § 23701. Exemption of Specified Organizations.

(a) Organizations which are organized and operated for nonprofit purposes within the provisions of a specific section of this article, or are defined in Section 23701h (relating to certain title-holding companies) or Section 23701x (relating to certain title-holding companies), are exempt from taxes imposed under this part, except as provided in this article or in Article 2 (commencing with Section 23731) of this chapter if both of the following occur:

(1) An application for exemption is submitted in the form prescribed by the Franchise Tax Board.

(2) The Franchise Tax Board issues a determination exempting the organization from tax.

(b) (1) Notwithstanding subdivision (a), an organization organized and operated for nonprofit purposes in accordance with Section 23701a, 23701d, 23701e, 23701f, 23701g, or 23701w shall be exempt from taxes imposed by this part, except as provided in this article or in Article 2 (commencing with Section 23731), upon its submission to the Franchise Tax Board of one of the following:

(A) A copy of the determination letter or ruling issued by the Internal Revenue Service recognizing the organization's exemption from federal income tax under Section 501(a) of the Internal Revenue Code, as an organization described in Section 501(c)(3), (c)(4), (c)(5), (c)(6), (c)(7), or (c)(19) of the Internal Revenue Code.

(B) A copy of the group exemption letter issued by the Internal Revenue Service that states that both the central organization and all of its subordinates are tax-exempt under Section 501(c)(3), (c)(4), (c)(5),(c)(6), (c)(7), or (c)(19) of the Internal Revenue Code and substantiation that the organization is included in the federal group exemption letter as a subordinate organization.

(2) (A) Upon receipt of the documents required in subparagraph (A) or (B) of paragraph (1), the Franchise Tax Board shall issue an acknowledgment that the organization is exempt from taxes imposed by this part, except as provided in this article or in Article 2 (commencing with Section 23731). The acknowledgment may refer to the organization's recognition by the Internal Revenue Service of exemption from federal income tax as an organization described in Section 501(c)(3), (c)(4), (c)(5), (c)(6), (c)(7), or (c)(19) of the Internal Revenue Code and, if applicable, the organization's subordinate organization status under a federal group exemption letter. The effective date of an organization's exemption from state income tax pursuant to this subdivision shall be no later than the effective date of the organization's recognition of exemption from federal income tax as an organization described in Section 501(c)(3), (c)(4), (c)(5), (c)(6), (c)(7), or (c)(19) of the Internal Revenue Code, or its status as a subordinate organization under a federal group exemption letter, as applicable.

(B) Notwithstanding any other provision of this subdivision, an organization formed as a California corporation or qualified to do business in California that, as of the date of receipt by the

Franchise Tax Board of the documents required under paragraph (1), is listed by the Secretary of State or Franchise Tax Board as "suspended" or "forfeited" may not establish its exemption under paragraph (1) and shall not receive an acknowledgment referred to under subparagraph (A) from the Franchise Tax Board until that corporation is listed by the Secretary of State and the Franchise Tax Board as an "active" corporation.

(3) If, for federal income tax purposes, an organization's exemption from tax as an organization described in Section 501(c)(3), (c)(4), (c)(5), (c)(6), (c)(7), or (c)(19) of the Internal Revenue Code is suspended or revoked, the organization shall notify the Franchise Tax Board of the suspension or revocation, in the form and manner prescribed by the Franchise Tax Board. Upon notification, the board shall suspend or revoke, whichever is applicable, for state income tax purposes, the organization's exemption under paragraph (1).

(4) This subdivision shall not be construed to prevent the Franchise Tax Board from revoking the exemption of an organization that is not organized or operated in accordance with California law, this chapter, or Section 501(c)(3), (c)(4), (c)(5), (c)(6), (c)(7), or (c)(19) of the Internal Revenue Code.

(5) If the Franchise Tax Board suspends or revokes the exemption of an organization pursuant to paragraph (3) or (4), the exemption shall be reinstated only upon compliance with this section, regardless of whether the organization can establish exemption under paragraph (1).

(c) This section shall not prevent a determination from having retroactive effect and does not prevent the issuance of a determination with respect to a domestic organization which was in existence prior to January 1, 1970, and exempt under prior law without the submission of a formal application or payment of a filing fee. For the purpose of this section, the term "domestic" means created or organized under the laws of this state.

(d) The Franchise Tax Board may prescribe rules and regulations to implement the provisions of this article.

(e) The amendments made to this section by the act adding this subdivision shall become operative on January 1, 2021.

Rev. & Tax. Code § 23701t. Homeowners' Associations.

(a) A homeowners' association organized and operated to provide for the acquisition, construction, management, maintenance, and care of residential association property if all of the following apply:

(1) Sixty percent or more of the gross income of the organization for the taxable year consists solely of amounts received as membership dues, fees and assessments from either of the following:

(A) Tenant-stockholders or owners of residential units, residences, or lots.

(B) Owners of time-share rights to use, or time-share ownership interests in, association property in the case of a time-share association.

(2) Ninety percent or more of the expenditures of the organization for the taxable year are expenditures for the acquisition, construction, management, maintenance, and care of association property and, in the case of a time-share association, for activities provided to or on behalf of members of the association.

(3) No part of the net earnings inures (other than by providing management, maintenance and care of association property or by a rebate of excess membership dues, fees or assessments) to the benefit of any private shareholder or individual.

(4) Amounts received as membership dues, fees and assessments not expended for association purposes during the taxable year are transferred to and held in trust to provide for the management, maintenance, and care of association property and common areas.

(b) The term "association property" means:

(1) Property held by the organization.

(2) Property held in common by the members of the organization.

(3) Property within the organization privately held by the members of the organization.

In the case of a time-share association, "association property" includes property in which the time-share association, or members of the association, have rights arising out of recorded easements, covenants, or other recorded instruments to use property related to the time-share project.

(c) A homeowners association shall be subject to tax under this part with respect to its "homeowners association taxable income," and that income shall be subject to tax as provided by Chapter 3 (commencing with Section 23501).

(1) For purposes of this section, the term "homeowners' association taxable income" of any organization for any taxable year means an amount equal to the excess over one hundred dollars ($100) (if any) of-

(A) The gross income for the taxable year (excluding any exempt function income), over

(B) The deductions allowed by this part which are directly connected with the production of the gross income (excluding exempt function income).

(2) For purposes of this section, the term "exempt function income" means any amount received as membership fees, dues and assessments from tenant-shareholders or owners of residential units, residences or lots, or owners of time-share rights to use, or time-share ownership interests in, association property in the case of a time-share association.

(d) The term "homeowners' association" includes a condominium management association, a residential real estate management association, a time-share association, and a cooperative housing corporation.

(e) "Cooperative housing corporation" includes, but is not limited to, a limited-equity housing cooperative, as defined in Section 33007.5 of the Health and Safety Code, organized either as a nonprofit public benefit corporation pursuant to Part 2 (commencing with Section 5110) of Division 2 of Title 1 of the Corporations Code, or a nonprofit mutual benefit corporation pursuant to Part 3 (commencing with Section 7110) of Division 2 of Title 1 of the Corporations Code.

(f) The term "time-share association" means any organization (other than a condominium management association) organized and operated to provide for the acquisition, construction, management, maintenance, and care of

Misc. Codes

association property if any member thereof holds a time-share right to use, or a time-share ownership interest in, real property constituting association property.

(g) The amendments made to this section by the act adding this subdivision shall apply to taxable years beginning on or after January 1, 1998.

5

VEHICLE CODE REGULATIONS

Veh. Code § 22658. Vehicle Removal from Private Property.

(a) The owner or person in lawful possession of private property, including an association of a common interest development as defined in Sections 4080 and 4100 or Section 6528 and 6534 of the Civil Code, may cause the removal of a vehicle parked on the property to a storage facility that meets the requirements of subdivision (n) under any of the following circumstances:

(1) There is displayed, in plain view at all entrances to the property, a sign not less than 17 inches by 22 inches in size, with lettering not less than one inch in height, prohibiting public parking and indicating that vehicles will be removed at the owner's expense, and containing the telephone number of the local traffic law enforcement agency and the name and telephone number of each towing company that is a party to a written general towing authorization agreement with the owner or person in lawful possession of the property. The sign may also indicate that a citation may also be issued for the violation.

(2) The vehicle has been issued a notice of parking violation, and 96 hours have elapsed since the issuance of that notice.

(3) The vehicle is on private property and lacks an engine, transmission, wheels, tires, doors, windshield, or any other major part or equipment necessary to operate safely on the highways, the owner or person in lawful possession of the private property has notified the local traffic law enforcement agency, and 24 hours have elapsed since that notification.

(4) The lot or parcel upon which the vehicle is parked is improved with a single-family dwelling.

(b) The tow truck operator removing the vehicle, if the operator knows or is able to ascertain from the property owner, person in lawful possession of the property, or the registration records of the Department of Motor Vehicles the name and address of the registered and legal owner of the vehicle, shall immediately give, or cause to be given, notice in writing to the registered and legal owner of the fact of the removal, the grounds for the removal, and indicate the place to which the vehicle has been removed. If the vehicle is stored in a storage facility, a copy of the notice shall be given to the proprietor of the storage facility. The notice provided for in this section shall include the amount of mileage on the vehicle at the time of removal and the time of the removal from the property. If the tow truck operator does not know and is not able to ascertain the name of the owner or for any other reason is unable to give the notice to the owner as provided in this section, the tow truck operator shall comply with the requirements of subdivision (c) of Section 22853 relating to notice in the same manner as applicable to an officer removing a vehicle from private property.

(c) This section does not limit or affect any right or remedy that the owner or person in lawful possession of private property may have by virtue of other provisions of law authorizing the removal of a vehicle parked upon private property.

(d) The owner of a vehicle removed from private property pursuant to subdivision (a) may recover for any damage to the vehicle resulting from any intentional or negligent act of any person causing the removal of, or removing, the vehicle.

(e) (1) An owner or person in lawful possession of private property, or an association of a common interest development, causing the removal of a vehicle parked on that property is liable for double the storage or towing charges whenever there has been a failure to comply with paragraph (1), (2), or (3) of subdivision (a) or to state the grounds for the removal of the vehicle if requested by the legal or registered owner of the vehicle as required by subdivision (f).

(2) A property owner or owner's agent or lessee who causes the removal of a vehicle parked on that property pursuant to the exemption set forth in subparagraph (A) of paragraph (1) of subdivision (l) and fails to comply with that subdivision is guilty of an infraction, punishable by a fine of one thousand dollars ($1,000).

(f) An owner or person in lawful possession of private property, or an association of a common interest development, causing the removal of a vehicle parked on that property shall notify by telephone or, if impractical, by the most expeditious means available, the local traffic law enforcement agency within one hour after authorizing the tow. An owner or person in lawful possession of private property, an association of a common interest development, causing the removal of a vehicle parked on that property, or the tow truck operator who removes the vehicle, shall state the grounds for the removal of the vehicle if requested by the legal or registered owner of that vehicle. A towing company that removes a vehicle from private property in compliance with subdivision (l) is not responsible in a situation relating to the validity of the removal. A towing company that removes the vehicle under this section shall be responsible for the following:

(1) Damage to the vehicle in the transit and subsequent storage of the vehicle.

(2) The removal of a vehicle other than the vehicle specified by the owner or other person in lawful possession of the private property.

(g) (1) (A) Possession of a vehicle under this section shall be deemed to arise when a vehicle is removed from private property and is in transit.

(B) Upon the request of the owner of the vehicle or that owner's agent, the towing company or its driver shall immediately and unconditionally release a vehicle that is not yet removed from the private property and in transit.

(C) A person failing to comply with subparagraph (B) is guilty of a misdemeanor.

(2) If a vehicle is released to a person in compliance with subparagraph (B) of paragraph (1), the vehicle owner or authorized agent shall immediately move that vehicle to a lawful location.

(h) A towing company may impose a charge of not more than one-half of the regular towing charge for the towing of a vehicle at the request of the owner, the owner's agent, or the person in lawful possession of the private property pursuant to this section if the owner of the vehicle or the vehicle owner's agent returns to the vehicle after the vehicle is coupled to the tow truck by means of a regular hitch, coupling device, drawbar, portable dolly, or is lifted off the ground by means of a conventional trailer, and before it is removed from the private property. The regular towing charge may only be imposed after the vehicle has been removed from the property and is in transit.

(i) (1) (A) A charge for towing or storage, or both, of a vehicle under this section is excessive if the charge exceeds the greater of the following:

(i) That which would have been charged for that towing or storage, or both, made at the request of a law enforcement agency under an agreement between a towing company and the law enforcement agency that exercises primary jurisdiction in the city in which is located the private property from which the vehicle was, or was attempted to be, removed, or if the private property is not located within a city, then the law enforcement agency that exercises primary jurisdiction in the county in which the private property is located.

(ii) That which would have been charged for that towing or storage, or both, under the rate approved for that towing operator by the Department of the California Highway Patrol for the jurisdiction in which the private property is located and from which the vehicle was, or was attempted to be, removed.

(B) A towing operator shall make available for inspection and copying his or her rate approved by the California Highway Patrol, if any, within 24 hours of a request without a warrant to law enforcement, the Attorney General, district attorney, or city attorney.

(2) If a vehicle is released within 24 hours from the time the vehicle is brought into the storage facility, regardless of the calendar date, the storage charge shall be for only one day. Not more than one day's storage charge may be required for a vehicle released the same day that it is stored.

(3) If a request to release a vehicle is made and the appropriate fees are tendered and documentation establishing that the person requesting release is entitled to possession of the vehicle, or is the owner's insurance representative, is presented within the initial 24 hours of storage, and the storage facility fails to comply with the request to release the vehicle or is not open for business during normal business hours, then only one day's storage charge may be required to be paid until after the first business day. A business day is any day in which the lienholder is open for business to the public for at least eight hours. If a request is made more than 24 hours after the vehicle is placed in storage, charges may be imposed on a full calendar day basis for each day, or part thereof, that the vehicle is in storage.

(j) (1) A person who charges a vehicle owner a towing, service, or storage charge at an excessive rate, as described in subdivision (h) or (i), is civilly liable to the vehicle owner for four times the amount charged.

(2) A person who knowingly charges a vehicle owner a towing, service, or storage charge at an excessive rate, as described in subdivision (h) or (i), or who fails to make available his or her rate as required in subparagraph (B) of paragraph (1) of subdivision (i), is guilty of a misdemeanor, punishable by a fine of not more than two thousand five hundred dollars ($2,500), or by imprisonment in a county jail for not more than three months, or by both that fine and imprisonment.

(k) (1) A person operating or in charge of a storage facility where vehicles are stored pursuant to this section shall accept a valid bank credit card or cash for payment of towing and storage by a registered owner, the legal owner, or the owner's agent claiming the vehicle. A credit card shall be in the name of the person presenting the card. "Credit card" means "credit card" as defined in subdivision (a) of Section 1747.02 of the Civil Code, except for the purposes of this section, credit card does not include a credit card issued by a retail seller.

(2) A person described in paragraph (1) shall conspicuously display, in that portion of the storage facility office where business is conducted with the public, a notice advising that all valid credit cards and cash are acceptable means of payment.

(3) A person operating or in charge of a storage facility who refuses to accept a valid credit card or who fails to post the required notice under paragraph (2) is guilty of a misdemeanor, punishable by a fine of not more than two thousand five hundred dollars ($2,500), or by imprisonment in a county jail for not more than three months, or by both that fine and imprisonment.

(4) A person described in paragraph (1) who violates paragraph (1) or (2) is civilly liable to the registered owner of the vehicle or the person who tendered the fees for four times the amount of the towing and storage charges.

(5) A person operating or in charge of the storage facility shall have sufficient moneys on the premises of the primary storage facility during normal business hours to accommodate, and make change in, a reasonable monetary transaction.

(6) Credit charges for towing and storage services shall comply with Section 1748.1 of the Civil Code. Law enforcement agencies may include the costs of providing for payment by credit when making agreements with towing companies as described in subdivision (i).

(l) (1) (A) A towing company shall not remove or commence the removal of a vehicle from private property without first obtaining the written authorization from the property owner or lessee, including an association of a common interest development, or an employee or agent thereof, who shall be present at the time of removal and verify the alleged violation, except that presence and verification is not required if the person authorizing the tow is the property owner, or the owner's agent who is not a tow operator, of a residential rental property of 15 or fewer units that does not have an onsite owner, owner's agent or employee, and the tenant has verified the violation, requested the tow from that tenant's assigned parking space, and provided a signed request or electronic mail, or has called and provides a signed request or electronic mail within 24 hours, to the property owner or owner's agent, which the owner or agent shall provide to the towing company within 48 hours of authorizing the tow. The signed request or electronic mail shall contain the name and address of the tenant, and the date and time the tenant requested the tow. A towing company shall obtain within 48 hours of receiving the written authorization to tow a copy of a tenant request required pursuant to this subparagraph. For the purpose of this subparagraph, a person providing the written authorization who is required to be present on the private property at the time of the tow does not have to be physically present at the specified location of where the vehicle to be removed is located on the private property.

(B) The written authorization under subparagraph (A) shall include all of the following:

(i) The make, model, vehicle identification number, and license plate number of the removed vehicle.

(ii) The name, signature, job title, residential or business address and working telephone number of the person, described in subparagraph (A), authorizing the removal of the vehicle.

(iii) The grounds for the removal of the vehicle.

(iv) The time when the vehicle was first observed parked at the private property.

(v) The time that authorization to tow the vehicle was given.

(C) (i) When the vehicle owner or his or her agent claims the vehicle, the towing company prior to payment of a towing or storage charge shall provide a photocopy of the written authorization to the vehicle owner or the agent.

(ii) If the vehicle was towed from a residential property, the towing company shall redact the information specified in clause (ii) of subparagraph (B) in the photocopy of the written authorization provided to the vehicle owner or the agent pursuant to clause (i).

(iii) The towing company shall also provide to the vehicle owner or the agent a separate notice that provides the telephone number of the appropriate local law enforcement or prosecuting agency by stating "If you believe that you have been wrongfully towed, please contact the local law enforcement or prosecuting agency at [insert appropriate telephone number]." The notice shall be in English and in the most populous language, other than English, that is spoken in the jurisdiction.

(D) A towing company shall not remove or commence the removal of a vehicle from private property described in subdivision (a) of Section 22953 unless the towing company has made a good faith inquiry to determine that the owner or the property owner's agent complied with Section 22953.

(E) (i) General authorization to remove or commence removal of a vehicle at the towing company's discretion shall not be delegated to a towing company or its affiliates except in the case of a vehicle unlawfully parked within 15 feet of a fire hydrant or in a fire lane, or in a manner which interferes with an entrance to, or exit from, the private property.

(ii) In those cases in which general authorization is granted to a towing company or its affiliate to undertake the removal or commence the removal of a vehicle that is unlawfully parked within 15 feet of a fire hydrant or in a fire lane, or that interferes with an entrance to, or exit from, private property, the towing company and the property owner, or owner's agent, or person in lawful possession of the private property shall have a written agreement granting that general authorization.

(2) If a towing company removes a vehicle under a general authorization described in subparagraph (E) of paragraph (1) and that vehicle is unlawfully parked within 15 feet of a fire hydrant or in a fire lane, or in a manner that interferes with an entrance to, or exit from, the private property, the towing company shall take, prior to the removal of that vehicle, a photograph of the vehicle that clearly indicates that parking violation. Prior to accepting payment, the towing company shall keep one copy of the photograph taken pursuant to this paragraph, and shall present that photograph and provide, without charge, a photocopy to the owner or an agent of the owner, when that person claims the vehicle.

(3) A towing company shall maintain the original written authorization, or the general authorization described in subparagraph (E) of paragraph (1) and the photograph of the violation, required pursuant to this section, and any written requests from a tenant to the property owner or owner's agent required by subparagraph (A) of paragraph (1), for a period of three years and shall make them available for inspection and copying within 24 hours of a request without a warrant to law enforcement, the Attorney General, district attorney, or city attorney.

(4) A person who violates this subdivision is guilty of a misdemeanor, punishable by a fine of not more than two thousand five hundred dollars ($2,500), or by imprisonment in the county jail for not more than three months, or by both that fine and imprisonment.

(5) A person who violates this subdivision is civilly liable to the owner of the vehicle or his or her agent for four times the amount of the towing and storage charges.

(m) (1) A towing company that removes a vehicle from private property under this section shall notify the local law enforcement agency of that tow after the vehicle is removed from the private property and is in transit.

(2) A towing company is guilty of a misdemeanor if the towing company fails to provide the notification required under paragraph (1) within 60 minutes after the vehicle is removed from the private property and is in transit or 15 minutes after arriving at the storage facility, whichever time is less.

(3) A towing company that does not provide the notification under paragraph (1) within 30 minutes after the vehicle is removed from the private property and is in transit is civilly liable to the registered owner of the vehicle, or the person who tenders the fees, for three times the amount of the towing and storage charges.

(4) If notification is impracticable, the times for notification, as required pursuant to paragraphs (2) and (3), shall be tolled for the time period that notification is impracticable. This paragraph is an affirmative defense.

(n) A vehicle removed from private property pursuant to this section shall be stored in a facility that meets all of the following requirements:

(1) (A) Is located within a 10-mile radius of the property from where the vehicle was removed.

(B) The 10-mile radius requirement of subparagraph (A) does not apply if a towing company has prior general written approval from the law enforcement agency that exercises primary jurisdiction in the city in which is located the private property from which the vehicle was removed, or if the private property is not located within a city, then the law enforcement agency that exercises primary jurisdiction in the county in which is located the private property.

(2) (A) Remains open during normal business hours and releases vehicles after normal business hours.

(B) A gate fee may be charged for releasing a vehicle after normal business hours, weekends, and state holidays. However, the maximum hourly charge for releasing a vehicle after normal business hours shall be one-half of the hourly tow rate charged for initially towing the vehicle, or less.

(C) Notwithstanding any other provision of law and for purposes of this paragraph, "normal business hours" are Monday to Friday, inclusive, from 8 a.m. to 5 p.m., inclusive, except state holidays.

(3) Has a public pay telephone in the office area that is open and accessible to the public.

(o) (1) It is the intent of the Legislature in the adoption of subdivision (k) to assist vehicle owners or their agents by, among other things, allowing payment by credit cards for towing and storage services, thereby expediting the recovery of towed vehicles and concurrently promoting the safety and welfare of the public.

(2) It is the intent of the Legislature in the adoption of subdivision (l) to further the safety of the general public by ensuring that a private property owner or lessee has provided his or her authorization for the removal of a vehicle from his or her property, thereby promoting the safety of those persons involved in ordering the removal of the vehicle as well as those persons removing, towing, and storing the vehicle.

(3) It is the intent of the Legislature in the adoption of subdivision (g) to promote the safety of the general public by requiring towing companies to unconditionally release a vehicle that is not lawfully in their possession, thereby avoiding the likelihood of dangerous and violent confrontation and physical injury to vehicle owners and towing operators, the stranding of vehicle owners and their passengers at a dangerous time and location, and impeding expedited vehicle recovery, without wasting law enforcement's limited resources.

(p) The remedies, sanctions, restrictions, and procedures provided in this section are not exclusive and are in addition to other remedies, sanctions, restrictions, or procedures that may be provided in other provisions of law, including, but not limited to, those that are provided in Sections 12110 and 34660.

(q) A vehicle removed and stored pursuant to this section shall be released by the law enforcement agency, impounding agency, or person in possession of the vehicle, or any person acting on behalf of them, to the legal owner or the legal owner's agent upon presentation of the assignment, as defined in subdivision (b) of Section 7500.1 of the Business and Professions Code; a release from the one responsible governmental agency, only if required by the agency; a government-issued photographic identification card; and any one of the following as determined by the legal owner or the legal owner's agent: a certificate of repossession of the vehicle, a security agreement for the vehicle, or title, whether paper or electronic, showing proof of legal ownership for the vehicle. Any documents presented may be originals, photocopies, or facsimile copies, or may be transmitted electronically. The storage facility shall not require any documents to be notarized. The storage facility may require the agent of the legal owner to produce a photocopy or facsimile copy of its repossession agency license or registration issued pursuant to Chapter 11 (commencing with Section 7500) of Division 3 of the Business and Professions Code, or to demonstrate, to the satisfaction of the storage facility, that the agent is exempt from licensure pursuant to Section 7500.2 or 7500.3 of the Business and Professions Code.

Veh. Code § 22658.1. Damage to Fence While Removing Vehicle; Location and Notification of Property Owner by Towing Company.

(a) Any towing company that, in removing a vehicle, cuts, removes, otherwise damages, or leaves open a fence without the prior approval of the property owner or the person in charge of the property shall then and there do either of the following:

(1) Locate and notify the owner or person in charge of the property of the damage or open condition of the fence, the name and address of the towing company, and the license, registration, or identification number of the vehicle being removed.

(2) Leave in a conspicuous place on the property the name and address of the towing company, and the license, registration, or identification number of the vehicle being removed, and shall without unnecessary delay, notify the police department of the city in which the property is located, or if the property is located in unincorporated territory, either the sheriff or the local headquarters of the Department of the California Highway Patrol, of that information and the location of the damaged or opened fence.

(b) Any person failing to comply with all the requirements of this section is guilty of an infraction.

Vehicle

Veh. Code § 22853. Notice to Department of Justice and Proprietor of Storage Garage; Reports; Notice to Owner.

(a) Whenever an officer or an employee removing a California registered vehicle from a highway or from public property for storage under this chapter does not know and is not able to ascertain the name of the owner or for any other reason is unable to give notice to the owner as required by Section 22852, the officer or employee shall immediately notify, or cause to be notified, the Department of Justice, Stolen Vehicle System, of its removal. The officer or employee shall file a notice with the proprietor of any public garage in which the vehicle may be stored. The notice shall include a complete description of the vehicle, the date, time, and place from which removed, the amount of mileage on the vehicle at the time of removal, and the name of the garage or place where the vehicle is stored.

(b) Whenever an officer or an employee removing a vehicle not registered in California from a highway or from public property for storage under this chapter does not know and is not able to ascertain the owner or for any other reason is unable to give the notice to the owner as required by Section 22852, the officer or employee shall immediately notify, or cause to be notified, the Department of Justice, Stolen Vehicle System. If the vehicle is not returned to the owner within 120 hours, the officer or employee shall immediately send, or cause to be sent, a written report of the removal by mail to the Department of Justice at Sacramento and shall file a copy of the notice with the proprietor of any public garage in which the vehicle may be stored. The report shall be made on a form furnished by that department and shall include a complete description of the vehicle, the date, time, and place from which the vehicle was removed, the amount of mileage on the vehicle at the time of removal, the grounds for removal, and the name of the garage or place where the vehicle is stored.

(c) Whenever an officer or employee or private party removing a vehicle from private property for storage under this chapter does not know and is not able to ascertain the name of the owner or for any other reason is unable to give the notice to the owner as required by Section 22852 and if the vehicle is not returned to the owner within a period of 120 hours, the officer or employee or private party shall immediately send, or cause to be sent, a written report of the removal by mail to the Department of Justice at Sacramento and shall file a copy of the notice with the proprietor of any public garage in which the vehicle may be stored. The report shall be made on a form furnished by that department and shall include a complete description of the vehicle, the date,

Vehicle

time, and place from which the vehicle was removed, the amount of mileage on the vehicle at the time of removal, the grounds for removal, and the name of the garage or place where the vehicle is stored.

Veh. Code § 22953. Towing from Non-Residential Private Property Held Open to the Public.

(a) An owner or person in lawful possession of private property that is held open to the public, or a discernible portion thereof, for parking of vehicles at no fee, or an employee or agent thereof, shall not tow or remove, or cause the towing or removal, of a vehicle within one hour of the vehicle being parked.

(b) Notwithstanding subdivision (a), a vehicle may be removed immediately after being illegally parked within 15 feet of a fire hydrant, in a fire lane, in a manner that interferes with an entrance to, or an exit from, the private property, or in a parking space or stall legally designated for disabled persons.

(c) Subdivision (a) does not apply to property designated for parking at residential property, or to property designated for parking at a hotel or motel where the parking stalls or spaces are clearly marked for a specific room.

(d) It is the intent of the Legislature in the adoption of subdivision (a) to avoid causing the unnecessary stranding of motorists and placing them in dangerous situations, when traffic citations or other civil remedies are available, thereby promoting the safety of the general public.

(e) A person who violates subdivision (a) is civilly liable to the owner of the vehicle or his or her agent for two times the amount of the towing and storage charges.

Veh. Code § 40000.15. Violations Are Misdemeanors, Not Infractions.

A violation of any of the following provisions shall constitute a misdemeanor and not an infraction:

Subdivision (g), (j), (k), (l), or (m) of Section 22658, relating to unlawfully towed or stored vehicles.

[Remainder of section omitted.]

6

FAIR HOUSING LAWS

Reasonable Modifications

Summary of the Joint Statement of the Department of Housing and Urban Development and the Department of Justice: "Reasonable Modifications Under the Fair Housing Act" [1] (42 U.S.C. §§ 3601-3619) (March 5, 2008)

Introduction

The Department of Justice ("DOJ") and the Department of Housing and Urban Development ("HUD") are jointly responsible for enforcing the federal Fair Housing Act (the "Act"), which prohibits discrimination in housing on the basis of race, color, religion, sex, national origin, familial status, and disability. One type of disability discrimination prohibited by the Act is a refusal to permit, at the expense of the person with a disability, reasonable modifications of existing premises occupied or to be occupied by such person if such modifications may be necessary to afford such person full enjoyment of the premises. HUD and DOJ frequently respond to complaints alleging that housing providers have violated the Act by refusing reasonable modifications to persons with disabilities. This Statement provides technical assistance regarding the rights and obligations of persons with disabilities and housing providers under the Act relating to reasonable modifications.

Questions and Answers

1. What types of discrimination against persons with disabilities does the Act prohibit?

The Act prohibits housing providers from discriminating against housing applicants or residents because of their disability or the disability of anyone associated with them and from treating persons with disabilities less favorably than others because of their disability. The Act makes it unlawful for any person to refuse "to permit, at the expense of the [disabled] person, reasonable modifications of existing

[1] For brevity the Joint Statement has been selectively edited. The full statement may be reviewed online at www.hud.gov.

premises occupied or to be occupied by such person if such modifications may be necessary to afford such person full enjoyment of the premises, except that, in the case of a rental, the landlord may where it is reasonable to do so condition permission for a modification on the renter agreeing to restore the interior of the premises to the condition that existed before the modification, reasonable wear and tear excepted." The Act also makes it unlawful for any person to refuse "to make reasonable accommodations in rules, policies, practices, or services, when such accommodations may be necessary to afford ... person(s) [with disabilities] equal opportunity to use and enjoy a dwelling." The Act also prohibits housing providers from refusing residency to persons with disabilities, or, with some narrow exceptions, placing conditions on their residency, because those persons may require reasonable modifications or reasonable accommodations.

2. What is a reasonable modification under the Fair Housing Act?

A reasonable modification is a structural change made to existing premises, occupied or to be occupied by a person with a disability, in order to afford such person full enjoyment of the premises. Reasonable modifications can include structural changes to interiors and exteriors of dwellings and to common and public use areas. A request for a reasonable modification may be made at any time during the tenancy. The Act makes it unlawful for a housing provider or homeowners' association to refuse to allow a reasonable modification to the premises when such a modification may be necessary to afford persons with disabilities full enjoyment of the premises.

To show that a requested modification may be necessary, there must be an identifiable relationship, or nexus, between the requested modification and the individual's disability. Further, the modification must be "reasonable." Examples of modifications that typically are reasonable include widening doorways to make rooms more accessible for persons in wheelchairs; installing grab bars in bathrooms; lowering kitchen cabinets to a height suitable for persons in wheelchairs; adding a ramp to make a primary entrance accessible for persons in wheelchairs; or altering a walkway to provide access to a public or common use area. These examples of reasonable modifications are not exhaustive.

3. Who is responsible for the expense of making a reasonable modification?

The Fair Housing Act provides that while the housing provider must permit the modification, the tenant is responsible for paying the cost of the modification.

4. Who qualifies as a person with a disability under the Act?

The Act defines a person with a disability to include (1) individuals with a physical or mental impairment that substantially limits one or more major life activities; (2) individuals who are regarded as having such an impairment; and (3) individuals with a record of such an impairment.

The term "physical or mental impairment" includes, but is not limited to, such diseases and conditions as orthopedic, visual, speech and hearing impairments, cerebral palsy, autism, epilepsy, muscular dystrophy, multiple sclerosis, cancer, heart disease, diabetes, Human Immunodeficiency Virus infection, mental retardation, emotional illness, drug addiction (other than addiction caused by current, illegal use of a controlled substance) and alcoholism.

The term "substantially limits" suggests that the limitation is "significant" or "to a large degree."

The term "major life activity" means those activities that are of central importance to daily life, such as seeing, hearing, walking, breathing, performing manual tasks, caring for one's self, learning, and speaking. This list of major life activities is not exhaustive.

5. Who is entitled to a reasonable modification under the Fair Housing Act?

Persons who meet the Fair Housing Act's definition of "person with a disability" may be entitled to a reasonable modification under the Act. However, there must be an identifiable relationship, or nexus, between the requested modification and the individual's disability. If no such nexus exists, then the housing provider may refuse to allow the requested modification.

6. If a disability is not obvious, what kinds of information may a housing provider request from the person with a disability in support of a requested reasonable modification?

A housing provider may not ordinarily inquire as to the nature and severity of an individual's disability. However, in response to a request for a reasonable modification, a housing provider may request reliable disability-related information that (1) is necessary to verify that the person meets the Act's definition of disability (i.e., has a physical or mental impairment that substantially limits one or more major life activities), (2) describes the needed modification, and (3) shows the relationship between the person's disability and the need for the requested modification. Depending on the individual's circumstances, information verifying that the person meets the Act's definition of disability can usually be provided by the individual herself (e.g., proof that an individual under 65 years of age receives Supplemental Security Income or Social Security Disability Insurance benefits or a credible statement by the individual). A doctor or other medical professional, a peer support group, a non-medical service agency, or a reliable third party who is in a position to know about the individual's disability may also provide verification of a disability. In most cases, an individual's medical records or detailed information about the nature of a person's disability is not necessary for this inquiry.

Once a housing provider has established that a person meets the Act's definition of disability, the provider's request for documentation should seek only the information that is necessary to evaluate if the reasonable modification is needed because of a disability. Such information must be kept confidential and must not be shared with other persons unless they need the information to make or assess a decision to grant or deny a reasonable modification request or unless disclosure is required by law (e.g., a court-issued subpoena requiring disclosure).

7. **What kinds of information, if any, may a housing provider request from a person with an obvious or known disability who is requesting a reasonable modification?**

A housing provider is entitled to obtain information that is necessary to evaluate whether a requested reasonable modification may be necessary because of a disability. If a person's disability is obvious, or otherwise known to the housing provider, and if the need for the requested modification is also readily apparent or known, then the provider may not request any additional information about the requester's disability or the disability-related need for the modification.

If the requester's disability is known or readily apparent to the provider, but the need for the modification is not readily apparent or known, the provider may request only information that is necessary to evaluate the disability-related need for the modification.

8. **Who must comply with the Fair Housing Act's reasonable modification requirements?**

Any person or entity engaging in prohibited conduct – i.e., refusing to allow an individual to make reasonable modifications when such modifications may be necessary to afford a person with a disability full enjoyment of the premises – may be held liable unless they fall within an exception to the Act's coverage. Courts have applied the Act to individuals, corporations, associations and others involved in the provision of housing and residential lending, including property owners, housing managers, homeowners and condominium associations, lenders, real estate agents, and brokerage services. Courts have also applied the Act to state and local governments, most often in the context of exclusionary zoning or other land-use decisions.

9. What is the difference between a reasonable accommodation and a reasonable modification under the Fair Housing Act?

Under the Fair Housing Act, a reasonable modification is a structural change made to the premises whereas a reasonable accommodation is a change, exception, or adjustment to a rule, policy, practice, or service. A person with a disability may need either a reasonable accommodation or a reasonable modification, or both, in order to have an equal opportunity to use and enjoy a dwelling, including public and common use spaces. Generally, under the Fair Housing Act, the housing provider is responsible for the costs associated with a reasonable accommodation unless it is an undue financial and administrative burden, while the tenant or someone acting on the tenant's behalf, is responsible for costs associated with a reasonable modification.

10. Are reasonable modifications restricted to the interior of a dwelling?

No. Reasonable modifications are not limited to the interior of a dwelling. Reasonable modifications may also be made to public and common use areas such as widening entrances to fitness centers or laundry rooms, or for changes to exteriors of dwelling units such as installing a ramp at the entrance to a dwelling.

11. Is a request for a parking space because of a physical disability a reasonable accommodation or a reasonable modification?

Courts have treated requests for parking spaces as requests for a reasonable accommodation and have placed the responsibility for providing the parking space on the housing provider, even if provision of an accessible or assigned parking space results in some cost to the provider. For example, courts have required a housing provider to provide an assigned space even though the housing provider had a policy of not assigning parking spaces or had a waiting list for available parking. However, housing providers may not require persons with disabilities to pay extra fees as a condition of receiving accessible parking spaces.

Providing a parking accommodation could include creating signage, repainting markings, redistributing spaces, or creating curb cuts. This list is not exhaustive.

12. What if the structural changes being requested by the tenant or applicant are in a building that is subject to the design and construction requirements of the Fair Housing Act and the requested structural changes are a feature of accessible design that should have already existed in the unit or common area, e.g., doorways wide enough to accommodate a wheelchair, or an accessible entryway to a unit?

The Fair Housing Act provides that covered multifamily dwellings built for first occupancy after March 13, 1991, shall be designed and constructed to meet certain minimum accessibility and adaptability standards. If any of the structural changes needed by the tenant are ones that should have been included in the unit or public and common use area when constructed then the housing provider may be responsible for providing and paying for those requested structural changes. However, if the requested structural changes are not a feature of accessible design that should have already existed in the building pursuant to the design and construction requirements under the Act, then the tenant is responsible for paying for the cost of the structural changes as a reasonable modification.

Although the design and construction provisions only apply to certain multifamily dwellings built for first occupancy since 1991, a tenant may request reasonable modifications to housing built prior to that date. In such cases, the housing provider must allow the modifications, and the tenant is responsible for paying for the costs under the Fair Housing Act.

13. Who is responsible for expenses associated with a reasonable modification, e.g., for upkeep or maintenance?

The tenant is responsible for upkeep and maintenance of a modification that is used exclusively by her. If a modification is made to a common area that is normally maintained by the housing provider, then the housing provider is responsible for the upkeep and maintenance of the modification. If a modification is made to a common area that is not normally maintained by the housing provider, then the housing provider has no responsibility under the Fair Housing Act to maintain the modification.

14. In addition to current residents, are prospective tenants and buyers of housing protected by the reasonable modification provisions of the Fair Housing Act?

Yes. A person may make a request for a reasonable modification at any time. An individual may request a reasonable modification of the dwelling at the time that the potential tenancy or purchase is discussed. Under the Act, a housing provider cannot deny or restrict access to housing because a request for a reasonable modification is made. Such conduct would constitute discrimination. The modification does not have to be made, however, unless it is reasonable.

15. When and how should an individual request permission to make a modification?

Under the Act, a resident or an applicant for housing makes a reasonable modification request whenever she makes clear to the housing provider that she is requesting permission to make a structural change to the premises because of her disability. She should explain that she has a disability, if not readily apparent or not known to the housing provider, the type of modification she is requesting, and the relationship between the requested modification and her disability.

An applicant or resident is not entitled to receive a reasonable modification unless she requests one. However, the Fair Housing Act does not require that a request be made in a particular manner or at a particular time. A person with a disability need not personally make the reasonable modification request; the request can be made by a family member or someone else who is acting on her behalf. An individual making a reasonable modification request does not need to mention the Act or use the words "reasonable modification." However, the requester must make the request in a manner that a reasonable person would understand to be a request for permission to make a structural change because of a disability.

Although a reasonable modification request can be made orally or in writing, it is usually helpful for both the resident and the housing provider if the request is made in writing. This will help prevent misunderstandings regarding what is being requested, or whether the request was made. To facilitate the processing and consideration of the request, residents or prospective residents may wish to check with a housing provider in advance to determine if the provider has a preference regarding the manner in which the request is made. However, housing providers must give appropriate consideration to reasonable modification requests even if the requester makes the request orally or does not use the provider's preferred forms or procedures for making such requests.

16. Does a person with a disability have to have the housing provider's approval before making a reasonable modification to the dwelling?

Yes. A person with a disability must have the housing provider's approval before making the modification. However, if the person with a disability meets the requirements under the Act for a reasonable modification and provides the relevant documents and assurances, the housing provider cannot deny the request.

17. What if the housing provider fails to act promptly on a reasonable modification request?

A provider has an obligation to provide prompt responses to a reasonable modification request. An undue delay in responding to a reasonable modification request may be deemed a failure to permit a reasonable modification.

18. What if the housing provider proposes that the tenant move to a different unit in lieu of making a proposed modification?

The housing provider cannot insist that a tenant move to a different unit in lieu of allowing the tenant to make a modification that complies with the requirements for reasonable modifications.

19. What if the housing provider wants an alternative modification or alternative design for the proposed modification that does not cost more but that the housing provider considers more aesthetically pleasing?

In general, the housing provider cannot insist on an alternative modification or an alternative design if the tenant complies with the requirements for reasonable modifications. If the modification is to the interior of the unit and must be restored to its original condition when the tenant moves out, then the housing provider cannot require that its design be used instead of the tenant's design. However, if the modification is to a common area or an aspect of the interior of the unit that would not have to be restored because it would not be reasonable to do so, and if the housing provider's proposed design imposes no additional costs and still meets the tenant's needs, then the modification should be done in accordance with the housing provider's design.

20. What if the housing provider wants a more costly design for the requested modification?

If the housing provider wishes a modification to be made with more costly materials, in order to satisfy the landlord's aesthetic standards, the tenant must agree only if the housing provider pays those additional costs. Housing providers may require that the tenant obtain all necessary building permits and may require that the work be performed in a workmanlike manner. If the housing provider requires more costly materials be used to satisfy her workmanship preferences beyond the requirements of the applicable local codes, the tenant must agree only if the housing provider pays for those additional costs as well. In such a case, however, the housing provider's design must still meet the tenant's needs.

21. What types of documents and assurances may a housing provider require regarding the modification before granting the reasonable modification?

A housing provider may require that a request for a reasonable modification include a description of the proposed modification both before changes are made to the dwelling and before granting the modification. A description of the modification to be made may be provided to a housing provider either orally or in writing depending on the extent and nature of the proposed modification. A housing provider may also require that the tenant obtain any building permits needed to make the modifications, and that the work be performed in a workmanlike manner.

The regulations implementing the Fair Housing Act state that housing providers generally cannot impose conditions on a proposed reasonable modification. For example, a housing provider cannot require that the tenant obtain additional insurance or increase the security deposit as a condition that must be met before the modification will be allowed. However, the Preamble to the Final Regulations also indicates that there are some conditions that can be placed on a tenant requesting a reasonable modification. For example, in certain limited and narrow circumstances, a housing provider may require that the tenant deposit money into an interest bearing account to ensure that funds are available to restore the interior of a dwelling to its previous state, ordinary wear and tear excepted. Imposing conditions not contemplated by the Fair Housing Act and its implementing regulations may be the same as an illegal refusal to permit the modification.

22. May a housing provider or homeowner's association condition approval of the requested modification on the requester obtaining special liability insurance?

No. Imposition of such a requirement would constitute a violation of the Fair Housing Act.

23. Once the housing provider has agreed to a reasonable modification, may she insist that a particular contractor be used to perform the work?

No. The housing provider cannot insist that a particular contractor do the work. The housing provider may only require that whoever does the work is reasonably able to complete the work in a workmanlike manner and obtain all necessary building permits.

24. If a person with a disability has made reasonable modifications to the interior of the dwelling, must she restore all of them when she moves out?

The tenant is obligated to restore those portions of the interior of the dwelling to their previous condition only where "it is reasonable to do so" and where the housing provider has requested the restoration. The tenant is not responsible for expenses associated with reasonable wear and tear. In general, if the modifications do not affect the housing provider's or subsequent tenant's use or enjoyment of the premises, the tenant cannot be required to restore the modifications to their prior state. A housing provider may choose to keep the modifications in place at the end of the tenancy.

25. Of the reasonable modifications made to the interior of a dwelling that must be restored, must the person with a disability pay to make those restorations when she moves out?

Yes. Reasonable restorations of the dwelling required as a result of modifications made to the interior of the dwelling must be paid for by the tenant unless the next occupant of the dwelling wants to retain the reasonable modifications and where it is reasonable to do so, the next occupant is willing to establish a new interest bearing escrow account. The subsequent tenant would have to restore the modifications to the prior condition at the end of his tenancy if it is reasonable to do so and if requested by the housing provider.

26. If a person with a disability has made a reasonable modification to the exterior of the dwelling, or a common area, must she restore it to its original condition when she moves out?

No. The Fair Housing Act expressly provides that housing providers may only require restoration of modifications made to interiors of the dwelling at the end of the tenancy. Reasonable modifications such as ramps to the front door of the dwelling or modifications made to laundry rooms or building entrances are not required to be restored.

27. May a housing provider increase or require a person with a disability to pay a security deposit if she requests a reasonable modification?

No. The housing provider may not require an increased security deposit as the result of a request for a reasonable modification, nor may a housing provider require a tenant to pay a security deposit when one is not customarily required. However, a housing provider may be able to take other steps to ensure that money will be available to pay for restoration of the interior of the premises at the end of the tenancy.

28. May a housing provider take other steps to ensure that money will be available to pay for restoration of the interior of the premises at the end of the tenancy?

Where it is necessary in order to ensure with reasonable certainty that funds will be available to pay for the restorations at the end of the tenancy, the housing provider may negotiate with the tenant as part of a restoration agreement a provision that requires the tenant to make payments into an interest-bearing escrow account. A housing provider may not routinely require that tenants place money in escrow accounts when a modification is sought. Both the amount and the terms of the escrow payment are subject to negotiation between the housing provider and the tenant.

Simply because an individual has a disability does not mean that she is less creditworthy than an individual without a disability. The decision to require that money be placed in an escrow account should be based on the following factors: 1) the extent and nature of the proposed modifications; 2) the expected duration of the lease; 3) the credit and tenancy history of the individual tenant; and 4) other information that may bear on the risk to the housing provider that the premises will not be restored.

If the housing provider decides to require payment into an escrow account, the amount of money to be placed in the account cannot exceed the cost of restoring the modifications, and the period of time during which the tenant makes payment into the escrow account must be reasonable. Although a housing provider may require that funds be placed in escrow, it does not automatically mean that the full amount of money needed to make the future restorations can be required to be paid at the time that the modifications are sought. In addition, it is important to note that interest from the account accrues to the benefit of the tenant. If an escrow account is established, and the housing provider later decides not to have the unit restored, then all funds in the account, including the interest, must be promptly returned to the tenant.

29. What if a person with a disability moves into a rental unit and wants the carpet taken up because her wheelchair does not move easily across carpeting? Is that a reasonable accommodation or modification?

Depending on the circumstances, removal of carpeting may be either a reasonable accommodation or a reasonable modification.

30. Who is responsible for paying for the costs of structural changes to a dwelling unit that has not yet been constructed if a purchaser with a disability needs different or additional features to make the unit meet her disability-related needs?

If the dwelling unit is not subject to the design and construction requirements (i.e., a detached single family home or a multi-story townhouse without an elevator), then the purchaser is responsible for the additional costs associated with the structural changes. The purchaser is responsible for any additional cost that the structural changes might create over and above what the original design would have cost.

If the unit being purchased is subject to the design and construction requirements of the Fair Housing Act, then all costs associated with incorporating the features required by the Act are borne by the builder. If a purchaser with a disability needs different or additional features added to a unit under construction or about to be constructed beyond those already required by the Act, and it would cost the builder more to provide the requested features, the structural changes would be considered a reasonable modification and the additional costs would have to be borne by the purchaser. The purchaser is responsible for any additional cost that the structural changes might create over and above what the original design would have cost.

31. Are the rules the same if a person with a disability lives in housing that receives federal financial assistance and the needed structural changes to the unit or common area are the result of the tenant having a disability?

Housing that receives federal financial assistance is covered by both the Fair Housing Act and Section 504 of the Rehabilitation Act of 1973. Under regulations implementing Section 504, structural changes needed by an applicant or resident with a disability in housing receiving federal financial assistance are considered reasonable accommodations. They must be paid for by the housing provider unless providing them would be an undue financial and administrative burden or a fundamental alteration of the program or unless the housing provider can accommodate the individual's needs through other means. Housing that receives federal financial assistance and that is provided by state or local entities may also be covered by Title II of the Americans with Disabilities Act.

Reasonable Accommodations

Summary of the Joint Statement of the Department of Housing and Urban Development and the Department of Justice: "Reasonable Accommodations Under the Fair Housing Act" [2] (42 U.S.C. §§ 3601-3619) (May 17, 2004)

Introduction

The Department of Justice ("DOJ") and the Department of Housing and Urban Development ("HUD") are jointly responsible for enforcing the federal Fair Housing Act1 (the "Act"), which prohibits discrimination in housing on the basis of race, color, religion, sex, national origin, familial status, and disability. One type of disability discrimination prohibited by the Act is the refusal to make reasonable accommodations in rules, policies, practices, or services when such accommodations may be necessary to afford a person with a disability the equal opportunity to use and enjoy a dwelling. HUD and DOJ frequently respond to complaints alleging that housing providers have violated the Act by refusing reasonable accommodations to persons with disabilities. This Statement provides technical assistance regarding the rights and obligations of persons with disabilities and housing providers under the Act relating to reasonable accommodations.

[2] For brevity the Joint Statement has been selectively edited. The full statement may be reviewed online at www.hud.gov.

Questions and Answers

1. What types of discrimination against persons with disabilities does the Act prohibit?

The Act prohibits housing providers from discriminating against applicants or residents because of their disability or the disability of anyone associated with them and from treating persons with disabilities less favorably than others because of their disability. The Act also makes it unlawful for any person to refuse "to make reasonable accommodations in rules, policies, practices, or services, when such accommodations may be necessary to afford ... person(s) [with disabilities] equal opportunity to use and enjoy a dwelling." The Act also prohibits housing providers from refusing residency to persons with disabilities, or placing conditions on their residency, because those persons may require reasonable accommodations. In addition, in certain circumstances, the Act requires that housing providers allow residents to make reasonable structural modifications to units and public/common areas in a dwelling when those modifications may be necessary for a person with a disability to have full enjoyment of a dwelling. With certain limited exceptions (see response to question 2 below), the Act applies to privately and publicly owned housing, including housing subsidized by the federal government or rented through the use of Section 8 voucher assistance.

2. Who must comply with the Fair Housing Act's reasonable accommodation requirements?

Any person or entity engaging in prohibited conduct – i.e., refusing to make reasonable accommodations in rules, policies, practices, or services, when such accommodations may be necessary to afford a person with a disability an equal opportunity to use and enjoy a dwelling – may be held liable unless they fall within an exception to the Act's coverage. Courts have applied the Act to individuals, corporations, associations and others involved in the provision of housing and residential lending, including property owners, housing managers, homeowners and condominium associations, lenders, real estate agents, and brokerage services. Courts have also applied the Act to state and local governments, most often in the context of exclusionary zoning or other land-use decisions. Under specific exceptions to the Fair Housing Act, the reasonable accommodation requirements of the Act do not apply to a private individual owner who sells his own home so long as he (1) does not own more than three single-family homes; (2) does not use a real estate agent and does not employ any discriminatory advertising or notices; (3) has not engaged in a similar sale of a home within a 24-month period; and (4) is not in the business of selling or renting dwellings. The reasonable accommodation requirements of the Fair Housing Act also do not apply to owner-occupied buildings that have four or fewer dwelling units.

3. Who qualifies as a person with a disability under the Act?

The Act defines a person with a disability to include (1) individuals with a physical or mental impairment that substantially limits one or more major life activities; (2) individuals who are regarded as having such an impairment; and (3) individuals with a record of such an impairment. The term "physical or mental impairment" includes, but is not limited to, such diseases and conditions as orthopedic, visual, speech and hearing impairments, cerebral palsy, autism, epilepsy, muscular dystrophy, multiple sclerosis, cancer, heart disease, diabetes, Human Immunodeficiency Virus infection, mental retardation, emotional illness, drug addiction (other than addiction caused by current, illegal use of a controlled substance) and alcoholism. The term "substantially limits" suggests that the limitation is "significant" or "to a large degree." The term "major life activity" means those activities that are of central importance to daily life, such as seeing, hearing, walking, breathing, performing manual tasks, caring for one's self, learning, and speaking. This list of major life activities is not exhaustive.

4. Does the Act protect juvenile offenders, sex offenders, persons who illegally use controlled substances, and persons with disabilities who pose a significant danger to others?

No, juvenile offenders and sex offenders, by virtue of that status, are not persons with disabilities protected by the Act. Similarly, while the Act does protect persons who are recovering from substance abuse, it does not protect persons who are currently engaging in the current illegal use of controlled substances. Additionally, the Act does not protect an individual with a disability whose tenancy would constitute a "direct threat" to the health or safety of other individuals or result in substantial physical damage to the property of others unless the threat can be eliminated or significantly reduced by reasonable accommodation.

5. How can a housing provider determine if an individual poses a direct threat?

The Act does not allow for exclusion of individuals based upon fear, speculation, or stereotype about a particular disability or persons with disabilities in general. A determination that an individual poses a direct threat must rely on an individualized assessment that is based on reliable objective evidence (e.g., current conduct, or a recent history of overt acts). The assessment must consider: (1) the nature, duration, and severity of the risk of injury; (2) the probability that injury will actually occur; and (3) whether there are any reasonable accommodations that will eliminate the direct threat. Consequently, in evaluating a recent history of overt acts, a provider must take into account whether the individual has received intervening treatment or medication that has eliminated the direct threat (i.e., a significant risk of substantial harm). In such a situation, the provider may request that the individual document how the circumstances have changed so that he no longer poses a direct threat. A provider may also obtain satisfactory assurances that the individual will not pose a direct threat during the tenancy. The housing provider must have reliable, objective evidence that a person with a disability poses a direct threat before excluding him from housing on that basis.

6. What is a "reasonable accommodation" for purposes of the Act?

A "reasonable accommodation" is a change, exception, or adjustment to a rule, policy, practice, or service that may be necessary for a person with a disability to have an equal opportunity to use and enjoy a dwelling, including public and common use spaces. Since rules, policies, practices, and services may have a different effect on persons with disabilities than on other persons, treating persons with disabilities exactly the same as others will sometimes deny them an equal opportunity to use and enjoy a dwelling. The Act makes it unlawful to refuse to make reasonable accommodations to rules, policies, practices, or services when such accommodations may be necessary to afford persons with disabilities an equal opportunity to use and enjoy a dwelling. To show that a requested accommodation may be necessary, there must be an identifiable relationship, or nexus, between the requested accommodation and the individual's disability.

7. Are there any instances when a provider can deny a request for a reasonable accommodation without violating the Act?

Yes. A housing provider can deny a request for a reasonable accommodation if the request was not made by or on behalf of a person with a disability or if there is no disabilityrelated need for the accommodation. In addition, a request for a reasonable accommodation may be denied if providing the accommodation is not reasonable – i.e., if it would impose an undue financial and administrative burden on the housing provider or it would fundamentally alter the nature of the provider's operations. The determination of undue financial and administrative burden must be made on a case-by-case basis involving various factors, such as the cost of the requested accommodation, the financial resources of the provider, the benefits that the accommodation would provide to the requester, and the availability of alternative accommodations that would effectively meet the requester's disability-related needs. When a housing provider refuses a requested accommodation because it is not reasonable, the provider should discuss with the requester whether there is an alternative accommodation that would effectively address the requester's disability-related needs without a fundamental alteration to the provider's operations and without imposing an undue financial and administrative burden. If an alternative accommodation would effectively meet the requester's disability-related needs and is reasonable, the provider must grant it. An interactive process in which the housing provider and the requester discuss the requester's disability-related need for the requested accommodation and possible alternative accommodations is helpful to all concerned because it often results in an effective accommodation for the requester that does not pose an undue financial and administrative burden for the provider.

8. What is a "fundamental alteration"?

A "fundamental alteration" is a modification that alters the essential nature of a provider's operations.

9. What happens if providing a requested accommodation involves some costs on the part of the housing provider?

Courts have ruled that the Act may require a housing provider to grant a reasonable accommodation that involves costs, so long as the reasonable accommodation does not pose an undue financial and administrative burden and the requested accommodation does not constitute a fundamental alteration of the provider's operations. The financial resources of the provider, the cost of the reasonable accommodation, the benefits to the requester of the requested accommodation, and the availability of other, less expensive alternative accommodations that would effectively meet the applicant or resident's disability-related needs must be considered in determining whether a requested accommodation poses an undue financial and administrative burden.

10. What happens if no agreement can be reached through the interactive process?

A failure to reach an agreement on an accommodation request is in effect a decision by the provider not to grant the requested accommodation. If the individual who was denied an accommodation files a Fair Housing Act complaint to challenge that decision, then the agency or court receiving the complaint will review the evidence in light of applicable law and decide if the housing provider violated that law. For more information about the complaint process, see question 19 below.

11. May a housing provider charge an extra fee or require an additional deposit from applicants or residents with disabilities as a condition of granting a reasonable accommodation?

No. Housing providers may not require persons with disabilities to pay extra fees or deposits as a condition of receiving a reasonable accommodation.

12. When and how should an individual request an accommodation?

Under the Act, a resident or an applicant for housing makes a reasonable accommodation request whenever she makes clear to the housing provider that she is requesting an exception, change, or adjustment to a rule, policy, practice, or service because of her disability. She should explain what type of accommodation she is requesting and, if the need for the accommodation is not readily apparent or not known to the provider, explain the relationship between the requested accommodation and her disability. An applicant or resident is not entitled to receive a reasonable accommodation unless she requests one. However, the Fair Housing Act does not require that a request be made in a particular manner or at a particular time. A person with a disability need not personally make the reasonable accommodation request; the request can be made by a family member or someone else who is acting on her behalf. An individual making a reasonable accommodation request does not need to mention the Act or use the words "reasonable accommodation." However, the requester must make the request in a manner that a reasonable person would understand to be a request for an exception, change, or adjustment to a rule, policy, practice, or service because of a disability. Although a reasonable accommodation request can be made orally or in writing, it is usually helpful for both the resident and the housing provider if the request is made in writing. This will help prevent misunderstandings regarding what is being requested, or whether the request was made. To facilitate the processing and consideration of the request, residents or prospective residents may wish to check with a housing provider in advance to determine if the provider has a preference regarding the manner in which the request is made. However, housing providers must give appropriate consideration to reasonable accommodation requests even if the requester makes the request orally or does not use the provider's preferred forms or procedures for making such requests.

13. Must a housing provider adopt formal procedures for processing requests for a reasonable accommodation?

No. The Act does not require that a housing provider adopt any formal procedures for reasonable accommodation requests. However, having formal procedures may aid individuals with disabilities in making requests for reasonable accommodations and may aid housing providers in assessing those requests so that there are no misunderstandings as to the nature of the request, and, in the event of later disputes, provide records to show that the requests received proper consideration. A provider may not refuse a request, however, because the individual making the request did not follow any formal procedures that the provider has adopted. If a provider adopts formal procedures for processing reasonable accommodation requests, the provider should ensure that the procedures, including any forms used, do not seek information that is not necessary to evaluate if a reasonable accommodation may be needed to afford a person with a disability equal opportunity to use and enjoy a dwelling. See Questions 16 - 18, which discuss the disability related information that a provider may and may not request for the purposes of evaluating a reasonable accommodation request.

14. Is a housing provider obligated to provide a reasonable accommodation to a resident or applicant if an accommodation has not been requested?

No. A housing provider is only obligated to provide a reasonable accommodation to a resident or applicant if a request for the accommodation has been made. A provider has notice that a reasonable accommodation request has been made if a person, her family member, or someone acting on her behalf requests a change, exception, or adjustment to a rule, policy, practice, or service because of a disability, even if the words "reasonable accommodation" are not used as part of the request.

15. What if a housing provider fails to act promptly on a reasonable accommodation request?

A provider has an obligation to provide prompt responses to reasonable accommodation requests. An undue delay in responding to a reasonable accommodation request may be deemed to be a failure to provide a reasonable accommodation.

16. What inquiries, if any, may a housing provider make of current or potential residents regarding the existence of a disability when they have not asked for an accommodation?

Under the Fair Housing Act, it is usually unlawful for a housing provider to (1) ask if an applicant for a dwelling has a disability or if a person intending to reside in a dwelling or anyone associated with an applicant or resident has a disability, or (2) ask about the nature or severity of such persons' disabilities. Housing providers may, however, make the following inquiries, provided these inquiries are made of all applicants, including those with and without disabilities:

- An inquiry into an applicant's ability to meet the requirements of tenancy;
- An inquiry to determine if an applicant is a current illegal abuser or addict of a controlled substance;
- An inquiry to determine if an applicant qualifies for a dwelling legally available only to persons with a disability or to persons with a particular type of disability; and
- An inquiry to determine if an applicant qualifies for housing that is legally available on a priority basis to persons with disabilities or to persons with a particular disability.

17. What kinds of information, if any, may a housing provider request from a person with an obvious or known disability who is requesting a reasonable accommodation?

A provider is entitled to obtain information that is necessary to evaluate if a requested reasonable accommodation may be necessary because of a disability. If a person's disability is obvious, or otherwise known to the provider, and if the need for the requested accommodation is also readily apparent or known, then the provider may not request any additional information about the requester's disability or the disability-related need for the accommodation. If the requester's disability is known or readily apparent to the provider, but the need for the accommodation is not readily apparent or known, the provider may request only information that is necessary to evaluate the disability-related need for the accommodation.

18. If a disability is not obvious, what kinds of information may a housing provider request from the person with a disability in support of a requested accommodation?

A housing provider may not ordinarily inquire as to the nature and severity of an individual's disability (see Answer 16, above). However, in response to a request for a reasonable accommodation, a housing provider may request reliable disability-related information that (1) is necessary to verify that the person meets the Act's definition of disability (i.e., has a physical or mental impairment that substantially limits one or more major life activities), (2) describes the needed accommodation, and (3) shows the relationship between the person's disability and the need for the requested accommodation. Depending on the individual's circumstances, information verifying that the person meets the Act's definition of disability can usually be provided by the individual himself or herself (e.g., proof that an individual under 65 years of age receives Supplemental Security Income or Social Security Disability Insurance benefits or a credible statement by the individual). A doctor or other medical professional, a peer support group, a non-medical service agency, or a reliable third party who is in a position to know about the individual's disability may also provide verification of a disability. In most cases, an individual's medical records or detailed information about the nature of a person's disability is not necessary for this inquiry. Once a housing provider has established that a person meets the Act's definition of disability, the provider's request for documentation should seek only the information that is necessary to evaluate if the reasonable accommodation is needed because of a disability. Such information must be kept confidential and must not be shared with other persons unless they need the information to make or assess a decision to grant or deny a reasonable accommodation request or unless disclosure is required by law (e.g., a court-issued subpoena requiring disclosure).

19. If a person believes she has been unlawfully denied a reasonable accommodation, what should that person do if she wishes to challenge that denial under the Act?

When a person with a disability believes that she has been subjected to a discriminatory housing practice, including a provider's wrongful denial of a request for reasonable accommodation, she may file a complaint with HUD within one year after the alleged denial or may file a lawsuit in federal district court within two years of the alleged denial. If a complaint is filed with HUD, HUD will investigate the complaint at no cost to the person with a disability.

Service and Assistance Animals

The Department of Housing and Urban Development Notice Regarding Service Animals and Assistance Animals for People with Disabilities (April 25, 2013)

Section I: Reasonable Accommodations for Assistance Animals under the FHAct and Section 504

The FHAct and the U.S. Department of Housing and Urban Development's (HUD) implementing regulations prohibit discrimination because of disability and apply regardless of the presence of Federal financial assistance. Section 504 and HUD's Section 504 regulations apply a similar prohibition on disability discrimination to all recipients of financial assistance from HUD. The reasonable accommodation provisions of both laws must be considered in situations where persons with disabilities use (or seek to use) assistance animals4 in housing where the provider forbids residents from having pets or otherwise imposes restrictions or conditions relating to pets and other animals.

An assistance animal is not a pet. It is an animal that works, provides assistance, or performs tasks for the benefit of a person with a disability, or provides emotional support that alleviates one or more identified symptoms or effects of a person's disability. Assistance animals perform many disability-related functions, including but not limited to, guiding individuals who are blind or have low vision, alerting individuals who are deaf or hard of hearing to sounds, providing protection or rescue assistance, pulling a wheelchair, fetching items, alerting persons to impending seizures, or providing emotional support to persons with disabilities who have a disability-related need for such support. For purposes of reasonable accommodation requests, neither the FHAct nor Section 504 requires an assistance animal to be individually trained or certified. While dogs are the most common type of assistance animal, other animals can also be assistance animals.

Housing providers are to evaluate a request for a reasonable accommodation to possess an assistance animal in a dwelling using the general principles applicable to all reasonable accommodation requests. After receiving such a request, the housing provider must consider the following:

(1) Does the person seeking to use and live with the animal have a disability-i.e., a physical or mental impaim1cnt that substantially limits one or more major life activities?

(2) Does the person making the request have a disability-related need for an assistance animal? In other words, does the animal work, provide assistance, perform tasks or services for the benefit of a person with a disability, or provide emotional support that alleviates one or more of the identified symptoms or effects of a person's existing disability?

If the answer to question (l) or (2) is "no," then the FHAct and Section 504 do not require a modification to a provider's "no pets" policy, and the reasonable accommodation request may be denied.

Where the answers to questions (1) **and** (2) are "yes," the FHAct and Section 504 require the housing provider to modify or provide an exception to a "no pets" rule or policy to permit a person with a disability to live with and use an assistance animal(s) in all areas of the premises where persons are normally allowed to go, unless doing so would impose an undue financial and administrative burden or would fundamentally alter the nature of the housing provider's services. The request may *also* be denied if: (1) the specific assistance animal in question poses a direct threat to the health or safety of others that cannot be reduced or eliminated by another reasonable accommodation, or (2) the specific assistance animal in question would cause substantial physical damage to the property of others that cannot be reduced or eliminated by another reasonable accommodation. Breed, size, and weight limitations may not be applied to an assistance animal. A determination that an assistance animal poses a direct threat of harm to others or would cause substantial physical damage to the property of others must be based on an individualized assessment that relies on objective evidence about the specific animal's actual conduct - not on mere speculation or fear about the types of harm or damage an animal may cause and not on evidence about harm or damage that other animals have caused. Conditions and restrictions that housing providers apply to pets may not be applied to assistance animals. For example, while housing providers may require applicants or residents to pay a pet deposit, they may not require applicants and residents to pay a deposit for an assistance animal.

A housing provider may not deny a reasonable accommodation request because he or she is uncertain whether or not the person seeking the accommodation bas a disability or a disability related need for an assistance animal. Housing providers may ask individuals who have disabilities that are not readily apparent or known to the provider to submit reliable documentation of a disability and their disability-related need for an assistance animal. If the disability is readily apparent or known but the disability-related need for the assistance animal is not, the housing provider may ask the individual to provide documentation of the disability related need for an assistance animal. For example, the housing provider may ask persons who are seeking a reasonable accommodation for an assistance animal that provides emotional support to provide documentation from a physician, psychiatrist, social worker, or other mental health professional that the animal provides emotional support that alleviates one or more of the identified symptoms or effects of an existing disability. Such documentation is sufficient if it establishes that an individual has a disability and that the animal in question will provide some type of disability-related assistance or emotional support.

However, a housing provider may not ask a tenant or applicant to provide documentation showing the disability or disability-related need for an assistance animal *if* the disability or disability-related need is readily apparent or already known to the provider. For example, persons who are blind or have low vision may not be asked to provide documentation of their disability or their disability-related need for a guide dog. A housing provider also may not ask an applicant or tenant to provide access to medical records or medical providers or provide detailed or extensive information or documentation of a person's physical or mental impairments. Like all reasonable accommodation requests, the determination of whether a person has a disability-related need for an assistance animal involves an individualized assessment. A request for a reasonable accommodation may not be unreasonably denied, or conditioned on payment of a fee or deposit or other terms and conditions applied to applicants or residents with pets, and a response may not be unreasonably delayed. Persons with disabilities who believe a request for a reasonable accommodation has been improperly denied may file a complaint with HUD.

Section II: The ADA Definition of "Service Animal"

In addition to their reasonable accommodation obligations under the FHAct and Section 504, housing providers may also have separate obligations under the ADA. DOJ's revised ADA regulations define "service animal" narrowly as any dog that is individually trained to do work or perform tasks for the benefit of an individual with a disability, including a physical, sensory, psychiatric, intellectual, or other mental disability. The revised regulations specify that "the provision of emotional support, well-being, comfort, or companionship do not constitute work or tasks for the purposes of this definition." Thus, trained dogs are the only species of animal that may qualify as service animals under the ADA (there is a separate provision regarding trained miniature horses\ and emotional support animals are expressly precluded from qualifying as service animals under the ADA. The ADA definition of "service animal" applies to state and local government programs, services activities, and facilities and to public accommodations, such as leasing offices, social service center establishments, universities, and other places or education. Because the ADA requirements relating to service animals are different from the requirements relating to assistance animals under the FHAct and Section 504, an individual's use of a service animal in an ADA covered facility must not be handled as a request for a reasonable accommodation under the FHAct or Section 504. Rather, in ADA-covered facilities, an animal need only meet the definition of "service animal" to be allowed into a covered facility.

To determine if an animal is a service animal, a covered entity shall not ask about the nature or extent of a person's disability, but may make two inquiries to determine whether an animal qualifies as a service animal. A covered entity may ask: (1) Is this a service animal that is required because of a disability? and (2) What work or tasks has the animal been trained to perform? A covered entity shall not require documentation, such as proof that the animal has been certified, trained, or licensed as a service animal. These are the only two inquiries that an ADA-covered facility may make even when an individual's disability and the work or tasks performed by the service animal are not readily apparent (e.g., individual with a seizure disability using a seizure alert service animal, individual with a psychiatric disability using psychiatric service animal, individual with an autism-related disability using an autism service animal).

A covered entity may not make the two permissible inquiries set out above when it is readily apparent that the animal is trained to do work or perform tasks for an individual with a disability (e.g., the dog is observed guiding an individual who is blind or has low vision, pulling a person's wheelchair, or providing assistance with stability or balance to an individual with an observable mobility disability). The animal may not be denied access to the ADA-covered facility unless: (1) the animal is out of control and its handler does not take effective action to control it; (2) the animal is not housebroken (i .e., trained so that, absent illness or accident, the animal controls its waste elimination); or (3) the animal poses a direct threat to the health or safety of others that cannot be eliminated or reduced to an acceptable level by a reasonable modification to other policies, practices and procedures. A determination that a service animal poses a direct threat must be based on an individualized assessment of the specific service animal's actual conduct - not on fears, stereotypes, or generalizations. The service animal must be permitted to accompany the individual with a disability to all areas of the facility where members of the public are normally allowed to go.

Section III. Applying Multiple Laws

Certain entities will be subject to both the service animal requirements of the ADA and the reasonable accommodation provisions of the FHAct and/or Section 504. These entities include, but are not limited to, public housing agencies and some places *of* public accommodation, such as rental offices, shelters, residential homes, some types of multifamily housing, assisted living facilities, and housing at places of education. Covered entities must ensure compliance with all relevant civil rights laws. As noted above, compliance with the FHAct and Section 504 does not ensure compliance with the ADA. Similarly, compliance with the ADA's regulations does not ensure compliance with the FHAct or Section 504.

The preambles to DOJ' s 2010 Title II and Title Ill ADA regulations state that public entities or public accommodations that operate housing facilities "may not use the ADA definition [of "service animal"] as a justification for reducing their FHAct obligations.

The revised ADA regulations also do not change the reasonable accommodation analysis under the FHAct or Section 504. The preambles to the 2010 ADA regulations specifically note that under the FHAct, "an individual with a disability may have the right to have an animal other than a dog in his or her home if the animal qualifies as a 'reasonable accommodation' that is necessary to afford the individual equal opportunity to use and enjoy a dwelling, assuming that the use of the animal does not pose a direct threat." In addition, the preambles state that emotional support animals that do not qualify as service animals under the ADA may "nevertheless qualify as permitted reasonable accommodations for persons with disabilities under the FHAct." While the preambles expressly mention only the FHAct, the same analysis applies to Section 504.

In cases where all three statutes apply, to avoid possible ADA violations the housing provider should apply the ADA service animal test first. This is because the covered entity may ask only whether the animal is a service animal that is required because of a disability, and if so, what work or tasks the animal has been been trained to perform. If the animal meets the test for "service animal," the animal must be permitted to accompany the individual with a disability to all areas of the facility where persons are normally allowed to go, unless (1) the animal is out of control and its handler does not take effective action to control it; (2) the animal is not housebroken (i.e., trained so that, absent illness or accident, the animal controls its waste elimination); or (3) the animal poses a direct threat to the health or safety of others that cannot be eliminated or reduced to an acceptable level by a reasonable modification lo other policies, practices and procedures.

If the animal does not meet the ADA service animal test, then the housing provider must evaluate the request in accordance with the guidance provided in Section I of this notice.

It is the housing provider's responsibility to know the applicable laws and comply with each of them.

Section IV. Conclusion

The definition of "service animal" contained in ADA regulations does not limit housing providers' obligations to grant reasonable accommodation requests for assistance animals in housing under either the FHAct or Section 504. Under these laws, rules, policies, or practices must be modified to permit the use of an assistance animal as a reasonable accommodation in housing when its use may be necessary to afford a person with a disability an equal opportunity to use and enjoy a dwelling and/or the common areas of a dwelling, or may be necessary to allow a qualified individual with a disability to participate in, or benefit from, any housing program or activity receiving financial assistance from **HUD**.

Selected Provisions of the California Unruh Civil Rights Act

Civ. Code § 51. Unruh Civil Rights Act.

(a) This section shall be known, and may be cited, as the Unruh Civil Rights Act.

(b) All persons within the jurisdiction of this state are free and equal, and no matter what their sex, race, color, religion, ancestry, national origin, disability, medical condition, genetic information, marital status, sexual orientation citizenship, primary language, or immigration status are entitled to the full and equal accommodations, advantages, facilities, privileges, or services in all business establishments of every kind whatsoever.

(c) This section shall not be construed to confer any right or privilege on a person that is conditioned or limited by law or that is applicable alike to persons of every sex, color, race, religion, ancestry, national origin, disability, medical condition, marital status, or sexual orientation citizenship, primary language, or immigration status, or to persons regardless of their genetic information.

(d) Nothing in this section shall be construed to require any construction, alteration, repair, structural or otherwise, or modification of any sort whatsoever, beyond that construction, alteration, repair, or modification that is otherwise required by other provisions of law, to any new or existing establishment, facility, building, improvement, or any other structure, nor shall anything in this section be construed to augment, restrict, or alter in any way the authority of the State Architect to require construction, alteration, repair, or modifications that the State Architect otherwise possesses pursuant to other laws.

(e) For purposes of this section:

(1) "Disability" means any mental or physical disability as defined in Sections 12926 and 12926.1 of the Government Code.

(2) (A) "Genetic information" means, with respect to any individual, information about any of the following:

(i) The individual's genetic tests.

(ii) The genetic tests of family members of the individual.

(iii) The manifestation of a disease or disorder in family members of the individual.

(A) "Genetic information" includes any request for, or receipt of, genetic services, or participation in clinical research that includes genetic services, by an individual or any family member of the individual.

(B) "Genetic information" does not include information about the sex or age of any individual.

(3) "Medical condition" has the same meaning as defined in subdivision (h) of Section 12926 of the Government Code.

(4) "Religion" includes all aspects of religious belief, observance, and practice.

(5) "Sex" includes, but is not limited to, pregnancy, childbirth, or medical conditions related to pregnancy or childbirth. "Sex" also includes, but is not limited to, a person's gender. "Gender" means sex, and includes a person's gender identity and gender expression. "Gender expression" means a person's gender-related appearance and behavior whether or not stereotypically associated with the person's assigned sex at birth.

(6) "Sex, race, color, religion, ancestry, national origin, disability, medical condition, genetic information, marital status, or sexual orientation" includes a perception that the person has any particular characteristic or characteristics within the listed categories or that the person is associated with a person who has, or is perceived to have, any particular characteristic or characteristics within the listed categories.

(7) "Sexual orientation" has the same meaning as defined in subdivision (r) of Section 12926 of the Government Code.

(f) A violation of the right of any individual under the federal Americans with Disabilities Act of 1990 (P.L. 101-336) shall also constitute a violation of this section.

Civ. Code § 51.2. Housing Discrimination Based on Age Prohibited.

(a) Section 51 shall be construed to prohibit a business establishment from discriminating in the sale or rental of housing based upon age. Where accommodations are designed to meet the physical and social needs of senior citizens, a business establishment may establish and preserve that housing for senior citizens, pursuant to Section 51.3, except housing as to which Section 51.3 is preempted by the prohibition in the federal Fair Housing Amendments Act of 1988 (Public Law 100-430) and implementing regulations against discrimination on the basis of familial status. For accommodations constructed before February 8, 1982, that meet all the criteria for senior citizen housing specified in Section 51.3, a business establishment may establish and preserve that housing development for senior citizens without the housing development being designed to meet physical and social needs of senior citizens.

(b) This section is intended to clarify the holdings in *Marina Point, Ltd. v. Wolfson* (1982) 30 Cal. 3d 72 and *O'Connor v. Village Green Owners Association* (1983) 33 Cal. 3d 790.

(c) This section shall not apply to the County of Riverside.

(d) A housing development for senior citizens constructed on or after January 1, 2001, shall be presumed to be designed to meet the physical and social needs of senior citizens if it includes all of the following elements:

(1) Entryways, walkways, and hallways in the common areas of the development, and doorways and paths of access to and within the housing units, shall be as wide as required by current laws applicable to new multifamily housing construction for provision of access to persons using a standard-width wheelchair.

(2) Walkways and hallways in the common areas of the development shall be equipped with standard height railings or grab bars to assist persons who have difficulty with walking.

(3) Walkways and hallways in the common areas shall have lighting conditions which are of sufficient brightness to assist persons who have difficulty seeing.

(4) Access to all common areas and housing units within the development shall be provided without use of stairs, either by means of an elevator or sloped walking ramps.

(5) The development shall be designed to encourage social contact by providing at least one common room and at least some common open space.

(6) Refuse collection shall be provided in a manner that requires a minimum of physical exertion by residents.

(7) The development shall comply with all other applicable requirements for access and design imposed by law, including, but not limited to, the Fair Housing Act (42 U.S.C. Sec. 3601 et seq.), the Americans with Disabilities Act (42 U.S.C. Sec. 12101 et seq.), and the regulations promulgated at Title 24 of the California Code of Regulations that relate to access for persons with disabilities or handicaps. Nothing in this section shall be construed to limit or reduce any right or obligation applicable under those laws.

(e) Selection preferences based on age, imposed in connection with a federally approved housing progam, do not constitute age discrimination in housing.

Civ. Code § 51.3. Establishing and Preserving Accessible Housing For Senior Citizens.

(a) The Legislature finds and declares that this section is essential to establish and preserve specially designed accessible housing for senior citizens. There are senior citizens who need special living environments and services, and find that there is an inadequate supply of this type of housing in the state.

(b) For the purposes of this section, the following definitions apply:

(1) "Qualifying resident" or "senior citizen" means a person 62 years of age or older, or 55 years of age or older in a senior citizen housing development.

(2) "Qualified permanent resident" means a person who meets both of the following requirements:

(A) Was residing with the qualifying resident or senior citizen prior to the death, hospitalization, or other prolonged absence of, or the dissolution of marriage with, the qualifying resident or senior citizen.

(B) Was 45 years of age or older, or was a spouse, cohabitant, or person providing primary physical or economic support to the qualifying resident or senior citizen.

(3) "Qualified permanent resident" also means a disabled person or person with a disabling illness or injury who is a child or grandchild of the senior citizen or a qualified permanent resident as defined in paragraph (2) who needs to live with the senior citizen or qualified permanent resident because of the disabling condition, illness, or injury. For purposes of this section, "disabled" means a person who has a disability as defined in subdivision (b) of Section 54. A "disabling injury or illness" means an illness or injury which results in a condition meeting the definition of disability set forth in subdivision (b) of Section 54.

(A) For any person who is a qualified permanent resident under this paragraph whose disabling condition ends, the owner, board of directors, or other governing body may require the formerly disabled resident to cease residing in the development upon receipt of six months' written notice; provided, however, that the owner, board of directors, or other governing body may allow the person to remain a resident for up to one year after the disabling condition ends.

(B) The owner, board of directors, or other governing body of the senior citizen housing development may take action to prohibit or terminate occupancy by a person who is a qualified permanent resident under this paragraph if the owner, board of directors, or other governing body finds, based on credible and objective evidence, that the person is likely to pose a significant threat to the health or safety of others that cannot be ameliorated by means of a reasonable accommodation; provided, however, that the action to prohibit or terminate the occupancy may be taken only after doing both of the following:

(i) Providing reasonable notice to and an opportunity to be heard for the disabled person whose occupancy is being challenged, and reasonable notice to the coresident parent or grandparent of that person.

(ii) Giving due consideration to the relevant, credible, and objective information provided in the hearing. The evidence shall be taken and held in a confidential manner, pursuant to a closed session, by the owner, board of directors, or other governing body in order to preserve the privacy of the affected persons. The affected persons shall be entitled to have present at the hearing an attorney or any other person authorized by them to speak on their behalf or to assist them in the matter.

(4) "Senior citizen housing development" means a residential development developed, substantially rehabilitated, or substantially renovated for, senior citizens that has at least 35 dwelling units. Any senior citizen housing development which is required to obtain a public report under Section 11010 of the Business and Professions Code and which submits its application for a public report after July 1, 2001, shall be required to have been issued a public report as a senior citizen housing development under Section 11010.05 of the Business and Professions Code. No housing development constructed prior to January 1, 1985, shall fail to qualify as a senior citizen housing development because it was not originally developed or put to use for occupancy by senior citizens.

(5) "Dwelling unit" or "housing" means any residential accommodation other than a mobilehome.

(6) "Cohabitant" refers to persons who live together as husband and wife, or persons who are domestic partners within the meaning of Section 297 of the Family Code.

(7) "Permitted health care resident" means a person hired to provide live-in, long-term, or terminal health care to a qualifying resident, or a family member of the qualifying resident providing that care. For the purposes of this section, the care provided by a permitted health care resident must be substantial in nature and must provide either assistance with necessary daily activities or medical treatment, or both. A permitted health care resident shall be entitled to continue his or her occupancy, residency, or use of the dwelling unit as a permitted resident in the absence of the senior citizen from the dwelling unit only if both of the following are applicable:

(A) The senior citizen became absent from the dwelling due to hospitalization or other necessary medical treatment and expects to return to his or her residence within 90 days from the date the absence began.

(B) The absent senior citizen or an authorized person acting for the senior citizen submits a written request to the owner, board of directors, or governing board stating that the senior citizen desires that the permitted health care resident be allowed to remain in order to be present when the senior citizen returns to reside in the development. Upon written request by the senior citizen or an authorized person acting for the senior citizen, the owner, board of directors, or governing board shall have the discretion to allow a permitted health care resident to remain for a time period longer than 90 days from the date that the senior citizen's absence began, if it appears that the senior citizen will return within a period of time not to exceed an additional 90 days.

(c) The covenants, conditions, and restrictions and other documents or written policy shall set forth the limitations on occupancy, residency, or use on the basis of age. Any such limitation shall not be more exclusive than to require that one person in residence in each dwelling unit may be required to be a senior citizen and that each other resident in the same dwelling unit may be required to be a qualified permanent resident, a permitted health care resident, or a person under 55 years of age whose occupancy is permitted under subdivision (h) of this section or under subdivision (b) of Section 51.4. That limitation may be less exclusive, but shall at least require that the persons commencing any occupancy of a dwelling unit include a senior citizen who intends to reside in the unit as his or her primary residence on a permanent basis. The application of the rules set forth in this subdivision regarding limitations on occupancy may result in less than all of the dwellings being actually occupied by a senior citizen.

(d) The covenants, conditions, and restrictions or other documents or written policy shall permit temporary residency, as a guest of a senior citizen or qualified permanent resident, by a person of less than 55 years of age for periods of time, not less than 60 days in any year, that are specified in the covenants, conditions, and restrictions or other documents or written policy.

(e) Upon the death or dissolution of marriage, or upon hospitalization, or other prolonged absence of the qualifying resident, any qualified permanent resident shall be entitled to continue his or her occupancy, residency, or use of the dwelling unit as a permitted resident. This subdivision shall not apply to a permitted health care resident.

(f) The condominium, stock cooperative, limited-equity housing cooperative, planned development, or multiple-family residential rental property shall have been developed for, and initially been put to use as, housing for senior citizens, or shall have been substantially rehabilitated or renovated for, and immediately afterward put to use as, housing for senior citizens, as provided in this section; provided, however, that no housing development constructed prior to January 1, 1985, shall fail to qualify as a senior citizen housing development because it was not originally developed for or originally put to use for occupancy by senior citizens.

(g) The covenants, conditions, and restrictions or other documents or written policies applicable to any condominium, stock cooperative, limited-equity housing cooperative, planned development, or multiple-family residential property that contained age restrictions on January 1, 1984, shall be enforceable only to the extent permitted by this section, notwithstanding lower age restrictions contained in those documents or policies.

(h) Any person who has the right to reside in, occupy, or use the housing or an unimproved lot subject to this section on January 1, 1985, shall not be deprived of the right to continue that residency, occupancy, or use as the result of the enactment of this section.

(i) The covenants, conditions, and restrictions or other documents or written policy of the senior citizen housing development shall permit the occupancy of a dwelling unit by a permitted health care resident during any period that the person is actually providing live-in, long-term, or hospice health care to a qualifying resident for compensation. For purposes of this subdivision, the term "for compensation" shall include provisions of lodging and food in exchange for care.

(j) Notwithstanding any other provision of this section, this section shall not apply to the County of Riverside.

Civ. Code § 51.4. Senior Housing Constructed Prior To 1982 - Exemption From Design Requirements.

(a) The Legislature finds and declares that the requirements for senior housing under Sections 51.2 and 51.3 are more stringent than the requirements for that housing under the federal Fair Housing Amendments Act of 1988 (Public Law 100-430) in recognition of the acute shortage of housing for families with children in California. The Legislature further finds and declares that the special design requirements for senior housing under Sections 51.2 and 51.3 may pose a hardship to some housing developments which were constructed before the decision in *Marina Point Ltd. v. Wolfson* (1982), 30 Cal. 3d 721. The Legislature further finds and declares that the requirement for specially designed accommodations in senior housing under Sections 51.2 and 51.3 provides important benefits to senior citizens and also ensures that housing exempt from the prohibition of age discrimination is carefully tailored to meet the compelling societal interest in providing senior housing.

(b) Any person who resided in, occupied, or used, prior to January 1, 1990, a dwelling in a senior citizen housing development which relied on the exemption to the special design requirement provided by this section prior to January 1, 2001, shall not be deprived of the right to continue that residency, occupancy, or use as the result of the changes made to this section by the enactment of Chapter 1004 of the Statutes of 2000.

(c) This section shall not apply to the County of Riverside.

Civ. Code § 52. Penalty for Discrimination.

(a) Whoever denies, aids or incites a denial, or makes any discrimination or distinction contrary to Section 51 or 51.5, or 51.6,is liable for each and every offense for the actual damages, and any amount that may be determined by a jury, or a court sitting without a jury, up to a maximum of three times the amount of actual damage but in no case less than four thousand dollars ($4,000), and any attorney's fees that may be determined by the court in addition thereto, suffered by any person denied the rights provided in Section 51 or 51.5, or 51.6.

(b) Whoever denies the right provided by Section 51.7 or 51.9, or aids, incites, or conspires in that denial, is liable for each and every offense for the actual damages suffered by any person denied that right and, in addition, the following:

(1) An amount to be determined by a jury, or a court sitting without a jury, for exemplary damages.

(2) A civil penalty of twenty-five thousand dollars ($25,000) to be awarded to the person denied the right provided by Section 51.7 in any action brought by the person denied the right, or by the Attorney General, a district attorney, or a city attorney. An action for that penalty brought pursuant to Section 51.7 shall be commenced within three years of the alleged practice.

(3) Attorney's fees as may be determined by the court.

(c) Whenever there is reasonable cause to believe that any person or group of persons is engaged in conduct of resistance to the full enjoyment of any of the rights described in this section, and that conduct is of that nature and is intended to deny the full exercise of those rights , the Attorney General, any district attorney or city attorney, or any person aggrieved by the conduct may bring a civil action in the appropriate court by filing with it a complaint. The complaint shall contain the following:

(1) The signature of the officer, or, in his or her absence, the individual acting on behalf of the officer, or the signature of the person aggrieved.

(2) The facts pertaining to the conduct.

(3) A request for preventive relief, including an application for a permanent or temporary injunction, restraining order, or other order against the person or persons responsible for the conduct, as the complainant deems necessary to ensure the full enjoyment of the rights described in this section.

(d) Whenever an action has been commenced in any court seeking relief from the denial of equal protection of the laws under the Fourteenth Amendment to the Constitution of the United States on account of race, color, religion, sex, national origin, or disability, the Attorney General or any district attorney or city attorney for or in the name of the people of the State of California may intervene in the action upon timely application if the Attorney General of any district attorney or city attorney certifies that the case is of general public importance. In that action the people of the State of California shall be entitled to the same relief as if it had instituted the action.

(e) Actions brought pursuant to this section are independent of any other actions, remedies or procedures that may be available to an aggrieved party pursuant to any other law.

(f) Any person claiming to be aggrieved by an alleged unlawful practice in violation of Section 51 or 51.7 may also file a verified complaint with the Department of Fair Employment and Housing pursuant to Section 12948 of the Government Code.

(g) This section does not require any construction, alteration, repair, structural or otherwise, or modification of any sort whatsoever beyond that construction, alteration, repair, or modification that is otherwise required by other provisions of law, to any new or existing establishment, facility, building, improvement, or any other structure, nor does this section augment, restrict, or alter in any way the authority of the State Architect to require construction, alteration, repair, or modifications that the State Architect otherwise possesses pursuant to other laws.

(h) For the purposes of this section, "actual damages" means special and general damages. This subdivision is declaratory of existing law.

(i) Subdivisions (b) to (f), inclusive, shall not be waived by contract except as provided in Section 51.7.

Civ. Code § 52.1. Housing Discrimination Based on Age Prohibited.

(a) This section shall be known, and may be cited, as the Tom Bane Civil Rights Act.

(b) If a person or persons, whether or not acting under color of law, interferes by threat, intimidation, or coercion, or attempts to interfere by threat, intimidation, or coercion, with the exercise or enjoyment by any individual or individuals of rights secured by the Constitution or laws of the United States, or of the rights secured by the Constitution or laws of this state, the Attorney General, or any district attorney or city attorney may bring a civil action for injunctive and other appropriate equitable relief in the name of the people of the State of California, in order to protect the peaceable exercise or enjoyment of the right or rights secured. An action brought by the Attorney General, any district attorney, or any city attorney may also seek a civil penalty of twenty-five thousand dollars ($25,000). If this civil penalty is requested, it shall be assessed individually against each person who is determined to have violated this section and the penalty shall be awarded to each individual whose rights under this section are determined to have been violated.

(c) Any individual whose exercise or enjoyment of rights secured by the Constitution or laws of the United States, or of rights secured by the Constitution or laws of this state, has been interfered with, or attempted to be interfered with, as described in subdivision (a), may institute and prosecute in his or her own name and on his or her own behalf a civil action for damages, including, but not limited to, damages under Section 52, injunctive relief, and other appropriate equitable relief to protect the peaceable exercise or enjoyment of the right or rights secured, including appropriate equitable and declaratory relief to eliminate a pattern or practice of conduct as described in subdivision (a).

(d) An action brought pursuant to subdivision (a) or (b) may be filed either in the superior court for the county in which the conduct complained of occurred or in the superior court for the county in which a person whose conduct complained of resides or has his or her place of business. An action brought by the Attorney General pursuant to subdivision (a) also may be filed in the superior court for any county wherein the Attorney General has an office, and in that case, the jurisdiction of the court shall extend throughout the state.

(e) If a court issues a temporary restraining order or a preliminary or permanent injunction in an action brought pursuant to subdivision (a) or (b), ordering a defendant to refrain from conduct or activities, the order issued shall include the following statement: VIOLATION OF THIS ORDER IS A CRIME PUNISHABLE UNDER SECTION 422.77 OF THE PENAL CODE.

(f) The court shall order the plaintiff or the attorney for the plaintiff to deliver, or the clerk of the court to mail, two copies of any order, extension, modification, or termination thereof granted pursuant to this section, by the close of the business day on which the order, extension, modification, or termination was granted, to each local law enforcement agency having jurisdiction over the residence of the plaintiff and any other locations where the court determines that acts of violence against the plaintiff are likely to occur. Those local law enforcement agencies shall be designated by the plaintiff or the attorney for the plaintiff. Each appropriate law enforcement agency receiving any order, extension, or modification of any order issued pursuant to this section shall serve forthwith one copy thereof upon the defendant. Each appropriate law enforcement agency shall provide to any law enforcement officer responding to the scene of reported violence, information as to the existence of, terms, and current status of, any order issued pursuant to this section.

(g) A court shall not have jurisdiction to issue an order or injunction under this section, if that order or injunction would be prohibited under Section 527.3 of the Code of Civil Procedure.

(h) An action brought pursuant to this section is independent of any other action, remedy, or procedure that may be available to an aggrieved individual under any other provision of law, including, but not limited to, an action, remedy, or procedure brought pursuant to Section 51.7.

(i) In addition to any damages, injunction, or other equitable relief awarded in an action brought pursuant to subdivision (b), the court may award the petitioner or plaintiff reasonable attorney's fees.

(j) A violation of an order described in subdivision (d) may be punished either by prosecution under Section 422.77 of the Penal Code, or by a proceeding for contempt brought pursuant to Title 5 (commencing with Section 1209) of Part 3 of the Code of Civil Procedure. However, in any proceeding pursuant to the Code of Civil Procedure, if it is determined that the person proceeded against is guilty of the contempt charged, in addition to any other relief, a fine may be imposed not exceeding one thousand dollars ($1,000), or the person may be ordered imprisoned in a county jail not exceeding six months, or the court may order both the imprisonment and fine.

(k) Speech alone is not sufficient to support an action brought pursuant to subdivision (a) or (b), except upon a showing that the speech itself threatens violence against a specific person or group of persons; and the person or group of persons against whom the threat is directed reasonably fears that, because of the speech, violence will be committed against them or their property and that the person threatening violence had the apparent ability to carry out the threat.

(l) No order issued in any proceeding brought pursuant to subdivision (a) or (b) shall restrict the content of any person's speech. An order restricting the time, place, or manner of any person's speech shall do so only to the extent reasonably necessary to protect the peaceable exercise or enjoyment of constitutional or statutory rights, consistent with the constitutional rights of the person sought to be enjoined.

(m) The rights, penalties, remedies, forums, and procedures of this section shall not be waived by contract except as provided in Section 51.7.

Civ. Code § 53. Discriminatory Provisions on Ownership or Use of Real Property Void.

(a) Every provision in a written instrument relating to real property that purports to forbid or restrict the conveyance, encumbrance, leasing or mortgaging of that real property to any person because of any characteristic listed or defined in subdivision (b) or (e) of Section 51 is void, and every restriction or prohibition as to the use or occupation of real property because of any characteristic listed or defined in subdivision (b) or (e) of Section 51 is void.

(b) Every restriction or prohibition, whether by way of covenant, condition upon use or occupation, or upon transfer of title to real property, which restriction or prohibition directly or indirectly limits the acquisition, use or occupation of that property because of any characteristic listed or defined in subdivision (b) or (e) of Section 51 is void.

(c) In any action to declare that a restriction or prohibition specified in subdivision (a) or (b) is void, the court shall take judicial notice of the recorded instrument or instruments containing the prohibitions or restrictions in the same manner that is takes judicial notice of the matters listed in Section 452 of the Evidence Code.

Selected Provisions of the Fair Employment and Housing Act

Gov't Code § 12955. Discrimination in Housing Prohibited.

It shall be unlawful:

(a) For the owner of any housing accommodation to discriminate against or harass any person because of the race, color, religion, sex, gender, gender identity, gender expression, sexual orientation, marital status, national origin, ancestry, familial status, source of income, disability, veteran or military status, or genetic information of that person.

(b) For the owner of any housing accommodation to make or to cause to be made any written or oral inquiry concerning the race, color, religion, sex, gender, gender identity, gender expression, sexual orientation, marital status, national origin, ancestry, familial status, disability, veteran or military status, or genetic information of any person seeking to purchase, rent, or lease any housing accommodation.

(c) For any person to make, print, or publish, or cause to be made, printed, or published any notice, statement, or advertisement, with respect to the sale or rental of a housing accommodation that indicates any preference, limitation, or discrimination based on race, color, religion, sex, gender, gender identity, gender expression, sexual orientation, marital status, national origin, ancestry, familial status, source of income, disability, veteran or military status, or genetic information or an intention to make that preference, limitation, or discrimination.

(d) For any person subject to the provisions of Section 51 of the Civil Code, as that section applies to housing accommodations, to discriminate against any person on the basis of sex, gender, gender identity, gender expression, sexual orientation, color, race, religion, ancestry, national origin, familial status, marital status, disability, genetic information, source of income, veteran or military status, or on any other basis prohibited by that section. Selection preferences based on age, imposed in connection with a federally approved housing program, do not constitute age discrimination in housing.

(e) For any person, bank, mortgage company, or other financial institution that provides financial assistance for the purchase, refinance, organization, or construction of any housing accommodation to discriminate against any person or group of persons because of the race, color, religion, sex, gender, gender identity, gender expression, sexual orientation, marital status, national origin, ancestry, familial status, source of income, disability, veteran or military status, or genetic information in the terms, conditions, or privileges relating to the obtaining or use of that financial assistance.

(f) For any owner of housing accommodations to harass, evict, or otherwise discriminate against any person in the sale or rental of housing accommodations when the owner's dominant purpose is retaliation against a person who has opposed practices unlawful under this section, informed law enforcement agencies of practices believed unlawful under this section, has testified or assisted in any proceeding under this part, or has aided or encouraged a person to exercise or enjoy the rights secured by this part. Nothing herein is intended to cause or permit the delay of an unlawful detainer action.

(g) For any person to aid, abet, incite, compel, or coerce the doing of any of the acts or practices declared unlawful in this section, or to attempt to do so.

(h) For any person, for profit, to induce any person to sell or rent any dwelling by representations regarding the entry or prospective entry into the neighborhood of a person or persons of a particular race, color, religion, sex, gender, gender identity, gender expression, sexual orientation, marital status, ancestry, disability, genetic information, source of income, familial status, veteran or military status, or national origin.

(i) (1) For any person or other organization or entity whose business involves real estate-related transactions to discriminate against any person in making available a transaction, or in the terms and conditions of a transaction, because of race, color, religion, sex, gender, gender identity, gender expression, sexual orientation, marital status, national origin, ancestry, source of income, familial status, disability, veteran or military status, or genetic information.

(2) For any person or other entity whose business includes performing appraisals, as defined in subdivision (b) of Section 11302 of the Business and Professions Code, of residential real property to discriminate against any person in making available those services, or in the performance of those services, because of race, color, religion, sex, gender, gender identity, gender expression, sexual orientation, familial status, source of income, disability, genetic information, veteran or military status, or national origin.

(j) To deny a person access to, or membership or participation in, a multiple listing service, real estate brokerage organization, or other service because of race, color, religion, sex, gender, gender identity, gender expression, sexual orientation, marital status, ancestry, disability, genetic information, familial status, source of income, veteran or military status, or national origin.

(k) To otherwise make unavailable or deny a dwelling based on discrimination because of race, color, religion, sex, gender, gender identity, gender expression, sexual orientation, familial status, source of income, disability, genetic information, veteran or military status, or national origin.

(l) To discriminate through public or private land use practices, decisions, and authorizations because of race, color, religion, sex, gender, gender identity, gender expression, sexual orientation, familial status, marital status, disability, genetic information, national origin, source of income, veteran or military status, or ancestry. Discrimination includes, but is not limited to, restrictive covenants, zoning laws, denials of use permits, and other actions authorized under the Planning and Zoning Law (Title 7 (commencing with Section 65000)), that make housing opportunities unavailable. Discrimination under this subdivision also includes the existence of a restrictive covenant, regardless of whether accompanied by a statement that the restrictive covenant is repealed or void.

(m) As used in this section, "race, color, religion, sex, gender, gender identity, gender expression, sexual orientation, marital status, national origin, ancestry, familial status, source of income, disability, veteran or military status, or genetic information," includes a perception that the person has any of those characteristics or that the person is associated with a person who has, or is perceived to have, any of those characteristics.

(n) To use a financial or income standard in the rental of housing that fails to account for the aggregate income of persons residing together or proposing to reside together on the same basis as the aggregate income of married persons residing together or proposing to reside together.

(o) In instances where there is a government rent subsidy, to use a financial or income standard in assessing eligibility for the rental of housing that is not based on the portion of the rent to be paid by the tenant.

(p) (1) For the purposes of this section, "source of income" means lawful, verifiable income paid directly to a tenant, or to a representative of a tenant, or paid to a housing owner or landlord on behalf of a tenant, including federal, state, or local public assistance, and federal, state, or local housing subsidies, including, but not limited to, federal housing assistance vouchers issued under Section 8 of the United States Housing Act of 1937 (42 U.S.C. Sec. 1437f). "Source of income" includes a federal Department of Housing and Urban Development Veterans Affairs Supportive Housing voucher. For the purposes of this section, a housing owner or landlord is not considered a representative of a tenant unless the source of income is a federal Department of Housing and Urban Development Veterans Affairs Supportive Housing voucher.

(2) For the purposes of this section, it shall not constitute discrimination based on source of income to make a written or oral inquiry concerning the level or source of income.

Gov't Code § 12955.1. "Discrimination" Defined.

(a) For purposes of Section 12955, "discrimination" includes, but is not limited to, a failure to design and construct a covered multifamily dwelling in a manner that allows access to, and use by, disabled persons by providing, at a minimum, the following features:

(1) All covered multifamily dwellings shall have at least one building entrance on an accessible route, unless it is impracticable to do so because of the terrain or unusual characteristics of the site. The burden of establishing impracticability because of terrain or unusual site characteristics is on the person or persons who designed or constructed the housing facility.

(2) All covered multifamily dwellings with a building entrance on an accessible route shall be designed and constructed in a manner that complies with all of the following:

(A) The public and common areas are readily accessible to and useable by persons with disabilities.

(B) All the doors designed to allow passage into and within all premises are sufficiently wide to allow passage by persons in wheelchairs.

(C) All premises within covered multifamily dwelling units contain the following features of adaptable design:

(i) An accessible route into and through the covered dwelling unit.

(ii) Light switches, electrical outlets, thermostats, and other environmental controls in accessible locations.

(iii) Reinforcements in bathroom walls to allow later installation of grab bars around the toilet, tub, shower stall, and shower seat, where those facilities are provided.

(iv) Useable kitchens and bathrooms so that an individual in a wheelchair can maneuver about the space.

(b) (1) For purposes of Section 12955, "discrimination" includes, but is not limited to, a failure to design and construct 10 percent of the multistory dwelling units in buildings without an elevator that consist of at least four condominium dwelling units or at least three rental apartment dwelling units in a manner that incorporates an accessible route to the primary entry level entrance and that meets the requirements of paragraph (2) of subdivision (a) with respect to the ground floor, at least one bathroom on the primary entry level and the public and common areas. Any fraction thereof shall be rounded up to the next whole number. For purposes of this subdivision, "elevator" does not include an elevator that serves only the first ground floor or any nonresidential area. In multistory dwelling units in these buildings without elevators, the "primary entry level entrance" means the principal entrance through which most people enter the dwelling unit, as designated by the California Building Standards Code or, if not designated by California Building Standards Code, by the building official. To determine the total number of multistory dwelling units subject to this subdivision, all multistory dwelling units in the buildings subject to this subdivision on a site shall be considered collectively. This subdivision shall not be construed to require an elevator within an individual multistory dwelling unit or within a building subject to this subdivision. This subdivision shall apply only to multistory dwelling units in a building subject to this subdivision for which an application for a construction permit is submitted on or after July 1, 2005.

(2) Notwithstanding subdivision (c), the Division of the State Architect and the Department of Housing and Community Development may adopt regulations to clarify, interpret, or implement this subdivision, if either of them deem it necessary and appropriate.

(c) Notwithstanding Section 12935, regulations adopting building standards necessary to implement, interpret, or make specific the provisions of this section shall be developed by the Division of the State Architect for public housing and by the Department of Housing and Community Development for all other residential occupancies, and shall be adopted pursuant to Chapter 4 (commencing with Section 18935) of Part 2.5 of the Health and Safety Code. Prior to the effective date of regulations adopted pursuant to this subdivision, existing federal accessibility standards that provide, to persons with disabilities, greater protections than existing state accessibility regulations shall apply. After regulations pursuant to this subdivision become effective, particular state regulations shall apply if they provide, to persons with disabilities, the same protections as, or greater protections than, the federal standards. If particular federal regulations provide greater protections than state regulations, then those federal standards shall apply. If the United States Department of Housing and Urban Development determines that any portion of the state regulations are not equivalent to the federal standards, the federal standards shall, as to those portions, apply to the design and construction of covered multifamily dwellings until the state regulations are brought into compliance with the federal standards. The appropriate state agency shall provide notice pursuant to the Administrative Procedures Act (Chapter 5 (commencing with Section 11500) of Part 5 of Division 3 of Title 2) of that determination.

(d) In investigating discrimination complaints, the department shall apply the building standards contained in the California Building Standards Code to determine whether a covered multifamily dwelling is designed and constructed for access to and use by disabled persons in accordance with this section.

(e) The building standard requirements for persons with disabilities imposed by this section shall meet or exceed the requirements under the federal Fair Housing Amendments Act of 1988 (Public Law 100-430) and its implementing regulations (24 C.F.R. 100.1 et seq.) and the existing state law building standards contained in the California Building Standards Code.

Gov't Code § 12955.1.1. "Covered Multifamily Dwellings" and "Multistory Dwelling Unit" Defined.

For purposes of Section 12955.1, the following definitions shall apply:

(a) "Covered multifamily dwellings" means both of the following:

(1) Buildings that consist of at least four condominium dwelling units or at least three rental apartment dwelling units if the buildings have at least one elevator. For purposes of this definition, dwelling units within a single structure separated by firewalls do not constitute separate buildings.

(2) The ground floor dwelling units in buildings that consist of at least four condominium dwelling units or at least three rental apartment dwelling units if the buildings do not have an elevator. For purposes of this definition, dwelling units within a single structure separated by firewalls do not constitute separate buildings.

(b) "Multistory dwelling unit" means a condominium dwelling unit or rental apartment with finished living space on one floor and the floor immediately above or below it or, if applicable, the floors immediately above and below it.

Gov't Code § 12955.2. "Familial Status" Defined.

For purposes of this part, "familial status" means one or more individuals under 18 years of age who reside with a parent, another person with care and legal custody of that individual, a person who has been given care and custody of that individual by a state or local governmental agency that is responsible for the welfare of children, or the designee of that parent or other person with legal custody of any individual under 18 years of age by written consent of the parent or designated custodian. The protections afforded by this part against discrimination on the basis of familial status also apply to any individual who is pregnant, who is in the process of securing legal custody of any individual under 18 years of age, or who is in the process of being given care and custody of any individual under 18 years of age by a state or local governmental agency responsible for the welfare of children.

Gov't Code § 12955.3. "Disability" Defined.

For purposes of this part, "disability" includes, but is not limited to, any physical or mental disability as defined in Section 12926.

Gov't Code § 12955.4. Religious Preference Allowed.

Nothing in this part shall prohibit a religious organization, association or society, or any nonprofit institution or organization operated, supervised, or controlled by or in conjunction with a religious organization, association, or society, from limiting the sale, rental, or occupancy of dwellings that it owns or operates for other than a commercial purpose to persons of the same religion or from giving preference to those persons, unless membership in that religion is restricted on account of race, color, or national origin.

Gov't Code § 12955.5. Data Collection By Government Allowed.

Nothing in this part shall preclude the government from establishing programs to collect information relating to discriminatory housing practices.

Gov't Code § 12955.6. Fair Housing Amendments Acts of 1988 Is Minimum Standard.

Nothing in this part shall be construed to afford to the classes protected under this part, fewer rights or remedies than the federal Fair Housing Amendments Act of 1988 (P.L. 100-430) and its implementing regulations (24 C.F.R. 100.1 et seq.), or state law relating to fair employment and housing as it existed prior to the effective date of this section. Any state law that purports to require or permit any action that would be an unlawful practice under this part shall to that extent be invalid. This part may be construed to afford greater rights and remedies to an aggrieved person than those afforded by federal law and other state laws.

Gov't Code § 12955.7. Retaliation for Compliance Prohibited.

It shall be unlawful to coerce, intimidate, threaten, or interfere with any person in the exercise or enjoyment of, or on account of that person having exercised or enjoyed, or on account of that person having aided or encouraged any other person in the exercise or enjoyment of, any right granted or protected by Section 12955 or 12955.1.

Gov't Code § 12955.8. Elements of Violation of Article.

For purposes of this article, in connection with unlawful practices:

(a) Proof of an intentional violation of this article includes, but is not limited to, an act or failure to act that is otherwise covered by this part, that demonstrates an intent to discriminate in any manner in violation of this part. A person intends to discriminate if race, color, religion, sex, gender, gender identity, gender expression, sexual orientation, marital status, national origin, ancestry, familial status, source of income, disability, veteran or military status, or genetic information is a motivating factor in committing a discriminatory housing practice even though other factors may have also motivated the practice. An intent to discriminate may be established by direct or circumstantial evidence.

(b) Proof of a violation causing a discriminatory effect is shown if an act or failure to act that is otherwise covered by this part, and that has the effect, regardless of intent, of unlawfully discriminating on the basis of race, color, religion, sex, gender, gender identity, gender expression, sexual orientation, marital status, national origin, ancestry, familial status, source of income, disability, veteran or military status, or genetic information. A business establishment whose action or inaction has an unintended discriminatory effect shall not be considered to have committed an unlawful housing practice in violation of this part if the business establishment can establish that the action or inaction is necessary to the operation of the business and effectively carries out the significant business need it is alleged to serve. In cases that do not involve a business establishment, the person whose action or inaction has an unintended discriminatory effect shall not be considered to have committed an unlawful housing practice in violation of this part if the person can establish that the action or inaction is necessary to achieve an important purpose sufficiently compelling to override the discriminatory effect and effectively carries out the purpose it is alleged to serve.

(1) Any determination of a violation pursuant to this subdivision shall consider whether or not there are feasible alternatives that would equally well or better accomplish the purpose advanced with a less discriminatory effect.

(2) For purposes of this subdivision, the term "business establishment" shall have the same meaning as in Section 51 of the Civil Code.

Gov't Code § 12955.9. Qualifying Senior Housing Allowed to Discriminate Based on Familial Status.

(a) The provisions of this part relating to discrimination on the basis of familial status shall not apply to housing for older persons.

(b) As used in this section, "housing for older persons" means any of the following:

(1) Housing provided under any state or federal program that the Secretary of Housing and Urban Development determines is specifically designed and operated to assist elderly persons, as defined in the state or federal program.

(2) Housing that meets the standards for senior housing in Sections 51.2, 51.3, and 51.4 of the Civil Code, except to the extent that those standards violate the prohibition of familial status discrimination in the federal Fair Housing Amendments Act of 1988 (Public Law100-430) and implementing regulations.

(3) Mobilehome parks that meet the standards for "housing for older persons" as defined in the federal Fair Housing Amendments Act of 1988 and implementing regulations.

(c) For purposes of this section, the burden of proof shall be on the owner to prove that the housing qualifies as housing for older persons.

Gov't Code § 12956. Relevant Records Maintained During Legal Action.

Upon notice that a verified complaint against it has been filed under this part, any owner of housing accommodations shall maintain and preserve any and all rental records or any other written materials relevant to the complaint, until the complaint is fully and finally disposed of and all appeals or related proceedings terminated.

Gov't Code § 12956.1. Amending Documents to Remove Discriminatory Language.

(a) As used in this section.

(1) "Association," "governing documents," and "declaration" have the same meanings as set forth in Sections 4080, 4135, and 4150 of the Civil Code.

(2) "Redaction" means the process of rerecording of a document that originally contained unlawful restrictive language, and when presented to the county recorder for rerecording, no longer contains the unlawful language or the unlawful language is masked so that it is not readable or visible.

(3) "Redacted" means the result of the rerecording of a document that originally contained unlawful restrictive language, and when presented to the county recorder for rerecording, no longer contains the unlawful language or the unlawful language is masked so that it is not readable or visible.

(b) (1) A county recorder, title company, escrow company, real estate broker, real estate agent, or association that provides a copy of a declaration, governing document, or deed to any person shall place a cover page or stamp on the first page of the previously recorded document or documents stating, in at least 14-point boldface type, the following:

"If this document contains any restriction based on age, race, color, religion, sex, gender, gender identity, gender expression, sexual orientation, familial status, marital status, disability, veteran or military status, genetic information, national origin, source of income as defined in subdivision (p) of Section 12955, or ancestry, that restriction violates state and federal fair housing laws and is void, and may be removed pursuant to Section 12956.2 of the Government Code by submitting a "Restrictive Covenant Modification" form, together with a copy of the attached document with the unlawful provision redacted to the county recorder's office. The "Restrictive Covenant Modification" form can be obtained from the county recorder's office and may be available on its internet website. The form may also be available from the party that provided you with this document. Lawful restrictions under state and federal law on the age of occupants in senior housing or housing for older persons shall not be construed as restrictions based on familial status."

(2) The requirements set forth in paragraph (1) shall not apply to documents being submitted for recordation to a county recorder.

(3) A title company, escrow company, or association that delivers a copy of a declaration, governing document, or deed directly to a person who holds an ownership interest of record in property shall also provide a Restrictive Covenant Modification form with procedural information for appropriate processing along with the document.

(c) Any person who records a document for the express purpose of adding a racially restrictive covenant is guilty of a misdemeanor. The county recorder shall not incur any liability for recording the document. Notwithstanding any other provision of law, a prosecution for a violation of this subdivision shall commence within three years after the discovery of the recording of the document.

Gov't Code § 12956.2. Recording a Restrictive Covenant Modification.

(a) (1) A person who holds or is acquiring an ownership interest of record in property that the person believes is the subject of an unlawfully restrictive covenant in violation of subdivision (l) of Section 12955 may record a document titled Restrictive Covenant Modification. A title company, escrow company, county recorder, real estate broker, real estate agent, or other person also may record the modification document provided for in this section. The county recorder may waive the fee prescribed for recording and indexing instruments pursuant to Section 27361 in the case of a restrictive covenant modification document. The modification document shall include a complete copy of the original document containing the unlawfully restrictive language with the unlawfully restrictive covenant language redacted.

(2) Beginning July 1, 2022, if a title company, escrow company, real estate broker, or real estate agent has actual knowledge that a declaration, governing document, or deed that is being directly delivered to a person who holds or is acquiring an ownership interest in property includes a possible unlawfully restrictive covenant, they shall notify the person who holds or is acquiring the ownership interest in the property of the existence of that covenant and their ability to have it removed through the restrictive covenant modification process. There shall be no presumption that a party providing a document has read the document or has actual knowledge of its content.

(3) Beginning July 1, 2022, if requested before the close of escrow, the title company or escrow company directly involved in the pending transaction shall assist in the preparation of a Restrictive Covenant Modification pursuant to this section, but the title company or escrow company shall have no liability associated with the recordation of a Restrictive Covenant Modification that contains modifications not authorized by this section on behalf of the requester.

(b) (1) Before recording the Restrictive Covenant Modification document, the county recorder shall submit the modification document and the original document to the county counsel who shall determine whether the language in the original document contains an unlawful restriction based on age, race, color, religion, sex, gender, gender identity, gender expression, sexual orientation, familial status, marital status, disability, veteran or military status, national origin, source of income as defined in subdivision (p) of Section 12955, or ancestry. The county counsel shall return the documents and inform the county recorder of its determination within a period of time specified in paragraph (2). The county recorder shall refuse to record the modification document if the county counsel or their designee finds that the original document does not contain an unlawful restriction as specified in this subdivision or the modification document contains modifications not authorized by this section.

(2) For documents recorded pursuant to subdivision (a), the period of time shall be a reasonable period of time, not to exceed three months, from the date the request for recordation is made, unless extraordinary circumstances apply.

(c) If a person requests to record a modification document, that person shall provide a return address in order for the county recorder to notify this person of the action taken by the county counsel on the respective property. The notice required pursuant to this subdivision may be made on a postcard mailed by first-class mail.

(d) The modification document shall be indexed in the same manner as the original document being modified. It shall contain a recording reference to the original document in the form of a book and page or instrument number, and date of the recording.

(e) Subject to covenants, conditions, and restrictions that were recorded after the recording of the original document that contains the unlawfully restrictive language and subject to covenants, conditions, and restrictions that will be recorded after the Restrictive Covenant Modification, the restrictions in the Restrictive Covenant Modification, once recorded, are the only restrictions having effect on the property. The effective date of the terms and conditions of the modification document shall be the same as the effective date of the original document.

(f) A Restrictive Covenant Modification form shall be prepared and accepted for submission and recordation in all counties in substantially the following form:

RESTRICTIVE COVENANT MODIFICATION:

The following reference document contains a restriction based on age, race, color, religion, sex, gender, gender identity, gender expression, sexual orientation, familial status, marital status, disability, veteran or military status, genetic information, national origin, source of income as defined in Section 12955 of the Government Code, or ancestry, that violates state and federal fair housing laws and is void. Pursuant to Section 12956.2 of the Government Code, this document is being recorded solely for the purpose of redacting and eliminating that restrictive covenant as shown on page(s) ___ of the document recorded on ____________(date) in book ________ and page _____ or instrument number _________ of the official records of the County of __________________, State of California.

Attached hereto is a true, correct and complete copy of the document referenced above, with the unlawful restrictive covenant redacted.

This modification document shall be indexed in the same manner as the original document being modified, pursuant to subdivision (d) of Section 12956 of the Government Code.

The effective date of the terms and conditions of the modification document shall be the same as the effective date of the original document.

(Signature of submitting party)

_______ County Counsel, or their designee, pursuant to paragraph (1) of subdivision (b) of Section 12956.2 of the Government Code, hereby states that it has determined that the original document referenced above contains an unlawful restriction and this modification may be recorded.

Or

________County Counsel, or their designee, pursuant to paragraph (1) of subdivision (b) of Section 12956.2 of the Government Code, finds that the original document does not contain an unlawful restriction, or the modification document contains modifications not authorized, and this modification may not be recorded.

County Counsel

By:

Date:

(g) The county recorder shall make available to the public Restrictive Covenant Modification forms onsite in an appropriately designated area, or online on the county recorder's internet website, either of which shall be deemed to satisfy the requirement of paragraphs (1) and (2) of subdivision (b) of Section 12956.1 to provide a Restrictive Covenant Modification form if the procedural information for appropriate processing is attached to the form. Those forms shall permit multiple submissions on behalf of different homes and for processing homes in batches with respect to a modification document that affects multiple homes or lots. The forms shall also permit the submission of a restrictive covenant modification form for a homeowners' association or a common interest development to modify covenants, conditions, and restrictions that will correct unlawfully restrictive covenants for multiple dwellings within a subdivision.

(h) If a person causes to be recorded a modified document pursuant to this section that contains modifications not authorized by this section, the county recorder shall not incur liability for recording the document. The liability that may result from the unauthorized recordation is the sole responsibility of the person who caused the modified recordation as provided in subdivision (a).

(i) (1) A restrictive covenant modification that is approved by county counsel or their designee and recorded pursuant to this section removes the illegal covenant from all property affected by the original covenant regardless of who submits the modification.

(2) This section does not affect the obligations of the governing board of a common interest development as defined in Section 4100 or 6534 of the Civil Code if the board of directors of that common interest development is subject to the requirements of subdivision (b) of Section 4225 or of subdivision (b) of Section 6606 of the Civil Code.

(j) For purposes of this section, "redaction" and "redacted" mean the same as defined in Section 12956.1

Gov't Code § 12956.3. Removal of Discriminatory Restrictions.

(a) The county recorder of each county shall establish a restrictive covenant program to assist in the redaction of unlawfully restrictive covenants in violation of subdivision (l) of Section 12955.

(b) Each county recorder as part of their restrictive covenant program shall undertake all of the following:

(1) By July 1, 2022, prepare an implementation plan, which shall be publicly available and may be posted on the internet website of the county recorder, that does all of the following:

(A) Outlines how the county recorder will carry out the identification and redaction of unlawfully restrictive covenants.

(B) Provides timelines for when elements of their plan will be accomplished.

(C) Provides how the county recorder's office plans to track and maintain a record of homes with unlawfully restrictive covenants once they have been identified.

(2) Identify unlawfully restrictive covenants in violation of subdivision (l) of Section 12955 in the records of the county recorder's office.

(3) Beginning January 1, 2022, index a restrictive covenant modification document under the title of "Restrictive Covenant Modification" and shall make that index available in their office for the public, and if the county recorder has an index online, include the title in the online index.

(4) Redact unlawfully restrictive covenants in the records of the respective county recorder's office, subject to county counsel approval, by rerecording a copy of the original document with the unlawfully restrictive language redacted so that it is not readable or visible, using a Restrictive Covenant Modification Form substantially similar to the form set forth in subdivision (f) of Section 12956.2.

(c) The county recorder shall retain each nonredacted record for future reference and public request needs.

(d) (1) The County Recorders Association of California shall submit status reports on the progress of each county's restrictive covenant program established pursuant to this section by January 1, 2023, and January 1, 2025, to the Legislature. The report may describe the number of documents identified for redaction, and the implementation timelines for actions taken by each county recorder's office.

(2) The County Recorders Association of California shall convene a best practices meeting to share concepts on implementation of this section no later than December 31, 2022, with all California county recorder offices and meet annually thereafter until December 31, 2027.

(e) Nothing in this section shall be construed to restrict, delay, or modify access to any official record, or modify any existing agreements regarding access to any official record.

(f) For purposes of this section "redaction" and "redacted" mean the same as defined in Section 12956.1.

(g) The failure of a county recorder to identify or redact illegal restrictive covenants, as required by this section, or the county recorder's identification or redaction of any restrictive covenants that are later determined not to be illegal, shall not result in any liability against the county recorder or the county.

Gov't Code § 12987. Penalty Provisions for Acts of Discrimination - Repealed

(a) If the commission, after hearing, finds that a respondent has engaged in any unlawful practice as defined in this part, the commission shall state its findings of fact and shall issue and cause to be served on the respondent an order requiring the respondent to cease and desist from the practice and to take those actions, as, in the judgment of the commission, will effectuate the purpose of this part, including, but not limited to, any of the following:

(1) The sale or rental of housing accommodation if it is still available, or the sale or rental of a like housing accommodation, if one is available, or the provision of financial assistance, terms, conditions, or privileges previously denied in violation of subdivision (f) of Section 12955 in the purchase, organization, or construction of the housing accommodation, if available.

(2) Affirmative or prospective relief, including injunctive or other equitable relief.

(3) The payment to the complainant of a civil penalty against any named respondent, not to exceed sixteen thousand dollars ($16,000), unless, in a separate accusation, the respondent has been adjudged to have, with intent, committed a prior violation of Section 12955. If the respondent has, in a separate accusation, been adjudged to have committee a prior violation of Section 12955 within the five years preceding the filing of the complaint, the amount of the civil penalty may exceed sixteen thousand dollars ($16,000), but may not exceed thirty-seven thousand five hundred dollars ($37,500). If the respondent, in separate accusations, has been adjudged to have, with intent, violated Section 12955 two or more times within the seven-year period preceding the filing of the complaint, the civil penalty may exceed thirty-seven thousand five hundred dollars ($37,500), but may not exceed sixty-five thousand dollars ($65,000). All civil penalties awarded under this provision shall be collected by the department. The commission may

award the prevailing party, other than the state, reasonable attorney's fees and costs against any party other than the state, including expert witness fees.

(4) The payment of actual damages to the complainant.

(b) In determining whether to assess a civil penalty pursuant to this section, the commission shall find that the respondent has been guilty of oppression, fraud, or malice, expressed or implied, as required by Section 3294 of the Civil Code. In determining the amount of a civil penalty, the commission shall consider Section 12955.6 and relevant evidence of, including, but not limited to, the following:

(1) Willful, intentional, or purposeful conduct.

(2) Refusal to prevent or eliminate discrimination.

(3) Conscious disregard for fair housing rights.

(4) Commission of unlawful conduct.

(5) Intimidation or harassment.

(6) Conduct without just cause or excuse.

(7) Multiple violations of the Fair Employment and Housing Act.

(c) If the commission finds that the respondent has engaged in an unlawful practice under this part, and the respondent is licensed or granted a privilege by an agency of the state or the federal government to do business, provide a service, or conduct activities, and the unlawful practice is determined to have occurred in connection with the exercise of that license or privilege, the commission shall provide the licensing or privilege granting agency with a copy of its decision or order.

(d) If the commission finds that the respondent has engaged in an unlawful practice under this part and is liable for actual damages or a civil penalty, any amount due to the respondent by a state agency may be offset to satisfy the commission's final order or decision.

(e) No remedy shall be available to the aggrieved person unless the aggrieved person waives any and all rights or claims under Section 52 of the Civil Code prior to receiving a remedy, and signs a written waiver to that effect.

(f) The commission may require a report of the manner of compliance.

(g) If the commission finds that a respondent has not engaged in any practice which constitutes a violation of this part, the commission shall state its findings of fact and shall issue and cause to be served on the complainant an order dismissing the accusation as to that respondent.

(h) Any order issued by the commission shall have printed on its face references to the provisions of the Administrative Procedure Act which prescribe the rights of appeal of any party to the proceeding to whose position the order is adverse.

7

FILING CIVIL ACTIONS

STATUTES OF LIMITATION

Civ. Proc. § 336. Five Year Statute of Limitation on Violation of Restriction on Use of Real Property.

Within five years:

(a) An action for mesne profits of real property.

(b) An action for violation of a restriction, as defined in Section 784 of the Civil Code. The period prescribed in this subdivision runs from the time the person seeking to enforce the restriction discovered or, through the exercise of reasonable diligence, should have discovered the violation. A failure to commence an action for violation of a restriction within the period prescribed in this subdivision does not waive the right to commence an action for any other violation of the restriction and does not, in itself, create an implication that the restriction is abandoned, obsolete, or otherwise unenforceable. This subdivision shall not bar commencement of an action for violation of a restriction before January 1, 2001, and until January 1, 2001, any other applicable statutory or common law limitation shall continue to apply to that action.

Civ. Proc. § 337. Four Year Statute of Limitation on Written Contract and Accounts.

Within four years:

(a) An action upon any contract, obligation or liability founded upon an instrument in writing, except as provided in Section 336a; provided, that the time within which any action for a money judgment for the balance due upon an obligation for the payment of which a deed of trust or mortgage with power of sale upon real property or any interest therein was given as security, following the exercise of the power of sale in such deed of trust or mortgage, may be brought shall not extend beyond three months after the time of sale under such deed of trust or mortgage.

(b) An action to recover (1) upon a book account whether consisting of one or more entries; (2) upon an account stated based upon an account in writing, but the acknowledgment of the account stated need not be in writing; (3) a balance due upon a mutual, open and current account, the items of which are in writing; provided, however, that if an account stated is based upon an account of one item, the time shall begin to run from the date of the item, and if an account stated is based upon an account of more than one item, the time shall begin to run from the date of the last item.

(c) An action based upon the rescission of a contract in writing. The time begins to run from the date upon which the facts that entitle the aggrieved party to rescind occurred. Where the ground for rescission is fraud or mistake, the time shall not begin to run until the discovery by the aggrieved party of the facts constituting the fraud or mistake. Where the ground for rescission is misrepresentation under Section 359 of the Insurance Code, the time shall not begin to run until the representation becomes false.

(d) When the period in which an action must be commenced under this section has run, a person shall not bring suit or initiate anarbitration or other legal proceeding to collect the debt. The period in which an action may be commenced under this section shall only be extended pursuant to Section 360.

Civ. Proc. § 337.1. Four Year Statute of Limitation on Injury or Death from Deficient Planning or Construction.

(a) Except as otherwise provided in this section, no action shall be brought to recover damages from any person performing or furnishing the design, specifications, surveying, planning, supervision or observation of construction or construction of an improvement to real property more than four years after the substantial completion of such improvement for any of the following:

(1) Any patent deficiency in the design, specifications, surveying, planning, supervision or observation of construction or construction of an improvement to, or survey of, real property;

(2) Injury to property, real or personal, arising out of any such patent deficiency; or

(3) Injury to the person or for wrongful death arising out of any such patent deficiency.

(b) If by reason of such patent deficiency, an injury to property or the person or an injury causing wrongful death occurs during the fourth year after such substantial completion, an action in tort to recover damages for such an injury or wrongful death may be brought within one year after the date on which such injury occurred, irrespective of the date of death, but in no event may such an action be brought more than five years after the substantial completion of construction of such improvement.

(c) Nothing in this section shall be construed as extending the period prescribed by the laws of this state for the bringing of any action.

(d) The limitation prescribed by this section shall not be asserted by way of defense by any person in actual possession or the control, as owner, tenant or otherwise, of such an improvement at the time any deficiency in such an improvement constitutes the proximate cause of the injury or death for which it is proposed to bring an action.

(e) As used in this section, "patent deficiency" means a deficiency which is apparent by reasonable inspection.

(f) Subdivisions (a) and (b) shall not apply to any owner-occupied single-unit residence.

Civ. Proc. § 337.15. Ten Year Statute of Limitation on Actions to Recover Damages From Construction Defects.

(a) No action may be brought to recover damages from any person, or the surety of a person, who develops real property or performs or furnishes the design, specifications, surveying, planning, supervision, testing, or observation of construction or construction of an improvement to real property more than 10 years after the substantial completion of the development or improvement for any of the following:

(1) Any latent deficiency in the design, specification, surveying, planning, supervision, or observation of construction or construction of an improvement to, or survey of, real property.

(2) Injury to property, real or personal, arising out of any such latent deficiency.

(b) As used in this section, "latent deficiency" means a deficiency which is not apparent by reasonable inspection.

(c) As used in this section, "action" includes an action for indemnity brought against a person arising out of that person's performance or furnishing of services or materials referred to in this section, except that a cross-complaint for indemnity may be filed pursuant to subdivision (b) of Section 428.10 in an action which has been brought within the time period set forth in subdivision (a) of this section.

(d) Nothing in this section shall be construed as extending the period prescribed by the laws of this state for bringing any action.

(e) The limitation prescribed by this section shall not be asserted by way of defense by any person in actual possession or the control, as owner, tenant or otherwise, of such an improvement, at the time any deficiency in the improvement constitutes the proximate cause for which it is proposed to bring an action.

(f) This section shall not apply to actions based on willful misconduct or fraudulent concealment.

(g) The 10-year period specified in subdivision (a) shall commence upon substantial completion of the improvement, but not later than the date of one of the following, whichever first occurs:

(1) The date of final inspection by the applicable public agency.

(2) The date of recordation of a valid notice of completion.

(3) The date of use or occupation of the improvement.

(4) One year after termination or cessation of work on the improvement.

The date of substantial completion shall relate specifically to the performance or furnishing design, specifications, surveying, planning, supervision, testing, observation of construction or construction services by each profession or trade rendering services to the improvement.

Civ. Proc. § 338. Three Year Statute of Limitation on Statutory Suit, Trespass or Injury to Real Property, Fraud and Mistake, Official Bonds, Slander of Title, False Advertising, Water Quality Control or Physical Damage to Private Property.

Within three years:

(a) An action upon a liability created by statute, other than a penalty or forfeiture.

(b) An action for trespass upon or injury to real property.

(c) (1) An action for taking, detaining, or injuring goods or chattels, including an action for the specific recovery of personal property.

(2) The cause of action in the case of theft, as described in Section 484 of the Penal Code, of any article of historical, interpretative, scientific, or artistic significance is not deemed to have accrued until the discovery of the whereabouts of the article by the aggrieved party, the aggrieved party's agent, or the law enforcement agency that originally investigated the theft.

(3) (A) Notwithstanding paragraphs (1) and (2), an action for the specific recovery of a work of fine art brought against a museum, gallery, auctioneer, or dealer, in the case of an unlawful taking or theft, as described in Section 484 of the Penal Code, of a work of fine art, including a taking or theft by means of fraud or duress, shall be commenced within six years of the actual discovery by the claimant or the claimant's agent, of both of the following:

(i) The identity and the whereabouts of the work of fine art. In the case where there is a possibility of misidentification of the object of fine art in question, the identity can be satisfied by the identification of facts sufficient to determine that the work of fine art is likely to be the work of fine art that was unlawfully taken or stolen.

(ii) Information or facts that are sufficient to indicate that the claimant has a claim for a possessory interest in the work of fine art that was unlawfully taken or stolen.

(B) The provisions of this paragraph shall apply to all pending and future actions commenced on or before December 31, 2017, including any actions dismissed based on the expiration of statutes of limitations in effect prior to the date of enactment of this statute if the judgment in that action is not yet final or if the time for filing an appeal from a decision on that action has not expired, provided that the action concerns a work of fine art that was taken within 100 years prior to the date of enactment of this statute.

(C) For purposes of this paragraph:

(i) "Actual discovery," notwithstanding Section 19 of the Civil Code, does not include any constructive knowledge imputed by law.

(ii) "Auctioneer" means any individual who is engaged in, or who by advertising or otherwise holds the individual out as being available to engage in, the calling for, the recognition of, and the acceptance of, offers for the purchase of goods at an auction as defined in subdivision (b) of Section 1812.601 of the Civil Code.

(iii) "Dealer" means a person who holds a valid seller's permit and who is actively and principally engaged in, or conducting the business of, selling works of fine art.

(iv) "Duress" means a threat of force, violence, danger, or retribution against an owner of the work of fine art in question, or the owner's family member, sufficient to coerce a reasonable person of ordinary susceptibilities to perform an act that otherwise would not have been performed or to acquiesce to an act to which the person would otherwise not have acquiesced.

(v) "Fine art" has the same meaning as defined in paragraph (1) of subdivision (d) of Section 982 of the Civil Code.

(vi) "Museum or gallery" shall include any public or private organization or foundation operating as a museum or gallery.

(4) Section 361 shall not apply to an action brought pursuant to paragraph (3).

(5) A party in an action to which paragraph (3) applies may raise all equitable and legal affirmative defenses and doctrines, including, without limitation, laches and unclean hands.

(d) An action for relief on the ground of fraud or mistake. The cause of action in that case is not to be deemed to have accrued until the discovery, by the aggrieved party, of the facts constituting the fraud or mistake.

(e) An action upon a bond of a public official except any cause of action based on fraud or embezzlement is not to be deemed to have accrued until the discovery, by the aggrieved party or the aggrieved party's agent, of the facts constituting the cause of action upon the bond.

(f) (1) An action against a notary public on the notary public's bond or in the notary public's official capacity except that any cause of action based on malfeasance or misfeasance is not deemed to have accrued until discovery, by the aggrieved party or the aggrieved party's agent, of the facts, constituting the cause of action

(2) Notwithstanding paragraph (1), an action based on malfeasance or misfeasance shall be commenced within one year from discovery, by the aggrieved party or the aggrieved party's agent, of the facts constituting the cause of action or within three years from the performance of the notarial act giving rise to the action, whichever is later.

(3) Notwithstanding paragraph (1), an action against a notary public on the notary public's bond or in the notary public's official capacity shall be commenced within six years.

(g) An action for slander of title to real property.

(h) An action commenced under Section 17536 of the Business and Professions Code. The cause of action in that case shall not be deemed to have accrued until the discovery by the aggrieved party, the Attorney General, the district attorney, the county counsel, the city prosecutor, or the city attorney of the facts constituting grounds for commencing such an action.

(i) An action commenced under the Porter-Cologne Water Quality Control Act (Division 7 (commencing with Section 13000) of the Water Code). The cause of action in that case shall not be deemed to have accrued until the discovery by the State Water Resources Control Board or a regional water quality control board of the facts constituting grounds for commencing actions under their jurisdiction.

(j) An action to recover for physical damage to private property under Section 19 of Article I of the California Constitution.

(k) An action commenced under Division 26 (commencing with Section 39000) of the Health and Safety Code. These causes of action shall not be deemed to have accrued until the discovery by the State Air Resources Board or by a district, as defined in Section 39025 of the Health and Safety Code, of the facts constituting grounds for commencing the action under its jurisdiction.

(l) An action commenced under Section 1603.1, 1615, or 5650.1 of the Fish and Game Code. These causes of action shall not be deemed to have accrued until discovery by the agency bringing the action of the facts constituting the grounds for commencing the action.

(m) An action challenging the validity of the levy upon a parcel of a special tax levied by a local agency on a per parcel basis.

(n) An action commencing under Section 51.7 of the Civil Code.

(o) An action commenced under Section 4601.1 of the Public Resources Code, if the underlying violation is of Section 4571, 4581, or 4621 of the Public Resources Code, or of Section 1103.1 of Title 14 of the California Code of Regulations, and the underlying violation is related to the conversion of timberland to nonforestry-related agricultural uses. These causes of action shall not be deemed to have accrued until discovery by the Department of Forestry and Fire Protection.

(p) An action for civil penalties commenced under Section 26038 of the Business and Professions Code.

Civ. Proc. § 339. Two Year Statute of Limitation on Oral Contracts, Abstract or Guaranty of Title, Title Insurance or Rescission.

Within two years:

1. An action upon a contract, obligation or liability not founded upon an instrument of writing, except as provided in Section 2725 of the Commercial Code or subdivision 2 of Section 337 of this code; or an action founded upon a contract, obligation or liability, evidenced by a certificate, or abstract or guaranty of title of real property, or by a policy of title insurance; provided, that the cause of action upon a contract, obligation or liability evidenced by a certificate, or abstract or guaranty of title of real property or policy of title insurance shall not be deemed to have accrued until the discovery of the loss or damage suffered by the aggrieved party thereunder.

2. An action against a sheriff or coroner upon a liability incurred by the doing of an act in an official capacity and in virtue of office, or by the omission of an official duty including the nonpayment of money collected in the enforcement of a judgment.

3. An action based upon the rescission of a contract not in writing. The time begins to run from the date upon which the facts that entitle the aggrieved party to rescind occurred. Where the ground for rescission is fraud or mistake, the time does not begin to run until the discovery by the aggrieved party of the facts constituting the fraud or mistake.

Civ. Proc. § 339.5. Lease Not In Writing; Period for Action after Breach.

Where a lease of real property is not in writing, no action shall be brought under Section 1951.2 of the Civil Code more than two years after the breach of the lease and abandonment of the property, or more than two years after the termination of the right of the lessee to possession of the property, whichever is the earlier time.

SERVICE OF SUMMONS

Civ. Proc. § 415.10. Personal Delivery of Summons.

A summons may be served by personal delivery of a copy of the summons and of the complaint to the person to be served. Service of a summons in this manner is deemed complete at the time of such delivery.

The date upon which personal delivery is made shall be entered on or affixed to the face of the copy of the summons at the time of its delivery. However, service of a summons without such date shall be valid and effective.

Civ. Proc. § 415.20. Service of Summons in Lieu of Personal Delivery.

(a) In lieu of personal delivery of a copy of the summons and complaint to the person to be served as specified in Section 416.10, 416.20, 416.30, 416.40, or 416.50, a summons may be served by leaving a copy of the summons and complaint during usual office hours in his or her office or, if no physical address is known, at his or her usual mailing address, other than a United States Postal Service post office box, with the person who is apparently in charge thereof, and by thereafter mailing a copy of the summons and complaint by first-class mail, postage prepaid to the person to be served at the place where a copy of the summons and complaint were left. When service is effected by leaving a copy of the summons and complaint at a mailing address, it shall be left with a person at least 18 years of age, who shall be informed of the contents thereof. Service of a summons in this manner is deemed complete on the 10th day after the mailing.

(b) If a copy of the summons and complaint cannot with reasonable diligence be personally delivered to the person to be served, as specified in Section 416.60, 416.70, 416.80, or 416.90, a summons may be served by leaving a copy of the summons and complaint at the person's dwelling house, usual place of abode, usual place of business, or usual mailing address other than a United States Postal Service post office box, in the presence of a competent member of the household or a person apparently in charge of his or her office, place of business, or usual mailing address other than a United States Postal Service post office box, at least 18 years of age, who shall be informed of the contents thereof, and by thereafter mailing a copy of the summons and of the complaint by first-class mail, postage prepaid to the person to be served at the place where a copy of the summons and complaint were left. Service of a summons in this manner is deemed complete on the 10th day after the mailing.

(c) Notwithstanding subdivision (b), if the only address reasonably known for the person to be served is a private mailbox obtained through a commercial mail receiving agency, service of process may be effected on the first delivery attempt by leaving a copy of the summons and complaint with the commercial mail receiving agency in the manner described in subdivision (d) of Section 17538.5 of the Business and Professions Code.

Civ. Proc. § 415.21. Access to Gated Community for Service of Process.

(a) Notwithstanding any other provision of law any person shall be granted access to a gated community or a covererd multifamily dwelling for a reasonable period of time for the purpose of performing lawful service of process or service of a subpoena upon displaying a current driver's license or other identification, and one of the following:

(1) A badge or other confirmation that the individual is acting in the individual's capacity as a representative of a county sheriff or marshal.

(2) Evidence of current registration as a process server pursuant to Chapter 16 (commencing with Section 22350) of Division 8 of the Business and Professions Code or of licensure as a private investigator pursuant to Chapter 11.3 (commencing with Section 7512) of Division 3 of the Business and Professions Code.

(b) This section shall only apply to a gated community or a covered multifamily dwelling that is staffed at the time service of process is attempted by a guard or other security personnel assigned to control access to the community or dwelling.

(c) For purposes of this section, "covered multifamily dwelling" means either of the following:

(1) An apartment building, including a timeshare apartment building not considered a place of public accommodation or transient lodging, with three or more dwelling units.

(2) A condominium, including a timeshare condominium not considered a place of public accommodation or transient lodging, with four or more dwelling units.

CLAIMS AGAINST VOLUNTEER DIRECTOR

Civ. Proc. § 425.15. Cause of Action Against Volunteer Director or Officer of Nonprofit Corporation.

(a) No cause of action against a person serving without compensation as a director or officer of a nonprofit corporation described in this section, on account of any negligent act or omission by that person within the scope of that person's duties as a director acting in the capacity of a board member, or as an officer acting in the capacity of, and within the scope of the duties of, an officer, shall be included in a complaint or other pleading unless the court enters an order allowing the pleading that includes that claim to be filed after the court determines that the party seeking to file the pleading has established evidence that substantiates the claim. The court may allow the filing of a pleading that includes that claim following the filing of a verified petition therefor accompanied by the proposed pleading and supporting affidavits stating the facts upon which the liability is based. The court shall order service of the petition upon the party against whom the action is proposed to be filed and permit that party to submit opposing affidavits prior to making its determination. The filing of the petition, proposed pleading, and accompanying affidavits shall toll the running of any applicable statute of limitations until the final determination of the matter, which ruling, if favorable to the petitioning party, shall permit the proposed pleading to be filed.

(b) Nothing in this section shall affect the right of the plaintiff to discover evidence on the issue of damages.

(c) Nothing in this section shall be construed to affect any action against a nonprofit corporation for any negligent action or omission of a volunteer director or officer occurring within the scope of the person's duties.

(d) For the purposes of this section, "compensation" means remuneration whether by way of salary, fee, or other consideration for services rendered. However, the payment of per diem, mileage, or other reimbursement expenses to a director or officer shall not constitute compensation.

(e) (1) This section applies only to officers and directors of nonprofit corporations that are subject to Part 2 (commencing with Section 5110), Part 3 (commencing with Section 7110), or Part 4 (commencing with Section 9110) of Division 2 of Title 1 of the Corporations Code that are organized to provide charitable, educational, scientific, social, or other forms of public service and that are exempt from federal income taxation under Section 501(c)(1), except any credit union, or Section 501(c)(4), 501(c)(5), 501(c)(7), or 501(c)(19) of the Internal Revenue Code.

(2) This section does not apply to any corporation that unlawfully restricts membership, services, or benefits conferred on the basis of political affiliation, age, or any characteristic listed or defined in subdivision (b) or (e) of Section 51 of the Civil Code.

Civ. Proc. § 425.16. Motion to Strike Pursuant to Free Speech Clause Under California and U.S. Constitutions.

(a) The Legislature finds and declares that there has been a disturbing increase in lawsuits brought primarily to chill the valid exercise of the constitutional rights of freedom of speech and petition for the redress of grievances. The Legislature finds and declares that it is in the public interest to encourage continued participation in matters of public significance, and that this participation should not be chilled through abuse of the judicial process. To this end, this section shall be construed broadly.

(b) (1) A cause of action against a person arising from any act of that person in furtherance of the person's right of petition or free speech under the United States or California Constitution in connection with a public issue shall be subject to a special motion to strike, unless the court determines that the plaintiff has established that there is a probability that the plaintiff will prevail on the claim.

(2) In making its determination, the court shall consider the pleadings, and supporting and opposing affidavits stating the facts upon which the liability or defense is based.

(3) If the court determines that the plaintiff has established a probability that the plaintiff will prevail on the claim, neither that determination nor the fact of that determination shall be admissible in evidence at any later stage of the case, or in any subsequent action, and no burden of proof or degree of proof otherwise applicable shall be affected by that determination in any later stage of the case or in any subsequent proceeding.

(c) (1) Except as provided in paragraph (2), in any action subject to subdivision (b), a prevailing defendant on a special motion to strike shall be entitled to recover that defendant's attorney's fees and costs. If the court finds that a special motion to strike is frivolous or is solely intended to cause unnecessary delay, the court shall award costs and reasonable attorney's fees to a plaintiff prevailing on the motion, pursuant to Section 128.5.

(2) A defendant who prevails on a special motion to strike in an action subject to paragraph (1) shall not be entitled to attorney's fees and costs if that cause of action is brought pursuant to Section 6259, 11130, 11130.3, 54960, or 54960.1 of the Government Code, or pursuant to Chapter 2 (commencing with Section 7923.100) of Part 4 of Division 10 of Title 1 of the Government Code. Nothing in this paragraph shall be construed to prevent a prevailing defendant from recovering attorney's fees and costs pursuant to Section 7923.115, 11130.5, or 54960.5 of the Government Code.

(d) This section shall not apply to any enforcement action brought in the name of the people of the State of California by the Attorney General, district attorney, or city attorney, acting as a public prosecutor.

(e) As used in this section, "act in furtherance of a person's right of petition or free speech under the United States or California Constitution in connection with a public issue" includes:

(1) any written or oral statement or writing made before a legislative, executive, or judicial proceeding, or any other official proceeding authorized by law;

(2) any written or oral statement or writing made in connection with an issue under consideration or review by a legislative, executive, or judicial body, or any other official proceeding authorized by law;

(3) any written or oral statement or writing made in a place open to the public or a public forum in connection with an issue of public interest; or

(4) any other conduct in furtherance of the exercise of the constitutional right of petition or the constitutional right of free speech in connection with a public issue or an issue of public interest.

(f) The special motion may be filed within 60 days of the service of the complaint or, in the court's discretion, at any later time upon terms it deems proper. The motion shall be scheduled by the clerk of the court for a hearing not more than 30 days after the service of the motion unless the docket conditions of the court require a later hearing.

(g) All discovery proceedings in the action shall be stayed upon the filing of a notice of motion made pursuant to this section. The stay of discovery shall remain in effect until notice of entry of the order ruling on the motion. The court, on noticed motion and for good cause shown, may order that specified discovery be conducted notwithstanding this subdivision.

(h) For purposes of this section, "complaint" includes "cross-complaint" and "petition," "plaintiff" includes "cross-complainant" and "petitioner," and "defendant" includes "cross-defendant" and "respondent."

(i) An order granting or denying a special motion to strike shall be appealable under Section 904.1.

(j) (1) Any party who files a special motion to strike pursuant to this section, and any party who files an opposition to a special motion to strike, shall, promptly upon so filing, transmit to the Judicial Council, by email or facsimile, a copy of the endorsed, filed caption page of the motion or opposition, a copy of any related notice of appeal or petition for a writ, and a conformed copy of any order issued pursuant to this section, including any order granting or denying a special motion to strike, discovery, or fees.

(2) The Judicial Council shall maintain a public record of information transmitted pursuant to this subdivision for at least three years, and may store the information on microfilm or other appropriate electronic media.

SMALL CLAIMS COURT

Civ. Proc. § 116.220. Jurisdiction.

(a) The small claims court has jurisdiction in the following actions:

(1) Except as provided in subdivisions (c), (e), and (f), for recovery of money, if the amount of the demand does not exceed five thousand dollars ($5,000).

(2) Except as provided in subdivisions (c), (e), and (f), to enforce payment of delinquent unsecured personal property taxes in an amount not to exceed five thousand dollars ($5,000), if the legality of the tax is not contested by the defendant.

(3) To issue the writ of possession authorized by Sections 1861.5 and 1861.10 of the Civil Code if the amount of the demand does not exceed five thousand dollars ($5,000).

(4) To confirm, correct, or vacate a fee arbitration award not exceeding five thousand dollars ($5,000) between an attorney and client that is binding or has become binding, or to conduct a hearing de novo between an attorney and client after nonbinding arbitration of a fee dispute involving no more than five thousand dollars ($5,000) in

controversy, pursuant to Article 13 (commencing with Section 6200) of Chapter 4 of Division 3 of the Business and Professions Code.

(5) or an injunction or other equitable relief only when a statute expressly authorizes a small claims court to award that relief.

(b) In any action seeking relief authorized by paragraphs (1) to (4), inclusive, of subdivision (a), the court may grant equitable relief in the form of rescission, restitution, reformation, and specific performance, in lieu of, or in addition to, money damages. The court may issue a conditional judgment. The court shall retain jurisdiction until full payment and performance of any judgment or order.

(c) Notwithstanding subdivision (a), the small claims court has jurisdiction over a defendant guarantor as follows:

(1) For any action brought by a natural person against the Registrar of the Contractors' State License Board as the defendant guarantor, the small claims jurisdictional limit stated in Section 116.221 shall apply.

(2) For any action against a defendant guarantor that does not charge a fee for its guarantor or surety services, if the amount of the demand does not exceed two thousand five hundred dollars ($2,500).

(3) For any action brought by a natural person against a defendant guarantor that charges a fee for its guarantor or surety services, if the amount of the demand does not exceed six thousand five hundred dollars ($6,500).

(4) For any action brought by an entity other than a natural person against a defendant guarantor that charges a fee for its guarantor or surety services or against the Registrar of the Contractors' State License Board as the defendant guarantor, if the amount of the demand does not exceed four thousand dollars ($4,000).

(d) In any case in which the lack of jurisdiction is due solely to an excess in the amount of the demand, the excess may be waived, but any waiver is not operative until judgment.

(e) Notwithstanding subdivision (a), in any action filed by a plaintiff incarcerated in a Department of Corrections and Rehabilitation facility, the small claims court has jurisdiction over a defendant only if the plaintiff has alleged in the complaint that he or she has exhausted his or her administrative remedies against that department, including compliance with Sections 905.2 and 905.4 of the Government Code. The final administrative adjudication or determination of the plaintiff's administrative claim by the department may be attached to the complaint at the time of filing in lieu of that allegation.

(f) In any action governed by subdivision (e), if the plaintiff fails to provide proof of compliance with the requirements of subdivision (e) at the time of trial, the judicial officer shall, at his or her discretion, either dismiss the action or continue the action to give the plaintiff an opportunity to provide that proof.

(g) For purposes of this section, "department" includes an employee of a department against whom a claim has been filed under this chapter arising out of his or her duties as an employee of that department

Civ. Proc. § 116.221. Additional Jurisdiction.

In addition to the jurisdiction conferred by Section 116.220, the small claims court has jurisdiction in an action brought by a natural person, if the amount of the demand does not exceed ten thousand dollars ($10,000), except ***as*** otherwise prohibited by subdivision (c) of Section 116.220 or subdivision (a) of Section 116.231.

Civ. Proc. § 116.540. Small Claims Court; Representatives Appearing for Corporate Parties.

(a) Except as permitted by this section, no individual other than the plaintiff and the defendant may take part in the conduct or defense of a small claims action.

(b) Except as additionally provided in subdivision (i), a corporation may appear and participate in a small claims court action only through a regular employee, or a duly appointed or elected officer or director, who is employed, appointed, or elected for purposes other than solely representing the corporation in small claims court.

. . .

(i) A party that is an association created to manage a common interest development, as defined in Section 4100 or in Sections 6528 and 6534 of the Civil Code, may appear and participate in a small claims action through an agent, a management company representative, or bookkeeper who appears on behalf of that association.

(j) At the hearing of a small claims action, the court shall require any individual who is appearing as a representative of a party under subdivisions (b) to (i), inclusive, to file a declaration stating (1) that the individual is authorized to appear for the party, and (2) the basis for that authorization. If the representative is appearing under subdivision (b), (c), (d), (h), or (i), the declaration shall also state that the individual is not employed solely to represent the party in small claims court.

[Remainder of section omitted.]

8

CONSTRUCTION DEFECT LITIGATION

TITLE 7. REQUIREMENTS FOR ACTIONS FOR CONSTRUCTION DEFECTS

CHAPTER 1.

DEFINITIONS

Civ. Code § 895. Definitions.

(a) "Structure" means any residential dwelling, other building, or improvement located upon a lot or within a common area.

(b) "Designed moisture barrier" means an installed moisture barrier specified in the plans and specifications, contract documents, or manufacturer's recommendations.

(c) "Actual moisture barrier" means any component or material, actually installed, that serves to any degree as a barrier against moisture, whether or not intended as such.

(d) "Unintended water" means water that passes beyond, around, or through a component or the material that is designed to prevent that passage.

(e) "Close of escrow" means the date of the close of escrow between the builder and the original homeowner. With respect to claims by an association, as defined in Section 4080, "close of escrow" means the date of substantial completion, as defined in Section 337.15 of the Code of Civil Procedure, or the date the builder relinquishes control over the association's ability to decide whether to initiate a claim under this title, whichever is later.

(f) "Claimant" or "homeowner" includes the individual owners of single-family homes, individual unit owners of attached dwellings and, in the case of a common interest development, any association as defined in Section 4080.

CHAPTER 2.

ACTIONABLE DEFECTS

Civ. Code § 896. Standards for Residential Construction.

In any action seeking recovery of damages arising out of, or related to deficiencies in, the residential construction, design, specifications, surveying, planning, supervision, testing, or observation of construction, a builder, and to the extent set forth in Chapter 4 (commencing with Section 910), a general contractor, subcontractor, material supplier, individual product manufacturer, or design professional, shall, except as specifically set forth in this title, be liable for, and the claimant's claims or causes of action shall be limited to violation of, the following standards, except as specifically set forth in this title. This title applies to original construction intended to be sold as an individual dwelling unit. As to condominium conversions, this title does not apply to or does not supersede any other statutory or common law.

(a) With respect to water issues:

(1) A door shall not allow unintended water to pass beyond, around, or through the door or its designed or actual moisture barriers, if any.

(2) Windows, patio doors, deck doors, and their systems shall not allow water to pass beyond, around, or through the window, patio door, or deck door or its designed or actual moisture barriers, including, without limitation, internal barriers within the systems themselves. For purposes of this paragraph, "systems" include, without limitation, windows, window assemblies, framing, substrate, flashings, and trim, if any.

(3) Windows, patio doors, deck doors, and their systems shall not allow excessive condensation to enter the structure and cause damage to another component. For purposes of this paragraph, "systems" include, without limitation, windows, window assemblies, framing, substrate, flashings, and trim, if any.

(4) Roofs, roofing systems, chimney caps, and ventilation components shall not allow water to enter the structure or to pass beyond, around, or through the designed or actual moisture barriers, including, without limitation, internal barriers located within the systems themselves. For purposes of this paragraph, "systems" include, without limitation, framing, substrate, and sheathing, if any.

(5) Decks, deck systems, balconies, balcony systems, exterior stairs, and stair systems shall not allow water to pass into the adjacent structure. For purposes of this paragraph, "systems" include, without limitation, framing, substrate, flashing, and sheathing, if any.

(6) Decks, deck systems, balconies, balcony systems, exterior stairs, and stair systems shall not allow unintended water to pass within the systems themselves and cause damage to the systems. For purposes of this paragraph, "systems" include, without limitation, framing, substrate, flashing, and sheathing, if any.

(7) Foundation systems and slabs shall not allow water or vapor to enter into the structure so as to cause damage to another building component.

(8) Foundation systems and slabs shall not allow water or vapor to enter into the structure so as to limit the installation of the type of flooring materials typically used for the particular application.

(9) Hardscape, including paths and patios, irrigation systems, landscaping systems, and drainage systems, that are installed as part of the original construction, shall not be installed in such a way as to cause water or soil erosion to enter into or come in contact with the structure so as to cause damage to another building component.

(10) Stucco, exterior siding, exterior walls, including, without limitation, exterior framing, and other exterior wall finishes and fixtures and the systems of those components and fixtures, including, but not limited to, pot shelves, horizontal surfaces, columns, and plant-ons, shall be installed in such a way so as not to allow unintended water to pass into the structure or to pass beyond, around, or through the designed or actual moisture barriers of the system, including any internal barriers located within the system itself. For purposes of this paragraph, "systems" include, without limitation, framing, substrate, flashings, trim, wall assemblies, and internal wall cavities, if any.

(11) Stucco, exterior siding, and exterior walls shall not allow excessive condensation to enter the structure and cause damage to another component. For purposes of this paragraph, "systems" include, without limitation, framing, substrate, flashings, trim, wall assemblies, and internal wall cavities, if any.

(12) Retaining and site walls and their associated drainage systems shall not allow unintended water to pass beyond, around, or through its designed or actual moisture barriers including, without limitation, any internal barriers, so as to cause damage. This standard does not apply to those portions of any wall or drainage system that are designed to have water flow beyond, around, or through them.

(13) Retaining walls and site walls, and their associated drainage systems, shall only allow water to flow beyond, around, or through the areas designated by design.

(14) The lines and components of the plumbing system, sewer system, and utility systems shall not leak.

(15) Plumbing lines, sewer lines, and utility lines shall not corrode so as to impede the useful life of the systems.

(16) Sewer systems shall be installed in such a way as to allow the designated amount of sewage to flow through the system.

(17) Showers, baths, and related waterproofing systems shall not leak water into the interior of walls, flooring systems, or the interior of other components.

(18) The waterproofing systems behind or under ceramic tile and tile countertops shall not allow water into the interior of walls, flooring systems, or other components so as to cause damage. Ceramic tile systems shall be designed and installed so as to deflect intended water to the waterproofing system.

(b) With respect to structural issues:

(1) Foundations, load bearing components, and slabs, shall not contain significant cracks or significant vertical displacement.

(2) Foundations, load bearing components, and slabs shall not cause the structure, in whole or in part, to be structurally unsafe.

(3) Foundations, load bearing components, and slabs, and underlying soils shall be constructed so as to materially comply with the design criteria set by applicable government building codes, regulations, and ordinances for chemical deterioration or corrosion resistance in effect at the time of original construction.

(4) A structure shall be constructed so as to materially comply with the design criteria for earthquake and wind load resistance, as set forth in the applicable government building codes, regulations, and ordinances in effect at the time of original construction.

(c) With respect to soil issues:

(1) Soils and engineered retaining walls shall not cause, in whole or in part, damage to the structure built upon the soil or engineered retaining wall.

(2) Soils and engineered retaining walls shall not cause, in whole or in part, the structure to be structurally unsafe.

(3) Soils shall not cause, in whole or in part, the land upon which no structure is built to become unusable for the purpose represented at the time of original sale by the builder or for the purpose for which that land is commonly used.

(d) With respect to fire protection issues:

(1) A structure shall be constructed so as to materially comply with the design criteria of the applicable government building codes, regulations, and ordinances for fire protection of the occupants in effect at the time of the original construction.

(2) Fireplaces, chimneys, chimney structures, and chimney termination caps shall be constructed and installed in such a way so as not to cause an unreasonable risk of fire outside the fireplace enclosure or chimney.

(3) Electrical and mechanical systems shall be constructed and installed in such a way so as not to cause an unreasonable risk of fire.

(e) With respect to plumbing and sewer issues: Plumbing and sewer systems shall be installed to operate properly and shall not materially impair the use of the structure by its inhabitants. However, no action may be brought for a violation of this subdivision more than four years after close of escrow.

(f) With respect to electrical system issues: Electrical systems shall operate properly and shall not materially impair the use of the structure by its inhabitants. However, no action shall be brought pursuant to this subdivision more than four years from close of escrow.

(g) With respect to issues regarding other areas of construction:

(1) Exterior pathways, driveways, hardscape, sidewalls, sidewalks, and patios installed by the original builder shall not contain cracks that display significant vertical displacement or that are excessive. However, no action shall be brought upon a violation of this paragraph more than four years from close of escrow.

(2) Stucco, exterior siding, and other exterior wall finishes and fixtures, including, but not limited to, pot shelves, horizontal surfaces, columns, and plant-ons, shall not contain significant cracks or separations.

(3) (A) To the extent not otherwise covered by these standards, manufactured products, including, but not limited to, windows, doors, roofs, plumbing products and fixtures, fireplaces, electrical fixtures, HVAC units, countertops, cabinets, paint, and appliances shall be installed so as not to interfere with the products' useful life, if any.

(B) For purposes of this paragraph, "useful life" means a representation of how long a product is warranted or represented, through its limited warranty or any written representations, to last by its manufacturer, including recommended or required maintenance. If there is no representation by a manufacturer, a builder shall install manufactured products so as not to interfere with the product's utility.

(C) For purposes of this paragraph, "manufactured product" means a product that is completely manufactured offsite.

(D) If no useful life representation is made, or if the representation is less than one year, the period shall be no less than one year. If a manufactured product is damaged as a result of a violation of these standards, damage to the product is a recoverable element of damages. This subparagraph does not limit recovery if there has been damage to another building component caused by a manufactured product during the manufactured product's useful life.

(E) This title does not apply in any action seeking recovery solely for a defect in a manufactured product located within or adjacent to a structure.

(4) Heating shall be installed so as to be capable of maintaining a room temperature of 70 degrees Fahrenheit at a point three feet above the floor in any living space.

(5) Living space air-conditioning, if any, shall be provided in a manner consistent with the size and efficiency design criteria specified in Title 24 of the California Code of Regulations or its successor.

(6) Attached structures shall be constructed to comply with interunit noise transmission standards set by the applicable government building codes, ordinances, or regulations in effect at the time of the original construction. If there is no applicable code, ordinance, or regulation, this paragraph does not apply. However, no action shall be brought pursuant to this paragraph more than one year from the original occupancy of the adjacent unit.

(7) Irrigation systems and drainage shall operate properly so as not to damage landscaping or other external improvements. However, no action shall be brought pursuant to this paragraph more than one year from close of escrow.

(8) Untreated wood posts shall not be installed in contact with soil so as to cause unreasonable decay to the wood based upon the finish grade at the time of original construction. However, no action shall be brought pursuant to this paragraph more than two years from close of escrow.

(9) Untreated steel fences and adjacent components shall be installed so as to prevent unreasonable corrosion. However, no action shall be brought pursuant to this paragraph more than four years from close of escrow.

(10) Paint and stains shall be applied in such a manner so as not to cause deterioration of the building surfaces for the length of time specified by the paint or stain manufacturers' representations, if any. However, no action shall be brought pursuant to this paragraph more than five years from close of escrow.

(11) Roofing materials shall be installed so as to avoid materials falling from the roof.

(12) The landscaping systems shall be installed in such a manner so as to survive for not less than one year. However, no action shall be brought pursuant to this paragraph more than two years from close of escrow.

(13) Ceramic tile and tile backing shall be installed in such a manner that the tile does not detach.

(14) Dryer ducts shall be installed and terminated pursuant to manufacturer installation requirements. However, no action shall be brought pursuant to this paragraph more than two years from close of escrow.

(15) Structures shall be constructed in such a manner so as not to impair the occupants' safety because they contain public health hazards as determined by a duly authorized public health official, health agency, or governmental entity having jurisdiction. This paragraph does not limit recovery for any damages caused by a violation of any other paragraph of this section on the grounds that the damages do not constitute a health hazard.

Civ. Code § 897. Inclusion of Items not Addressed in Chapter.

The standards set forth in this chapter are intended to address every function or component of a structure. To the extent that a function or component of a structure is not addressed by these standards, it shall be actionable if it causes damage.

CHAPTER 3.

OBLIGATIONS

Civ. Code § 900. Warranty Covering Fit and Finish Items.

As to fit and finish items, a builder shall provide a homebuyer with a minimum one-year express written limited warranty covering the fit and finish of the following building components. Except as otherwise provided by the standards specified in Chapter 2 (commencing with Section 896), this warranty shall cover the fit and finish of cabinets, mirrors, flooring, interior and exterior walls, countertops, paint finishes, and trim, but shall not apply to damage to those components caused by defects in other components governed by the other provisions of this title. Any fit and finish matters covered by this warranty are not subject to the provisions of this title. If a builder fails to provide the express warranty required by this section, the warranty for these items shall be for a period of one year.

Civ. Code § 901. Enhanced Protection Agreement.

A builder may, but is not required to, offer greater protection or protection for longer time periods in its express contract with the homeowner than that set forth in Chapter 2 (commencing with Section 896). A builder may not limit the application of Chapter 2 (commencing with Section 896) or lower its protection through the express contract with the homeowner. This type of express contract constitutes an "enhanced protection agreement."

Civ. Code § 902. Applicability of Civil Code Sections 896 and 897.

If a builder offers an enhanced protection agreement, the builder may choose to be subject to its own express contractual provisions in place of the provisions set forth in Chapter 2 (commencing with Section 896). If an enhanced protection agreement is in place, Chapter 2 (commencing with Section 896) no longer applies other than to set forth minimum provisions by which to judge the enforceability of the particular provisions of the enhanced protection agreement.

Civ. Code § 903. Enhanced Protection Agreement; Builder Duties.

If a builder offers an enhanced protection agreement in place of the provisions set forth in Chapter 2 (commencing with Section 896), the election to do so shall be made in writing with the homeowner no later than the close of escrow. The builder shall provide the homeowner with a complete copy of Chapter 2 (commencing with Section 896) and advise the homeowner that the builder has elected not to be subject to its provisions. If any provision of an enhanced protection agreement is later found to be unenforceable as not meeting the minimum standards of Chapter 2 (commencing with Section 896), a builder may use this chapter in lieu of those provisions found to be unenforceable.

Civ. Code § 904. Enforcement of Construction Standards.

If a builder has elected to use an enhanced protection agreement, and a homeowner disputes that the particular provision or time periods of the enhanced protection agreement are not greater than, or equal to, the provisions of Chapter 2 (commencing with Section 896) as they apply to the particular deficiency alleged by the homeowner, the homeowner may seek to enforce the application of the standards set forth in this chapter as to those claimed deficiencies. If a homeowner seeks to enforce a particular standard in lieu of a provision of the enhanced protection agreement, the homeowner shall give the builder written notice of that intent at the time the homeowner files a notice of claim pursuant to Chapter 4 (commencing with Section 910).

Civ. Code § 905. Action to Enforce Construction Standards.

If a homeowner seeks to enforce Chapter 2 (commencing with Section 896), in lieu of the enhanced protection agreement in a subsequent litigation or other legal action, the builder shall have the right to have the matter bifurcated, and to have an immediately binding determination of his or her responsive pleading within 60 days after the filing of that pleading, but in no event after the commencement of discovery, as to the application of either Chapter 2 (commencing with Section 896) or the enhanced protection agreement as to the deficiencies claimed by the homeowner. If the builder fails to seek that determination in the timeframe specified, the builder waives the right to do so and the standards set forth in this title shall apply. As to any non-original homeowner, that homeowner shall be deemed in privity for purposes of an enhanced protection agreement only to the extent that the builder has recorded the enhanced protection agreement on title or provided actual notice to the non-original homeowner of the enhanced protection agreement. If the enhanced protection agreement is not recorded on title or no actual notice has been provided, the standards set forth in this title apply to any non-original homeowners' claims.

Civ. Code § 906. Builder's Election.

A builder's election to use an enhanced protection agreement addresses only the issues set forth in Chapter 2 (commencing with Section 896) and does not constitute an election to use or not use the provisions of Chapter 4 (commencing with Section 910). The decision to use or not use Chapter 4 (commencing with Section 910) is governed by the provisions of that chapter.

Civ. Code § 907. Homeowner Maintenance Obligations.

A homeowner is obligated to follow all reasonable maintenance obligations and schedules communicated in writing to the homeowner by the builder and product manufacturers, as well as commonly accepted maintenance practices. A failure by a homeowner to follow these obligations, schedules, and practices may subject the homeowner to the affirmative defenses contained in Section 944.

CHAPTER 4.

PRELITIGATION PROCEDURE

Civ. Code § 910. Procedures Required Prior to Filing Action for Violation of Construction Standards.

Prior to filing an action against any party alleged to have contributed to a violation of the standards set forth in Chapter 2 (commencing with Section 896), the claimant shall initiate the following pre-litigation procedures:

(a) The claimant or his or her legal representative shall provide written notice via certified mail, overnight mail, or personal delivery to the builder, in the manner prescribed in this section, of the claimant's claim that the construction of his or her residence violates any of the standards set forth in Chapter 2 (commencing with Section 896). That notice shall provide the claimant's name, address, and preferred method of contact, and shall state that the claimant alleges a violation pursuant to this part against the builder, and shall describe the claim in reasonable detail sufficient to determine the nature and location, to the extent known, of the claimed violation. In the case of a group of homeowners or an association, the notice may identify the claimants solely by address or other description sufficient to apprise the builder of the locations of the subject residences. That document shall have the same force and effect as a notice of commencement of a legal proceeding.

(b) The notice requirements of this section do not preclude a homeowner from seeking redress through any applicable normal customer service procedure as set forth in any contractual, warranty, or other builder-generated document; and, if a homeowner seeks to do so, that request shall not satisfy the notice requirements of this section.

Civ. Code § 911. "Builder" Defined.

(a) For purposes of this title, except as provided in subdivision (b), "builder" means any entity or individual, including, but not limited to a builder, developer, general contractor, contractor, or original seller, who, at the time of sale, was also in the business of selling residential units to the public for the property that is the subject of the homeowner's claim or was in the business of building, developing, or constructing residential units for public purchase for the property that is the subject of the homeowner's claim.

(b) For the purposes of this title, "builder" does not include any entity or individual whose involvement with a residential unit that is the subject of the homeowner's claim is limited to his or her capacity as general contractor or contractor and who is not a partner, member of, subsidiary of, or otherwise similarly affiliated with the builder. For purposes of this title, these nonaffiliated general contractors and nonaffiliated contractors shall be treated the same as subcontractors, material suppliers, individual product manufacturers, and design professionals.

Civ. Code § 912. Builder's Duties.

A builder shall do all of the following:

(a) Within 30 days of a written request by a homeowner or his or her legal representative, the builder shall provide copies of all relevant plans, specifications, mass or rough grading plans, final soils reports, Bureau of Real Estate public reports, and available engineering calculations, that pertain to a homeowner's residence specifically or as part of a larger development tract. The request shall be honored if it states that it is made relative to structural, fire safety, or soils provisions of this title. However, a builder is not obligated to provide a copying service, and reasonable copying costs shall be borne by the requesting party. A builder may require that the documents be copied onsite by the requesting party, except that the homeowner may, at his or her option, use his or her own copying service, which may include an offsite copy facility that is bonded and insured. If a builder can show that the builder maintained the documents, but that they later became unavailable due to loss or destruction that was not the fault of the builder, the builder may be excused from the requirements of this subdivision, in which case the builder shall act with reasonable diligence to assist the homeowner in obtaining those documents from any applicable government authority or from the source that generated the document. However, in that case, the time limits specified by this section do not apply.

(b) At the expense of the homeowner, who may opt to use an offsite copy facility that is bonded and insured, the builder shall provide to the homeowner or his or her legal representative copies of all maintenance and preventative maintenance recommendations that pertain to his or her residence within 30 days of service of a written request for those documents. Those documents shall also be provided to the homeowner in conjunction with the initial sale of the residence.

(c) At the expense of the homeowner, who may opt to use an offsite copy facility that is bonded and insured, a builder shall provide to the homeowner or his or her legal representative copies of all manufactured products maintenance, preventive maintenance, and limited warranty information within 30 days of a written request for those documents. These documents shall also be provided to the homeowner in conjunction with the initial sale of the residence.

(d) At the expense of the homeowner, who may opt to use an offsite copy facility that is bonded and insured, a builder shall provide to the homeowner or his or her legal representative copies of all of the builder's limited contractual warranties in accordance with this part in effect at the time of the original sale of the residence within 30 days of a written request for those documents. Those documents shall also be provided to the homeowner in conjunction with the initial sale of the residence.

(e) A builder shall maintain the name and address of an agent for notice pursuant to this chapter with the Secretary of State or, alternatively, elect to use a third party for that notice if the builder has notified the homeowner in writing of the third party's name and address, to whom claims and requests for information under this section may be mailed. The name and address of the agent for notice or third party shall be included with the original sales documentation and shall be initialed and acknowledged by the purchaser and the builder's sales representative.

This subdivision applies to instances in which a builder contracts with a third party to accept claims and act on the builder's behalf. A builder shall give actual notice to the homeowner that the builder has made such an election, and shall include the name and address of the third party.

(f) A builder shall record on title a notice of the existence of these procedures and a notice that these procedures impact the legal rights of the homeowner. This information shall also be included with the original sales documentation and shall be initialed and acknowledged by the purchaser and the builder's sales representative.

(g) A builder shall provide, with the original sales documentation, a written copy of this title, which shall be initialed and acknowledged by the purchaser and the builder's sales representative.

(h) As to any documents provided in conjunction with the original sale, the builder shall instruct the original purchaser to provide those documents to any subsequent purchaser.

(i) Any builder who fails to comply with any of these requirements within the time specified is not entitled to the protection of this chapter, and the homeowner is released from the requirements of this chapter and may proceed with the filing of an action, in which case the remaining chapters of this part shall continue to apply to the action.

Civ. Code § 913. Written Acknowledgment of Notice of Claim.

A builder or his or her representative shall acknowledge, in writing, receipt of the notice of the claim within 14 days after receipt of the notice of the claim. If the notice of the claim is served by the claimant's legal representative, or if the builder receives a written representation letter from a homeowner's attorney, the builder shall include the attorney in all subsequent substantive communications, including, without limitation, all written communications occurring pursuant to this chapter, and all substantive and procedural communications, including all written communications, following the commencement of any subsequent complaint or other legal action, except that if the builder has retained or involved legal counsel to assist the builder in this process, all communications by the builder's counsel shall only be with the claimant's legal representative, if any.

Civ. Code § 914. Nonadversarial Procedure.

(a) This chapter establishes a nonadversarial procedure, including the remedies available under this chapter which, if the procedure does not resolve the dispute between the parties, may result in a subsequent action to enforce the other chapters of this title. A builder may attempt to commence nonadversarial contractual provisions other than the nonadversarial procedures and remedies set forth in this chapter, but may not, in addition to its own nonadversarial contractual provisions, require adherence to the nonadversarial procedures and remedies set forth in this chapter, regardless of whether the builder's own alternative nonadversarial contractual provisions are successful in resolving the dispute or ultimately deemed enforceable. At the time the sales agreement is executed, the builder shall notify the homeowner whether the builder intends to engage in the nonadversarial procedure of this section or attempt to enforce alternative nonadversarial contractual provisions. If the builder elects to use alternative nonadversarial contractual provisions in lieu of this chapter, the election is binding, regardless of whether the builder's alternative nonadversarial contractual provisions are successful in resolving the ultimate dispute or are ultimately deemed enforceable.

(b) Nothing in this title is intended to affect existing statutory or decisional law pertaining to the applicability, viability, or enforceability of alternative dispute resolution methods, alternative remedies, or contractual arbitration, judicial reference, or similar procedures requiring a binding resolution to enforce the other chapters of this title or any other disputes between homeowners and builders. Nothing in this title is intended to affect the applicability, viability, or enforceability, if any, of contractual arbitration or judicial reference after a nonadversarial procedure or provision has been completed.

Civ. Code § 915. Actions Resulting in Nonapplication of Chapter.

If a builder fails to acknowledge receipt of the notice of a claim within the time specified, elects not to go through the process set forth in this chapter, or fails to request an inspection within the time specified, or at the conclusion or cessation of an alternative nonadversarial proceeding, this chapter does not apply and the homeowner is released from the requirements of this chapter and may proceed with the filing of an action. However, the standards set forth in the other chapters of this title shall continue to apply to the action.

Civ. Code § 916. Builder's Investigation of Claimed Unmet Standards.

(a) If a builder elects to inspect the claimed unmet standards, the builder shall complete the initial inspection and testing within 14 days after acknowledgment of receipt of the notice of the claim, at a mutually convenient date and time. If the homeowner has retained legal representation, the inspection shall be scheduled with the legal representative's office at a mutually convenient date and time, unless the legal representative is unavailable during the relevant time periods. All costs of builder inspection and testing, including any damage caused by the builder inspection, shall be borne by the builder. The builder shall also provide written proof that the builder has liability insurance to cover any damages or injuries occurring during inspection and testing. The builder shall restore the property to its pretesting condition within 48 hours of the testing. The builder shall, upon request, allow the inspections to be observed and electronically recorded, video recorded, or photographed by the claimant or his or her legal representative.

(b) Nothing that occurs during a builder's or claimant's inspection or testing may be used or introduced as evidence to support a spoliation defense by any potential party in any subsequent litigation.

(c) If a builder deems a second inspection or testing reasonably necessary, and specifies the reasons therefor in writing within three days following the initial inspection, the builder may conduct a second inspection or testing. A second inspection or testing shall be completed within 40 days of the initial inspection or testing. All requirements concerning the initial inspection or testing shall also apply to the second inspection or testing.

(d) If the builder fails to inspect or test the property within the time specified, the claimant is released from the requirements of this section and may proceed with the filing of an action. However, the standards set forth in the other chapters of this title shall continue to apply to the action.

(e) If a builder intends to hold a subcontractor, design professional, individual product manufacturer, or material supplier, including an insurance carrier, warranty company, or service company, responsible for its contribution to the unmet standard, the builder shall provide notice to that person or entity sufficiently in advance to allow them to attend the initial, or if requested, second inspection of any alleged unmet standard and to participate in the repair process. The claimant and his or her legal representative, if any, shall be advised in a reasonable time prior to the inspection as to the identity of all persons or entities invited to attend. This subdivision does not apply to the builder's insurance company. Except with respect to any claims involving a repair actually conducted under this chapter, nothing in this subdivision shall be construed to relieve a subcontractor, design professional, individual product manufacturer, or material supplier of any liability under an action brought by a claimant.

Civ. Code § 917. Offer to Repair.

Within 30 days of the initial or, if requested, second inspection or testing, the builder may offer in writing to repair the violation. The offer to repair shall also compensate the homeowner for all applicable damages recoverable under Section 944, within the timeframe for the repair set forth in this chapter. Any such offer shall be accompanied by a detailed, specific, step-by-step statement identifying the particular violation that is being repaired, explaining the nature, scope, and location of the repair, and setting a reasonable completion date for the repair. The offer shall also include the names, addresses, telephone numbers, and license numbers of the contractors whom the builder intends to have perform the repair. Those contractors shall be fully insured for, and shall be responsible for, all damages or injuries that they may cause to occur during the repair, and evidence of that insurance shall be provided to the homeowner upon request. Upon written request by the homeowner or his or her legal representative, and within the timeframes set forth in this chapter, the builder shall also provide any available technical documentation, including, without limitation, plans and specifications, pertaining to the claimed violation within the particular home or development tract. The offer shall also advise the homeowner in writing of his or her right to request up to three additional contractors from which to select to do the repair pursuant to this chapter.

Civ. Code § 918. Homeowner Acceptance of Offer to Repair.

Upon receipt of the offer to repair, the homeowner shall have 30 days to authorize the builder to proceed with the repair. The homeowner may alternatively request, at the homeowner's sole option and discretion, that the builder provide the names, addresses, telephone numbers, and license numbers for up to three alternative contractors who are not owned or financially controlled by the builder and who regularly conduct business in the county where the structure is located. If the homeowner so elects, the builder is entitled to an additional noninvasive inspection, to occur at a mutually convenient date and time within 20 days of the election, so as to permit the other proposed contractors to review the proposed site of the repair. Within 35 days after the request of the homeowner for alternative contractors, the builder shall present the homeowner with a choice of contractors. Within 20 days after that presentation, the homeowner shall authorize the builder or one of the alternative contractors to perform the repair.

Civ. Code § 919. Offer To Mediate.

The offer to repair shall also be accompanied by an offer to mediate the dispute if the homeowner so chooses. The mediation shall be limited to a four-hour mediation, except as otherwise mutually agreed before a nonaffiliated mediator selected and paid for by the builder. At the homeowner's sole option, the homeowner may agree to split the cost of the mediator, and if he or she does so, the mediator shall be selected jointly. The mediator shall have sufficient availability such that the mediation occurs within 15 days after the request to mediate is received and occurs at a mutually convenient location within the county where the action is pending. If a builder has made an offer to repair a violation, and the mediation has failed to resolve the dispute, the homeowner shall allow the repair to be performed either by the builder, its contractor, or the selected contractor.

Civ. Code § 920. Actions Resulting in Filing of Action by Homeowner.

If the builder fails to make an offer to repair or otherwise strictly comply with this chapter within the times specified, the claimant is released from the requirements of this chapter and may proceed with the filing of an action. If the contractor performing the repair does not complete the repair in the time or manner specified, the claimant may file an action. If this occurs, the standards set forth in the other chapters of this part shall continue to apply to the action.

Civ. Code § 921. Procedure When Resolution Involves Repair by Builder.

(a) In the event that a resolution under this chapter involves a repair by the builder, the builder shall make an appointment with the claimant, make all appropriate arrangements to effectuate a repair of the claimed unmet standards, and compensate the homeowner for all damages resulting therefrom free of charge to the claimant. The repair shall be scheduled through the claimant's legal representative, if any, unless he or she is unavailable during the relevant time periods. The repair shall be commenced on a mutually convenient date within 14 days of acceptance or, if an alternative contractor is selected by the homeowner, within 14 days of the selection, or, if a mediation occurs, within seven days of the mediation, or within five days after a permit is obtained if one is required. The builder shall act with reasonable diligence in obtaining any such permit.

(b) The builder shall ensure that work done on the repairs is done with the utmost diligence, and that the repairs are completed as soon as reasonably possible, subject to the nature of the repair or some unforeseen event not caused by the builder or the contractor performing the repair. Every effort shall be made to complete the repair within 120 days.

Civ. Code § 922. Observation and Electronic Recording of Repair Allowed.

The builder shall, upon request, allow the repair to be observed and electronically recorded, video recorded, or photographed by the claimant or his or her legal representative. Nothing that occurs during the repair process may be used or introduced as evidence to support a spoliation defense by any potential party in any subsequent litigation.

Civ. Code § 923. Full Disclosure of Repairs.

The builder shall provide the homeowner or his or her legal representative, upon request, with copies of all correspondence, photographs, and other materials pertaining or relating in any manner to the repairs.

Civ. Code § 924. Written Explanation of Unrepaired Items.

If the builder elects to repair some, but not all of, the claimed unmet standards, the builder shall, at the same time it makes its offer, set forth with particularity in writing the reasons, and the support for those reasons, for not repairing all claimed unmet standards.

Civ. Code § 925. Failure to Complete Repairs in Time Specified.

If the builder fails to complete the repair within the time specified in the repair plan, the claimant is released from the requirements of this chapter and may proceed with the filing of an action. If this occurs, the standards set forth in the other chapters of this title shall continue to apply to the action.

Civ. Code § 926. No Release or Waiver in Exchange for Repair Work.

The builder may not obtain a release or waiver of any kind in exchange for the repair work mandated by this chapter. At the conclusion of the repair, the claimant may proceed with filing an action for violation of the applicable standard or for a claim of inadequate repair, or both, including all applicable damages available under Section 944.

Civ. Code § 927. Statute of Limitations.

If the applicable statute of limitations has otherwise run during this process, the time period for filing a complaint or other legal remedies for violation of any provision of this title, or for a claim of inadequate repair, is extended from the time of the original claim by the claimant to 100 days after the repair is completed, whether or not the particular violation is the one being repaired. If the builder fails to acknowledge the claim within the time specified, elects not to go through this statutory process, or fails to request an inspection within the time specified, the time period for filing a complaint or other legal remedies for violation of any provision of this title is extended from the time of the original claim by the claimant to 45 days after the time for responding to the notice of claim has expired. If the builder elects to attempt to enforce its own nonadversarial procedure in lieu of the procedure set forth in this chapter, the time period for filing a complaint or other legal remedies for violation of any provision of this part is extended from the time of the original claim by the claimant to 100 days after either the completion of the builder's alternative nonadversarial procedure, or 100 days after the builder's alternative nonadversarial procedure is deemed unenforceable, whichever is later.

Civ. Code § 928. Mediation Procedure.

If the builder has invoked this chapter and completed a repair, prior to filing an action, if there has been no previous mediation between the parties, the homeowner or his or her legal representative shall request mediation in writing. The mediation shall be limited to four hours, except as otherwise mutually agreed before a nonaffiliated mediator selected and paid for by the builder. At the homeowner's sole option, the homeowner may agree to split the cost of the mediator and if he or she does so, the mediator shall be selected jointly. The mediator shall have sufficient availability such that the mediation will occur within 15 days after the request for mediation is received and shall occur at a mutually convenient location within the county where the action is pending. In the event that a mediation is used at this point, any applicable statutes of limitations shall be tolled from the date of the request to mediate until the next court day after the mediation is completed, or the 100-day period, whichever is later.

Civ. Code § 929. Cash Offer in Lieu of Repair.

(a) Nothing in this chapter prohibits the builder from making only a cash offer and no repair. In this situation, the homeowner is free to accept the offer, or he or she may reject the offer and proceed with the filing of an action. If the latter occurs, the standards of the other chapters of this title shall continue to apply to the action.

(b) The builder may obtain a reasonable release in exchange for the cash payment. The builder may negotiate the terms and conditions of any reasonable release in terms of scope and consideration in conjunction with a cash payment under this chapter.

Civ. Code § 930. Strict Construction of Time Periods.

(a) The time periods and all other requirements in this chapter are to be strictly construed, and, unless extended by the mutual agreement of the parties in accordance with this chapter, shall govern the rights and obligations under this title. If a builder fails to act in accordance with this section within the timeframes mandated, unless extended by the mutual agreement of the parties as evidenced by a postclaim written confirmation by the affected homeowner demonstrating that he or she has knowingly and voluntarily extended the statutory timeframe, the claimant may proceed with filing an action. If this occurs, the standards of the other chapters of this title shall continue to apply to the action.

(b) If the claimant does not conform with the requirements of this chapter, the builder may bring a motion to stay any subsequent court action or other proceeding until the requirements of this chapter have been satisfied. The court, in its discretion, may award the prevailing party on such a motion, his or her attorney's fees and costs in bringing or opposing the motion.

Civ. Code § 931. Claim Combined with other Causes of Action.

If a claim combines causes of action or damages not covered by this part, including, without limitation, personal injuries, class actions, other statutory remedies, or fraud-based claims, the claimed unmet standards shall be administered according to this part, although evidence of the property in its unrepaired condition may be introduced to support the respective elements of any such cause of action. As to any fraud-based claim, if the fact that the property has been repaired under this chapter is deemed admissible, the trier of fact shall be informed that the repair was not voluntarily accepted by the homeowner. As to any class action claims that address solely the incorporation of a defective component into a residence, the named and unnamed class members need not comply with this chapter.

Civ. Code § 932. Subsequently Discovered Claims.

Subsequently discovered claims of unmet standards shall be administered separately under this chapter, unless otherwise agreed to by the parties. However, in the case of a detached single family residence, in the same home, if the subsequently discovered claim is for a violation of the same standard as that which has already been initiated by the same claimant and the subject of a currently pending action, the claimant need not reinitiate the process as to the same standard. In the case of an attached project, if the subsequently discovered claim is for a violation of the same standard for a connected component system in the same building as has already been initiated by the same claimant, and the subject of a currently pending action, the claimant need not reinitiate this process as to that standard.

Civ. Code § 933. Evidence of Repair Work.

If any enforcement of these standards is commenced, the fact that a repair effort was made may be introduced to the trier of fact. However, the claimant may use the condition of the property prior to the repair as the basis for contending that the repair work was inappropriate, inadequate, or incomplete, or that the violation still exists. The claimant need not show that the repair work resulted in further damage nor that damage has continued to occur as a result of the violation.

Civ. Code § 934. Evidence of Parties' Conduct.

Evidence of both parties' conduct during this process may be introduced during a subsequent enforcement action, if any, with the exception of any mediation. Any repair efforts undertaken by the builder, shall not be considered settlement communications or offers of settlement and are not inadmissible in evidence on such a basis.

Civ. Code § 935. Similar Requirements of Civil Code Section 6000.

To the extent that provisions of this chapter are enforced and those provisions are substantially similar to provisions in Section 6000 of the Civil Code, but an action is subsequently commenced under Section 6000 of the Civil Code, the parties are excused from performing the substantially similar requirements under Section 6000 of the Civil Code.

Civ. Code § 936. Liability of Subcontractors.

Each and every provision of the other chapters of this title apply to general contractors, subcontractors, material suppliers, individual product manufacturers, and design professionals to the extent that the subcontractors, material suppliers, individual product manufacturers, and design professionals caused, in whole or in part, a violation of a particular standard as the result of a negligent act or omission or a breach of contract. In addition to the affirmative defenses set forth in Section 945.5, a general contractor, subcontractor, material supplier, design professional, individual product manufacturer, or other entity may also offer common law and contractual defenses as applicable to any claimed violation of a standard. All actions by a claimant or builder to enforce an express contract, or any provision thereof, against a general contractor, subcontractor, material supplier, individual product manufacturer, or design professional is preserved.

Nothing in this title modifies the law pertaining to joint and several liability for builders, general contractors, subcontractors, material suppliers, individual product manufacturer, and design professionals that contribute to any specific violation of this title. However, the negligence standard in this section does not apply to any general contractor, subcontractor, material supplier, individual product manufacturer, or design professional with respect to claims for which strict liability would apply.

Civ. Code § 937. Claims and Damages not Covered by Title.

Nothing in this title shall be interpreted to eliminate or abrogate the requirement to comply with Section 411.35 of the Code of Civil Procedure or to affect the liability of design professionals, including architects and architectural firms, for claims and damages not covered by this title.

Civ. Code § 938. Application to Units Purchased After January 1, 2003.

This title applies only to new residential units where the purchase agreement with the buyer was signed by the seller on or after January 1, 2003.

CHAPTER 5.

PROCEDURE

Civ. Code § 941. Time Limit for Bringing Construction Defect Action.

(a) Except as specifically set forth in this title, no action may be brought to recover under this title more than 10 years after substantial completion of the improvement but not later than the date of recordation of a valid notice of completion.

(b) As used in this section, "action" includes an action for indemnity brought against a person arising out of that person's performance or furnishing of services or materials referred to in this title, except that a cross-complaint for indemnity may be filed pursuant to subdivision (b) of Section 428.10 of the Code of Civil Procedure in an action which has been brought within the time period set forth in subdivision (a).

(c) The limitation prescribed by this section may not be asserted by way of defense by any person in actual possession or the control, as owner, tenant or otherwise, of such an improvement, at the time any deficiency in the improvement constitutes the proximate cause for which it is proposed to make a claim or bring an action.

(d) Sections 337.15 and 337.1 of the Code of Civil Procedure do not apply to actions under this title.

(e) Existing statutory and decisional law regarding tolling of the statute of limitations shall apply to the time periods for filing an action or making a claim under this title, except that repairs made pursuant to Chapter 4 (commencing with Section 910), with the exception of the tolling provision contained in Section 927, do not extend the period for filing an action, or restart the time limitations contained in subdivision (a) or (b) of Section 7091 of the Business and Professions Code. If a builder arranges for a contractor to perform a repair pursuant to Chapter 4 (commencing with Section 910), as to the builder the time period for calculating the statute of limitation in subdivision (a) or (b) of Section 7091 of the Business and Professions Code shall pertain to the substantial completion of the original construction and not to the date of repairs under this title. The time limitations established by this title do not apply to any action by a claimant for a contract or express contractual provision. Causes of action and damages to which this chapter does not apply are not limited by this section.

Civ. Code § 942. Claims Involving Residential Construction Standards.

In order to make a claim for violation of the standards set forth in Chapter 2 (commencing with Section 896), a homeowner need only demonstrate, in accordance with the applicable evidentiary standard, that the home does not meet the applicable standard, subject to the affirmative defenses set forth in Section 945.5. No further showing of causation or damages is required to meet the burden of proof regarding a violation of a standard set forth in Chapter 2 (commencing with Section 896), provided that the violation arises out of, pertains to, or is related to, the original construction.

Civ. Code § 943. Limitation on Causes of Action Under Section 944.

(a) Except as provided in this title, no other cause of action for a claim covered by this title or for damages recoverable under Section 944 is allowed. In addition to the rights under this title, this title does not apply to any action by a claimant to enforce a contract or express contractual provision, or any action for fraud, personal injury, or violation of a statute. Damages awarded for the items set forth in Section 944 in such other cause of action shall be reduced by the amounts recovered pursuant to Section 944 for violation of the standards set forth in this title.

(b) As to any claims involving a detached single-family home, the homeowner's right to the reasonable value of repairing any nonconformity is limited to the repair costs, or the diminution in current value of the home caused by the nonconformity, whichever is less, subject to the personal use exception as developed under common law.

Civ. Code § 944. Claim for Damages.

If a claim for damages is made under this title, the homeowner is only entitled to damages for the reasonable value of repairing any violation of the standards set forth in this title, the reasonable cost of repairing any damages caused by the repair efforts, the reasonable cost of repairing and rectifying any damages resulting from the failure of the home to meet the standards, the reasonable cost of removing and replacing any improper repair by the builder, reasonable relocation and storage expenses, lost business income if the home was used as a principal place of a business licensed to be operated from the home, reasonable investigative costs for each established violation, and all other costs or fees recoverable by contract or statute.

Civ. Code § 945. Original Purchasers and Successors-In-Interest.

The provisions, standards, rights, and obligations set forth in this title are binding upon all original purchasers and their successors-in-interest. For purposes of this title, associations and others having the rights set forth in Sections ***5980*** and ***5985*** shall be considered to be original purchasers and shall have standing to enforce the provisions, standards, rights, and obligations set forth in this title.

Civ. Code § 945.5. Affirmative Defenses.

A builder, general contractor, subcontractor, material supplier, individual product manufacturer, or design professional, under the principles of comparative fault pertaining to affirmative defenses, may be excused, in whole or in part, from any obligation, damage, loss, or liability if the builder, general contractor, subcontractor, material supplier, individual product manufacturer, or design professional, can demonstrate any of the following affirmative defenses in response to a claimed violation:

(a) To the extent it is caused by an unforeseen act of nature which caused the structure not to meet the standard. For purposes of this section an "unforeseen act of nature" means a weather condition, earthquake, or manmade event such as war, terrorism, or vandalism, in excess of the design criteria expressed by the applicable building codes, regulations, and ordinances in effect at the time of original construction.

(b) To the extent it is caused by a homeowner's unreasonable failure to minimize or prevent those damages in a timely manner, including the failure of the homeowner to allow reasonable and timely access for inspections and repairs under this title. This includes the failure to give timely notice to the builder after discovery of a violation, but does not include damages due to the untimely or inadequate response of a builder to the homeowner's claim.

(c) To the extent it is caused by the homeowner or his or her agent, employee, general contractor, subcontractor, independent contractor, or consultant by virtue of their failure to follow the builder's or manufacturer's recommendations, or commonly accepted homeowner maintenance obligations. In order to rely upon this defense as it relates to a builder's recommended maintenance schedule, the builder shall show that the homeowner had written notice of these schedules and recommendations and that the recommendations and schedules were reasonable at the time they were issued.

(d) To the extent it is caused by the homeowner or his or her agent's or an independent third party's alterations, ordinary wear and tear, misuse, abuse, or neglect, or by the structure's use for something other than its intended purpose.

(e) To the extent that the time period for filing actions bars the claimed violation.

(f) As to a particular violation for which the builder has obtained a valid release.

(g) To the extent that the builder's repair was successful in correcting the particular violation of the applicable standard.

(h) As to any causes of action to which this statute does not apply, all applicable affirmative defenses are preserved.

Civ. Code § 43.99. Liability Of Independent Quality Review Provider.

(a) There shall be no monetary liability on the part of, and no cause of action for damages shall arise against, any person or other legal entity that is under contract with an applicant for a residential building permit to provide independent quality review of the plans and specifications provided with the application in order to determine compliance with all applicable requirements imposed pursuant to the State Housing Law (Part 1.5 (commencing with

Section 17910) of Division 13 of the Health and Safety Code), or any rules or regulations adopted pursuant to that law, or under contract with that applicant to provide independent quality review of the work of improvement to determine compliance with these plans and specifications, if the person or other legal entity meets the requirements of this section and one of the following applies:

(1) The person, or a person employed by any other legal entity, performing the work as described in this subdivision, has completed not less than five years of verifiable experience in the appropriate field and has obtained certification as a building inspector, combination inspector, or combination dwelling inspector from the International Conference of Building Officials (ICBO) and has successfully passed the technical written examination promulgated by ICBO for those certification categories.

(2) The person, or a person employed by any other legal entity, performing the work as described in this subdivision, has completed not less than five years of verifiable experience in the appropriate field and is a registered professional engineer, licensed general contractor, or a licensed architect rendering independent quality review of the work of improvement or plan examination services within the scope of his or her registration or licensure.

(3) The immunity provided under this section does not apply to any action initiated by the applicant who retained the qualified person.

(4) A "qualified person" for purposes of this section means a person holding a valid certification as one of those inspectors.

(b) Except for qualified persons, this section shall not relieve from, excuse or lessen in any manner, the responsibility or liability of any person, company, contractor, builder, developer, architect, engineer, designer, or other individual or entity who develops, improves, owns, operates, or manages any residential building for any damages to persons or property caused by construction or design defects. The fact that an inspection by a qualified person has taken place may not be introduced as evidence in a construction defect action, including any reports or other items generated by the qualified person. This subdivision shall not apply in any action initiated by the applicant who retained the qualified person.

(c) Nothing in this section, as it relates to construction inspectors or plans examiners, shall be construed to alter the requirements for licensure, or the jurisdiction, authority, or scope of practice, of architects pursuant to Chapter 3 (commencing with Section 5500) of Division 3 of the Business and Professions Code, professional engineers pursuant to Chapter 7 (commencing with Section 6700) of Division 3 of the Business and Professions Code, or general contractors pursuant to Chapter 9 (commencing with Section 7000) of Division 3 of the Business and Professions Code.

(d) Nothing in this section shall be construed to alter the immunity of employees of the Department of Housing and Community Development under the Tort Claims Act (Division 3.6 (commencing with Section 810) of Title 1 of the Government Code) when acting pursuant to Section 17965 of the Health and Safety Code.

(e) The qualifying person shall engage in no other construction, design, planning, supervision, or activities of any kind on the work of improvement, nor provide quality review services for any other party on the work of improvement.

(f) The qualifying person, or other legal entity, shall maintain professional errors and omissions insurance coverage in an amount not less than two million dollars ($2,000,000).

(g) The immunity provided by subdivision (a) does not inure to the benefit of the qualified person for damages caused to the applicant solely by the negligence or willful misconduct of the qualified person resulting from the provision of services under the contract with the applicant.

Civ. Code § 1134. Required Disclosure Before Sale Of Converted Unit.

(a) As soon as practicable before transfer of title for the first sale of a unit in a residential condominium, community apartment project, or stock cooperative which was converted from an existing dwelling to a condominium project, community apartment project, or stock cooperative, the owner or subdivider, or agent of the owner or subdivider, shall deliver to a prospective buyer a written statement listing all substantial defects or malfunctions in the major systems in the unit and common areas of the premises, or a written statement disclaiming knowledge of any such substantial defects or malfunctions. The disclaimer may be delivered only after the owner or subdivider has inspected the unit and the common areas and has not discovered a substantial defect or malfunction which a reasonable inspection would have disclosed.

(b) If any disclosure required to be made by this section is delivered after the execution of an agreement to purchase, the buyer shall have three days after delivery in person or five days after delivery by deposit in the mail, to terminate his or her agreement by delivery of written notice of that termination to the owner, subdivider, or agent. Any disclosure delivered after the execution of an agreement to purchase shall contain a statement describing the buyer's right, method and time to rescind as prescribed by this subdivision.

(c) For the purposes of this section:

(1) "Major systems" includes, but is not limited to, the roof, walls, floors, heating, air conditioning, plumbing, electrical systems or components of a similar or comparable nature, and recreational facilities.

(2) Delivery to a prospective buyer of the written statement required by this section shall be deemed effected when delivered personally or by mail to the prospective buyer or to an agent thereof, or to a spouse unless the agreement provides to the contrary. Delivery shall also be made to additional prospective buyers who have made a request therefor in writing.

(3) "Prospective buyer" includes any person who makes an offer to purchase a unit in the condominium, community apartment project, or stock cooperative.

(d) Any person who willfully fails to carry out the requirements of this section shall be liable in the amount of actual damages suffered by the buyer.

(e) Nothing in this section shall preclude the injured party from pursuing any remedy available under any other provision of law.

(f) No transfer of title to a unit subject to the provisions of this chapter shall be invalid solely because of the failure of any person to comply with the requirements of this section.

(g) The written statement required by this section shall not abridge or limit any other obligation of disclosure created by any other provision of law or which is or may be required to avoid fraud, deceit, or misrepresentation in the transaction.

CONSTRUCTION DEFECT LITIGATION FOR COMMON INTEREST DEVELOPMENTS

For actions for damages against common interest development builders, developers or general contractors, see Chapter 2, beginning at Civil Code § 6000.

9

SIGNIFICANT JUDICIAL DECISIONS AFFECTING COMMON INTEREST DEVELOPMENTS

(Cases decided within the past year are shown entirely in ***bold italicized*** print.)

Published court decisions play an important role in the American legal system by creating law and providing precedent upon which courts in the future may rely in deciding similar disputes. To appreciate the significance of a particular judicial decision it is helpful to understand the basic structure of the judicial system. There are two independent judicial systems in the United States that operate concurrently – the state court system and the federal court system. State courts generally handle matters of local concern, such as individual rights and property rights of state citizens. State court decisions comprise the vast majority of those involving common interest developments. Federal courts are generally concerned with enforcement of federal laws, such as federal constitutional rights, federal housing laws, bankruptcy, federal income taxation and disputes between citizens of different states. Federal courts sometimes touch upon matters involving common interest developments. Appellate courts in both systems review trial court decisions based upon evidence that is preserved in a judicial record. Ultimately, the final decision-making authority is a supreme court in both state and federal systems. The higher the court, the higher the value of its decision as precedent.

This chapter contains overviews of the most significant judicial decisions by the California Supreme Court and the California Courts of Appeal regarding common interest developments. They are organized by subject matter. The cases are also listed in the Index.

The cases discussed here are provided for information only and are current as of November 1, 2021. The subsequent history of a case should be checked before relying on it.

ADMINISTRATIVE AND TRANSFER FEES

Berryman v. Merit Property Management, Inc. (2007) 152 Cal.App.4th 1544. An owner of a home located in two associations was required by the property management company to pay $100 in document fees and $225 in transfer fees to each association on the sale of the home. The owner brought suit claiming that the charges were excessive and violated Civ. Code § 4575, which limits the amount of transfer fees an association can charge, and various other claims. The Court of Appeal found that Civ. Code § 4575 applies only to charges by an association and not by a third party vendor, such as a management company, because documentation and transfer fees by a management company are a product of market forces and not subject to statutory control. See also, *Brown v. Professional Community Management Co.* (2005) 127 Cal.App.4th 532.

Brown v. Professional Community Management Co. (2005) 127 Cal.App.4th 532. An owner sued the association and its property manager challenging the legality of certain fees imposed by the property manager on the owner for collection services the property manager provided to the association. The owner claimed that Civ. Code § 5600(b) prohibits an association from charging fees in excess of the actual costs incurred. The Court of Appeal held that Civ. Code § 5600(b) does not apply to a property manager or other third party vendors. Their charges are controlled by market forces and not by the Davis-Stirling Common Interest Development Act (Civ. Code §§ 4000 et seq.). Such charges can be passed along to an owner in appropriate circumstances. See also, *Berryman v. Merit Property Management, Inc.* (2007) 152 Cal.App.4th 1544.

Dey v. Continental Central Credit (2009) 170 Cal.App.4th 721. An owner sued the association for unfair competition (Bus. & Prof. Code §§ 17200 et seq.) alleging the association imposed an illegal collection cost on him for collection of a debt he owed the association. The owner contended the fee was not reasonably related to the actual cost of collection as required by Civ. Code § 5600(b). The fee imposed was that charged by the association's management company. The Court of Appeal, relying on *Brown v. Professional Community Management, Inc.* (2005) 127 Cal.App.4th 532, ruled the fees imposed by a management company are not illegal unless they exceed the association's costs, and the association's costs necessarily include fees charged by management for its services. In a broader sense, the amounts charged by third party vendors are controlled by market forces, not Civ. Code § 5600(b), and such charges can be passed along to owners in appropriate circumstances.

Fowler v. M&C Association Management Services, Inc. (2013) 220 Cal.App.4th 1152. An association's managing agent may charge a "transfer fee" directly to an individual buyer for costs incurred processing paperwork, filing documentation and updating association records following a sale. The court concluded that the term "transfer fee" has multiple meanings, and that the fees charged by the managing agent were not transfer fees within the meaning of Civ. Code §1098, and as such was not obligated to record notice of the transfer fee.

ASSESSMENT ALLOCATION

Bodily v. Parkmont Village Green Homeowners Association, Inc. (1980) 104 Cal.App.3d 348. An agreement between a developer and an association suspending the developer's obligation to pay assessments on unsold lots is a material change in the public offering that requires the prior approval of the Bureau of Real Estate. Without such approval the association may disregard the agreement and recover all unpaid assessments.

Cebular v. Cooper Arms Homeowners Association (2006) 142 Cal.App.4th 106. A stock cooperative was converted into condominiums. Under its new CC&Rs, assessments were allocated among the members according to their voting rights as had been done among the shareholders of the stock cooperative. A member challenged the allocation as "wholly arbitrary" because the division did not reflect the value, location, square footage, elevation or ocean views of units. The Court of Appeal held that the unusual method of allocation was justified for historical reasons, and when judged against the presumption of reasonableness given to CC&R provisions, the allocation was not "wholly arbitrary" and did not violate any public policy. The court noted that the plaintiff "should have considered the governing documents to determine his rights and liabilities" when he purchased his unit.

ASSESSMENT OBLIGATION

Park Place Estates Homeowners Association v. Naber (1994) 29 Cal.App.4th 427. An owner may not withhold assessments owed to the association on the grounds that the owner is entitled to recover money or damages from the association for some other obligation. The Davis-Stirling Common Interest Development Act establishes a strong public policy against allowing an owner to offset assessments against any other obligation allegedly owed by the association to the owner.

ASSESSMENT COLLECTION

Basave de Guillen (2019) 604 B.R. 826. The Davis-Stirling Common Interest Development Act does not authorize a continuing lien securing future assessments accruing after the recordation of the lien. Civ. Code § 5675(a) limits the lien to the amounts specified in the notice of delinquent assessment, and the notice must include an itemized statement showing the delinquent assessments (and related fees and costs) owing at the time of notice. Therefore, post-lien assessments are unsecured and dischargeable in bankruptcy.

Diamond v. Superior Court (2013) 217 Cal.App.4th 1172. An association's assessment lien was invalid and unenforceable in a judicial foreclosure action because the association failed to strictly comply with the mandatory notice and other requirements of Civ. Code §§ 5675 and 5705. Strict compliance is required because of the summary nature of the dispossession. The association was required to start over from scratch with a new assessment lien and pay the owner's costs in defending against the foreclosure of the invalid lien.

Diamond Heights Village Association v. Financial Freedom Senior Funding Corporation (2011) 196 Cal.App.4th 290. In a judicial action to foreclose an assessment lien, the assessment lien merged into the judgment of foreclosure. For the association to maintain lien priority after entry of judgment, it must record an abstract of judgment pursuant to Code of Civ. Proc. § 674.

Fidelity Mortgage Trustee Service, Inc. v. Ridgegate East Homeowners Association (1994) 27 Cal.App.4th 503. In the absence of an agreement to the contrary, a trustee service may recover its legal expense from an association and/or its property manager in successfully defending an action for wrongful foreclosure of an assessment lien, even where the association, property manager and the trustee service all acted properly. An agent (i.e., the foreclosure service) forced to defend a suit based upon actions taken at the direction of a principal (i.e., the association or property manager) is entitled to indemnification for such expenses under principles of agency law.

Huntington Continental Townhouse Association v. Miner (2014) 230 Cal. App.4th 590. A homeowners association must accept and apply partial payments that reduce delinquent assessments owed first and then to any other amounts due, such as late fees, interest, and attorneys' fees and costs in accordance with Civ. Code § 5655.

Multani v. Witkin & Neal (2013) 215 Cal.App.4th 1428. Under Civ. Code § 5715(b), an owner has 90 days to redeem his or her property after it has been sold through non-judicial foreclosure if the owner pays all of the arrearage and related costs. In this case, the association's non-judicial foreclosure was invalid absent evidence that it notified the owners of their statutory right of redemption before the property was sold.

Thaler v. Household Finance Corp. (2000) 80 Cal.App.4th 1093. An assessment lien does not have priority over a prior recorded mortgage or deed of trust, regardless of language in the CC&Rs purporting to give an assessment lien priority over a prior recorded encumbrance.

Wilton v. Mountain Wood Homeowners Association (1993) 18 Cal.App.4th 565. Recording an assessment lien by an association is absolutely privileged under Civ. Code § 47(b) and not actionable even if the lien is without merit.

BOARD DECISION MAKING

Affan v. Portofino Cove Homeowners Association (2010) 189 Cal.App.4th 930. A managing agent of a homeowners association has no claim to judicial deference under *Lamden.*

Beehan v. Lido Isle Community Association (1977) 70 Cal.App.3d 858. An association may exercise prudent business discretion in deciding whether or not to sue for a violation of the governing documents.

Clark v. Rancho Santa Fe Association (1989) 216 Cal.App.3d 606. A board may exercise its discretion and aesthetic judgment in deciding whether to approve or disapprove an application for an architectural modification, provided its decision is reasonable and made in good faith. In making such determinations, a board has wide latitude in its decision-making. See also *Dolan-King v. Rancho Santa Fe Association* (2000) 81 Cal.App.4th 948.

Ekstrom v. Marquesa at Monarch Beach Homeowners Association (2009) 168 Cal.App.4th 1111. Owners in a planned development sued to enforce a CC&R provision requiring all trees to be trimmed to a height that did not exceed the roof line, unless the tree did not obstruct a neighbor's view. The association took the position that the restriction did not apply to palm trees because trimming a palm tree from the top down would effectively kill the tree. The court ruled in favor of the owners and ordered the association to enforce restrictions against palm trees as well as other types of trees. The court stated that the "judicial deference rule" of *Lamden v. La Jolla Shores Clubdominium Association* cannot be used to justify a direct violation of the CC&Rs. Rather it applies to the discretionary decision-making in areas such as maintenance and repair. The court also found that the 4-year statute of limitations (Code of Civ. Proc. § 337) applicable to a CC&R enforcement action did not commence to run until the owners demanded enforcement rather than the date of violation.

Eith v. Ketelhut (2019) 31 Cal.App.5th 1. The judicial deference rule applies to an association board's decision that growing grapes on private property does not constitute business or commercial activity prohibited under the association's CC&Rs.

Franklin v. Marie Antoinette Condominium Association (1993) 19 Cal. App.4th 824. An association may assert an exculpatory clause in the CC&Rs as a defense to an action for breach of contract based upon allegations of failure to maintain the common area as required by the CC&Rs. The association here was found free of fault in the discharge of its duties. The exculpatory clause merely shifted the risk of a no-fault loss to the owner. But see *Cohen v. Kite Hill Community Association* (1983) 142 Cal.App.3d 642, holding that an exculpatory clause may not be used to protect an association from at-fault liability.

Lamden v. La Jolla Shores Clubdominium Association (1999) 21 Cal.4th 249. A court will defer to a board's authority and presumed expertise in discretionary decisions regarding the maintenance and repair of a common interest development, provided that the decisions are based upon reasonable investigation, made in good faith and with regard to the best interest of the association, and are within the scope of authority given to the board under the relevant statutes and CC&Rs.

Palm Spring Villas II Homeowners Association, Inc. v. Parth (2016) 248 Cal.App.4th 268. The President of the Association's Board of Directors hired contractors, signed promissory notes, and fired a property manager without the Board's approval and without investigating whether she had the power to do so under the CC&Rs and Bylaws as President and member of the Board. The Board refused to ratify one of the contracts, and the contractor sued. The Association cross-complained against the President asserting breach of fiduciary duty and breach of the CC&Rs and Bylaws. The President argued that she was protected under the business judgment rule. The Court of Appeal held that a director who fails to act as an ordinarily prudent person and/or make a reasonable inquiry as indicated by the circumstances is not protected from liability by the business judgment rule. The Court determined the President failed to act with reasonable diligence and found her liable for her actions.

BOARD MEETINGS

SB Liberty, LLC v. Isla Verde Association, Inc. (2013) 217 Cal.App.4th 272. An attorney representing a limited liability company that owned a condominium was properly excluded from a board of directors meeting because he was neither the managing member of the limited liability company nor the holder of a valid proxy. A letter from the limited liability company authorizing the attorney to represent its interests at the meeting was legally insufficient to meet the requirements of a valid proxy.

BOARD-ADOPTED OPERATING RULES

Bear Creek Planning Committee v. Ferwerda (2011) 193 Cal.App.4th 1178. An association has the power to adopt architectural standards in the form of rules that go beyond those contained in the CC&Rs provided the rules do not conflict with the CC&Rs. But an association does not have the power to adopt a rule authorizing recovery of attorneys' fees in a dispute over the architectural standards when no authority for such an award exists in the CC&Rs.

Dolan-King v. Rancho Santa Fe Association (2000) 81 Cal.App.4th 965. An owner challenging the architectural decision of an association has the burden of proving that the association's decision was unreasonable and arbitrary under the circumstances. A decision is unreasonable and arbitrary "when it bears no rational relationship to the protection, preservation, operation or purpose of the affected land." Unrecorded use restrictions (e.g., rules, guidelines, etc.) may not be given a presumption of reasonableness, but evaluated under a straight "reasonableness" test.

Liebler v. Point Loma Tennis Club (1995) 40 Cal.App.4th 1600. An association has the authority to adopt or amend rules prohibiting nonresident owners from using the common recreational facilities where the intent of the CC&Rs is to have one set of users per unit. The association has the authority to impose fines based upon a rule authorizing the fines. This case may be in conflict with *MaJor v. Miraverde Homeowners Association* (1992) 7 Cal.App.4th 618.

MaJor v. Miraverde Homeowners Association (1992) 7 Cal.App.4th 618. A rule prohibiting a nonresident owner from using the common area recreation facilities when the unit is occupied by another family member is unenforceable. The family member in this case was an 82-year old woman who did not utilize the recreational facilities and there was no issue of double usage. The case did not rule on whether an owner who leases a unit and delegates all rights of use to the common area may be prohibited from using the facilities but indicated that a different rule might apply in such a case. This case may be in conflict with *Liebler v. Point Loma Tennis Club* (1995) 40 Cal.App.4th 1600.

Rancho Santa Fe Association v. Dolan-King (2004) 115 Cal.App.4th 28. Unrecorded rules designed as guidelines for architectural modifications are subject to the test of reasonableness, and, provided they meet that test, are enforceable against the members. In a lawsuit over the proper interpretation of rules, the prevailing party is entitled to attorneys' fees and court costs. In this case, the Court of Appeal upheld an attorneys' fee award in favor of the association in the amount of $318,293.50.

Sui v. Price (2011) 196 Cal.App.4th 933. An association enacted a rule prohibiting the parking of inoperative vehicles on association property. The owner of the single inoperable vehicle sued alleging discrimination because the rule was intended to apply only to him. The court upheld the rule on the ground that it was reasonable when considered by reference to the common interest development as a whole rather than by reference to a particular individual.

Tesoro del Valle Master Association v. Griffin (2011) 200 Cal.App.4th 619. Civ. Code §§ 714 and 5975 allow reasonable restrictions on solar energy systems, including aesthetic impacts, and the association's guidelines in this case were found reasonable. Nothing in either statute requires an association to propose a comparable alternative system when it denies an application.

Watts v. Oak Shores Community Association (2015) 235 Cal.App.4th 466, 185 Cal.Rptr.3d 376. The Oak Shores Community Association adopted rules which limited short term rentals within the development to a period of seven days, and which imposed an annual fee of $135 on owners who rent their lots. The Court of Appeal, applying the judicial deference rule established in *Lamden v. La Jolla Shores Clubdominium Association*, found the rule to be reasonable based upon the evidence and testimony presented by the association, and upheld the rule based upon the language of the CC&Rs, which gave the board broad powers to adopt rules for the development.

CC&R ENFORCEMENT, ARCHITECTURAL CONTROLS

Chapala Management Corp. v. Stanton (2010) 186 Cal.App.4th 1532. An association, acting through its architectural committee, acted properly in requiring an owner to remove two new casement windows that did not comply with the association's approved scheme for windows and awarded the association its attorneys' fees and costs.

Clear Lake Riviera Community Association v. Cramer (2010) 182 Cal.App.4th 459. Owners constructed a home in violation of a height restriction in the association's architectural rules despite prior warnings not to do so. The home exceeded the height restriction by 9 feet and impinged on neighbors' views. In an enforcement action, the court ruled in favor of the association finding that the height restriction was enforceable even though adopted as a rule rather than a CC&R provision. The court required the owners to modify the home to conform to the restrictions even though the modifications were estimated to cost some $200,000.

Cohen v. Kite Hill Community Association (1983) 142 Cal.App.3d 642. An association must exercise authority to approve or disapprove architectural modifications in a manner consistent with the CC&Rs. The association cannot grant approvals prohibited by the CC&Rs. Nor can it immunize itself from liability by standing behind an exculpatory clause in the CC&Rs purporting to insulate it from any liability for improper action.

Deane Gardenhome Association v. Denktas (1993) 13 Cal.App.4th 1394. An association may be prevented from enforcing architectural restrictions where, through informal action of its officers or directors, the association leads an owner to believe that architectural approval has been granted and the owner carries out modifications in reliance on that belief. In order to avoid this problem, officers and directors should follow established procedures for review of architectural submissions by the full board or architectural committee.

Ryland Mews Homeowners Association v. Munoz (2015) 234 Cal.App.4th 705. Owner installed hardwood floor without seeking prior approval from the architectural review committee as was required by the CC&Rs. The modification caused a significant increase in sound transfer and noise and CC&Rs had express provisions barring activities constituting a nuisance and prohibiting any unit from being altered in such a manner that would increase sound transmission to another unit "including modification of flooring. The Court ordered the owner to submit an application for approval to modify his hardwood flooring and, as an interim remedy, ordered that rugs be placed on 80% of the floor areas.

Seligman v. Tucker (1970) 6 Cal.App.3d 691. A CC&R view restriction forbidding the erection of any structure to a height which unreasonably obstructs the view from any other lot is not too vague or uncertain to be enforceable, but a specific height limitation is more easily applied.

Woodridge Escondido Property Owners Association v. Nielsen (2005) 130 Cal.App.4th 559. An owner in a planned development constructed a wood deck that encroached on a shared easement area between two adjacent homes with the permission of the association's architectural committee. The CC&Rs prohibited the installation of "any permanent structure other than irrigation systems" in the easement area. The board of directors later realized the architectural committee's mistaken approval of the deck, ordered it removed, and offered to pay the owner's cost of removal. The owner refused and the association sued to enforce the removal. The court found that because the CC&Rs expressly prohibit the construction of a permanent structure in the easement area, the association did not act arbitrarily in demanding its removal even after approving it. The court further found that the association did not have the authority to approve the construction of any structure in the easement area in violation of the CC&Rs. The association was allowed to recover its attorneys' fees as the prevailing party.

CC&R ENFORCEMENT, GENERALLY

Alfaro v. Community Housing Improvement System & Planning Association, Inc. (2009) 171 Cal.App.4th 1356. Plaintiffs were owners of 22 single-family residences in an affordable housing development. Plaintiffs claimed they weren't told of the affordable housing restrictions and no mention was made of it in the purchase documents. However, some deeds contained the restrictions while others did not. The owners whose deeds did disclose the restrictions were denied relief because their actual or imputed knowledge of the restrictions was a matter of law. But those owners whose deeds did not contain the restrictions were allowed to proceed with an action for nondisclosure. But see *Citizens for Covenant Compliance v. Anderson* (1995) 12 Cal.4th 345.

Almanor Lakeside Villas Owners Association v. Carson (2016) 246 Cal. App.4th 761. The principal issue in this case was whether the association was the prevailing party in an action to collect fines where it was awarded over $100,000 in attorneys' fees and costs. The Carsons owned a lodge and chalets within the development. Per the CC&Rs, commercial use was allowed on the Carsons' lots as this use preexisted the development. The CC&Rs prohibited short-term rentals and imposed reporting requirements for tenants and leases. The commercial properties were exempted from the short-term rental prohibition but not the reporting requirements. The Carsons believed the CC&Rs did not apply to them and failed to comply with the requirements. The board levied substantial fines and ultimately sued to collect $54,000 in dues, fines, fees and interest. The Carsons cross-complained against the association. The court ruled against the Carsons on their cross-complaint but also rejected as unreasonable many of the fines that the association had sought to impose, awarding the association only $6,620 in fines. Davis-Stirling mandates attorneys' fees and costs to the prevailing party in a CC&R enforcement action. On the parties' competing motions for attorneys' fees, the court determined the association was the prevailing party and awarded it $101,803.15 in attorney's fees and costs. The Carsons appealed. The court found that the pivotal issue was whether the association's fines were enforceable under the law. It concluded that even though the association recovered only a fraction of the fines sought, the association has authority to promulgate and enforce reasonable rules. The court also mentioned that it ruled entirely in favor of the association on the Carsons' cross-complaint. The court affirmed the both the attorneys' fees award and the judgment on the cross-complaint.

Biagini v. Hyde (1970) 3 Cal.App.3d 877. No physical damage or financial harm need be shown in a CC&R enforcement action.

Broadmoor San Clemente Homeowners Association v. Nelson (1994) 25 Cal. App.4th 1. California Fair Employment & Housing Act (Gov't Code § 12955 et seq.) and the Federal Fair Housing Act of 1968 (42 United States Code § 3604(f)(1)) authorize the operation of residential care facilities for the elderly even where a CC&R provision prohibits business or commercial activity within a subdivision.

Citizens for Covenant Compliance v. Anderson (1995) 12 Cal.4th 345. Formerly a CC&R restriction could only be enforced if it was referenced in a deed. In this case, the California Supreme Court held that a CC&R restriction could be enforced even though it was not referenced in a deed if the restriction is a matter of public record at the time of purchase. This rule was made retroactive so that it applies to all past and future transfers.

City of Oceanside v. McKenna (1989) 215 Cal.App.3d 1420. A CC&R provision restricting leasing of units to persons of low and moderate income is valid and enforceable in a condominium project subsidized by local redevelopment funds and designed to further redevelopment goals of providing low-cost housing for permanent local residents. The restriction does not violate Civ. Code § 711, prohibiting unreasonable restraints on transfers of property if uniformly applied.

Duffey v. Superior Court (1992) 3 Cal.App.4th 425. An association may sue to enforce CC&R provisions without joining all of the individual owners other than the owner directly in violation. Other owners may or may not choose to become involved in the enforcement action, but whether the other owners join or not, the decision of the court will be binding on all owners.

Eisen v. Tavangarian (2019) 36 Cal.App.5th 626. Property owners brought an action against their neighbors, seeking an injunction to stop them from completing renovations to their home, alleging the renovations violated the CC&Rs. A provision in the CC&Rs required owners to obtain approvals from the association's Architectural Committee before altering exiting buildings on their property; another provision said the powers of the Architectural Committee would cease at the end of 1980; and another provision prohibited the erection of any structure which would obstruct views from any other lot. The trial court interpreted the various provisions of the CC&Rs and concluded the renovations violated the CC&Rs because they obstructed the plaintiffs' views. Their neighbors appealed, and the Court of Appeal reversed. The Court of Appeal held that the CC&R provisions protecting views applied to new structures, and not alterations of existing structures, and that approval for alterations (or renovations) to existing structures was no longer required after 1980. In reaching its holding, the Court of Appeals stated that CC&Rs must be read "as a whole" and the construction that "gives effect to every part of the CC&Rs" should be adopted.

Grossman v. Park Fort Washington Association (2012) 212 Cal.App.4th 1128. The prevailing party in a CC&R enforcement action is entitled to recover pre-litigation attorneys' fees and costs incurred in alternative dispute resolution pursuant to Civ. Code §§ 5925 et seq. Note that the case does not address the language of Civ. Code § 5940 that the costs of the alternative dispute resolution shall be borne by the parties, in the plural. Perhaps fees and costs can be recovered by the prevailing party only if ADR fails and there is a subsequent enforcement action.

Ironwood Owners Association IX v. Solomon (1986) 178 Cal.App.3d 766. An association must follow its own internal disciplinary procedures before seeking relief in court.

Nahrstedt v. Lakeside Village Condominium Association (1994) 8 Cal.4th 361. CC&R restrictions, including pet restrictions, are presumed reasonable and will be enforced uniformly against all association members unless the restrictions are arbitrary, impose burdens on the property that substantially outweigh the restriction's benefits to the development's residents or violate a fundamental public policy. See also *Villa De Las Palmas Homeowners Association v. Terifaj* (2004) 33 Cal.4th 73.

Pacifica Homeowners' Association v. Wesley Palms Retirement Community (1986) 178 Cal.App.3d 1147. A landowner has no natural right to air, light, or an unobstructed view unless created through an easement by the legislature, local government or by private parties in an agreement or deed restriction.

Rancho Mirage Country Club Homeowners Association v. Hazelbaker (2016) 2 Cal.App.5th 252. The principal issue in this case was whether an association was entitled to an award of attorneys' fees and costs under Davis-Stirling in an action to enforce a mediated settlement agreement concerning unauthorized architectural modifications. Defendants modified an exterior patio which the association contended was a violation of the CC&Rs. The parties mediated the dispute pursuant to Davis-Stirling which resulted in a written agreement. Subsequently, the association filed a lawsuit alleging the defendants failed to comply with their obligations under the mediation agreement to modify the property in certain ways. While the lawsuit was pending, the defendants made modifications to the patio to the satisfaction of the association but could not reach agreement regarding attorneys' fees. The association asserted it was entitled to its attorneys' fees as the prevailing party per the mediated settlement agreement and per the prevailing party attorneys' fees provision of Davis-Stirling which provides for such an award in an action to enforce the governing documents. The association filed a motion and was awarded $18,991 in attorneys' fees and $572 in costs. Defendants appealed and the appeals court affirmed. The court found that the association was the prevailing party because it achieved its main goals in the dispute notwithstanding that the goals were initially reached through a mediated settlement and the subsequent litigation involved enforcement of the settlement. The appellate court also found that the trial court lacked the discretion to deny attorneys' fees to the association after determining the association was the prevailing party in the action and concluded the award was reasonable.

Salawy v. Ocean Towers Housing Corporation (2004) 121 Cal.App.4th 664. While Civ. Code § 5975 only authorizes an award of attorneys' fees in an action to "enforce" the governing documents, it does not authorize such an award in an action by a member to enforce an oral promise by the association to reimburse a member for relocation expenses during a large-scale renovation project. But see *Kaplan v. Fairway Oaks Homeowners Association* (2002) 98 Cal.App.4th 715.

Starlight Ridge South Homeowners Association v. Hunter-Bloor (2009) 177 Cal.App.4th 440. In a planned development, the CC&Rs assigned responsibility for maintenance, repair and replacement of the "landscape maintenance areas" to the association. A separate CC&R provision required each owner to "maintain, repair, replace and keep free from debris or obstructions the drainage system and devices, if any, located on his Lot." A drainage channel over one owner's property was in poor condition and the association requested the owner to perform repairs. The owner declined on the ground that the drainage channel was in the "landscape maintenance areas" and an association maintenance responsibility. The association brought an enforcement action and the court ruled in favor of the association largely on the ground that in interpreting the CC&Rs, a court will resolve an ambiguity by reference to the rule of interpretation that a more specific provision will take precedence over a more general provision. Here, the CC&Rs specifically stated that the owner was responsible for maintaining the drainage channel, and that specificity overrode the more general provision that the association was responsible for the landscape maintenance areas.

Villa De Las Palmas Homeowners Association v. Terifaj (2004) 33 Cal.4th 73. A CC&R restriction adopted by an amendment after an owner acquires his unit is enforceable against that owner, even though the owner disagreed with the amendment and voted against it. Subsequently adopted CC&R restrictions, like the original CC&R provisions, are presumed valid and the burden of proving otherwise rests on the challenging owner.

Ward v. Superior Court (1997) 55 Cal.App.4th 60. An association may not record a "notice of noncompliance" or "notice of violation" against a property for a violation of the governing documents. Recordable documents are governed by statute. No statute authorizes the recordation of a "notice of noncompliance" or "notice of violation." Individuals cannot create a recordable document by private agreement or by a CC&R provision. See also, *California Riviera Homeowners Association v. Superior Court* (1996) 37 Cal.App.4th 1599.

CORPORATE SUSPENSION

Palm Valley Homeowners Association v. Design MTC (2001) 85 Cal.App.4th 553. A corporation suspended for failure to file a required information statement with the California Secretary of State, as well as for non-payment of taxes and fees, may not prosecute or defend a lawsuit. Counsel who knowingly violates this rule may be subject to sanctions by the trial court.

DISCLOSURE

Kovich v. Paseo Del Mar Homeowners' Association (1996) 41 Cal.App.4th 863. An association has no legal duty to disclose the existence of construction defects or related litigation to a prospective purchaser, at least where it does not voluntarily undertake to provide such information. The duty to disclose such information is on the seller; not the association.

Ostayan v. Nordhoff Townhomes Homeowners Association (2003) 110 Cal.App.4th 120. An association is not required to notify its members when filing suit against its insurance company for damages, unless a contrary provision is present in the association's governing documents.

Smith v. Laguna Sur Villas Community Association (2000) 79 Cal.App.4th 639. An incorporated association is a separate legal entity distinct from its members, and it may assert the attorney-client privilege to protect all communications (including billings) between the attorney and the association against disclosure to the members. Directors who have an absolute right to request privileged information in their capacity as directors lose that right when they cease to be directors.

FAIR HOUSING ISSUES

Auburn Woods I Homeowners Association v. Fair Employment & Housing Commission (Elebiari) (2004) 121 Cal.App.4th 1578. The California Fair Employment & Housing Act (FEHA) (Gov. Code § 12900 et seq.) requires an association "to make reasonable accommodations in rules, policies, practices, or services when such accommodations may be necessary to afford a disabled person equal opportunity to use and enjoy a dwelling." Two condominium owners filed a complaint with the Fair Employment & Housing Commission (FEHC) alleging that an association violated the FEHA by attempting to enforce a CC&R no-pet restriction prohibiting them from keeping a small dog. The therapeutic effect of the pet was supported by a physician's statement, although it was not a "service dog" as defined in Civ. Code § 54.1. The FEHC ruled against the association, and the ruling was upheld on appeal. The Court of Appeals noted: "We reiterate that the FEHC did not rule that companion pets are always a reasonable accommodation for individuals with mental disabilities. Each inquiry is fact-specific and requires a case-by-case determination." However, the court provided little guidance for future cases.

Bliler v. Covenant Control Commission (1988) 205 Cal.App.3d 18. Age restrictions that meet the requirements of Civ. Code § 51.3 may be imposed on a subdivision converted to senior citizen housing, even though age restrictions were not originally imposed on the development.

C.L. v. Del Amo Hospital, Inc. (2021) WL 4026761 (Only Westlaw citation is currently available, not yet reported). While not directly pertaining to service animals in homeowners association, this case involved a disabled woman with PTSD who attempted on multiple occasions to bring her dog into a voluntary psychiatric treatment hospital. Despite the woman's disability, the hospital refused the service animal on the grounds that it would fundamentally alter the treatment provided to the woman. She sued on the grounds the hospital discriminated against her and failed to provide a reasonable accommodation. The Court of Appeal held that while the dog did qualify as a service animal (i.e., one that was specifically trained to ameliorate the disabled person's symptoms), the type of intensive and interactive treatment offered by the hospital would have been fundamentally altered and thus the hospital was justified in its refusal to provide an accommodation and allow the service animal in.

Nelson v. Avondale Homeowners Association (2009) 172 Cal.App.4th 857. An owner conducted business from his condominium as both a religious and medical counselor. The association's governing documents prohibited a "home business". The owner made no attempt to obtain the association's approval or the local municipality's approval. The association imposed a $200 fine for the violation, revoked all guest passes and offered to make "reasonable accommodation" for the owner to service his clientele by mail while he re-establish an outside office. The owner filed suit claiming discrimination based on disability and religion in violation of the California Fair Employment and Housing Act (Gov't Code §§ 12900 et seq.) and sought injunctive relief. The Court of Appeal affirmed a trial court ruling denying injunctive relief stating that the owner was unlikely to prevail on the merits and therefore injunctive relief was inappropriate.

Walnut Creek Manor v. Fair Employment and Housing Commission (1991) 54 Cal.3d 245. The California Fair Employment and Housing Act (FEHA) (Gov't Code §§ 12900 et seq.) authorizes the Fair Employment Commission to award compensatory damages for out-of-pocket expenses but not for emotional distress. It may award a maximum of $1,000 for a single "course of discriminatory conduct against the same individual on the same unlawful basis." The commission is not authorized to impose multiple, cumulative penalties based upon a single course of conduct.

GOVERNING DOCUMENT AMENDMENTS

Costa Serena Owners Coalition v. Costa Serena Architectural Committee (2009) 175 Cal.App.4th 1175. Costa Serena is a planned development built in seven phases with separate CC&Rs. In 1987, the seven phases were unified into a single community with a single set of CC&Rs which contained a termination provision of December 31, 2006. In 1999, the unified CC&Rs were amended to allow an extension of the termination date by a majority vote of the members. In 2006 the CC&Rs were amended by a majority vote to extend the termination date to December 31, 2039. Several members challenged the 1987 restatement of the CC&Rs and the extension amendment in an effort to eliminate an age restriction limiting occupancy to seniors. The court ruled that any challenge to the irregularities in adopting the 1987 CC&Rs was barred by the 4-year statute of limitation (Code of Civ. Proc. § 343) and the amendment extending the term to

2039 was valid. (Editor's note: The court may have been influenced by Civ. Code § 4265(a) which states: "The Legislature further finds and declares that it is in the public interest to provide a vehicle for extending the term of the declaration if the extension is approved by a majority of all members, pursuant to Section 4065.")

Mission Shores Association v. Pheil (2008) 166 Cal.App.4th 789. An association filed a petition in Superior Court to reduce the percentage of votes necessary to amend its CC&Rs pursuant to Civ. Code § 4275. The association sought to limit residential leases to a minimum of 30 days. The amendment garnered 59% of the vote but not the 67% required by the CC&Rs to change leasing rights. An owner objected on the grounds that he had purchased in reliance on the developer's representations that he was free to rent for any term without restriction. The Court of Appeal held that the rent restriction was reasonable, and was not arbitrary or capricious, and a valid way to ensure that the property would not become "akin to a hotel" and to preserve the character of the community. The court noted that similar restrictions are found in many city and county ordinances, and are not contrary to public policy. Notably, the court also stated that the enforcement remedies in the CC&Rs apply to tenants as well as owners and may be enforced against both by the association, so long as the enforcement does not violate public policy.

Orchard Estate Homes, Inc. v. Orchard Homeowner Alliance (2019) 32 Cal. App.5th 471. Voter apathy or voter non-participation are not required either explicitly or implicitly for a petition to approve CC&R amendments under Civ. Code § 4275.

Peak Investments v. South Peak Homeowners Association (2006) 140 Cal. App.4th 1363. Civ. Code § 4275 allows the association or a member to petition the court for an order reducing the percentage required to amend the CC&Rs when the CC&Rs require a super-majority (e.g., 67%, 75%, etc.) to approve the amendment; but, before petitioning the court the amendment first must be put to a vote and approved by a majority of the members. The question addressed in this case is whether the pre-petition vote must result in approval by a majority of the total voting power of the association or by a majority of the votes actually cast. The Court of Appeal held that the statute requires pre-petition approval by a majority of all members; not a majority of those casting votes.

Quail Lakes Owners Association v. Kozina (2012) 204 Cal.App.4th 1132. An association filed a petition pursuant to Civ. Code § 4275 seeking to reduce a super-majority voting requirement to amend its CC&Rs. 1,409 votes were cast; 1,209 were in favor of the new CC&Rs. Civ. Code § 4275 authorized the court to lower the voting percentage requirement if certain criteria were met. One member objected asserting the unreasonableness of the proposed changes and their defeat on a prior vote. After the association corrected several deficiencies in the petition, and after several court hearings on the reasonableness of the changes, the trial court granted the petition finding, among other things, insufficient opposition. The Court of Appeal affirmed the decision and further held that a single member does not have standing to assert objections on behalf of other members who do not participate in the proceeding.

GOVERNMENT PERMITS

Ocean Harbor House Homeowners Association v. California Coastal Commission (2008) 163 Cal.App.4th 215. An owners association sought a coastal development permit from the California Coastal Commission to build a seawall to protect the condominium complex from erosion that threatened its structural integrity. The commission granted the permit, but as a condition required the association to pay a mitigation fee to the state that over five years would total $5.3 million in present value. The association appealed the amount of the mitigation fee. The Court of Appeal affirmed the amount of the fee finding that it was roughly proportional to the value of one acre of beach front property the seawall would eliminate over time.

INDEMNITY

Crawford v. Weather Shield Mfg., Inc. (2008) 44 Cal.4th 541. An association brought a construction defect claim against a developer and its subcontractor. The court held that the provisions of the subcontract obliged the subcontractor to defend the developer in lawsuits brought against both parties where plaintiffs alleged construction defects arising from the subcontractor's negligence, even if a trier of fact finds that the subcontractor was not negligent.

Queen Villas Homeowners Association v. TCB Property Management (2007) 149 Cal.App.4th 1. An association brought suit against its property manager for failure to disclose and thwart a single board member from self-dealing in providing services in connection with a separate construction defect lawsuit. Apparently, the director was paid for her "services" by the property manager without proper board approval. The property manager defended based upon a standard indemnification clause in the property management agreement under which the association agreed to defend, indemnify and hold harmless the manager from all claims arising out of the manager's performance of its duties, excluding only claims involving the manager's sole negligence or willful misconduct. The Court of Appeal held this type of classic indemnity clause relates only to third party claims and not to claims between the association and the manager themselves. Such protection can only be achieved by a very clearly drafted exculpatory clause not present in the agreement involved here. The court pointed out that to rule otherwise would allow the manager to disregard with impunity its duties under the management agreement. (Note: exculpatory clauses may be subject to challenge as contrary to public policy under Civ. Code § 1668.)

INSURANCE

Atain Specialty Ins. Co. v. Lake Lindero Homeowners Assn. (2022) Unpublished. A management company submitted the association's annual insurance certification to association's carrier but failed to disclose a legal dispute that, while not a pending lawsuit, had involved a threat of legal action by an owner against the association. When the lawsuit was later filed by the owner, the association tendered defense of the matter but its carrier declined to cover the dispute claiming the association's failure to disclose the issue on its annual certification was material. The Court of Appeal upheld the carrier's denial of coverage on the basis the association's failure to disclose was a material fact.

Foothill Village Homeowners Association v. Bishop (1999) 68 Cal.App.4th 1364. A lender holding a security interest in a condominium has no right to the proceeds of an earthquake insurance policy without a specific provision to that effect in the loan agreement.

Larkspur Isle Condominium Owners' Association v. Farmers Insurance Group (1994) 31 Cal.App.4th 106. First party insurance is coverage that insures the policyholder's own property. Third party insurance is coverage that insures the policyholder against his own liability for negligent injury to property of another. In a first party case, only the first policy on the risk during a progressive loss spanning several policy periods is available to provide coverage. Coverage is "triggered" when the loss "manifests" or becomes apparent upon reasonable inspection. This is called the "manifestation rule." A different rule applies in third party coverage cases. See *Montrose Chemical Corp. v. Admiral Insurance Co.* (1995) 10 Cal.4th 645.

Marina Green Homeowners Association v. State Farm Fire & Casualty Co. (1994) 25 Cal.App.4th 200. California Insurance Code § 10087 requires an insurance company providing homeowner insurance to also offer earthquake coverage; however, the requirements of Section 10087 do not apply to an association master policy in a development of more than four units. Section

10087 applies only to individually owned condominium units and residential structures of not more than four units.

Marquez Knolls Property Owners Association, Inc. v. Executive Risk Indemnity, Inc. (2007) 153 Cal.App.4th 228. A dispute arose between adjacent owners over the construction of a patio enclosure that partially blocked the view of the adjacent owner. The adversely affected owner sued the owner who constructed the enclosure and the association to require its removal. The association tendered its defense and indemnity of the claim to its insurance carrier. The carrier denied coverage on the basis of an exclusion from coverage of any claim arising out of the "design, construction, renovation or rehabilitation of any building, structure or other improvement on the property." The Court of Appeal ruled that the exclusion did not apply because the activities of the association involved only the review and approval/disapproval of the alteration and was not involved in any way in the design, construction, renovation or rehabilitation of the physical enclosure. Therefore, the claim was covered by the policy.

Oak Park Calabasas Condominium Association v. State Farm Fire & Casualty Co. (2006) 137 Cal.App.4th 557. An association may not simply refuse to pay a contractor and, when the contractor sues, tender the claim to its insurance carrier thereby transferring its contractual liability from itself to the insurance carrier. Moreover, the association's deliberate act in not paying its contractor lacked the fortuity of unanticipated consequences normally required to trigger insurance coverage.

Palacin v. Allstate Insurance Co. (2004) 119 Cal.App.4th 855. An owner sued her insurance carrier for wrongfully denying coverage for water damage to the walls and floors of her condominium unit. The policy covered all items "which are your insurance responsibility as expressed or implied under the governing rules of the condominium." The carrier claimed that damage to the walls and floors were the association's insurance responsibility and there was no coverage under the owner's policy. The Court of Appeal held that the owner's insurance obligations may be determined not only from the language of the policy involved but also from the language of the governing documents, and the actual practices of the owners and the association.

Parkwoods Community Association v. California Insurance Guarantee Association (2006) 141 Cal.App.4th 1362. California Insurance Guarantee Association (CIGA) is a quasi-governmental agency created to pay covered claims against insolvent property and casualty insurance carriers authorized to do business in California. However, financial assistance is available from CIGA only when no other insurance is available to cover the claim. The court held that a partially exhausted policy of excess insurance constitutes "other insurance available to cover the claim" to the extent that its limits have not been completely exhausted and therefore CIGA had no obligation to contribute to settlement of a construction defect lawsuit.

San Miguel Community Association v. State Farm General Insurance Co. (2013) 220 Cal.App.4th 798. An association's general liability policy that obligated the insurance company to defend any claim seeking damages did not obligate the insurer to defend a lawsuit seeking only injunctive relief and punitive damages but no compensatory damages. In addition, since the complaint did not seek compensatory damages, punitive damages were barred from coverage as a matter of law.

Villa Los Alamos Homeowners Association v. State Farm General Insurance Co. (2011) 198 Cal.App.4th 522. An association sued its insurance carrier to recover some portion of $650,000 it incurred in removing acoustical "popcorn" ceiling material that was discovered to contain asbestos. While the insurance policy did not contain a specific exclusion for asbestos-related claims, it did contain a more general exclusion for claims arising from environmental pollution. The court found this exclusion sufficient to preclude coverage and awarded judgment for the insurance company.

LEGAL STANDING

Adelman v. Associated International Insurance Co. (2001) 90 Cal.App.4th 352. Individual owners have no right to sue an insurance company under an association's insurance policy in which they are not named as insureds. The insurance company's duty runs only to the association, and the association is the proper party to bring an enforcement action if the policy is breached.

B.C.E. Dev., Inc. v. Smith (1989) 215 Cal.App.3d 1142. A developer who no longer has any ownership interest in a common interest development may nonetheless sue to enforce architectural restrictions if the CC&Rs provide standing.

Farber v. Bay View Terrace Homeowners Association (2006) 141 Cal.App.4th 1007. A former owner was sued by the new owner for nondisclosure of a roof leak. The former owner sued, among others, the association seeking a declaration of her rights and responsibilities vis-à-vis the association and obligating the association to perform the roof repairs. Her action against the association was dismissed.

The court ruled that once an owner divests herself of any ownership interest in a common interest development, that person loses standing to enforce the CC&Rs.

Martin v. Bridgeport Community Association, Inc. (2009) 173 Cal.App.4th 1024. The owners purchased a home in a planned development for occupancy by their daughter and son-in-law, and gave those occupants a power of attorney to deal with the association on the owners' behalf. It was later determined that the size of the lot was smaller than represented in the purchase documents. In negotiations with the developer and the association, the daughter and son-in-law reached an agreement on a lot line adjustment that would increase the lot size by approximately 5,600 square feet. The association reneged on the agreement and the occupants sued to enforce the agreement. Although the occupants held an assignment of all rights from the owners to prosecute the litigation, the Court of Appeal ruled that the "occupants", as distinct from the "owners", did not have standing to pursue claims of the owners to recover an interest in real property, which is not assignable. Under Civ. Code § 5975, enforcement rights lie with the association and owners alone. Occupants without an ownership interest do not have standing to enforce the governing documents.

Posey v. Leavitt (1991) 229 Cal.App.3d 1236. An association or a member can bring an action to enforce a CC&R provision prohibiting construction of a deck encroaching on common area, even if the association previously approved the construction. Civ. Code § 5975 provides that unless the CC&Rs state otherwise, CC&R restrictions may be enforced by either the association or a member.

LIABILITY

Alpert v. Villa Romano Homeowners Association (2000) 81 Cal.App.4th 1320. An association has a duty to warn or protect resident and nonresident pedestrians from known trip and fall hazards on association property.

Cadam v. Somerset Gardens Townhouse Homeowners Association (2011) 200 Cal.App.4th 383. An owner sued an association for injuries she suffered when she tripped on 3/4" to 7/8" horizontal separation between two sections of a concrete walkway leading from her garage to her front door. There was no vertical displacement. The court ruled against the owner finding the separation was "minor" and "trivial", and that the association was not required to maintain its walkways in perfect condition.

Chee v. Amanda Gold Property Management (2006) 143 Cal.App.4th 1360. An owner leased his condominium unit to a tenant through the property management company. The tenant owned a terrier that attacked another elderly resident. The injured resident sued the association, the condominium owner, the property manager and the dog owner. The dog owner filed for bankruptcy. The action against the other parties was dismissed because the injured plaintiff could not establish that any of them had actual knowledge of the dog's dangerous propensities or the ability to control or prevent the attack.

Cohen v. S & S Construction Co. (1983) 151 Cal.App.3d 941. A developer who controls an association board is liable to the individual owners for failure to enforce the CC&Rs and the developer cannot immunize itself by an exculpatory clause in the CC&Rs.

Coley v. Eskaton (2020) 51 Cal.App.5th 943. An association director acting with a material conflict of interest is not protected from personal liability by the business judgment rule (BJR). Where directors are employees of an entity member which owns a majority of units and employee compensation is partly based on employer performance, the directors were incentivized to shift responsibility for certain costs away from their employer. This resulted in a material conflict of interest and the directors were personally liable for various breaches of fiduciary duties.

Davert v. Larson (1985) 163 Cal.App.3d 407. Individual owners of an unincorporated association may be personally liable for association liabilities. (This case is partially superseded by Civ. Code § 5805 which provides limited immunity to owners if specified insurance is maintained.)

Frances T. v. Village Green Owners Association (1986) 42 Cal.3d 490. The California Supreme Court likened an association to a landlord and held that a condominium association may be held to a landlord's standard of care as to the common areas under its control. Landlords must take reasonable steps to maintain common area in ways that prevent unreasonable risk of harm to persons.

Heiman v. Workers' Compensation Appeals Board (2007) 149 Cal.App.4th 724. A property manager unknowingly hired an unlicensed and uninsured contractor to perform work on an association building. An employee of the contractor fell and was seriously injured. The unlicensed contractor, the property manager and the association were all sued by the injured employee. They were all held to be co-employers of the injured worker under Labor Code § 2750.5 and responsible for payment of all workers' compensation benefits and tort damages of the injured employee.

Hellman v. La Cumbre Golf & Country Club (1992) 6 Cal.App.4th 1224. An owner living adjacent to a golf course cannot compel the golf course operator to change the line of play so that golf balls do not land on his property, especially when the owner purchased the property with knowledge of the hazard and when he is unable to prove a continuing nuisance resulting in actual damage.

Issakhani v. Shadow Glen Homeowners Assn. (2021) 63 Cal. App. 5th 917. Guest of owner was unable to find parking inside the community, so she parked across a 5-lane street and was seriously injured when she jaywalked to cross the street and enter the association. The injured guest claimed the association was negligent for failing to provide sufficient parking for guests and because the number of guest parking spaces was lower than what the Association's conditions of approval required. The Court of Appeal held a landowner does not have an affirmative duty to provide onsite parking to protect invitees from dangers in crossing streets to access the property. The Court of Appeal also confirmed that even though the association did not provide enough guest parking spaces per its conditions of approval, this did not operate to create a duty of care to protect the injured guest or provide enough parking spaces.

Pamela W. v. Millson (1994) 25 Cal. App.4th 950. An association does not have a duty to take steps to protect against criminal activity absent prior knowledge of similar criminal activity in the neighborhood, even though a condominium project may be located in a high crime area. But a duty may arise when the association becomes aware that criminal acts are likely to occur on its property in the absence of crime prevention measures.

Raven's Cove Townhomes, Inc. v. Knuppe Dev. Co. (1981) 114 Cal.App.3d 783. Developer appointed directors can be held personally liable for decisions that benefit the developer's interests at the expense of the association and its members. Also, the cost of repair is the proper measure of damage in a construction defect lawsuit.

Ruoff v. Harbor Creek Community Association (1992) 10 Cal.App.4th 1624. Members, as well as the association, may be held individually liable for injuries sustained as a result of hazardous conditions in the common area. Civ. Code § 5805, enacted in response to the Ruoff case provides limited immunity to individual members if the association carries certain limits of liability insurance; however, the limited immunity extends only to tort claims.

Sands v. Walnut Gardens Condominium Assn. Inc. (2019) 35 Cal.App.5th 174. Outside the CC&Rs, an association has no independent duty as to common areas arising from tort law. Thus, a breach of contract is tortious only when some independent duty arising from tort law is violated, as laid out in Erlich v. Menezes (1999) 21 Cal.4th 543.

Tilley v. CZ Master Association (2005) 131 Cal.App.4th 464. A security guard sued an association for negligence, negligent supervision and premises liability after he suffered injuries when responding to complaints about a youth party. He attempted to arrest two party-goers and was assaulted. The court dismissed the action finding the association had no duty to restrict youth parties, no control over the party, and did not require the security guard to confront potentially violent persons. The basic scope of the guard's duties was to observe and report misconduct.

Titus v. Canyon Lake Property Owners Association (2004) 118 Cal.App.4th 906. An association had no duty to protect a passenger in a private vehicle driven by an intoxicated driver on association property where neither the association nor its security company acted in any way to increase the risk of such an accident and neither had reason to foresee that such an accident would occur. The mere authority to make and enforce traffic rules within the community was insufficient to create a heightened standard of care on the part of the association.

LITIGATION, CONSTRUCTION DEFECT

Aas v. Superior Court (2001) 24 Cal.4th 627. An association may not recover under common law remedies (e.g., negligence, strict liability, etc.) for construction defects that have not yet resulted in property damage. The remedy for non-damage related defects lies in theories of breach of contract and breach of express and implied warranty and, more recently, under the Right to Repair Act (Civ. Code §§ 895 et seq.).

Acqua Vista Homeowners Association v. MWI, Inc. (2017) 7 Cal.App.5th 1129. A homeowners association brought suit against a material supplier under the SB 800 Right to Repair Act. The court held that pursuant to Civil Code §936, a party suing a material supplier under SB 800 for violation of one or more construction standards must prove that the violation of the construction standard was caused in whole or in part by a negligent act or omission, or breach of contract. Absent this showing, a material supplier cannot be held liable under SB 800.

Baeza v. Superior Court (2012) 201 Cal.App.4th 1214. In a construction defect lawsuit, where owners signed purchase agreements offering two non-adversarial pre-litigation procedures, one statutory (see Civ. Code §§ 910 et seq.) and the other contractual, and the builder opts out of the statutory procedure in favor of its own contractual procedures, the homeowners must participate in the contractual non-adversarial procedures and the builder is excused from participation in the statutory non-adversarial procedures. Any unlawful provisions in the contractual procedures did not invalidate the entire contractual procedure, but rather the unlawful provisions could be severed if found unenforceable in a subsequent trial.

Beacon Residential Community Association v. Skidmore, Owings & Merrill, LLP (2014) 59 Cal.4th 568. A homeowners association sued a developer and various other parties, including two architectural firms, over construction design defects that allegedly made the homes unsafe and uninhabitable for significant portions of the year. The architectural firms, which allegedly designed the homes in a negligent manner but did not make the final decisions on how the homes should be built, challenged the suit on the grounds that they owed no duty to the homeowners with whom they had no contractual relationship. The California Supreme Court held that an architect owes a duty of care to future homeowners in the design of residential housing where the architect is a principal architect on the project and not subordinate to other design professionals. The duty of care extends to such architects even when they do not actually build the project or exercise ultimate control over its construction.

Belasco v. Wells (2015) 234 Cal.App.4th 409, 183 Cal.Rptr.3d 840. An owner purchased a newly constructed home in 2004 and in 2006 filed a complaint against the developer alleging construction defects. Before trial the parties entered into a settlement agreement in which defendant agreed to pay plaintiff $25,000 in exchange for a release of all liability for the disputed defects, and a Civil Code Section 1542 waiver of all known and unknown claims. At the time of settlement, defendant did not disclose that it, and not a subcontractor, installed the roof of the residence. In 2011 plaintiff again filed suit against the developer after discovering roof defects. Plaintiff argued that the Section 1542 waiver contained in the 2006 settlement agreement cannot be applied to latent defects under Section 929 of the Right to Repair Act, and that his rights under the Act could not be waived. The Court of Appeal upheld the trial court's grant of summary judgment in favor of defendant, finding that the 2006 settlement and Section 1542 waiver was a "reasonable release" under Section 929 of the Right to Repair Act.

Branches Neighborhood Corporation v. Calatlantic Group, Inc. (2018) 26 Cal.App.5th 743. The Court of Appeal held that an Arbitrator did not exceed his power in dismissing an association's claims against a developer on the ground that the association violated its own CC&Rs by bringing the claims without first having obtained the required approval of its members. The court held that the association does not have a right to have its members later ratify what was an unauthorized act.

Cancun Homeowners Association v. City of San Juan Capistrano (1989) 215 Cal.App.3d 1352. A municipal building inspector is immune from liability for failure to disapprove landfill with less than 90% compaction where city ordinance called for compaction to that standard but left the building official with some discretion on approval.

Clarendon America Insurance Co. v. Starnet Ins. Co. (2010) 186 Cal.App.4th 1397. The Calderon Act (Civ. Code §§ 6000 et seq.), requires common interest developments to notify a builder in writing of construction defect claims before commencing a lawsuit. The written notice commences a 180-day period during which the parties must attempt to resolve the dispute. The issue in this case was whether the written notice was sufficient to trigger coverage under the builder's general liability policy and thus require the participation of the carrier in pre-litigation negotiations. The Court of Appeal held that the written notice is commencement of a "civil proceeding" sufficient to invoke coverage under the policy.

Creekridge Townhome Owners Association, Inc. v. C. Scott Whitten, Inc. (2009) 177 Cal.App.4th 251. The discovery of a moisture problem in only 1 of 61 units in a townhome complex was insufficient to put an association on notice of latent construction defects for statute of limitation purposes. One moisture problem might well be a routine maintenance problem. The Court of Appeal distinguished the prior case of *Landale-Cameron Court, Inc. v. Ahonen* (2007) 155 C.A.4th 1401, where the discovery of leaks in at least 3 of a project's 8 condominium units, almost a 40% failure rate, was sufficient to put the association on notice for statute of limitation purposes.

Darling v. Superior Court (2012) 211 Cal.App.4th 69. The "Right to Repair Act" (Civ. Code §§ 895 et seq.) establishes a non-adversarial inspection and repair procedure that allows builders to attempt to resolve homeowners' construction defect claims in advance of litigation. The Act requires owners to serve the builder with a notice of the claim, requires the builder to produce copies of certain documents requested by the owners, and gives the builder an opportunity to repair the purported defects within a given time period. If the owners file a lawsuit before the pre-litigation procedure is completed, the builder may obtain a stay of the lawsuit. But if the builder fails to comply with the requirements of the pre-litigation procedure, the owner may proceed with a lawsuit without completing the pre-litigation process. Here, the owners failed to serve the builder with a notice of claim pursuant to Civ. Code § 910(a) and that failure excused the builder from producing documents required by Civ. Code § 912(a).

East Hilton Drive Homeowners Association v. Western Real Estate Exch., Inc. (1982) 136 Cal.App.3d 630. Legal claims based upon strict liability and breach of warranty apply only to the original builder/developer. They do not extend to subsequent owners/investors who acquire the subdivision after construction is complete, even though the units have never been occupied before sale by the subsequent owners/investors.

Eichler Homes, Inc. v. Anderson (1970) 9 Cal.App.3d 224. The sellers of component parts used in the construction of residential housing expressly and impliedly warrant that the component parts are reasonably fit for their intended purpose. Failure of those component parts will give rise to an action for breach of warranty and damages.

El Escorial Owners' Association v. DLC Plastering, Inc. (2007) 154 Cal. App.4th 1337. In a complicated case, the Court of Appeal held, among other things: (1) a suspended corporation may not prosecute or defend a construction defect lawsuit, but its insurance carrier may intervene in the lawsuit to protect its interest so long as it does so in its own name and not the name of the suspended corporation, (2) a trial court has considerable discretion to calculate and allocate damages in making a determination of a good faith settlement, (3) all parties responsible for construction defects, regardless of whether their acts are successive or contemporaneous, are jointly and severally liable as joint tortfeasors, (4) an association successful in a construction defect action is entitled to recover not only expert fees in formulating a repair plan but also for the expense of investigating and evaluating a construction defect claim, and (5) the trial court has discretion to allocate attorneys' fees to be awarded a party between those claims where attorneys' fees are recoverable and those where they are not.

Erlich v. Menezes (1999) 21 Cal.4th 543. Owners of residential property cannot recover for emotional distress from defective construction of a home. California does not allow emotional distress damages arising solely from property damage.

Geertz v. Ausonio (1992) 4 Cal.App.4th 1363. Different statutes of limitation apply to latent and patent defects. Whether a defect is latent or patent for statute of limitation purposes is a question that must be decided at trial on the basis of factual evidence.

Glen Oaks Estates Homeowners Association v. Re/Max Premier Properties, Inc. (2012) 203 Cal.App.4th 913. In a construction defect lawsuit, the association named as defendants, among others, two real estate brokers who acted as agents of the developers and assisted in the sale of lots. The brokers contended that the association had no standing to sue them as the association was not the "buyer" in the purchase agreements. The Court of Appeal held that the association had standing under Civ. Code § 5980 to sue the brokers based on allegations they had obtained inaccurate soils reports and misled the purchasers regarding defects in a common roadway and common area slopes.

Greenbriar Homes Communities, Inc. v. Superior Court (2004) 117 Cal. App.4th 337. A clause in a residential purchase agreement for a newly constructed home requiring all construction defect claims not resolved by mediation to be resolved by reference to an extra-judicial private referee/arbitrator is enforceable against original purchasers who signed the purchase agreement, but not against subsequent owners who bought after the original sale. A later case, *Tarrant Bell Property, LLC v. Superior Court* (2011) 51 Cal.4th 538, disapproves a portion of *Greenbriar* and holds that courts have the discretion to enforce (or in this case, not enforce) a pre-dispute judicial reference provision.

Haggis v. City of Los Angeles (2000) 22 Cal.4th 490. A municipality is immune from liability for failure to perform discretionary investigation and evaluation of site conditions which later result in damage to a residential structure.

Inco Development Corp. v. Superior Court (2005) 131 Cal.App.4th 1014. The 10-year statute of limitation (Code of Civ. Proc. § 337.15) for latent construction defects is not tolled or suspended while the developer/builder is in bankruptcy. Normally, the filing of a petition in bankruptcy operates as an automatic stay of any judicial proceeding against the debtor under 11 U.S.C § 362. However, Code of Civ. Proc. § 337.15 is treated differently from other statutes of limitation because it is a "statute of repose" or ultimate termination of claims. In such cases, 11 U.S.C. § 108 does allow any claim that cannot be brought during the pendency of bankruptcy to be brought within 30 days after the termination of the bankruptcy proceeding. Here, that was not done.

Jimenez v. Superior Court (2002) 29 Cal.4th 473. Manufacturers of component parts incorporated into mass-produced homes are subject to strict liability in tort if those parts cause damage to a residence. Here, plaintiff owners were allowed to recover for damage caused by defective windows to other parts of their homes.

Kriegler v. Eichler Homes, Inc. (1969) 269 Cal.App.2d 224. Builder/developers may be held strictly liable for construction defects in mass produced residential housing. Such housing also carries an implied warranty that it is reasonably fit for its intended purpose.

Landale-Cameron Court, Inc. v. Ahonen (2007) 155 Cal.App.4th 1401. A construction defect lawsuit was barred by the 3-year statute of limitation (Code of Civ. Proc. § 338) for property damage where the president of the association knew of water intrusion in at least 3 of the project's 8 condominium units (about a 40% failure rate) and observed a handyman trying to repair roof leaks more than three years before suit was filed. See also, *Creekridge Townhome Owners Association, Inc. v. C. Scott Whitten, Inc.* (2009)177 Cal.App.4th 251 (different result).

Lantzy v. Centex Homes (2003) 31 Cal.4th 363. In a construction defect lawsuit, equitable tolling is not available to toll or suspend the 10-year statute of limitations (Code of Civ. Proc. § 337.15) from running even if the developer promises or attempts to repair the defects. However, equitable estoppel may suspend the 10-year statute of limitations from running if there is fraud on the part of the developer.

Lauriedale Associates, Ltd. v. Wilson (1992) 7 Cal.App.4th 1439. A developer who is sued for construction defects and inadequate assessments cannot cross-complain for indemnity against the individual unit owners. The developer may obtain equivalent protection by asserting an affirmative defense which will allow an offset against the association's damage claim to the extent that the damage is caused or aggravated by the individual unit owners. Civ. Code § 5805 provides limited immunity from civil liability to individual owners if the association carries certain limits of liability insurance; however, the limited immunity extends only to tort claims and not other types of liability. See also *Jaffee v. Huxley Architecture* (1988) 200 Cal.App.3d 1188, and Civ. Code § 5800 for similar protection of association officers and directors.

Liberty Mutual Insurance Co. v. Brookfield Crystal Cove LLC (2013) 219 Cal.App.4th 98. The Right to Repair Act (Civ. Code §§ 895 et seq.) does not provide the exclusive remedies for construction defects in residential housing and a property owner may pursue common law rights and remedies in addition to those available under the Right to Repair Act.

McMillan Albany LLC v. Superior Court (2018) 4 Cal.5th 241. The California Supreme Court ruled that the Right to Repair Act provides the exclusive remedy for most property damage claims over construction defects. The Right to Repair Act does not affect suits for personal injury, breach of contract, or fraud. It does, however, displace traditional legal remedies for most claims over economic losses against homebuilders stemming from construction defects.

Montrose Chemical Corp. v. Admiral Insurance Co. (1995) 10 Cal.4th 645. All general liability insurance policies in force during a continuous or progressive loss to property over a period of time spanning several policy periods are available to provide coverage for the loss. The fact that the loss is known during an earlier policy period does not eliminate later coverage. All such policies are available to provide coverage and all must respond to a damage claim. This rule applies only to third party liability coverage; it does not apply to first party property damage coverage. See also, *Larkspur Isle Condominium Owners Association v. Farmers Insurance Group* (1994) 31 Cal.App.4th 106.

Oak Springs Villas Homeowners Association v. Advanced Truss Systems, Inc. (2012) 206 Cal.App.4th 1304. In a construction defect action for framing deficiencies in roof trusses, the association settled with the developer and other defendants but not the truss supplier who was a cross-defendant. The settling defendants obtained an order from the trial court that the settlement was entered into in "good faith" barring any further claims against them. The truss supplier appealed the "good faith" order. The Court of Appeal dismissed the appeal as premature because no final judgment had yet been entered against the truss supplier. The only way the merits of a "good faith" settlement can be challenged prior to entry of final judgment is by a writ pursuant to Code of Civ. Proc. § 877.6. The truss supplier chose the wrong procedure for challenging the "good faith" order.

Orndorff v. Christiana Community Builders (1990) 217 Cal.App.3d 683. The standard measure of damage to property is the cost of repair or diminution in value, whichever is less; however, when the injured property has special or unique value to the owner, the owner may elect between either measure of damage but may not recover both.

Paradise Hills Associates v. Procel (1991) 235 Cal.App.3d 1528. A developer may not stop distribution of truthful information about construction defects by owners who already live in the development. Such action is an unconstitutional prior restraint on the exercise of free speech guaranteed by the First Amendment of the United States Constitution. However, distribution of false information may be actionable trade defamation.

Pinnacle Museum Tower Association v. Pinnacle Market Development, LLC (2012) 55 Cal.4th 223. In a construction defect lawsuit, an arbitration clause in the CC&Rs could be enforced by the developer even though the association did not exist when the CC&Rs were recorded and the association did not "consent" to the arbitration clause. The court found the arbitration clause was covered by the Federal Arbitration Act (9 U.S.C. §§ 1, et seq.) which pre-empted any state law requiring judicial resolution of claims covered by the FAA. Notable quote: Section 2 of the FAA states that the act is "a congressional declaration of a liberal federal policy favoring arbitration agreements, notwithstanding any state substantive or procedural policies to the contrary."

Regents of the Univ. of Cal. v. Hartford Acc. & Indem. Co. (1978) 21 Cal.3d 624. An action for latent construction defects is subject to a two-step statute of limitations analysis. The action must be filed within three or four years of discovery of the defective condition(s), depending on whether the action is based on negligent injury to the property which has a 3-year statute of limitations (Code of Civ. Proc. § 338) or on breach of warranty which has a 4-year statute of limitations (Code of Civ. Proc. § 337). But in either case, the action must be filed within 10 years of substantial completion or it will be time barred by the absolute 10-year statute of limitations (Code of Civ. Proc. § 337.15).

Seahaus La Jolla Owners Association v. Superior Court (2014) 224 Cal.App.4th 754. A homeowners association sued the developer and others for construction defects. The association and its counsel conducted meetings with many of the individual homeowners to apprise them of the status and goals of the litigation. The defendants in discovery sought to inquire into the content and disclosures made at those informational litigation update meetings which were conducted by the association's counsel. The association objected on the grounds of attorney-client privilege. The Court of Appeal concluded that litigation meetings were protected by the attorney-client privilege (Evid. Code § 952) and defendants were not entitled to discover the content of discussions that took place at the meetings.

Siegel v. Anderson Homes (2004) 118 Cal.App.4th 994. Subsequent owners of homes sued for construction defects and an issue arose over whether the original owners or the subsequent owners had the right to bring the action. The Court of

Appeal held that subsequent owners could bring an action for construction defects provided that appreciable damage first became apparent during their period of ownership. If the damage first became apparent prior to their purchase, the claim for construction defects belonged to the prior owners. When the damage became apparent is a question of fact to be decided by the judge or jury at trial. The sale of property does not automatically transfer the right to bring an action for construction defects possessed by a prior owner, but the right can be transferred from the seller to the buyer in the purchase agreement.

Smart Corner Owners Assn. v. CJUF Smart Corner LLC (2021) 64 Cal. App. 5th 439. Association had CC&Rs that required membership approval prior to initiating construction defect action. The approval was not obtained. The Developer initially prevailed on a motion for summary judgment claiming the association failed to comply with CC&Rs and also that its motion for summary judgment was a final judicial decision. Following the legislature's adoption of Civ. Code sec. 5986, which applies retroactively, the Court of Appeal overturned the lower court ruling and held the association was not required to obtain a membership vote in order to initiate a construction defect action against the developer. The Court of Appeal also found that a final judicial decision is one that has been substantively litigated through its appeal processes as opposed to procedurally decided through motions or solely lower court rulings.

Stearman v. Centex Homes (2000) 78 Cal.App.4th 611. An association can recover under strict liability for defective components in a building that cause damage to other components of the building, regardless of whether damage has occurred to property apart from the structure itself. Also, expert fees incurred by the association in having professionals investigate construction defects and formulate an appropriate repair plan are recoverable as damages in a lawsuit.

Stonegate Homeowners Association v. Staben (2006) 144 Cal.App.4th 740. An association has a valid claim against a subcontractor arising from the subcontractor's defective work, even if there is no privity of contract between the association and the subcontractor. Regardless of the contractual arrangement between the general contractor and the subcontractor, the subcontractor has a duty to perform the work in a good and workmanlike manner according to industry standards. See also, *La Jolla Village Homeowners Association v. Superior Court* (1989) 212 Cal.App.3d 1131.

Trend Homes, Inc. v. Superior Court (2005) 131 Cal.App.4th 950. A clause in a purchase agreement for a new home requiring all claims for construction defects not resolved by mediation to be resolved by reference to an extra-judicial private referee/arbitrator is enforceable against original purchasers who signed the purchase agreement, but not enforceable against subsequent owners who bought after the original sale and did not sign the original purchase agreement. See also *Greenbriar Homes Communities, Inc. v. Superior Court* (2004) 117 Cal.App.4th 337; but see *Pardee Construction Co. v. Superior Court* (2002) 100 Cal.App.4th 1081, 1086, for a contrary ruling. See also *Tarrant Bell Property, LLC v. Superior Court* (2011) 51 Cal.4th 538, for a contrary ruling that disapproves a portion of *Trend Homes*.

Treo @ Kettner Homeowners Association v. Superior Court (2008) 166 Cal. App.4th 1055. An association sued the developer and others for construction defects. The developer-written CC&Rs required all disputes between the association and the developer be decided by a referral to a non-judicial third party (e.g., a retired judge, etc.) pursuant to Code of Civ. Proc. § 638. On appeal, the CC&R provision requiring non-judicial disposition violated Article I, Section 16, of the California Constitution and Code of Civ. Proc. § 631 which ensures the right to trial by jury unless the parties waive the protection after a dispute has arisen. See also *Grafton Partners v. Superior Court* (2005) 36 Cal.4th 944.

Vaughn v. Dome Construction Co. (1990) 223 Cal.App.3d 144. An owner who sues for construction defects may continue to prosecute the action even after that owner sells the property. Given the duty of disclosure in California, presumably the sale price will be reduced to reflect the existence of disclosed defects. If repairs have been carried out, the seller who actually paid for the repairs has suffered the damage.

Winston Square Homeowners Association v. Centex West, Inc. (1989) 213 Cal. App.3d 282. The trial court may award special master fees as a recoverable cost to the prevailing party in a construction defect action. Additionally, attempted repairs by a developer will only toll the applicable limitation period as to the specific defect repaired.

Ziani Homeowners Association v. Brookfield Ziani LLC (2015) 243 Cal. App.4th 274. In a construction defect suit initiated by a homeowners association, an owner can intervene in a case under Code Civ. Proc. Section 387 if the owner timely files an intervention motion. A court determines timeliness not from when individual condominium owners knew or should have known about the suit by their homeowners association but rather from the date they knew or should have known that their interests in the litigation were not being adequately represented.

LITIGATION, GENERALLY

Arias v. Katella Townhouse Homeowners Association, Inc. (2005) 127 Cal. App.4th 847. An owner brought an action against the association for failure to maintain and repair the common area that allowed toxic mold to develop around her unit. The association made a statutory settlement offer (Code of Civ. Proc. § 998) and the owner declined. After the settlement offer expired, the association made voluntarily payments to the owner for various items of loss but did not pay the full amount of the claim. By statute the prevailing party in such an action is entitled to recover attorneys' fees. The issue faced by the court was whether the amount of post-offer voluntary payments by the association should be added to the amount of the judgment obtained by the owner at trial to determine the owner's total recovery. The court found that the voluntary payments should be added to the judgment for the purpose of determining the prevailing party. Since the total of both exceeded the statutory settlement offer, the owner was the prevailing party and entitled to her attorneys' fees.

Bein v. Brechtel-Jochim Group, Inc. (1992) 6 Cal.App.4th 1387. A process server may serve a subpoena or other legal process on an individual living in a gated community by delivering it to the gate guard if the process server is refused entry to the subdivision. Code of Civ. Proc. § 415.21 provides that a process server, upon presentation of identification as a registered process server or a law enforcement official, must be granted access to a gated community to serve process.

Champir LLC v. Fairbanks Ranch Assn. (2021) 66 Cal. App. 5th 583. Owners sued their association concerning the association's attempt to install a traffic signal adjacent to their property. The owners contended the association failed to comply with the CC&Rs and obtain majority owner approval for the installation. The trial court granted the owner's request for a temporary restraining order and also issued a preliminary injunction. During the trial, the association later obtained the members' approval, so the owners dismissed their lawsuit. Both sides filed a motion to recover their attorneys' fees and costs. Despite voluntarily dismissing their claim, the court determined the owners were the prevailing party because they forced the association to obtain membership approval under the CC&Rs. Even though the association was ultimately able to install the traffic light it was not a prevailing party because they still had to obtain membership approval. The court looks to a party's substantive litigation objectives in determining who is a prevailing party. Also, because the owners dismissed their claims, the court held this precluded the association from being awarded attorney's fees under a contractual theory of recovery.

Elnekave v. Via Dolce Homeowners Association (2006) 142Cal.App.4th 1193. Code of Civ. Proc. § 664.6 provides that "[i]f parties to pending litigation stipulate, in writing signed by the parties outside the presence of the court or orally before the court, for settlement of the case, or part thereof, the court, upon motion, may enter judgment pursuant to the terms of the settlement." In this case an owner sued the association and others over the presence of mold and mold related expenses. A settlement was reached in open court. The association was represented in court by its property manager and its insurance carrier, both of whom agreed to the settlement and represented to the court that they possessed authority to settle on behalf of the association. One party sought to enforce the settlement; the other resisted. The Court of Appeal held that the words "the parties" in the statute mean the actual parties named in the lawsuit and that the presence of the property manager and insurance representative were insufficient to meet the requirement. For an in-court oral settlement agreement to be enforceable, an officer or director of the association must be present in court and approve it.

Heather Farms Homeowners Association v. Robinson (1994) 21 Cal.App.4th 1568. A court has discretion to determine whether or not there is a prevailing party for the purposes of awarding attorneys' fees when an action is resolved by settlement and mutual dismissals. Civ. Code § 5975 and many governing documents authorize an award of attorneys' fees to the prevailing party in a CC&R enforcement action. But a party must obtain a net benefit in order to be a prevailing party and court has wide discretion to determine whether either party is the "prevailing party" in the case of mutual dismissals.

James F. O'Toole Co., Inv. v. Los Angeles Kingsbury Court Owners Association (2005) 126 Cal.App.4th 549. The association refused to pay a $140,196.59 judgment obtained by an owner. The owner pursued post-judgment enforcement proceedings and the association claimed its assets were exempt from execution under Civ. Code § 5620 because all assessments went to "essential services". The Court of Appeals rejected the argument finding that the exemption applies only to "regular assessments" and not to "special assessments" or "emergency assessments". The court ordered the association to impose a special emergency assessment to pay the judgment and, when the association failed to do so, ordered the appointment of a receiver to carry out the trial court's order.

Kaplan v. Fairway Oaks Homeowners Association (2002) 98 Cal.App.4th 715. In actions brought to challenge the validity of an election of the board of directors, the prevailing party is entitled to attorneys' fees under Civ. Code § 5975, which was amended in 1993 to refer to "governing documents" rather than the "declaration." Thus, actions brought to enforce voting rights under the bylaws are treated the same as actions brought to enforce the CC&Rs.

Kaye v. Mount La Jolla Homeowners Association (1988) 204 Cal.App.3d 1476. In an action against the association for failure to maintain common area, owners cannot recover damages measured by both cost of repair and diminution in value, but are limited to one of the two.

Lewow v. Surfside III Condominium Owners Association, Inc. (2012) 203 Cal. App.4th 128. An owner brought an unsuccessful enforcement action against the association. After judgment was entered in the association's favor and before the association moved for an award of attorneys' fees, the owner filed for bankruptcy and then a few months later dismissed the bankruptcy proceeding. Because of the bankruptcy the association did not file a motion for attorneys' fees within the required time limit. The Court of Appeal affirmed a trial court ruling that the association's tardy filing was excusable based on a good faith belief that the bankruptcy had extended the time limit to file the attorneys' fee motion and upheld an award to the association of $292,205.50 in attorneys' fees.

Ranch at the Falls LLC v. O'Neal (2019) 38 Cal.App.5th 155. Homeowners in an association who own private streets within the development are necessary parties to a quiet title action for establishing an easement over those streets.

That v. Alders Maintenance Association (2012) 206 Cal.App.4th 1419. A member sued the association because he disagreed with the results of a recall election. The trial court dismissed the action and awarded the association approximately $15,000 in attorneys' fees. The Court of Appeal upheld the dismissal and found the owner's lawsuit frivolous, but reversed the attorneys' fee award because it was not an action to "enforce" the governing documents as required by Civ. Code § 5975.

Tract 19051 Homeowners Association v. Kemp (2015) 60 Cal.4th 1135, 343 P.3d 883. A homeowners association filed suit to enforce its governing documents against an owner undertaking home renovations. The trial court found that the association was not a common interest development and rendered judgment in favor of the owner, including an award of attorneys' fees under the Davis-Stirling Common Interest Development Act. The Supreme Court affirmed the trial court's decision and held that in an action to enforce governing documents the Act permits an award of attorneys' fees to a prevailing party, even if it is not established that the governing documents are of a common interest development.

Woodland Hills Residents Association v. City Council (1979) 23 Cal.3d 917. Code of Civ. Proc. § 1021.5, authorizing an award of attorneys' fees under the private attorney general doctrine, applies to an action by a community association that successfully challenges a city's improper action under the Subdivision Map Act.

MAINTENANCE

Dover Village Association v. Jennison (2010) 191 Cal.App.4th 123.

An association sued to require an owner to fix an underground sewer lateral that served only his condominium unit. The court ruled in favor of the owner finding that the sewer lateral was located in the common area for which the association was responsible.

Ritter & Ritter, Inc. Pension & Profit Plan v. The Churchill Condominium Association (2008) 166 Cal.App.4th. Members sued their association and individual directors for breach of the CC&Rs, breach of fiduciary duty and injunctive relief for failure to plug utility openings or penetrations in concrete slab floors that separated upper from lower units in a 13-story building. Odors from lower floors were able to pass through the openings and adversely affect the units above. The original construction plans called for the openings to be closed. Building codes in effect at the time of original construction did not require they be closed; current building codes did require closure in new buildings but not a retrofit of existing, nonconforming buildings. The retrofit work adjacent to plaintiffs' units could have been accomplished for $2,700 per unit. A jury found the association breached its duty to maintain the common areas by not undertaking repairs but also found the individual directors were not individually liable. The Court of Appeal affirmed the jury verdict and the trial court's award of $531,159 in attorneys' fees and legal expense against the association.

NUISANCE

Mendez v. Rancho Valncia Resort Partners, LLC (2016) 3 Cal.App.5th 248. After becoming frustrated with the noise emanating from a resort when it hosted outdoor events on a lawn created for that purpose, plaintiffs, who shared a property line with the resort, brought a private nuisance action against the resort, seeking to enjoin the resort from continuing to create noise that would travel onto plaintiffs' property and disturb them there. Following a bench trial, the trial court entered judgment in favor of the resort. The Court of Appeal affirmed the judgment. Because plaintiffs' complaint was based on the level of noise generated by the resort, the trial court appropriately placed due emphasis on that factor in assessing whether that noise violated the noise ordinance. Given all of the evidence, the trial court reasonably determined that it could not conclude that noise levels from the resort that otherwise complied with the general sound level limits of the noise ordinance were nonetheless disturbing, excessive, or offensive within the meaning of general noise prohibitions provision.

PROTECTED SPEECH

Country Side Villas Homeowners Association v. Ivie (2011) 193 Cal.App.4th 1110. An association sued an owner who publicly criticized the board for its handling of maintenance issues, advocating a recall and suggesting deliberate mismanagement. The case was dismissed on the grounds that it was an "anti-SLAPP" (i.e., strategic lawsuit against public participation) under Code of Civ. Proc. § 425.16. The court held that the owner's criticism was protected activity because she raised issues of public interest to all association members.

Cross v. Cooper (2011) 197 Cal.App.4th 357. The owner of a rented condominium listed it for sale. The tenant disclosed to a prospective purchaser that a registered sex offender lived nearby and the purchaser terminated the contract. The owner sued the tenant for interference with contract and other claims. The court dismissed the owner's suit on the grounds that it was an "anti-SLAPP" [i.e., strategic lawsuit against public participation] under Code of Civ. Proc. § 425.16. The court held that the disclosure was made in connection with the public interest in knowing the location of registered sex offenders.

Damon v. Ocean Hills Journalism Club (2000) 85 Cal.App.4th 468. A former association manager sued several association members, two board members and a private association journalism club for defamation. The action was dismissed pursuant to California's anti-SLAPP statute (Code of Civ. Proc. § 425.16), which prohibits litigation filed to dissuade the exercise of free speech rights. The anti-SLAPP statute applied here because the alleged defamatory statements were made "in a place open to the public or in a public forum" and concerned an issue of public interest. Interestingly, the "public forum" requirement was satisfied by an "open board meeting" pursuant to Civ. Code § 4900 and a newsletter distributed only to association members.

Laguna Publishing Co. v. Golden Rain Foundation (1982) 131 Cal.App.3d 816. A private, gated residential community can exclude unsolicited newspapers from being distributed within the community, provided it does not discriminate between similar newspapers engaged in similar activity.

Ruiz v. Harbor View Community Association (2005) 134 Cal.App.4th 1456. Members sued the association for defamation stemming from denial of the members' conceptual plans to rebuild their house. The defamation claims were based on two letters written by association counsel. The association challenged the suit on the grounds that the letters were in furtherance of free speech and protected by Code of Civ. Proc. § 425.16 (anti-SLAPP). That statute provides a special motion to strike a complaint against a person arising from any act by that person in furtherance of their right of petition or free speech under federal or state law. The statute protects all defendants, including corporate associations, from interference with the valid exercise of their legal rights, particularly the right of freedom of speech or the right to petition the government for redress of grievances. These are protections which extend to private conduct that impacts a private community as well as public community.

Turner v. Vista Pointe Ridge Homeowners Association (2009) 180 Cal.App.4th 676. Members sued an association alleging various claims for failure of the association to grant a variance for a modification to an outdoor patio, including a casita, built more than a foot higher than the approved height. The association denied a variance, in part, because of a protesting neighbor. The association responded to the suit by a motion to dismiss on the grounds that its actions in enforcing architectural restrictions were protected free speech activities and subject to dismissal pursuant to California's anti-SLAPP statute (Code of Civ. Proc. § 425.16). The Court of Appeal held that not every communication about the enforcement of architectural restrictions is protected freedom of speech. The court further found that the association's actions in this case were not taken in furtherance of its right of free speech and therefore not protected by the anti-SLAPP statute. See also, *Ruiz v. Harbor View Community Association* (2005) 134 Cal.App.4th 1456; and *Damon v. Ocean Hills Journalism Club* (2000) 85 Cal.App.4th 468.

RECORDS INSPECTION

Moran v. Oso Valley Greenbelt Association (2004) 117 Cal.App.4th 1029. In an action by an owner to recover costs and attorneys' fees in inspecting association records, the trial court has discretion whether or not to award such expenses depending on the facts of a particular case. The court will take into consideration such factors as delay in production, prevaricating tactics, and charging more than the reproduction cost.

Relzoff v. Moulton Parkway Residents' Assn., No. One. (2017) 14 Cal.App.5th 742. Plaintiffs filed suit against a homeowners association alleging failure to make certain association records available for inspection. The Association was declared the prevailing party in the suit and moved for and was awarded attorneys' fees and costs pursuant to Civil Code §5235(c). The Court of Appeal upheld the award of costs and reversed the attorneys' fees award, concluding that under Code of Civil Procedure §1021 attorneys' fees are awarded only when specifically provided for by statute, and Civil Code §5235(c) does not specifically provide for attorneys' fees.

RENTAL RESTRICTIONS

Brown v. Montage at Mission Hills (2021) 68 Cal. App. 5th 124. Over the course of many years, an owner in an association that did not have any rental prohibitions or restrictions rented her unit on a short-term basis. The association's members approved an amendment to the CC&Rs that imposed a minimum lease term, thus prohibiting the owner's short-term rentals, but not prohibiting leases altogether. The owner brought suit claiming Civ. Code §4740 prohibited the association from imposing any rental restrictions or prohibitions that were not in place when she purchased. The Court of Appeal found that the legislative history of Civ. Code §4740 intended broad rights and protections for owners to be able to rent their separate interests without restrictions, unless such restrictions were in place when they purchased or prior to 2012 when the law was implemented. In addition, the Court of Appeal held that notwithstanding the fact that Civ. Code §4741 does permit associations to impose bans on short-term rentals under 30-days, this does not otherwise permit associations to enact such a ban in violation of section 4740. Thus, the Court held that the amendment was unenforceable as to this owner.

Kracke v. City of Santa Barbara (2021) 63 Cal. App. 5th 1089. The City of Santa Barbara modified its treatment of short-term rentals in residential areas of the city in 2015 which substantially restricted the number of permitted short-term rentals. Prior to that, the City had permitted them and collected tax revenue from the rentals. Parts of Santa Barbara fall within the California Coastal Zone and are governed by the California Coastal Act. An operator of a short-term rental housing company sued the City to prohibit its enforcement of its municipal code changes claiming the changes to the code violated the Act. The Act includes in its objectives a goal to maximize public access to the beach and protecting lower cost visitor and recreational facilities. The California Coastal Commission enforces the Act. The Court of Appeal held that any changes (whether they come from the government or a homeowners association) that affect that density or intensity of housing within the Coastal Zone qualify as a "development" under the Act and thus, must be made by both the Commission and the City together. As this applies to common interest developments, associations located within the Coastal Zone cannot modify their rental restrictions without approval from the Commission for the changes.

STATUTE OF LIMITATIONS

Crestmar Owners Association v. Stapakis (2007) 157 Cal.App.4th 1223. An association sued to quiet title to two parking spaces. The CC&Rs provided that all parking spaces not transferred by the developer/converter to condominium buyers after a period of 3 years would be conveyed to the association. More than 20 years later two parking spaces had still not been conveyed. The developer/converter then conveyed the two parking spaces to itself. The association challenged the conveyance. The developer/converter defended on the grounds that the statute of limitation had run on the association's claim. The Court of Appeal affirmed a ruling that the statute of limitation for a quiet title action does not begin to run until an adverse claim is made on the property. Here the adverse claim was the developer/converter's conveyance to itself.

Cutujian v. Benedict Hills Estates Association (1996) 41 Cal.App.4th 1379. The statute of limitation for a claim against an association for failure to perform its duties under the CC&Rs begins to run when a demand is made on the association, not when damage occurs. (Note: Normally, the statute of limitation for property damage begins to run when appreciable property damage has occurred. This case is unique because the owner who brought suit acquired the property long after the damage began. The value of this case as precedent may be limited to similar cases where the owner's acquisition postdates injury and the owner takes action promptly after purchase.)

Pacific Hills Homeowners Association v. Prun (2008) 160 Cal.App.4th 1557. In a planned development, owners installed a gate and a fence in violation of the CC&Rs height and setback requirements and the architectural guidelines adopted as rules. More than four years transpired before the association commenced an enforcement action. The owners defended on the grounds that the 4-year statute of limitation (Code of Civ. Proc. § 337) that applies to written documents controlled rather than the 5-year statute of limitation (Code of Civ. Proc. § 336(b)) that applies to a restriction of the use of land. The Court of Appeal affirmed the trial court's ruling that the 5-year statute of limitation controls both the enforcement of CC&R provisions and the rules, and therefore the association's enforcement action was timely.

Smith v. Superior Court (1990) 217 Cal.App.3d 950. The statute of limitation for an action by a member against an association for breach of fiduciary duty and/or negligence is 3 years. Code of Civ. Proc. § 359 provides that an action against directors of a corporation must be brought within 3 years after the discovery of the wrongful acts by the aggrieved party. But see, *Briano v. Rubio* (1996) 46 Cal. App4th 1167, criticizing Smith.

VOTING AND ELECTIONS

Artus v. Gramercy Towers Condominium Assn. (2018) 19 Cal.App5th 923. A member who obtains preliminary relief in an action challenging a membership vote conducted pursuant to Civil Code section 5100 et seq. is not entitled to an award of attorneys' fees and costs if the member does not succeed in obtaining a final judgment in the member's favor. The Court of Appeal analyzed the legislative history of Civil Code section 5145 and concluded that the statute does not authorize an interim award of attorneys' fees and costs related to obtaining preliminary injunctive relief.

Chantiles v. Lake Forest II Master Homeowners Association (1995) 37 Cal. App.4th 914. There is no absolute right to inspect secret ballots after an annual election – even by an incumbent director – where less intrusive ways of verifying the vote count are available which preserve the privacy of member votes. Article I, Section 1, of the California Constitution guarantees association members the right to privacy in their voting decisions and that right must be balanced against the need to verify election results. Less intrusive inspection methods include a confidentiality agreement, obscuring voter names, or independent review by a neutral person or by the court.

Friars Village Homeowners Association v. Hansing (2013) 220 Cal.App.4th 405. In adopting an election rule that disqualified from candidacy for the board of directors any person related by blood or marriage to another board member or board candidate, the association acted within its authority under Civ. Code § 5105 to specify candidate qualifications, despite language in the statute that prohibits an election rule if it disallows any member from nominating himself or herself for election to the board of directors.

La Jolla Mesa Vista Improvement Association v. La Jolla Mesa Vista Homeowners Association (1990) 220 Cal.App.3d 1187. An owner's written consent to extending the term of the CC&Rs is irrevocable for a reasonable period of time while other owners' consents are being obtained, unless the governing documents specifically permit previously cast ballots to be revoked.

The rule promotes stability and certainty in continuous existence of common interest developments.

Wittenburg v. Beachwalk Homeowners Association (2013) 217 Cal.App.4th 654. A board of directors violated Civ. Code § 5105(a) by improperly denying members opposed to a bylaw amendment equal access to association media and facilities for campaign purposes while at the same time advocating approval of the bylaw amendment. The board's initial advocacy triggered the opposing members' equal access rights. The board violated the statute by charging a rental fee to use a common area for election activity. Even though the rental space was commonly rented out, the statute requires that rental fees should not be charged for election activities. In addition, the board violated the statute by denying use of a common area for election activity without explanation.

10

CALIFORNIA ASSOCIATION OF COMMUNITY MANAGERS, INC. (CACM) SAMPLE MANAGEMENT RETAINER AGREEMENT*

ARTICLE I
Recitals

A. REAL PROPERTY ("Property") COVERED BY THIS AGREEMENT:

Common Interest Development:
Location:
Declaration Recordation No.:
Tract No.:
# of CID Units:
Development Type (i.e., Condo, PD):
Developer (if any):
Address:

B. "ASSOCIATION" AS A PARTY TO THIS AGREEMENT:

Association: ______________________________,
a California Mutual Benefit, Non-Profit Corporation
Address:

C. "Company [INSERT actual name]" AS A PARTY TO THIS AGREEMENT:

Name:
Address:
Principal:

*Note: This sample agreement is reproduced with permission from the California Association of Community Managers (CACM), and may be found on CACM's website at www.cacm.org.

D. DEFINITIONS:

"Assessments" As used in this Agreement, the term "Assessments" shall mean those rates for general and special assessments established and approved by the Board, which the Association members are bound to pay as their share of the common expenses.

"Association" shall mean a corporation formed under the California State Corporations Code, or an unincorporated California Association, its successors and assigns. As used in this Agreement, "Association" shall specifically represent «CID Name».

"Base Fee" shall mean the monthly fee identified in Section 8, (Sections 8.1, 8.1.1-8.1.3) and covers Company's basic contractual services and usual and customary office expenses, exclusive of all extraordinary services that may occur by board direction as identified in Section 9 and Exhibit A of this Agreement.

"Board" shall mean the Board of Directors of the Association, elected pursuant to the Bylaws of the Association.

"Budget" shall mean a written, itemized estimate of the expenses to be incurred by the Association in performing its functions under its Declaration and Bylaws.

"Common Areas" shall mean all the real property and improvements, including without limitation, streets, open parking areas, landscape areas and recreational facilities, which are owned or controlled by the Association for the common use and enjoyment of all the owners.

"Common Interest Development" means any of the following:

1. A condominium project
2. A planned development
3. A stock cooperative

"Association," "Owner," or "Company," herein or any pronoun used in the place thereof, shall mean and include the masculine and the feminine, the singular or the plural number and jointly and severally, individuals, firms or corporations, and each of their respective successors, executors, administrators, and assignees as the context so indicates.

"Governing Documents" shall include but not be limited to the Declaration of Covenants, Conditions and Restrictions ("CC&Rs"), Bylaws, and operating rules of the Association, which govern the operation of the common interest development or Association.

"Managing Agent" shall refer to Company and as defined and referenced in the California Davis-Stirling Common Interest Development Act.

E. MISCELLANEOUS

In consideration of the covenants herein, the Association enters into this Agreement with Company to manage the Property for the compensation provided in Section 8 and for the term in Section 11, subject to the "Scope of Services," Terms and Conditions set forth hereafter.

This Agreement supersedes any and all prior representations, understandings and communications, and may be modified only by written agreement of the parties. Any oral agreements or modifications are expressly invalid.

This Agreement will be construed in accordance with, and governed by, the laws of the State of California. If any term, provision, covenant or condition of this Agreement, including the Scope of Services, should be found by a Court of competent jurisdiction to be invalid, all other provisions shall continue in full force and effect and shall in no way be affected, impaired or invalidated.

If any legal proceeding is necessary to enforce or interpret the provisions of this Agreement, the prevailing party shall be entitled to its reasonable attorney's fees and legal costs, in addition to any other relief to which such party may be entitled. The parties agree that this Agreement shall be effective as of the date set forth in Section 11.

If the Association is incorporated, it is understood and so assured by the signer that the person signing on behalf of Association is a duly elected officer thereof and has corporate authority to execute this Agreement. If the Association is un-incorporated, and this Agreement is signed by both parties prior to the first (organizational) homeowners meeting, it is understood and assured by the person signing on behalf of the Association that the Association automatically assumes or will assume the full legal obligations of this Agreement for the full term stated in this Agreement and that no provisions to the contrary are or will be included in the Association's CC&Rs or Bylaws.

ARTICLE II
Scope of Service

APPOINTMENT AND ACCEPTANCE

In consideration of the mutual promises, covenants, and conditions set forth herein and pursuant to the governing documents of Association, Association hereby appoints Company as its exclusive managing agent as that term is defined in California Civil Code section 4158 and Company hereby accepts the appointment as exclusive managing agent, on the terms and conditions set forth herein, to assist the Board of Directors in managing and maintaining the Property. Company will deliver services reasonably necessary to provide Association with management services on behalf of the Association's Board and strictly within the scope of this Agreement.

It is expressly understood and agreed that Company is to perform services as an independent contractor and is not to be deemed an employee of Association. It is further expressly understood and agreed that Company's employees, officers, directors, shareholders, and other representatives of Company are not parties to this Agreement, except to the extent that they have a right to indemnification under the terms of this Agreement.

Association shall provide certification to Company, within 10 days of the date of this Agreement, that Association is in good standing with all governmental agencies, including but not limited to, the Internal Revenue Service, the Franchise Tax Board, and the Secretary of State. In the event Association fails to provide such certification, Company shall verify that Association is in good standing and, if necessary, take steps to help reinstate Association to good standing. Association shall pay Company for all time and expenses incurred with respect to providing this service at the rates set forth in Exhibit A.

1. COMPANY'S SERVICES AND RESPONSIBILITIES

1.1 Management shall utilize its experience, professional skills and knowledge to assist Association's Board and its committees in accordance with generally accepted industry standards in the area of Common Interest Development Management.

1.2 The Association retains the primary responsibility for enforcement of provisions of the Association's governing documents and contractual agreements and assumes liability for any and all acts and occurrences which relate to the actions of the Association and its actions concerning the Property covered by this contract.

1.3 Company will undertake reasonable efforts to implement the lawful decisions of the Board of Directors and in accordance with the Terms and Conditions of this Agreement, subject to the compensation schedule set forth herein. Company will not be obligated to implement any decision which:

a. is contrary to the terms of this Agreement, industry standards, applicable laws or governing documents,

b. outside Company's expertise, knowledge or licenses, or

c. could involve transactions, activities, services or time that are not expressly set forth in this Agreement.

Company may hire other professionals, at Association's sole expense, as are necessary and proper in the discharge of its duties under this Agreement.

1.4 It will be the responsibility of Company, during the term of this Agreement, to perform the duties as set forth in this Agreement, consistent with the plans and directives of the Association's Directors, and to perform such other acts as are reasonably necessary to discharge Company's responsibilities.

2. FINANCIAL MANAGEMENT

2.1 **Maintenance Assessments:** Company will provide for the collection and deposit of all general and special assessments and any other appropriate charges/fees as they become due and payable or as otherwise directed by the Board.

2.2 **Association Operating Funds:** Company shall establish and maintain, in a bank or savings institution of Company's choice, one or more separate trust accounts in the name of Association. Said deposits shall be insured by the Federal Deposit Insurance Corporation or equivalent, and shall contain only Association trust funds collected on behalf of Association. Company shall have the authority to draw on these accounts for any payments which Company must make to discharge any liabilities or obligations incurred pursuant to the terms of this Agreement, including payment of Company's fees. Any service fees charged for banking services or account maintenance by the financial institution shall be the responsibility of the Association and shall be a charge against Association's operating and/or money market accounts.

2.3 **Delinquent Accounts:** Company is authorized to take reasonable steps for collection of delinquent accounts in accordance with Association's governing documents and delinquency policy, including but not limited to sending notices and assessing the delinquent account late charges, interest, and collection costs. Association shall pay Company for these services in accordance with the rates set forth in Exhibit A. As an accommodation to Association, along with seeking collection of the delinquent accounts, Company shall attempt to collect from the delinquent owner the fees incurred by Association in connection with collecting the delinquent assessments/accounts. In the event such efforts fail, Company will have authority to record a lien against the delinquent owner's unit in accordance with the Governing Documents and the approved collection policy.

Company shall have the authority to utilize attorneys and/or collection agencies in the pursuit of delinquent accounts upon specific resolution of the Board. Company is further authorized to pay, from funds in Association's bank accounts, all costs and attorney's fees incurred in the collection of the delinquent account. When allowable, said costs and fees are to be charged back to the account of the individual owner.

Company is authorized to assess the delinquent account a late charge and a delinquent processing charge, along with other charges for collection and lien fees, reflective of the costs of collection, accounting, payment plan monitoring and legal proceedings. All such assessments are to be deposited into the account of the Association. Company shall be paid <<__>> % of any late charges paid by the delinquent owner. Statutory interest may be charged commencing 30 days after any due date. Reasonable costs of collection, including attorney's fees, are authorized to be charged and collected per Exhibit A.

Association agrees to hold Company free and harmless from any and all liabilities, costs, expenses, obligations and/or attorney's fees incurred by Company in pursuit of the collection of delinquent accounts/assessments, including but not limited to staff time assisting legal counsel or attending court hearings. Association shall pay Company in accordance with the rates set forth in Exhibit A.

2.4 **Disbursement Authorization:** Company is authorized and shall make all disbursements from Association funds for liabilities incurred on behalf of Association. Association acknowledges Company's role as "Paymaster" [UNDEFINED]; accordingly, such disbursements may be made via paper drafts or electronically at the discretion of Company. Company is authorized to utilize all fraud control systems and methods available to Company for the protection of Association's funds. Company is hereby granted authority to make any non-budget expenditures as provided in this section at its own discretion up to <<$____.00>>. In addition, Company shall have the authority to make normal and usual expenditures as prescribed by the Board and/or by the Association's approved operating budget. Company will obtain approval for any extraordinary expenses of the Association as needed.

Emergency repairs involving imminent danger to life or property, or immediately necessary for the preservation and safety of the property, or for the safety of the Members, or required to avoid the suspension of any necessary service to the complex, may be made by the Company irrespective of the cost limitation imposed by this section.

Company will establish Association's reserve accounts at Association's direction. Company makes no warranty or representations regarding the security or yield of any reserve investment. Except for the disbursements provided for above, all reserve account disbursements will be signed by two members of the Board.

2.5 Accounting and Financial Statements: Company will maintain a set of accounting records in accordance with generally accepted industry standards.

a. Company will distribute monthly to all members of the Board a financial statement for the previous month, including copies of the Balance Sheet, Statement of Income and Expenses, Schedules of Cash Investments, reserve allocations, and a check register of disbursements. Company shall also report to Board any cash flow problems.

b. Company shall reconcile all bank statements received by Company and shall provide to the Board on a quarterly basis copies of the bank statements and reconciliations.

c. Company will cooperate with the Association's Certified Public Accountant in its review of Association's financial statement and preparation of the Association's tax returns. Association shall pay Company for this service as set forth in Exhibit A.

d. d. Company will, upon direction from the Board, distribute to all members (homeowners) of the Association, at Association expense, copies of annual financial statements, budgets, collection policies, and all other publications and reports deemed necessary by the Board and applicable laws.

2.6 **Budget Preparation:** Company will prepare and submit to the Board a proposed budget. Any budget draft will be subject to final approval by the Board and the Board shall retain full responsibility for the appropriateness of data contained in the budget. Any decision to adopt Company's proposed budget, or to amend it for adoption will be reserved to and exercised solely by the Board.

2.7 In the event Association elects to have an outside firm perform a reserve study, Company agrees to cooperate with said outside firm and to furnish any and all standard forms and documents in Company's possession, upon request.

3. PHYSICAL MANAGEMENT

3.1 Maintenance: Company will assist the Board in its responsibilities for the upkeep, maintenance and management of the Common Area and the equipment, pursuant to the Association's documents and within the scope of this Agreement.

3.2 Company will receive maintenance requests and/or complaints concerning the Common Areas, and communicate them to appropriate Association contractors and vendors for correction, repairs and maintenance.

3.3 Company will provide a 24-hours per day, 7 days per week call center to assist or refer emergencies in the Common Areas. Serious matters will be reported to the Association's Board with appropriate recommendations for the purpose of receiving further instructions from the Board on how to proceed.

3.4 Company will perform monthly general reviews of the Common Areas and facilities from ground level, and will submit findings, action taken and recommendations to the Board of Directors, to assist in preserving the aesthetics of the Common Areas. Company shall also make additional periodic reviews of the Common Area as it deems necessary to satisfy its duties under the terms of this Agreement. The Company shall not be required to review the Common Areas during its reviews from any other perspective than from ground level. Company is authorized to initiate routine repairs to the Common Areas and facilities, so long as such repairs and maintenance are in compliance with the Board's adopted management plan for the Association or Section 2.4 herein.

3.5 Bids and Quotations for Hiring, Supervising and Discharging Third Party Contractors and Vendors:

Company shall review and provide guidance and assistance to the Board concerning the bidding process to enter into contracts with third parties for goods, materials and services that are expected to exceed $<minimum amount>. The phrase "goods, materials and services" shall be broadly construed to include every kind of goods, materials and services including, but not limited to, those supplied by accountants, architects, attorneys, banks, bookkeepers, governmental agencies, insurance agents and companies, landscapers, maintenance workers, repair workers and all other similarly situated contractors/vendors of the Association.

Company shall assist the Association in obtaining one or more bids from contractors or vendors. Company shall use reasonable commercial efforts in researching vendors and contractors, but cannot and does not make any warranties or representation as to the capability or quality of the work or services of any particular vendor or contractor.

a. Company will, upon receipt of instructions or upon resolution of the Board, request bids from insured vendors/contractors of Company and Board's selection, with a minimum of two (2) and a maximum of three (3) bids for the types of third-party goods or services that Company believes, in its sole discretion, are likely to cost $<<amount>> or more. Those items for which the Board requests bids that are in the Company's sole discretion likely to less than $<<amount>> will not be let out for bid, and Company shall be under no duty to solicit bids for those items. Should the Board wish for Company to solicit bids for an item costing less than $<<amount>>, Company shall be entitled to an hourly fee in accordance with Section 9.1 of this Agreement. Specifications for all items shall be included with the Board's request, and the Board shall be solely responsible for establishing the standards, specifications or criteria for work to be let out for bid. Company will endeavor to make helpful suggestions; however, the Board shall make and be responsible for the final decision in establishing standards, specifications and criteria.

b. Company will, upon receipt of the Board's instructions or resolution, discharge Association vendors/contractors that the Board decides are not performing up to the standards, specifications or criteria established by the Board. Company, on the basis of an operation schedule, job standards and compensation rates approved by the Association, shall investigate, secure and pay third parties in order to maintain and operate the Association. Any contract for such third party will be a direct contract between the Association and the third party, and Company will act solely as the representative of the Association in negotiations and maintenance of said contracts, and not as a contracting party. Compensation for the services of all third-party contractors shall be paid by the Association. Under no circumstance does Company make any representations or warranties for the work performed by any third party contractor.

4. ADMINISTRATIVE MANAGEMENT AND CONSULTING

4.1 Association is responsible for obtaining and delivering to Company all records from prior management. Company shall not be required to locate information not turned over to Company and Company is relieved of any obligation to perform Services under the terms of this Agreement to the extent that performance of such Services is rendered impossible or unreasonably burdensome due to Association's failure to provide Company with its records.

Company shall organize the records and documents it receives from Association, or its prior management, in accordance with Company's normal procedures. The fee Association shall pay to Company for the initial setup is set forth in Exhibit A.

Within sixty (60) days from receipt of complete records, Company shall provide a statement of Association's financial condition or recommend to Association that its records need to be audited by a Certified Public Accountant ("CPA"). If Company expresses concern about the completeness and/or accuracy of Association's financial records, Association agrees to have an independent CPA perform an incoming audit of Association's financial records. If, in the sole opinion of Company, it cannot issue financial reports as a result of the condition of the books and records it receives at the inception of this Agreement, it is relieved of the obligation of issuing financial reports until such time the condition of the books and records is remedied following the independent audit.

Association agrees also to have an independent CPA perform an outgoing audit of Association's financial report should either party terminate this Agreement.

If requested by Board, Company shall obtain three (3) bids for performance of these audits. If a CPA firm is not selected by Board within ten (10) days of notification by Company then Company shall have the right to select the CPA, absent action by Association. Association agrees to pay for and shall be solely responsible for the cost of any audit which may be performed.

4.2 Company will write or delegate letters and communicate as necessary to assist the Board in carrying out its responsibilities.

4.3 Company will counsel and advise Board and its committees in their day-to-day operations.

4.4 Company will assist in interpretation of the rules of the Association and suggest possible steps of enforcement.

4.5 Company will provide, at Association's sole cost and expense, material and expertise in the development of methods of communication to the member homeowners (rules and regulations, etc.), as necessary.

4.6 At the request of the Board, and at the Association's sole cost and expense, Company will send notices of Association meetings, prepare the Agenda for said meeting, circulate minutes of any such meetings as prepared by the Recording Secretary, and implement instructions as approved by the Board.

4.7 Company will attend up to twelve (12) monthly meetings of the Board in any calendar year. Time in excess of two (2) hours per meeting or fraction thereof that lasts after <<_:00 p.m.>>, shall be charged at the rate schedule in accordance with Section 9.1 of this Agreement.

4.8 Company will attend meetings scheduled Monday through Thursday, except holidays. Meetings held on days other than those identified herein, and which the Company agrees to attend, will be charged at the rate on Section 9.1 of this Agreement.

4.9 Company shall endeavor to prepare and send to Board, five (5) days prior to a regularly scheduled Board meeting, a Board packet and report containing the following:

- A description and summary of action items completed since the last regular meeting;
- Copies of pertinent correspondence from homeowners, government agencies or third parties;
- Periodic reports from vendors or contractors providing services to Association;
- Copies of any bids;
- A report of Association's financial transactions since the previous meeting or board packet;
- Minutes of the previous meeting;
- Copies of new owner welcome letters; and
- A summary of all homeowners not current with their Assessments.

4.10 Company will not be obligated to attend special meetings of the membership or of the Board or the Association's committees. However, if Company is requested to attend and accepts, Association will pay Company at the rate schedule in accordance with Section 9.1 of this Agreement, per hour for each hour or fraction thereof that such meeting lasts, plus mileage at the IRS rate per mile in effect at that time.

4.11 At the Association's sole cost and expense, Company will assist in preparation for Association Annual Membership Meeting, including preparation of any appropriate/requested documents, and will attend and participate in conducting the meeting if so requested by the Board.

4.12 Company will not be responsible to record and/or type minutes of regular meetings of the Board or the Annual Meeting of the Association. Upon request by the Board, Company shall select a third party to serve as Recording Secretary, the costs for which shall be borne by the Association. At the request of Association, Company shall distribute a copy of the minutes to any owner, at the expense of Association, according to the rates forth in Exhibit A.

4.13 In the event any Board meeting is cancelled by Association ten (10) days or less prior to a scheduled meeting, for any reason whatsoever, then Association shall pay Company for any such rescheduled meeting at the rate for an extra meeting set forth in Exhibit A.

4.14 Company will maintain possession of all records of the affairs of the Association throughout the term of this Agreement. While Company will put forth every effort to maintain Association records in good order, Company makes no representation or warranty as to the accuracy and/or completeness of such records. Accuracy and completeness of the Association records remain the responsibility of the Association.

4.15 Company agrees to assist Association to enable Association to provide records that Association is required to provide owners under California law and shall make available for inspection and copying by an owner of Association, or the owner's authorized designated representative, Association's records during Company's normal business hours, provided Company receives reasonable notice in advance. Association will pay Company for providing these records and any services related thereto in accordance with the rates set forth in Exhibit A. It is understood and agreed that the services/documents described in this section do not include those services/documents provided to facilitate an owner's sales or refinancing as described in Section 6.2 of this Agreement.

4.16 Special Mailings and Newsletters requested by the Board as prepared by the Association shall be duplicated and mailed at the expense of the Association. All requests for duplication of additional copies of project documents, correspondence, reports, etc., will be at the expense of the Association.

5. TERMINATION OF AGREEMENT

5.1 Either party may terminate this Agreement by providing sixty (60) days written notice to the other. This termination provision may be invoked with or without cause. Upon such notice of termination, the parties agree that this Agreement shall remain in full force and effect for the entire sixty (60) days. In the event that Association does gives such notice to Company, Association shall pay to Company a cancellation sum equal to sixty (60) day's management fees.

5.2 In the event of a dispute over the performance and/or non-performance by either party in this agreement, the alleging party shall offer arbitration to the offending party prior to initiating legal action to gain compliance with the terms and conditions set forth by this agreement.

Prior to requesting arbitration, the alleging party must provide the offending party written notice of the dispute. Such notice shall allow for a reasonable time, not to exceed thirty (30) days, for the offending party to comply with this agreement. After the expiration of said thirty days the alleging party can proceed to binding arbitration or can elect to file suit. Upon acceptance of a written demand for arbitration the dispute shall be submitted to arbitration with a single arbitrator mutually selected by the parties from a list of five arbitrators submitted by the American Arbitration Association. The determination of the arbitrator shall be binding upon both parties. The arbitration shall be conducted pursuant to the rules of the American Arbitration Association and shall be submitted within 120 days of submission. Upon making a written demand for arbitration, the dispute shall be submitted promptly to an arbitrator mutually selected by the parties and the determination of the arbitrator shall be binding upon both parties. If the arbitrator shall determine that offending party has committed a material breach of this agreement, then such finding shall furnish the aggrieved party with the right to terminate the contract 30 days after the final decision of the arbitrator and the offending party shall bear all costs of the arbitration proceeding. In the event that the parties cannot mutually select a single arbitrator, the arbitrator will be selected by the American Arbitration Association from the remaining names. The arbitrator shall award the prevailing party its costs, including reasonable attorney fees.

5.3 The Association acknowledges that Company will incur extraordinary costs in the transition period after termination such as the generation of special reports identifying the inventory of records, the inventory of current activities, processing the transitional documents, mechanically and physically transporting books, records and documents, and meeting with the Association and/or Company's successor to describe, define and explain the Association's documents, instruments and records, and the functioning of the community. Consequently, Association agrees that all such transitional services shall be deemed to be extraordinary services for which Company shall be compensated as hereafter set forth. In any event, however, the compensation for these transitional services shall not exceed the sum of the most recent monthly fee, including extras, payable under the Agreement.

5.4 Should any party hereto retain counsel for the purpose of enforcing or preventing the breach of any provision of this Agreement, including, but not limited to, instituting any action or arbitration to enforce any provision hereof, for damages by reason of such party's rights or obligations hereunder or for any other judicial remedy, then the prevailing party shall be entitled to be reimbursed by the losing party for all such costs and expenses incurred thereby, including, but not limited to, reasonable attorney's fees and costs for services rendered to such prevailing party.

5.5 Upon taking of the entire or a substantial portion of the Property through lawful condemnation proceedings by any governmental party, either party may terminate this Agreement by serving 30 days written notice by certified mail to the other party.

6. RECORDS RETENTION

6.1 The Association's current records shall be kept at the Company's office. Such records shall be available for inspection and copying during Company's normal business hours in accordance with California state laws and Association document provisions, Monday through Friday. Company shall be entitled to charge and receive copying and document research costs, as set forth in Exhibit A, from anyone requesting copies of records or documents, before making such copies. Company shall be entitled to reasonable notice prior to such inspection or copying of records.

6.2 Company shall maintain a current list of members/homeowners name/ property address/mailing address) in accordance with the information supplied to Company. Reasonable efforts will be made to keep this list accurate, but it shall be the responsibility of the Association to advise Company of address or ownership changes. Company shall not be obligated to search official records for such transfers of ownership unless specifically requested to do so by the Board at hourly rates set forth in this Agreement. Company will record changes of address of ownership upon advice from owners or escrow, with supporting documentation.

Company agrees to assist Association to enable Association to prepare and provide documentation Association is required to maintain and/or provide under California law and as reasonably requested by escrow companies, appraisers, and lenders, in order to facilitate sales of individual residences located within Association, and in connection with a homeowner's re-financing needs. Association acknowledges that Company is providing this service as an accommodation and that Association will be charged by Company for these additional services. The fees Association is to pay Company for this service are set forth in Exhibit A or on the web site at <<www.__________>> and are subject to change at the sole discretion of Company.

As a further accommodation to Association, Company agrees to prepare a "demand statement" prior to the close of escrow, and upon notification of the close of escrow, Company agrees to transfer all information from the name of the seller(s) to the name of the buyer(s). Association shall pay Company for these services in accordance with the rate set forth Exhibit A.

As an accommodation to Association, Company will seek collection of the aforementioned fees from the owner through escrow/the escrow process. Association understands and agrees that in the event the fees are not collected from the owner, Association is responsible for payment of the fees to Company.

6.3 Company will maintain documents and complete files for all current correspondence relating to Association, such as incoming unit owner correspondence, violation and architectural control letters, contracts, purchase orders, filing with public agencies, insurance policies and information and other related documents.

6.4 All records and correspondence regarding Association are and will remain the sole property of Association. Company agrees to return any and all such records and correspondence to the Association, or to an entity or person designated by the Board upon termination of this Agreement. Such records will be available for pick up at Company's office or such other designated location as may be agreed upon. Electronic media, such as computer tape, discs, and general electronically stored databases are the sole property of the Company and any duplication or transference of information shall be at the sole discretion of the Company with all costs and charges to be paid by the requesting party.

6.5 Company agrees to maintain storage of Association records and correspondence at Association's sole cost and expense as set forth in Exhibit A.

7. INSURANCE AND INDEMNIFICATION

7.1 Management Insurance: Company will, throughout the term of this Agreement, and at Company's sole expense, maintain the following insurance coverage:

a. Fidelity insurance with coverage for all Company's employees, when applicable, to protect Association funds, if any;

b. Company's liability insurance and comprehensive general liability coverage, including automobile liability, completed operations, blanket contractual and personal injury coverage, with combined single limits of $1,000,000 property damage and liability;

c. Workers' Compensation Insurance in the statutory amount, covering any of Company's employees; and

d. Errors and Omissions coverage with limits of $1,000,000.

7.2 Association Insurance: The Association will, throughout the term of the Agreement and at the Association's sole expense, maintain the following insurance coverage:

a. Occurrence-based Commercial General Liability insurance with limits of at least $1,000,000 each occurrence and aggregate. The policy will include "your real estate manager" within the definition of insured;

b. Directors' and Officers' Liability insurance with limits of at least $1,000,000 per claim and aggregate. This coverage will be maintained for a period of three years following the termination of this Agreement.

c. Commercial Crime Insurance (or fidelity bond) including computer fraud and funds transfer fraud with limits of not less than the balance of the Association's reserve funds plus three months' total assessment revenue; and

d. Property and such other insurance as required by the Association's Declarations and applicable California law and as deemed appropriate to adequately protect the Association and Board.

The Association will provide a current and original certificate of insurance providing evidence of the Association's insurance, showing Company as additional insured for the Liability and Directors' and Officers' policies and also for any umbrella and automobile policies if the Association maintains these coverages such that Company is covered for any and all claims and losses indemnified by Association pursuant to Section 7.3. The policies will provide primary and non-contributing insurance to the additional insured. The liability policy and any Workers' Compensation policy will be endorsed with a waiver of subrogation naming Company.

7.3 Indemnification: The Association shall indemnify, defend at its sole cost (with counsel selected by Company) and hold Company and its employees, agents, representatives, officers, directors, and shareholders harmless from and against any and all claims, demands, actions, liabilities, losses, damages, injuries, costs and expenses (including, without limitation, actual attorney's fees and defense costs) arising directly or indirectly out of, or in connection with or related to, this Agreement or in connection with the management, operation, or condition of the Association, including any and all claims and damages and liability for injuries suffered or death or property damage incurred relating to the Property, except to the extent any such liability is due to the sole willful misconduct or gross negligence of Company and/or its employees. This provision to indemnify Manager and its employees, agents, representatives, officers, directors, and shareholders also relates to any and all acts, errors, or omissions, statements or representations made by Company in the performance and/or non-performance of this Agreement, Manager's duties, and relating to any and all contractual liabilities and non-contractual liabilities which may be alleged or imposed against Company or Association. The obligation of Association to indemnify, defend and hold harmless includes but is not limited to the obligation to pay for, on a current basis, all costs of defense of Company in any action, which costs include but are not limited to the payment of all fees and expenses for legal, expert, accounting or other professional services needed to defend any action brought by any person or entity for which indemnification and defense of Company is called for hereunder. Notwithstanding any other provision of this Agreement to the contrary, the Association's obligations under this Section shall survive the expiration and/or termination of this Agreement for any reason whatsoever and shall bind any and all of the heirs, successors, assigns and/or transferees of the Association. Further, this provision shall not be limited by any applicable insurance coverage available to the Association or Company hereunder.

Company will be responsible only for any willful misconduct and gross negligence where such liability is due to the sole conduct of Company and/or its employees in the performance of its duties under this Agreement.

8. COMPENSATION

8.1 In consideration of Company's acceptance of its appointment hereunder and the performance of services as set forth herein, the compensation to which the Company will be entitled will consist of fees for basic services (base fee) which are considered due upon execution of this Agreement, but are paid monthly, along with those fees and costs for special or extraordinary services as set forth in Exhibit A.

8.8.1 Association shall pay Company a base monthly fee of <<$fee>> in advance on the first day or each month. Association understands and agrees that the base monthly fee does not include payment and reimbursement for goods, supplies, materials and/or services as set forth in Exhibit A and on Company's website. Any costs incurred for such goods, supplies, materials and/or services shall be paid by Association to Company within << days>> days of said costs/expenses being incurred by Company.

Payments, including but not limited to, payment of the Base Fee, fees due in accordance with Exhibit A and Company's website, and fees due on notice of termination of this Agreement pursuant to Section 5 of this Agreement, not made by the fifteenth (15th) of the succeeding month shall accrue a late fee of ten percent (10%) plus bear interest at a rate of ten percent (10%) per annum. Association agrees that in the event of late payment, Company will incur costs and suffer damages, the amount of which costs and damages are impossible or difficult to precisely ascertain, and that the late fee and interest set forth herein is a reasonable estimation of such costs and damages.

Company is entitled to deduct its Base Fee and expenses when due from Association funds in its possession.

8.8.2 Upon the first day, of the first month, following completion of the first year of this Agreement, and every twelve (12) months thereafter, the Base Fee payable to Company shall automatically be increased by either <<___ percent (_%)>> or the cumulative measure of increase in the Bureau of Labor

Statistics Consumer Price Index for All Urban Consumers (CPI-U), whichever is greater. Notwithstanding anything contained herein, Company retains the right to a higher increase at anytime an increased workload can be documented or anticipated.

8.8.3 Company and Association agree that the Base Fee is based upon the estimated time necessary to fulfill Company's duties defined by this Agreement. Association and Company agree that time in excess of «Hours» hours in the aggregate, shall be billed to Association in accordance with Section 9.1 herein.

Company understands the time investment necessary to assist Association at the inception of this Agreement. Accordingly, Company will not charge for excessive time for a period of four months from the date of commencement.

9. SPECIAL OR EXTRAORDINARY SERVICES

9.1 Association shall pay Company compensation as follows:

Principals \$<<rate>> per hour, Community Administrator \$<<rate>> per hour, Accounting and Clerical Personnel \$<<rate>> per hour, or a specific rate as given below, for services performed on behalf of Association outside the normal course of operation or outside the parameters of this agreement.

9.2 Company may be required to perform additional services beyond the scope of this Agreement, for which the above fees, or the current rates that are then applicable, will be charged by the work performed. Examples of such services include, but are not limited to:

a. Assistance in adhering to requirements of laws and regulations which may be passed during the term of the Agreement that require Company participation.

b. Company will be paid per hour, portal to portal, for work performed by Company on behalf of Association, including but not limited to, appearance at court, at hearings, depositions, claims negotiations and processing of insurance losses or reconstruction, performing committee functions, such as monitoring, reporting and updating of any architectural progress and violations within the common areas, development status reports, bank loans, investments, maintenance, construction defect matters, financial reconstruction, discovery on Association's acts prior to the original commencement date of this agreement.

Company will only be paid for the services identified above if performing said services cannot be accomplished, along with Company's other duties defined herein, within the hours prescribed by Section 8.1.3 of this Agreement.

10. ASSOCIATION SET-UP FEE

10.1 Company shall be paid a one-time, non-refundable fee of $<<Set-up fee>> at the commencement of this Agreement to off-set the costs of setting up the Association's records. Not included in such set-up fee are bank charges or independent accountant's fee which may also be incurred.

11. TERM OF CONTRACT

11.1 This Agreement shall commence «Date» and shall continue in full force and effect for twelve months, and hereinafter from year to year. This agreement shall automatically renew for a like term at each anniversary of the commencement date, unless terminated before as set forth above in Section 5.

11.2 Company's compensation shall commence upon <<Date>>.

12. PROTECTION OF COMPANY CONFIDENTIAL INFORMATION

12.1 Association acknowledges that solely by reason of this Agreement, Association may/will come into possession of, obtain knowledge of, or contribute to Company "Confidential Information" as defined herein. "Confidential Information" means any and all information and data whether maintained in hard copy or electronic form, concerning Company's trade secrets, proprietary information, marketing and sales techniques, manuals, programs, design methods, processes, formulas, pricing, bidding methods, inventions, discoveries, improvements, research or development and test results, specifications, data, know-how, formats, marketing plans, business plans and strategies, forecasts, financial information, budgets, projections, employee compensation and benefits, and vendor/supplier lists, identities, characteristics, preferences, and agreements. Such information may be contained in lists, reports, or computer programs; or may constitute unwritten information, techniques, processes, practices or knowledge. Confidential Information includes all information that has or could have commercial value or other utility in the business in which Company is engaged or in which it contemplates engaging. Confidential Information also includes all information of which the unauthorized disclosure could be detrimental to the interests of Company, whether or not such information is identified as Confidential Information by Company.

12.2 Association agrees that at all times, during or after this Agreement, Association will hold in trust, keep confidential, and not, directly or indirectly, disclose to any third party or make any use or cause to permit the exploitation, dissemination, copying or summarizing of any Confidential Information, as defined herein, except for the benefit of Company.

12.3 Association agrees and understands that all of the Confidential Information is a valuable asset of Company and is, will be, and shall at all times remain, the sole and exclusive property of Company. Association is aware that the unauthorized disclosure of Company Confidential Information may be highly prejudicial to its interests, an invasion of privacy, and an improper disclosure. Association understands and agrees that it must maintain and preserve all of the Confidential Information and knowledge thereof as unavailable to Company's competitors, the industry, and the general public in order to protect Company's business, competitive position, and goodwill, since Company derives a competitive advantage in the marketplace by maintaining the Confidential Information and knowledge thereof as secret and unavailable to Company's competitors and the public.

12.4 Association also understands and agrees that but for entering into this Agreement with Company, the Confidential Information would not have been disclosed to Association.

13. NON SOLICITATION OF COMPANY STAFF

13.1 Association further agrees that, during and for a period of one (1) year after the term of this Agreement, Association will not, directly or indirectly, induce or attempt to induce any Company employee or consultant to discontinue its employment with Company or offer or accept for hire any of Company's employees. Association understands and agrees that Company spends a significant amount of time in hiring and training its employees and developing its relationships with its consultants.

13.2 Association understands and agrees that if Association, directly or indirectly, either for Association or for any other person or entity, induces or attempts to induce Company's employees or consultants to discontinue employment with Company, interferes with those relationships, or accepts for hire any of Company's employees, such conduct may cause irreparable harm. Association also understands and agrees that in addition to any equitable relief available to Company, because it may be difficult to ascertain and impractical or extremely difficult to fix an actual monetary amount of damages, Association shall be liable to Company in an amount, as liquidated damages, equal to the compensation paid to said employees/consultants for the twelve (12) months immediately preceding such event. This sum is agreed upon as compensation for the injury suffered by Company, not as a penalty, but to replace and retrain said employee and/or consultant.

14. MISCELLANEOUS

14.1 Company will not be required to perform any act or duty hereunder involving the expenditure of money unless Company shall have in its possession sufficient funds of the Association available. Therefore, if at any time the funds in the possession of Company are not sufficient to pay the charges incident to this Agreement, Company, shall not be responsible to advance its own funds for any reason, and the Association agrees, in such cases, that upon notice thereof by Company, the Association shall make immediate arrangements to make funds available to cover the insufficiency. Company shall promptly notify Association of any deficiency in the account necessary to pay the charges incident to this Agreement.

14.2 Company shall receive communications and directions from any Director and shall act with the assumption that said Director is acting on behalf of the entire Board. Should a conflict arise between Directors, Company shall consider the President as the authorized representative of the Board/Association with authority to act on behalf of Board/Association. Should the President be unavailable to resolve such a conflict, then the Vice President shall serve in this capacity. Company may, but is not required to, submit any matter, direction, instruction or the like to the Board and shall then follow the direction of the Board.

The Board understands its fiduciary duties and agrees to govern the Association in a businesslike manner, acting in good faith and in the best interest of the association and in accordance with the adopted community management plan, the Association's governing documents and applicable state and federal laws.

14.3 No right or remedy herein conferred upon, or reserved to either of the parties to this Agreement, is intended to be exclusive of any other right or remedy. Each and every right and remedy shall be cumulative, and in addition to any other right or remedy, given under this Agreement now or hereafter, legally existing upon the occurrence of any event of default under this Agreement. The failure of either party in the event of default under this Agreement to insist at any time upon the strict observance or performance of any of the provisions of this Agreement, or to exercise any right or remedy, shall not be construed as a waiver or relinquishment of such right or remedy with respect to subsequent defaults.

Every right and remedy given by this Agreement to the parties may be exercised from time to time and as often as may be deemed appropriate by those parties.

14.4 The execution, interpretation and performance of this Agreement shall in all respects be controlled and governed by the laws of the State of California. If any part of this Agreement shall be declared invalid or unenforceable, the invalid or unenforceable provisions shall be stricken from this Agreement without affecting any other provision.

14.5 Notices or other communications between the parties to this Agreement may be mailed by U.S. registered or certified mail with return receipt and postage prepaid, may be deposited in a U.S. Post Office or a depository regularly maintained by the post office, or sent via facsimile or email. Such notices may also be delivered by hand or by any other receipted method including common carriers such as UPS or FedEx or other means permitted by law. For purposes of this Agreement, notices shall be deemed been "given" or "delivered" upon personal delivery thereof or twenty-four (24) hours after having been sent by one of the means permitted by law.

If mailed to Company, the following address applies:

____

____

____

____

If mailed to Association, address of the Secretary of Association applies.

14.6 This Agreement, including any attachments/addendums, contains the entire agreement and understanding of the parties hereto and supersedes any and all prior representations, understandings and communications.

14.7 This Agreement may be modified only in a writing signed by both of the parties. Any oral agreements or modifications are expressly invalid.

14.8 Even though the date of this Agreement signed by each party may be different, the parties agree that this Agreement shall be effective as of the date set forth in Section 11.1 of this Agreement.

14.9 Association and Company acknowledge that they have carefully read and reviewed this Agreement and each term and provision contained herein and by execution of this Agreement show their informed and voluntary consent thereto. The parties hereby agree that, at the time this Agreement is executed, the terms of this Agreement are commercially reasonable and effectuate the intent and purposes of the Association and Company.

15. DISCLAIMER

No representation or recommendation is made by Company, its employees, or the California Association of Community Managers as to the legal sufficiency, legal effect, or other consequences of this Agreement. The parties shall rely solely upon the advice of their own legal counsel as to the legal and other consequences of this Agreement.

By affixing signatures below, both Association and Company agree to the terms, conditions and provisions specified by this Agreement.

ASSOCIATION: **«Association Name»**

BY: ______________________________

TITLE: ______________________________

DATE: ______________________________

COMPANY: **<<Management Company's Name>>**

By: ______________________________

TITLE: ______________________________

DATE: ______________________________

California Association of Community Managers, Inc.SM

23461 South Pointe Drive, Suite 200, Laguna Hills, CA 92653 | info@cacm.org | 949.916.2226 | www.cacm.org

SAMPLE EXHIBIT "A"

INDIVIDUAL PROPERTY OWNER CHARGES
(Billed Directly to Individual Property Owners):

A. Escrow Transactions

1.	Transfer & Set-up Fee *	$<<fee>> ($<<fee>> for new developments)
2.	Refinance Fee *	$<<fee>>
3.	Association Documents – Complete sets only **	$<<fee>>
4.	Homeowner Certifications	$<<fee>>

* Includes statement of account, budget, fidelity bond and financial statement.
** Includes CC&Rs, Bylaws, Articles of Incorporation, Rules & Regulations.

B. Collection Charges (Billed to Association for Homeowner Reimbursement)

1.	Intent to Lien Letter & Tracking Fee	$<<fee>>
2.	Preparation & Recording of Lien	$<<fee>>
3.	Late Charges	50% of amount collected from homeowner
4.	Payment Plan Administration	$<<fee>> per unit per month
5.	Processing Returned Checks	$<<fee>> per check + bank charges

C. Architectural Review Fees (Billed Directly to Homeowner upon Submittal)

1.	Plan Review and Packaging for ARC Submittal *(For custom home development only)*	$<<fee>> per submittal
2.	Modification and Addition Plan Review *(After initial construction of home)*	$<<fee>> per submittal
3.	Progress Reviews and Compliance Reports	No Charge

D. Reimbursable Association Administrative Operating Costs/Expenses

The following charges are reimbursable Administrative Operating Expenses incurred on behalf of the Association. An invoice to substantiate each charge at the time of payment will be provided.

Telephone Toll Calls	Actual Cost
Postage	Actual Cost
Certified/UPS/Fed Ex	$<<fee>> plus charges
Homeowners' Listings	$<<fee>> per page
Fax Charges (incoming & outgoing)	$<<fee>> per page
Distribution Stickers/Keys/Openers	$<<fee>> each plus costs
Labels/Address Sheets	$<<fee>> each (special mailings only)
Mailing Charges	$<<fee>> (special mailings only)
Fold/Staple	$<<fee>> (special mailings only)
Envelopes Small	$<<fee>> (special mailings only)
Large	$<<fee>>each
Special Check Processing	$<<fee>> per check
Photocopies	$<<fee>>per page
Folders/Postcards	$<<fee>> each
Year-end 1099s; Payroll Tax Returns	$<<fee>> each + costs
Special Assessments – First Month	$ N/A
Each Add'l Month	$ N/A
Check Stock/Micr Ink	$<<fee>> per check
Document Storage	$<<fee>> per box per month
Payroll Processing Fee	Greater – 10% of gross payroll or $<<fee>> per check
EDD/Vendor Filing Fee	$<<fee>> per vendor
Off-Site Document Retrieval	Actual Cost
SAMPLE EXHIBIT "A" (continued)	
Verification of Good Standing with Governmental Agencies	$<<fee>> per Agency plus charges
Review of Financial Statements/Preparation Of Tax Returns for CPA	$<<fee>> plus charges

Company is authorized to purchase supplies for Association including, but not limited to, check stock, data discs, copier use, and telephone toll calls made for Association business.

Note: The foregoing list is intended to identify the major areas of service that are extraordinary expenses. There may be additional services for which the Association will be charged. In such cases, the Company will provide cost estimates prior to engaging any additional service. The above fees may be subject to change without notice or subject to change due to implementation of new law(s).

Note: If the Company wishes to add language into their Management Contract that includes Mandatory Arbitration (Section 5.2), the paragraphs below serve as an example and are not intended to be legal advice. Please consult qualified and independent legal counsel for further advice and direction.

MANDATORY ARBITRATION

Except for any controversy, claim or dispute within the jurisdiction of the small claims court, any dispute arising out of or relating to this Agreement, or the alleged breach thereof, except as provided in this Agreement, arbitration shall be governed by and proceed in accordance with and be subject to the provisions of the Federal Arbitration Act; however, to the extent that the Federal Arbitration Act is inapplicable or held not to require arbitration of a particular dispute, the California Arbitration Act – Title 9 of Part III of the California Code of Civil Procedure (commencing at Section 1280 et seq.), or any successor or replacement statute(s), shall apply. The Parties shall be entitled to conduct discovery and take depositions pursuant to the provisions of Code of Civil Procedure Section 1283.05, without giving effect to the limitations contained in Code of Civil Procedure Section 1283.05(e).

Any arbitration shall be held in <<______>> County, California. If the Parties are unable to agree on a neutral arbitrator ("Arbitrator") within ten (10) days of the aggrieved party giving written notice to the other party, then the arbitration will be held under the auspices of one of the following organizations: the American Arbitration Association ("AAA") or Judicial Arbitration & Mediation Services ("JAMS"), or their successor-in-interest, with the designation of the organization to be made by the party who initiates the arbitration.

Any demand for arbitration shall be in writing and must be made within a reasonable time after the claim, dispute or other matter in question has arisen. In no event shall the demand for arbitration be made after the date that institution of legal or equitable proceedings based upon such claim, dispute or other matter would be barred by the applicable statute of limitations or the date specified in this Agreement, whichever is the earlier.

The Parties agree that, except as provided in this Agreement, the proceedings shall be conducted in accordance with the selected organization's then applicable arbitration procedures and rules. The Arbitrator shall be either a retired judge, or an attorney who is experienced in the area of dispute.

The Arbitrator shall apply the law of the state of California or federal law, or both, as applicable to the issues asserted and is without jurisdiction to apply any different substantive law or law of remedies. The Arbitrator shall have exclusive authority to resolve any dispute relating to the interpretation, applicability, enforceability or formation of this Agreement.

Notwithstanding the above, either party may file a request with a court of competent jurisdiction for equitable relief, including but not limited to injunctive relief, and expedited discovery pending resolution of any claim through the arbitration procedure set forth herein; however, in such cases, the trial on the merits of the claims will occur in front of, and will be decided by, the Arbitrator, who will have the same ability to order legal or equitable remedies as could a court of general jurisdiction.

The Arbitrator shall have jurisdiction to hear and rule on pre-hearing disputes and is authorized to hold pre-hearing conferences by telephone or in person, as the Arbitrator deems advisable. The Arbitrator shall have the authority to entertain a motion to dismiss and/or a motion for summary judgment by any party and shall apply the standards governing such motions under the California Rules of Civil Procedure. The Arbitrator may issue orders to protect the confidentiality of proprietary information, trade secrets or other sensitive information.

Although conformity to legal rules of evidence shall not be necessary, the Arbitrator shall determine the admissibility, relevance, and materiality of the evidence offered and may exclude evidence deemed by the Arbitrator to be cumulative or irrelevant, and shall take into account applicable principles of legal privilege, such as those involving the confidentiality of communications between a lawyer and client.

The Arbitrator shall render an award and written opinion, which will consist of a written statement signed by the Arbitrator regarding the disposition of each claim and the relief, if any, as to each claim and also contain a concise written statement of the reasons of the award, stating the essential findings and conclusions of law upon which the award is based, no later than thirty (30) days from the date the arbitration hearing concludes or the post-hearing briefs (if requested) are received, whichever is later. Costs and fees of the Arbitrator shall be borne by the non-prevailing party, unless the Arbitrator determines otherwise. The award of the Arbitrator, which may include equitable relief, shall be final and binding upon the Parties and judgment may be entered upon it in accordance with applicable law in any court having jurisdiction thereof. Either party may bring an action in any court of competent jurisdiction to compel arbitration and to enforce an arbitration award.

11

PARLIAMENTARY PROCEDURE

Parliamentary procedure originated in the English Parliament as a way of debating public affairs even when matters became heated. The rules were introduced to meetings in America with the first settlers from England and, as we know them today, were established in 1876 by Henry M. Robert when he published his first manual on parliamentary law entitled *Robert's Rules of Order*. The original procedural system has evolved into a sophisticated set of rules that has become the standard method of conducting business at organizational meetings.

The purpose of this segment of the book is to set forth the basic rules of parliamentary procedure so that they can easily be understood and adapted to fit the needs of your organization. It is important to remember that parliamentary procedure, while allowing for democratic rule, should be flexible enough to protect the rights of all members, including the opposition. A sense of fair play can be established by providing everyone with an opportunity to be heard. Like any system, parliamentary procedure works when it is used properly by those in charge and treats with respect the rights of all members.

This is a basic summary of a complex set of rules that will serve as a guide for most routine matters. However, when technical issues arise it may be necessary to consult a primary text on parliamentary procedure.

ORDER OF BUSINESS

Organizations using parliamentary procedure usually follow a fixed order of business. The following is a typical example:

1. CALL TO ORDER: The President or chairperson says, "The meeting will please come to order."

2. ROLL CALL: Members say "present" as their names are called.

3. READING AND APPROVAL OF MINUTES: The Secretary reads the minutes of the last meeting and calls for approval, modification or addition by motion.

4. OFFICERS' REPORTS: Officers may provide reports on their latest activities. This part of the meeting is usually limited to a report without discussion.

5. COMMITTEE REPORTS: "Standing" or permanent committees may provide reports on their latest activities, then "ad hoc" or special committees may report, usually in the order of importance. This part of the meeting is also usually limited to a report without discussion.

6. SPECIAL BUSINESS: The assembly then considers important business that was previously designated for consideration at the meeting, such as by a noticed agenda.

7. UNFINISHED BUSINESS: Business left over from prior meetings may then be discussed.

8. NEW BUSINESS: New topics may be introduced and discussed.

9. ANNOUNCEMENTS: Members of the assembly may then inform the members of other subjects and events germane to the business of the organization.

10. ADJOURNMENT: The meeting ends by vote or general consensus recorded in the minutes, or under special circumstances by the chair's decision if time of adjournment was decided by an earlier vote.

TYPES OF MOTIONS

There are four types of motions. Each type has a specific purpose and a relative priority. The order of precedence is: privileged motions, subsidiary motions and then main motions. Incidental motions have no order of precedence; they must be decided as soon as they arise.

1. MAIN MOTIONS introduce matters of business to the assembly for its consideration. They cannot be made when another motion is pending before the assembly, because only one main motion may be considered at a time. However, any main motion must yield to privileged, subsidiary and incidental motions. A main motion might be introduced as follows: "I move that we contract..."

2. SUBSIDIARY MOTIONS assist the assembly in handling the main motion and they are voted on before the main motion. Some examples are: a motion to amend, a motion to refer to committee, a motion to postpone, a motion to limit or extend debate, a motion to close debate and a motion to table. A subsidiary motion may be introduced by saying, "I move the question be amended by striking out…"

3. PRIVILEGED MOTIONS are the most urgent. They usually deal with a special or important matter not directly related to the pending business but which must be addressed immediately. Some examples are: a motion to recess, a motion to adjourn at a predetermined time, a motion to complain about heat, noise or other conditions, a motion to protest breach of rules or conduct, and a motion to avoid improper or embarrassing matter.

4. INCIDENTAL MOTIONS raise questions of procedure that relate to other pending motions and must be considered before a vote on the related motion. For example, an incidental motion may involve a motion to appeal the chair's decision to the assembly, a motion to suspend the rules, a point of order, a parliamentary inquiry, a request to withdraw a motion, a request for division of the motion into parts, or verification of a vote.

CONSIDERATION OF MOTIONS

Generally, a motion is in order if it relates to the business at hand and is presented at the right time. Under the Open Meeting Act, boards of common interest developments may only act on a motion if it relates to an agenda item, and the agenda and notice of the meeting were provided to the membership at least four days prior to the open meeting, or at least two days prior to the executive session. A motion must not be obstructive, frivolous or against the governing documents. Usually, a second is required. A second indicates that another member would like to consider the motion. A second is not required for certain types of motions, but if a second is required, the motion will die without a second. The procedure of a second prevents spending time on a question that interests only one person.

Once made, most motions can be amended by striking out, inserting, or both at once. Amendments must relate to the main motion, and both the main motion and all amendments to it are debatable. Parliamentary procedure guards the right to free and full debate on most motions, except for some privileged and incidental motions which are not debateable.

Some motions are so important that the speaker may be interrupted to make them. After the interruption has been attended to the original speaker regains the floor.

Most motions require a majority vote, unless the governing documents provide otherwise. . Once passed, most motions can be re-debated and re-voted to give the members an opportunity to change their minds. The move to reconsider, however, must come from a member of the winning side.

PRESENTING A MOTION

A motion proposes that the assembly take a stand or take action on some issue. A member can present a motion by making a proposal with the introduction, "I move…" A member may second a motion expressing support for the decision to discuss another member's motion. Following a second, if a second is required, a member may debate the pending motion or related business by giving an opinion or raising a question about the business at hand. Finally, a member may call for a vote on the disposition of the motion.

The procedure for presenting a motion is relatively simple. First, the member making the motion (the "mover") should wait until the last speaker is finished and obtain the floor by addressing the chair. The mover should say, "Mr. or (Ms.) Chairperson (or President)" and state his or her name. The chair will acknowledge the mover by repeating the mover's name. Next, the mover should state the motion in clear and concise terms. The mover should frame the motion affirmatively, not negatively. For example, the mover should say, "I move that we . . ." instead of, "I move that we do not . . ." The mover should avoid personalities, innuendo and irrelevancies in the motion.

Once the motion has been made, the mover should wait for a second. Another member will second the motion by saying, "I second the motion." Or, if a second is not immediately forthcoming, the chair will call for a second. If there is no second and a second is required for the motion, the motion will not be considered.

Following a second, the chair will say, "It is moved and seconded that we…" and debate will commence. The motion then becomes the property of the assembly ("assembly property") and it cannot be changed without the consent of the members by a vote.

A pending motion may be expanded. The mover is allowed to speak first. The mover should direct all comments to the chair, and obey the time limits for speaking as stated in the bylaws or as predetermined by the members or the chair. The other members may speak after the mover is finished, and the mover may speak again after all other members have finished speaking

At the conclusion of debate, the chair will ask, "Are you ready for the question?" If there is no more discussion, the chair will take the vote. Alternatively, a motion for a previous question may be adopted.

VOTING ON A MOTION

The method of voting on a motion depends on the situation and the bylaws. Generally, there are five methods of voting on a motion: 1) by a voice vote; 2) by a show of hands; 3) by a roll call; 4) by a ballot; and 5) by general consent. Any member may move for an exact count on any type of vote that is taken.

A voice vote is taken by the chair asking those in favor to say "Aye" and those opposed to say "No." This method may be used for a majority vote only. It may not be used for a 2/3 vote.

A vote by a show of hands is taken by members raising their hands as sight verification of or as an alternative to a voice vote. It does not require a count.

A vote by roll call is taken by the chair calling out the name of each member who then answers "Yes" or "No" as his or her name is called. The secretary will record the roll call vote as taken when a record of each person's vote is needed.

A vote taken by ballot requires the members to write their vote on a slip of paper. This method of voting should be used when secrecy is desired.

A vote by general consent is used when a motion is not likely to be opposed. It is introduced by the chair saying, "If there is no objection . . ." Members demonstrate agreement by their silence. If a member says, "I object," the matter must be put to a roll call or ballot vote.

A motion is pending so long as it has been stated by the chair but not yet voted on. The last motion stated by the chair is the first pending, and the main motion is always the last voted on.

TABLING AND INDEFINITELY POSTPONING A MOTION

A vote can be delayed for either a predetermined period or indefinitely. Postponement involves two types of motions: a motion to table or a motion to postpone indefinitely. A motion to table is often used in an attempt to "kill" a motion. However, there is always the option to "take from the table" later by a motion for reconsideration by the assembly. A tabled motion will remain tabled until reconsidered. A motion to postpone indefinitely allows members to dispose of a motion without making a decision for or against the matter presented. It is useful in the case of a badly chosen main motion for which either a "Yes" or "No" vote would have undesirable consequences. Again, a motion postponed indefinitely may be reconsidered when a motion for reconsideration is passed.

20 TIPS FOR A SUCCESSFUL MEETING

1. RESPECT TRADITION. Follow established parliamentary procedure.

2. HAVE A WRITTEN AGENDA and stick to it.

3. ALLOT A DESIGNATED AMOUNT OF TIME for each controversial matter and schedule after routine business.

4. RESTATE EACH MOTION so that it may be recorded accurately and understood fully. Repeat again if necessary.

5. CONTROL DISCUSSION and debate through the chair. Require recognition before allowing a member to speak.

6. LIMIT DISCUSSION to matters pertinent to the pending motion.

7. PERMIT FULL DEBATE even if it requires delaying a vote until the next meeting.

8. ALLOW ALL SIDES TO SUBMIT privileged, subsidiary and incidental motions.

9. RAISE A POINT OF ORDER whenever there is an error, mistake, omission or misunderstanding.

10. DO NOT USE parliamentary technicalities for tactical advantage alone.

11. CALL FOR A FINAL VOTE on all motions and in the proper order of their respective precedence.

12. DISPOSE OF ALL NON-CONTROVERSIAL MATTERS by a general consensus vote.

13. REQUIRE A VOTE BY BALLOT on all important contested matters.

14. ALLOW THE CHAIR to resolve procedural questions unless an appeal is taken to the assembly questioning the chair's action.

15. RECORD ALL MOTIONS whether they are defeated or succeed. Record non-controversial motions adopted by general consensus.

16. DO NOT RECORD individual opinion, personal criticism, comments made in debate, motives behind motions or motions that have been withdrawn.

17. PERMIT THE ENTIRE ASSEMBLY to decide when debate should end.

18. DO NOT SPEND VALUABLE MEETING TIME worrying about who is right or wrong. Nothing is as important as it seems at first.

19. BE WILLING TO LOSE A BATTLE OR TWO in order to win the war.

20. GET ACQUAINTED with a good lawyer, CPA and parliamentarian.

12

USEFUL FORMS AND CHECKLISTS

Note: The forms in this chapter are for informational purposes only and may not reflect the most current legal developments. These informational materials are not intended, and should not be taken, as legal advice. You should contact an attorney for advice on specific legal problems, before using these forms.

NOTICE OF BOARD MEETING

Date: ______________________

Dear Members,

Please be advised that the Board of Directors will be meeting in open/executive session on ___(date)___, at ___(time)___. The meeting will be held at the ___(name of facility)___, located at ___(address of facility)___. The business of the board shall be limited to those items contained in the attached agenda.

Board of Directors

Model Homeowners' Association

(SAMPLE)
BOARD MEETING AGENDA

______(Insert Date)______ Meeting

1. Open Homeowner Forum
2. Call to Order
3. Approval of Minutes of (insert date) Board Meeting
4. Reports
   a. Treasurer's Report
   b. Landscape Committee's Report
   c. Management Site Inspection Report
5. Old Business
   a. Parking Enforcement
6. New Business
   a. Appointment of Inspector of Election
   b. Painting Project
7. Adjournment

RESOLUTION OF THE BOARD OF DIRECTORS

RECITALS

Whereas, ______(state date, time of meeting)______

Whereas, ______(state facts upon which resolution is based)______

Whereas, (state additional facts, as necessary)

RESOLUTION

NOW, THEREFORE, the Board of Directors does hereby approve the following resolution: ______(state resolution)______.

RESOLVED FURTHER, ______(state additional resolutions, as necessary)______

RESOLVED FURTHER, ______(state additional resolutions, as necessary)______

This Resolution was adopted upon motion duly made, seconded and approved by a majority of a quorum of directors present at a duly noticed meeting held (insert date).

Executed this __________ day of __________, 2015

By: ________________________________

Secretary
Model Homeowners' Association

NOTICE OF ANNUAL MEMBERSHIP MEETING

Date: ______________________

Dear Members,

The Annual Membership Meeting of Model Homeowners Association will be held on ____(date)____ at ____(time)____. The meeting will be held at the ____(name of facility)____, located at ____(address of facility)____.

The purpose of the Annual Meeting is for the Inspector of Election to tabulate member votes for the annual election of directors and [list any other agenda items]. Your ballot and instructions for voting are enclosed. All ballots must be received by the Inspector of Election no later than (date and time of ballot deadline).

Board of Directors

Model Homeowners' Association

SAMPLE BALLOT

(Cumulative Voting Permitted)

THREE DIRECTORS will be elected. Cumulative voting is permitted. You may cast one vote for each of three candidates, or three votes for one candidate, or you may cast any combination that does not exceed a total of THREE VOTES. **MARK NO MORE THAN THREE BOXES TOTAL.**

CANDIDATE NAMES (*in alphabetical order*)	VOTES		
[Name]	☐	☐	☐
[Name]	☐	☐	☐
[Name]	☐	☐	☐
[Name]	☐	☐	☐
[Name]	☐	☐	☐

SECRET BALLOT VOTING INSTRUCTIONS

(Cumulative Voting Permitted)

Enclosed are your Secret Ballot and two return envelopes. Please be sure to follow all of the ballot instructions correctly so that your vote may be counted.

There are [number] positions on the Board to be filled. You may cast up to [number] votes and you may cumulate your votes (give more than one vote to a particular candidate or candidates, up to the total number of votes permitted).

State law requires use of a double envelope system. Mark your ballot and place it in the smaller envelope then place that envelope in the larger envelope with the return address on it. Remember to sign the outer envelope where indicated.

The deadline for returning your ballot is [date], at [time]. You may mail your ballot or you may hand-deliver it to [address of inspector of election].

SAMPLE BALLOT

(Cumulative Voting Not Permitted)

THREE DIRECTORS will be elected. You may cast only ONE vote for up-to three candidates. **MARK NO MORE THAN THREE BOXES TOTAL.**

CANDIDATE NAMES (*in alphabetical order*)	VOTES
[Name]	☐
[Name]	☐
[Name]	☐
[Name]	☐
[Name]	☐

SECRET BALLOT VOTING INSTRUCTIONS

(Cumulative Voting Not Permitted)

Enclosed are your Secret Ballot and two return envelopes. Please be sure to follow all of the ballot instructions correctly so that your vote may be counted.

There are [number] positions on the Board to be filled. You may vote for up to [number] of candidates. Do not cast more than one vote for any candidate.

State law requires use of a double envelope system. Mark your ballot and place it in the smaller envelope then place that envelope in the larger envelope with the return address on it. Remember to sign the outer envelope where indicated.

The deadline for returning your ballot is [date], at [time]. You may mail your ballot or you may hand-deliver it to [address of inspector of election].

SAMPLE AFFIDAVIT CERTIFYING ELECTION RESULTS

I, ________(name)________, am the Inspector of Election in the membership vote of the members of Model Homeowners' Association, the ballots for which were tabulated by me on______(date)______. The results of the vote are as follows:

Total Ballots Received: ________ Number of Ballots Disqualified: ________

Ballot Item:________ Votes in Favor: ________ Votes Against: ________

Name of Candidate	Votes Received
(name)	________
(name)	________
(name)	________

I declare under penalty of perjury under the laws of the State of California that the foregoing is true and correct. Executed this ______ day of ________, 201__, at ________________, California.

____

Signature

____

Print Name

BOARD MEMBER CODE OF ETHICS

As a board member, you need to be aware that more is expected of those in leadership roles. Review the following statements. Signing this Code of Ethics solidifies your commitment to honest board service.

As a member of this board, I will:

- Be committed to fulfilling the mission and vision of the XYZ HOA.
- Keep all confidential board information, confidential.
- Focus my efforts on the XYZ HOA and not my personal goals.
- Serve on a committee and/or task force in a leadership capacity.
- Refrain from using my service on this board for my own personal advantage or for the advantage of my friends or associates.
- Respect and support the majority decisions of the board.
- Immediately disclose to the board any perceived or real conflict of interest as soon as I have knowledge of the potential conflict.
- Approach all board issues with an open mind, prepared to make the best decisions for everyone involved.
- Do nothing to violate the trust of those who elected or appointed me to the board or of those we serve.
- Never exercise authority as a board member except when acting in a board meeting or as I am delegated by the board or its President.
- Continue to maintain the XYZ HOA board member candidate qualifications.
- Consider myself a trustee of this organization and do my best to ensure that it is well maintained, financially secure, growing and always operating within the best interest of those we serve.

______________________________ ____________

BOARD MEMBER SIGNATURE DATE

Note: This form is reproduced with permission from the California Association of Community Managers, Inc. (CACM), and may be found on CACM's website at www.cacm.org.

BOARD MEMBER COMMITMENT PLEDGE

I,____________________, recognizing the vital responsibility I am undertaking in serving as a member of the Board of Directors of the XYZ HOA, hereby pledge to carry out in a trustworthy and diligent manner the duties and obligations of my role as a board member.

My Role:

I acknowledge that my primary role as a board member is (1) to understand, support and ensure fidelity to the XYZ HOA mission and vision, and (2) to carry out the functions of the office of board member and/or officer as stated in the Bylaws.

My role as a board member will focus on the development of the broad policies (e.g., long-term vision, overall financial philosophy, etc.) that govern the implementation of institutional plans and purposes.

My Commitment:

I will exercise the duties and responsibilities of this office with integrity, fidelity and care.

I Pledge To:

- Maintain a good working relationship with other board members.
- Keep up to date on the organization's major programs and services.
- Follow trends and important developments in the HOA industry and substantive fields of interest.
- Educate myself about the needs of the constituents I serve.
- Act knowledgeably and prudently when making recommendations.
- Recommend qualified individuals with relevant skills and experience as possible nominees for the board.
- Prepare for and participate at board and committee meetings.
- Participate in the strategic planning process.

- Willingly volunteer and use my special skills to further the organization's mission and vision.
- Complete all assignments in a timely manner.
- Listen respectfully to others' points of view.
- Take advantage of opportunities to enhance the organization's public image by periodically speaking to leaders in the community about the work of the XYZ HOA.
- Respect the confidentiality of the board's executive sessions.
- Speak for the board or XYZ HOA only when authorized to do so.
- Suggest agenda items for future board and committee meetings.
- Aid and advise the President when my help is requested.
- Avoid burdening the staff with requests for special favors.
- Ensure any communication with the community association manager does not undermine the relationship between the board and the manager.
- Avoid, in fact and perception, conflicts of interest that might violate the trust of the board or organization, and disclose to the board, in a timely manner, any possible conflicts.

If, for any reason, I find myself unable to carry out the above duties as best as I can, I agree to resign my position as a board member/officer.

____________________________________ _____________

BOARD MEMBER SIGNATURE DATE

Note: This form is reproduced with permission from the California Association of Community Managers (CACM), and may be found on CACM's website at www.cacm.org.

SUMMARY OF STATUTORY DEFAULT MEET AND CONFER PROCEDURE

(Civil Code § 5915)

1. Either party to a dispute within the scope of this article may invoke the following procedure:

2. The party may request the other party to meet and confer in an effort to resolve the dispute. The request shall be in writing.

3. A member of an association may refuse a request to meet and confer. The association may not refuse a request to meet and confer.

4. The board shall designate a director to meet and confer.

5. The parties shall meet promptly at a mutually convenient time and place, explain their positions to each other, and confer in good faith in an effort to resolve the dispute. The parties may be assisted by an attorney or another person at their own cost when conferring.

6. A resolution of the dispute agreed to by the parties shall be memorialized in writing and signed by the parties, including the board designee on behalf of the association.

7. A written agreement reached under this section binds the parties and is judicially enforceable if it is signed by both parties and both of the following conditions are satisfied:

   (a) The agreement is not in conflict with law or the governing documents of the common interest development or association.

   (b) The agreement is either consistent with the authority granted by the board to its designee or the agreement is ratified by the board.

8. A member may not be charged a fee to participate in the process.

REQUEST TO MEET AND CONFER

(Internal Dispute Resolution Pursuant to Civil Code § 5915)

TO: ____________________

DISPUTE: ____________________ Association would like to meet and confer with you concerning ____ ____________________ (i.e. some violation of the governing documents). If this dispute cannot be resolved at this time, the next step is to meet with a neutral third party to try to resolve this dispute. The suggested meeting time is ____________. Please contract ________________ at ________________ to confirm the time and place of the meeting. If you do not confirm this meeting, it will be assumed that you do not wish to participate in this informal procedure.

OR

DISPUTE: I/We, owners of ____________________ would like to meet with the board or its designated representative to resolve the dispute concerning ____ ____.

Please contact me at ____________ to arrange a mutually convenient time and place to explain our positions and confer in good faith to resolve this dispute. (The board may not refuse this request to meet and confer.) (See Civil Code § 5915)

By: ________________________ Dated: ____________

SUMMARY OF ALTERNATIVE DISPUTE RESOLUTION REQUIREMENTS

(Civil Code §§ 5925-5965)

1. In general, an association or member of an association may not file an action in Superior Court to enforce the governing documents or to enforce certain laws that govern community associations, unless the parties first try to submit their dispute to alternative dispute resolution (ADR), which includes mediation, arbitration, conciliation, or other nonjudicial procedure that involves a neutral party in the decision making process. The form of ADR may be binding or non-binding, and costs are borne as agreed to by the parties involved.

2. This requirement does not generally apply to disputes within the jurisdiction of the Small Claims Court or disputes over assessments.

3. The ADR process is commenced by one party serving the other party with a Request for Resolution in accordance with Civil Code section 5935(b). It must contain the following:

    a. A brief description of the dispute;

    b. A request for ADR; and

    c. A notice that the party receiving the Request for Resolutionmust respond within 30 days or the Request For Resolution will be deemed rejected.

    d. If the person on whom the Request for Resolution is served is an owner, a copy of the statutes governing ADR.

4. Service of the Request for Resolution may be by personal delivery, first-class mail, express mail, facsimile or other means reasonably calculated to give the other party actual notice.

5. A party served with a Request for Resolution has 30 days to accept or reject the request. Failure to accept or reject is deemed a rejection.

6. If the Request for Resolution is accepted, ADR must be completed within 90 days from the date of acceptance. The deadline can be extended by a written agreement among all parties.

7. Should the association or owner wish to file a lawsuit for enforcement of the governing documents or a specified statute, the law requires the association or the individual to file a certificate with the court prior to the filing of the suit, stating: (1) that ADR has been completed, (2) that one of the other parties did not accept the terms offered for ADR, or (3) that urgent orders of the court were necessary. Failure to file this certificate can be grounds for dismissing the lawsuit.

8. Refusal to participate in ADR may result in the loss of the right to recover attorney fees in a subsequent Superior Court action.

FAILURE OF A MEMBER OF THE ASSOCIATION TO COMPLY WITH THE ALTERNATIVE DISPUTE RESOLUTION REQUIREMENTS OF SECTION 5930 OF THE CIVIL CODE MAY RESULT IN THE LOSS OF YOUR RIGHT TO SUE THE ASSOCIATION OR ANOTHER MEMBER OF THE ASSOCIATION REGARDING ENFORCEMENT OF THE GOVERNING DOCUMENTS OR THE APPLICABLE LAW.

CHECKLISTS

COMMUNITY ASSOCIATION DISCLOSURE CHECKLIST

* Annual Budget Report - 30 to 90 Days Before End of Fiscal Year

The Pro Forma Budget or Summary of the Pro Forma Budget	§5300(b)(1)
Summary of Association Reserves	§5300(b)(2);§5565
Summary of the Reserve Funding Plan	§5300(b)(3);§5550 (b)(5)
Statement of Any Board Decision to Defer or Not Undertake Certain Component Repairs	§5300(b)(4)
Statement of Any Anticipated Special Assessments	§5300(b)(5)
Statement of Method(s) of Reserve Funding	§5300(b)(6)
Statement Outlining Procedure Used to Calculate Reserves	§5300(b)(7);§5570(b)(4)
Association Loan Disclosure	§5300(b)(8)
Summary of Specified Insurance Coverages	§5300(b)(9)
Statement of FHA-approved status - Condominium Projects only (Effective 7/1/2016)	§5300(b)(10)
Statement of VA-approved status - Condominium Projects only (Effective 7/1/2016)	§5300(b)(11)
Copy of Completed "Charges for Documents Provided" Disclosure Form	§5300(b)(12);§4528
Assessment and Reserve Fund Disclosure Summary – Form	§5300(e);§5570

*Annual Policy Statement – 30 to 90 Days Before End of Fiscal Year

Name and Address of Person Designated to Receive Official Communications to the Association	§5310(a)(1);§4035
Notice of Right to Submit Secondary Address for Annual Disclosures and Collection Notices	§5130(a)(2);§4040(b)
Notice of Location, if any, Designated for Posting General Notices	§5310(a)(3);§4045
Notice of Right to Receive General Notices by Individual Delivery Upon Request	§5310(a)(4);§4045(b)
Notice of Right to Receive Minutes of Board Meetings	§5310(a)(5);§4950(b)
Notice of Collection Rights & Duties – Form	§5310(a)(6);§5730
Assessment Collection Policy	§5310(a)(7)
Discipline Policy, If Any, Including Schedule of Fines ("Fine Policy")	§5310(a)(8);§5850
Dispute Resolution Summary ("Meet and Confer" and Alternative Dispute Resolution)	§5310(a)(9)§5920;§5965
Architectural Guidelines and Procedures	§5310(a)(10);§4765(c)
Mailing Address for Overnight Payment of Assessments	§5310(a)(11);§5655(c)

***NOTE:** *These disclosures may alternatively be made in summary, generally describing their contents. Such a summary, if provided in lieu of complete reports, must include a notice, in 10-point boldface type on the first page, advising members how to request complete report(s) at no cost.*

Additional Financial Disclosures

Use of Reserve Funds	By General Notice After Decision	§5520
Intent to Borrow From Reserves	In General Notice of Board Meeting	§5515(a)
Intent to Postpone Repayment of Borrowed Reserves	Within 1 Year of Decision to Borrow, in General Notice of Board Meeting	§5515(d)
Review of Financial Statement	Within 120 Days After Close of Fiscal Year	§5305
Notice of Special Assessment or Increase in Regular Assessments	Not less than 30 Days and Not More Than 60 Days Before Due	§5615

Documents to Sellers and Members / Other

Disclosures to Sellers (Documents/Pricing Form)	Within 10 Days of Receiving Written Request	§4525;§4530
Statement of Non-Incorporation	If Applicable, With Disclosure to Sellers	§4525(a)(1)
Notice of Age Restrictions	If Applicable, With Disclosure to Sellers	§4525(a)(2)
Notice of Rental Restrictions	If Applicable, With Disclosure to Sellers	§4525(a)(9)
Statement Regarding Discriminatory Covenants - Form	When Providing Any Governing Document	Gov't Code §12956.1

Architectural Controls / Rule-Making

Architectural Guidelines and Procedures	In Annual Policy Statement	§4765(c) §5310(a)(10)
Notice of Right to Reconsideration of Denied Application, If Decision Not Made By Board	With Written Denial	§4765(a)(5)
Notice of Intent to Make Certain Rules Changes	By General Notice, At Least 30 Days Prior to Board Adoption; Emergency Rules Excepted	§4360(a)&(d)
Notice of Adoption of Certain Rule Changes	Provided by General Notice, Not More Than 15 Days After Adoption	§4360(c)

Member Addresses

Solicit member addresses	Annually, arguably 60 to 90 days before Annual Budget Report is issued	§4041(b)

Meetings

Notice and Agenda of Open Board Meetings	By General Notice, At Least 4 Days Prior to Board Meeting	§4920(a); §4930
Notice of Emergency Board Meeting	No Notice Required	§4920(b)(1)
Notice and Agenda of Executive Session Meeting	By General Notice, At Least 2 Days Prior to Board Meeting	§4920(b)(2) §4930
Notice of Right to Receive Minutes of Board Meetings	In Annual Policy Statement	§4950 §5310(a)(5)
Notice of Intent to Make Certain Rules Changes	By General Notice, At Least 30 Days Prior to Board Adoption	§4360(a)
Notice to Member of Board Meeting to Consider Imposing Discipline	By Individual Delivery, At Least 10 Days Prior to Board Meeting	§5855(a)

Member Discipline / Dispute Resolution

Enforcement Policy, If Any, Including Schedule of Monetary Penalties ("Fine Policy")	In Annual Policy Statement	§5850
Notice to Member of Board Meeting to Consider Imposing Discipline	By Individual Delivery, At Least 10 Days Prior to Board Meeting	§5855(a)
Notice to Member of Discipline Imposed	By Individual Delivery, Not More Than 15 Days After Decision	§5855(c)
Alternative Dispute Resolution Rights Summary	In Annual Policy Statement	§5310(a)(9) §5965
Internal Dispute Resolution ("Meet-and-Confer") Program Summary	In Annual Policy Statement	§5310(a)(9) §5920

Liens / Collections

Notice of Right to Submit Secondary Address For Collection Notices	In Annual Policy Statement	§5130(a)(2)
Pre-Lien Notice	At Least 30 Days Before Recording Lien	§5660
Assessment Collection Policy	In Annual Policy Statement / With Pre-Lien Notice	§5310(a)(7) §5660(a)
Notice of Right to Inspect Financial Records	With Pre-Lien Notice	§5660(a)
Notice of Right to Meet with Board to Discuss Delinquent Assessment Payment Plan	With Pre-Lien Notice	§5660(d)
Notice of Right to Dispute Assessment Debt by "Meet and Confer"	With Pre-Lien Notice	§5660(e)
Notice of Right to Request Post-Lien ADR	With Pre-Lien Notice	§5660(f)

Insurance

Summary of Specified Insurance Coverages	In Annual Budget Report	§5300(b)(9)

Construction Defects

Notice of Construction Defect Litigation	30 Days Before Suit is Filed	§6150
Notice of Construction Defect Resolution / Repair Plan and Timeline	As Soon as Reasonably Practicable After Resolution	§6100
Receipt / Expenditure of Construction Defect Award / Settlement Monies	In Annual Budget Report or Year-End Review of Financial Statement	§5565(b)(3)

Corporate Disclosures

Statement of Officers' Names, Addresses / Agent for Service of Process	File Every Other Year, Up to Five Months Prior to Anniversary Date of Initial Filing	Corp. Code §8210
Registry / Statement of CID Association	File with Secretary of State Every Other Year, with Statement of Officers' Names, etc. / Within 60 Days of Change in On-Site or Management Address	§5405

TRANSITION FROM DEVELOPER CONTROL

A. DOCUMENTS TO OBTAIN

- Original recorded CC&Rs and any amendments.
- Original corporate minute book containing articles of incorporation, bylaws, rules and regulations.
- Corporate seal, letterhead, books and records.
- Original recorded condominium plan or tract map.
- Original minutes of all board of director meetings.
- Original minutes of all member meetings.
- Membership roster from inception to date.
- All bank records, including: a) checkbooks, passbooks and other access documents; b) bank statements and reconciliations; c) cancelled checks and check registers; and d) bank account and borrowing resolutions.
- As-built plans and specifications.
- Inventory of moveable property.
- Tax records including: a) returns (Federal and State); b) board certifications to CPA; c) IRS and FTB correspondence; and d) audit materials.
- Insurance policies including: a) general liability policies; b) directors and officers liability; and c) fidelity bonds.
- Maintenance contracts and records.
- Management contracts and records.
- *Pro forma* operating budgets from inception to date.
- Reserve studies and updates from inception to date.
- Bonds - subdivision maintenance bond, etc.
- Warranties and written contracts with product suppliers.
- Records of accounts payable and accounts receivable from inception to date.
- Statement of known defective conditions.

B. FINANCIAL AUDIT

- Review financial statements.
- Review *pro forma* operating budget.
- Review bank statements and cancelled checks.
- Review segregation of operation revenue from reserves.
- Review prior reserve studies.
- Review balances on deposit in reserve accounts.
- Conduct an audit if discrepancies appear.

C. CONSTRUCTION AUDIT

- Review all major systems on spot check basis including the roof system, siding system, foundation system, electrical system, plumbing system, seismic restraint system, and the landscape and drainage system.
- Retain expert consultants as necessary.
- Define any problems and method of repair.
- Determine cost of repair.
- Make demand on developer for compensation.

D. ORGANIZATION OF ASSOCIATION

- Review governing documents for compliance with requirements for officers and directors.
- Review committee structure for effective use.
- Review management contracts for compliance with current needs.
- Review service providers for adequacy.
- Review professional consultant contracts for adequacy and conflicts of interest.
- Establish reporting procedures for management and committees.
- Delegate tasks to Board members and committee members.
- Develop long range plan for overall management of project.

13

RESOURCE LIST

California Association of Community Managers (CACM)
23461 South Pointe Dr., Ste. 200
Laguna Hills CA 92653
Tel: (949) 916-2226
Tel: (800) 363-9771 (toll free)
Email: info@cacm.org
www.cacm.org

Executive Council of Homeowners (ECHO)
1960 The Alameda, Suite 195
San Jose, CA 95126
Tel: (408) 297-3246
Fax: (408) 297-3517
Email: info@echo-ca.org
www.echo-ca.org

California Legislative Action Committee (CAI-CLAC)
1809 S Street, Suite 101-245
Sacramento, CA 95811
Tel: (888) 909-7403
Fax: (916) 550-9488
Email: office@caiclac.com
www.caiclac.com

The GovDoc Project
Berding & Weil LLP
2175 N. California Blvd. Suite 500
Walnut Creek, CA 94596
Tel: (800) 838-2090
Fax: (925) 820-5592
Email: govdocproject@berdingweil.com
www.berdingweil.com

Complimentary HOA Document Review and Defect Investigation
Berding & Weil LLP
2175 N. California Blvd. Suite 500
Walnut Creek, CA 94596
Tel: (800) 838-2090
Fax: (925) 820-5592
Email:
complimentary@berdingweil.com
www.berdingweil.com

Community Associations Institute (CAI) Websites:

National Chapter:
www.caionline.org

Bay Area/Central California Chapter: www.caibaycen.com

California North Chapter:
www.cai-cnc.org

Channel Islands Chapter:
www.cai-channelislands.org

Coachella Valley Chapter:
www.coachellavalleycai.org

Greater Inland Empire Chapter:
www.cai-grie.org

Greater Los Angeles Chapter:
www.cai-glac.org

Orange County Chapter:
www.caioc.org

San Diego Chapter:
www.cai-sd.org

Department of Real Estate
1651 Exposition Blvd.
Sacramento, CA 95815
Public Information Line:
Tel: (877) 373-4542
Fax: (916) 263-8943
www.dre.ca.gov

Official California Legislative Information
www.leginfo.ca.gov

Department of General Services Legislative Bill Room
State Capitol Room B32
Sacramento, CA 95814
Tel: (916) 445-2323
Fax: (916) 322-1257
www.dgs.ca.gov/osp/programs/billroom.aspx

Secretary of State
1500 11th Street
Sacramento, CA 95814-5701
Tel: (916) 653-6814
www.sos.ca.gov

Department of Consumer Affairs Consumer Information Center
1625 N. Market Blvd., Suite 112
Sacramento, CA 95834
Toll Free: (800) 952-5210
www.dca.ca.gov

California Association of Realtors (CAR) Legislative Offices
1121 L Street #600
Sacramento, CA 95814
Tel: (916) 492-5200
Fax: (916) 444-2033
www.car.org

Department of Insurance Consumer Hotline
300 South Spring Street,
South Tower
Los Angeles, CA 90013
Toll Free: (800) 927-HELP (4357)
www.insurance.ca.gov

California Housing Law Project
1107 9th Street, Suite 801
Sacramento, CA 95814
www.housingadvocates.org

California Association of Realtors (CAR) Executive Offices
525 South Virgil Ave.
Los Angeles, CA 90020
Tel: (213) 739-8200
Fax: (213) 480-7724
Hotline: (213) 739-8282
www.car.org

Davis-Stirling Common Interest Development Act

Cross-Reference Chart

Subject	New Code	Old Code
Citation	§4000	§1350
Headings	§4005	§1350.5
Effect of Act of Documents or Actions before 1/1/14	§4010	new
Construction of Zoning Ordinances	§4020	§1372
Delivery of Documents to Association	§4035	new
Individual Delivery or Individual Notice	§4040	new
Process for Updating Owner Address	§4041	new
General Delivery or General Notice	§4045	new
Completion of Delivery	§4050	new
Electronic Delivery	§4055	new
Approval by Majority Vote	§4065	new
Approval by Majority of a Quorum	§4070	new
Definitions	§4075	§1351 first sentence
Annual Budget Report	§4076	new
Annual Policy Statement	§4078	new
Association	§4080	§1351(a)
Board	§4085	new
Board Meeting	§4090	§1363.05(k)(2)
Common Area	§4095	§1351(b)
Common Interest Development	§4100	§1351(c)
Community Apartment Project	§4105	§1351(d)
Community Service Organization	§4110	§1368(c)(3)
Condominium Plan	§4120	new
Condominium Project	§4125	§1351(f)
Declarant	§4130	§1351(g)

Subject	New Code	Old Code
Declaration	§4135	§1351(h)
Directors	§4140	new
Exclusive Use Common Area	§4145	§1351(i)
General Notice	§4148	new
Governing Documents	§4150	§1351(j)
Individual Notice	§4153	new
Item of Business	§4155	§1363.05(k)(1)
Managing Agent	§4158	§1363.1(b); §1363.2(f)
Member	§4160	new
Person	§4170	new
Planned Development	§4175	§1351(k)
Reserve Accounts	§4177	§1365.5(f)
Reserve Account Requirements	§4178	§1365.5(g)
Separate Interest	§4185	§1351(l)
Stock Cooperative	§4190	§1351(m)
Application of Act; Creation of CID	§4200	§1352
Requirement of Common Area	§4201	§1374
Nonapplicable Provisions for Commercial CIDs	§4202	§1373
Controlling Authority	§4205	new
Statement Identifying Party Authorized to Receive Assessments	§4210	§1366.2
Liberal Construction of Documents	§4215	§1370
Boundaries of Units; Presumption	§4220	§1371
Discriminatory Restrictive Covenants	§4225	§1352.2
Amendment of Governing Documents for Certain Declarant Provisions	§4230	§1355.5
Amendment of Governing Documents to Reflect Changes in the Davis-Stirling Common Interest Development Act	§4235	new

Subject	New Code	Old Code
Contents of Declaration	§4250	§1353(a)(1) first two sentences; §1353(b)
Notice of Airport in Vicinity; Notice of San Francisco Bay Conservation and Development Commission Jurisdiction	§4255	1353(a)(1)-(4) not including first two sentences
Permissible Amendment of Declaration	§4260	§1355(b)
Extension of Term of Declaration	§4265	§1357(a)(b) and (d)
Amendment of Declaration; Effective Date	§4270	§1355(a)
Court Approval of Amendment of Declaration; Requirements	§4275	§1356
Articles of Incorporation, Requirements	§4280	§1363.5
Condominium Plan, Requirements	§4285	§1351(e) first paragraph
Certificate Consenting to Recordation of Condominium Plan	§4290	§1351(e)(A)-(D) not including the last paragraph of former section 1351(e)
Amendment or Revocation of Condominium Plan	§4295	§1351(e) last paragraph
Operating Rules, Definitions	§4340	§1357.100
Validity of Operation Rules	§4350	§1357.110
Applicability of Member Review and Comment Requirement	§4355	§1357.120
Notice of Rule Change	§4360	§1357.130
Reversal of Rule Change	§4365	§1357.140
Application of Article to Rule Changes after 1/1/04	§4370	§1357.150
Ownership of Common Area	§4500	§1362
Common Area Rights and Easements	§4505	§1361

Subject	New Code	Old Code
Access to Owners' Separate Interest	§4510	§1361.5
Peaceful Assembly	§4515	new
Owners' Disclosure of Specified Items to Prospective Purchasers	§4525	§1368(a)
Estimated Fees for Escrow Documents; Statutory Disclosure Form	§4528	§1368.2
Copies of Escrow Documents to Owners	§4530	§1368(b) not including 1368(b)(3)
Application of Civil Code sections 1133 and 1134 in Separate Interest Transfers	§4535	§1368(f)
Remedies for Violation of Article	§4540	§1368(d)
Validity of Title Transferred in Violation of Article	§4545	§1368(e)
Prohibition of Transfer Fees	§4575	§1368(c)(1)
Exceptions to the Prohibition of Transfer Fees	§4580	§1368(c)(2)
Grants of Exclusive Use of Common Area	§4600	§1363.07
Remedies for Violation of Section 4600	§4605	§1363.09(a)(b)
Restrictions on Common Area Partition	§4610	§1359
Liens for Labor and Materials	§4615	§1369
Transfer of Separate Interest in Community Apartment Project	§4625	§1358(a)
Transfer of Separate Interest in a Condominium Project	§4630	§1358(b)
Transfer of Separate Interest in Planned Development	§4635	§1358(c)
Transfer of Separate Interest in Stock Cooperative	§4640	§1358(d)
Transfer of Exclusive Use Area	§4645	Second to last paragraph of §1358
Restrictions on Partition	§4650	Last paragraph of §1358

Subject	New Code	Old Code
Limitations of Regulation of Separate Interest	§4700	new
Display of the Flag of the United States of America	§4705	§1353.5
Sign Restrictions	§4710	§1353.6
Pet Restrictions	§4715	§1360.5
Roof Coverings	§4720	§1353.7
Antenna and Satellite Restrictions	§4725	§1376
Marketing Restrictions	§4730	§1368.1
Low Water-Using Plants and Landscaping Restrictions	§4735	§1353.8
Pressure Washing Restrictions	§4736	new
Rental or Lease Restrictions	§4740	§1360.2
Electric Vehicle Charging Stations	§4745	§1353.9
Solar Energy Systems	§4746	new
Personal Agriculture	§4750	new
Clotheslines	§4753	new
Modification of Separate Interest	§4760	§1360
Architectural Review and Procedure for Approval	§4765	§1378
Association Responsibility for Repair, Replacement or Maintenance of Common Area.	§4775	§1364(a)
Application of Pesticides by Non-Licensed Persons	§4777	new
Damage by Wood-Destroying Pests or Organisms	§4780	§1364(b)(1)
Treatment of Wood-Destroying Pests or Organisms; Notice of Removal of Occupants	§4785	§1364(d)(e)
Access for Maintenance of Telephone Wiring	§4790	§1364(f)
CID to be Managed by Association	§4800	§1363(a)
Powers of Association	§4805	§1363(c)

Subject	New Code	Old Code
Membership Rights in Joint Neighborhood Associations	§4820	§1363(h)
Open Meeting Act	§4900	§1363.05(a)
Board Meeting Required for Action; Electronic Transmissions	§4910	§1363.05(j)
Notice of Board Meeting	§4920	§1363.05(f)
Emergency Board Meeting	§4923	§1363.05(g)
Member Attendance at Board Meetings	§4925	§1363.05(b) not including the mid-portion of the provision, which addresses executive sessions
Requirements for Action by Board	§4930	§1363.05(i)
Executive Session	§4935	§1363.05(b) not including the third sentence or the first part of the first sentence.
Minutes of Meeting	§4950	§1363.05(d)
Remedies for Violation of this Article	§4955	§1363.09(a)(b)
Member Meetings	§5000	§1363(d); §1363.05(h)
Secret Ballot Elections	§5100 Subdivision (b) is new	§1363.03(b) first sentence; §1363.03(l)(n)
Election Rules	§5105	§1363.05(a)
Inspector of Election	§5110	§1363.03(c)
Secret Ballot Procedures	§5115	§1363.03(c)
Counting Ballots	§5120	§1363(f)(g)
Custody of Ballots	§5125	§1363(h)(i)
Proxies	§5130	§1363(d)

Subject	New Code	Old Code
Prohibition of Association Funds for Campaign Purposes	§5135	§1363.04
Remedies for Violation of this Article	§5145	§1363.09(a)
Records Inspection Definitions	§5200 Paragraphs (a)(11)-(13) are new.	§1365.2(a)(1)
Availability of Records for Member Inspection and Copying	§5205	§1365.2(b)(c); §1365.2(a)(2); §1365.2(h)
Time Periods for Access to Records	§5210	§1365.2(i)(j)(k)
Permissible Redactions in Records	§5215	§1365.2(d)
Member Opt Out	§5220	§1365.2(a)(1)(I)(iii)
Reason for Request of Membership List	§5225	§1365.2(a)(1)(I)(ii)
Restriction on Use of Records	§5230	§1365(e)
Member Action	§5235	§1365(f)
Application of Corporations Code to Article	§5240	§1365(l)
Record Requests	§5260	new
Annual Budget Report	§5300	§1365(a) last paragraph; §1365(a)(1)(2); § 1365(b)
Review of the Financial Statement	§5305	§1365(c)
Annual Policy Statement	§5310	new
Delivery of Full Report or Summary of Annual Disclosures	§5320	new
Director Conflict of Interest	§5350	§1365.6
Prospective Managing Agent	§5375	§1363.1(a)
Managing Agent Disclosures	§5375.5	new
Managing Agent Facilitation of Disclosures	§5376	new
Management of Common Interest Funds	§5380	§1363.2(a)-(f)

Subject	New Code	Old Code
Meaning of Managing Agent	§5385	§1363.1(b)(1) and first clause of second sentence of §1363.2(f)
On-line Education for Directors	§5400	§1363.0001
Identification and Registration of Community Associations	§5405	§1363.6
Board of Directors; Duties	§5500	§1365.5(a)
Expenditure of Reserve Accounts	§5510	§1365.5(b)
Borrowing from Reserve Accounts	§5515	§1365.5(c)(2)
Use of Reserve Funds; Notice to Members	§5520	§1365.5(d)
Study of Reserve Accounts	§5550	§1365.5(e)(1)-(4)
Reserve Funding Plan	§5560	Second, third and fourth sentences of §1365.5(e)(5)
Summary of Reserves	§5565	§1365(a)(2)
Reserve Disclosures (Form)	§5570	§1365.2.5
Community Service Organization Financial Disclosures	§5580	§1365.3
Levy of Assessments	§5600	First sentence of §1366(a)
Limitation on Increases in Assessments	§5605	Second sentence of §1366(a) and first sentence of §1366(b)
Emergency Assessments	§5610	Third and fourth sentences and paragraphs (1)-(3) of §1366(b)
Notice of Increased or Special Assessment	§5615	§1366(d)
Assessment Exemption from Judgment	§5620	§1366(c)

Subject	New Code	Old Code
Assessments Based on Taxable Value of Separate Interest	§5625	§1366.4
Assessments; Debt of Owner; Association Recovery	§5650	First sentence of §1367.1(a)
Payment of Delinquent Assessments	§5655	§1367.1(b)
Payment Under Protest	§5658	§1367.6
Notice of Lien	§5660	§1367.1(a)(1)-(6)
Payment Plans	§5661	§1367.1(c)(3)
Meet and Confer	§5670	§1367.1(c)(1)(A)
Board Approval Requires to Record Lien	§5673	§1367.1(c)(2)
Lien; Notice of Delinquent Assessments	§5675	First five sentences of §1367.1(d)
Priority of Lien	§5680	§1367.1(f)
Release of Lien; Lien Recorded in Error	§5685	Sixth sentence of 1367.1(d); 1367.1(i); 1367.5
Failure to Comply; Requirement to Recommence Notice	§5690	§1367.1(l)
Enforcement of Lien	§5700	Second sentence of 1367.1(g); 1367.1(h)
Prior to Foreclosure of Liens, Offer to Meet and Confer; Approval by Board	§5705	§1367.4(a); §1367.4(c)(1); 1367.1(c)(1)(B); 1367.4(c)(2)

Subject	New Code	Old Code
Sale by Trustee	§5710	Third sentence of §1367.1(g); 1367.1(j); fourth sentence and paragraphs (1) and (2) of §1367.1(g)
Right of Redemption	§5715	§1367.4; §1367.4(c)(4)
Foreclosure of Liens; Amount and Time Thresholds	§5720	§1367.4(a)(b)(d)
Monetary Charge or Penalty Imposed by Association may become a Lien	§5725	Seventh and eight sentences of §1367.1(d); §1367.1(e)
Annual Policy Statement; Form Notice	§5730	§1365.1
Limitation on Assignment of Right to Collect	§5735	First sentence of 1367.1(g)
Application of Article on Lien Recorded On or After January 1, 2003	§5740	1367.1
Liability of Volunteer Officer or Director	§5800	§1365.7
Liability of Owner in Tenancy-In-Common Common Area	§5805	§1365.9
Notice of Insurance Policies	§5810	§1365(f)(2)
Schedule of Monetary Penalties	§5850	First sentence of §1363(f); subd. (b)-(d) are new
Disciplinary Actions and Monetary Charges Imposed by Board	§5855	§1363(g)
Application of §5850 and §5855	§5865	§1363(i)
Dispute Resolution	§5900	§1363.810
Fair, Reasonable, Expeditious Procedures	§5905	§1363.820
Minimum Requirements of Dispute Resolution Procedures	§5910	§1363.830
Statutory Default Procedure	§5915	§1363.840

Subject	New Code	Old Code
Description of Association Meet and Confer Program in Annual Policy Statement	§5920	§1363.850
Alternative Dispute Resolution Definitions	§5925	§1369.510
Litigation Pre-Filing Requirements	§5930	§1369.520
Request for Resolution	§5935	§1369.530
Completing the Process	§5940	§1369.540
Statutes of Limitation	§5945	§1369.550
Commencement of Action; Certificate	§5950	§1369.560
Post-Filing Reference to ADR	§5955	§1369.570
Refusal to Participate in Pre-Filing ADR	§5960	§1369.580
Summary of Article in Annual Policy Statement	§5965	§1369.590(a)
Enforcement of Governing Documents	§5975	§1354
Association Standing	§5980	§1363.3
Allocation of Damages	§5985	§1368.4
Design or Construction Defects; Pre-filing Procedure [Operative Until July 7, 2017]	§6000	§1375
Resolution of Design or Construction Defect Dispute; Disclosure to Members	§6100	§1375.1
Pre-Filing Notice to Members	§6150	§1368.5

Old Davis-Stirling Common Interest Development Act

Cross Reference Chart

Subject	Old Code	New Code
Citation	§1350	§4000
Headings	§1350.5	§4005
Methods of Delivering Notice; Applicable Sections of Law	§1350.7	n/a
Definitions	§1351	§4075, §4080; §4095; §4100, §4105; §4125; §4130; §4135; §4145; §4150; §4175; §4185; §4190; §4285
Application of Title; Creation of Common Interest Development	§1352	§4200
Discriminatory Restrictive Covenants; Removal from Governing Documents	§1352.5	§4225
Declaration; Contents	§1353	§4250; §4255
Display of Flag of the United States	§1353.5	§4705
Sign Restrictions	§1353.6	§4710
Roof Coverings; Fires and Fire Protection	§1353.7	§4720
Low Water-Usage Plants; Water-Efficient Landscape Ordinances; Emergency Water Use Regulations	§1353.8	§4735
Electric Vehicle Charging Stations	§1353.9	§4745
Covenants and Restrictions in Declaration as Equitable Servitudes; Enforcement; Attorneys' Fees	§1354	§5975
Amendment of Declaration	§1355	§4260; §4270
Amendment of Governing Documents for Certain Declarant Provisions	§1355.5	§4230

Subject	Old Code	New Code
Amendment of Declaration; Power of Court to Approve Amendment; Recording Amendment; Mailing	§1356	§4275
Extension of Term of Declaration	§1357	§4265
Operating Rules; Definition	§1357.100	§4340
Requirements to be Valid and Enforceable	§1357.110	§4350
Rule Changes for Certain Operating Rules; Applicability and Exceptions	§1357.120	§4355
Rule Changes; Procedures for Notice: Adoption; Emergency Rules Changes	§1357.130	§4360
Commencement of Rule Changes	§1357.150	§4370
Interests Included in Conveyance, Judicial Sale or Transfer of Separate Interests, Transfers of Exclusive Use Areas; Restrictions Upon Severability of Component Interests	§1358	§4625; §4630; §4635; §4640; §4645; §4650
Restrictions on Partition	§1359	§4610
Modification of Unit by Owner; Facilitation of Access for Handicapped; Approval by Project Association	§1360	§4760
Restrictions on Renting or Leasing	§1360.2	§4740
Restrictions on Pets	§1360.5	§4715
Rights and Easements of Ingress, Egress, and Support	§1361	§4505
Access to Owners' Separate Interests	§1361.5	§4510
Ownership of Common Areas	§1362	§4500
Management; Powers of Association; Membership Rights	§1363	§4800; §4805; §4820; §5000; §5120; §5125; §5130; §5850; §5855; §5865
On-Line Education for Directors	§1363.001	§5400

Subject	Old Code	New Code
Disclosure Documents Index	§1363.005	n/a
Election Rules; Secret Ballots; Inspectors of Election; Balloting	§1363.03	§5100; §5110; §5115
Association Funds and Campaigns	§1363.04	§5135
Common Interest Development Open Meeting Act	§1363.05	§4090; §4155; §4900; §4910; §4920; §4923; §4925; §4930; §4935; §4950; §5000; §5105
Grants of Exclusive Use Common Area	§1363.07	§4600
Remedies for Violation of Election Procedures, Campaign Fund Restrictions, CID Opening Meeting Act, Invalid Grants of Exclusive Use Common Area	§1363.09	§4605; §4955; §5145
Prospective Managing Agent; Written Disclosures	§1363.1	§4158; §5375; §5385
Managing Agent; Deposit of Funds Received; Requirements; Separate Records; Commingling Funds	§1363.2	§4158; §5380; §5385
Articles of Incorporation; Identifying Corporation as Association; Business Office Address; Managing Agent's Name and Address	§1363.5	§4280
Identification and Registration of Community Associations	§1363.6	§5405
Dispute Resolution; Application	§1363.810	§5900
Fair, Reasonable, and Expeditious Procedures	§1363.820	§5905
Minimum Requirements; Dispute Resolution Procedures	§1363.830	§5910
Statutory Default Procedure	§1363.840	§5915
Annual Notice, Description of Association Meet and Confer Program	§1363.850	§5920

Subject	Old Code	New Code
Responsibility for Repair, Replacement, or Maintenance; Damage by Wood-Destroying Pests or Organisms; Cost Allocation; Notice of Repair Requirements; Access for Maintenance of Telephone Wiring	§1364	§4775; §4780; §4785; §4790
Documents Prepared and Distributed by the Association	§1365	§5230; §5235; §5240; §5300; §5305; §5810
Statutory Notice; Assessment Collection and Foreclosure; Secondary Addresses for Purposes of Notices Required in This Article	§1365.1	§5730
Access to Association Records	§1365.2	§5200; §5205; §5210; §5215; §5220; §5225
Form; Assessment and Reserve Funding Disclosure Summary	§1365.2.5	§5570
Community Service Organizations; Financial Disclosures	§1365.3	§5580
Board of Directors; Duties; Operating and Reserve Accounts; Borrowing From Reserve Accounts; Notice to Members; Visual Inspection of Components; Study of Reserve Accounts	§1365.5	§5500; §5510; §5515; §5520; §5550; §5560; §5565
Interested Directors; Conflicts of Interest	§1365.6	§5350
Tortious Act or Omission of Volunteer Officer or Director of the Association Managing Residential Development; Liability; Criteria; Limitations	§1365.7	§5800
Member Limited Immunity; General Liability Insurance	§1365.9	§5805
Levy of Assessments; Limitation on Increases; Delinquent Assessments; Interest	§1366	§5600; §5605; §5610; §5615; §5620
Limitation on Imposition or Collection of Assessments or Fees	§1366.1	§5600(b)

Subject	Old Code	New Code
Statement Identifying Party Authorized to Receive Assessments	§1366.2	§4210
Disputed Assessments; Payment Under Protest; Notice	§1366.3	
Assessments Based on Taxable Value of Separate Interests	§1366.4	§5625
Assessments; Debt of Owner; Notice; Lien; Monetary Penalties; Enforcement of Liens; Application to Liens Recorded Prior to January 1, 2003	§1367	n/a
Assessments; Debt of Owner; Notice; Lien; Monetary Penalties; Enforcement of Liens; Application to Liens Recorded on or After January 1, 2003	§1367.1	§5650; §5655; §5660; §5661; §5670; §5673; §5675; §5680; §5685; §5690; §5700; §5710; §5725; §5735
Foreclosure of Liens for Assessment Debt Arising On or After January 1, 2006; Amount and Time Thresholds; Small Claims Court Judgments	§1367.4	§5705; §5715; §5720
Liens Recorded in Error	§1367.5	§5685
Payment Under Protest	§1367.6	§5658
Sale or Title Transfer; Provision of Specified Items to Prospective Purchasers; Copies; Fees; Violations; Penalty and Attorney Fees; Validity of Title Transferred in Violation; Additional Requirements	§1368	§4110; §4525; §4530; §4535; §4540; §4545; §4575; §4580
Marketing of Separate Interests	§1368.1	§4730
Estimated Fees for Escrow Documents; Statutory Disclosure Form	§1368.2	§4528
Standing	§1368.3	§5980
Allocation of Damages	§1368.4	§5985
Civil Action; Damage to Common Interest Development; Notice to Members	§1368.5	§6150

Subject	Old Code	New Code
Liens for Labor and Materials	§1369	§4515
Definitions	§1369.510	§5925
Litigation Pre-Filing Requirements	§1369.520	§5930
Initiating the Process; Requests for Resolution	§1369.530	§5935
Completing the Process; Costs	§1369.540	§5940
Statutes of Limitation	§1369.550	§5945
Certificate; Commencement of Action	§1369.560	§5950
Post-Filing Reference	§1369.570	§5955
Refusal to Participate in Pre-Filing Alternative Dispute Resolution	§1369.580	§5960
Annual Disclosure	§1369.590	§5965
Liberal Construction of Instruments	§1370	§4215
Boundaries of Units; Presumptions	§1371	§4220
Construction of Zoning Ordinances	§1372	§4020
Development Expressly Zoned as Industrial or Commercial and Limited to Such Purposes; Exclusion	§1373	§4202
Application of Act; Common Area Requirement	§1374	§4201
Design or Construction Defects; Prefiling Procedure [Operative Until July 1, 2017]	§1375	§6000
Design and Construction Defects; Procedures in Litigation	§1375.05	
Disclosure to Members; Resolution or Design or Construction Defect Dispute	§1375.1	§6100
Video or Television Antennas; Satellite Dish Systems; Restrictions on Installation; Application for Approval	§1376	§4725
Architectural or Design Review; Procedures for Approval	§1378	§4765

TABLE OF STATUTES

INTERNAL REVENUE CODE

BUSINESS AND PROFESSIONS CODE

CIVIL CODE

CODE OF CIVIL PROCEDURE

CORPORATIONS CODE

GOVERNMENT CODE

REVENUE & TAXATION CODE

VEHICLE CODE

CASE LAW INDEX

ADMINISTRATIVE AND TRANSFER FEES

ASSESSMENT ALLOCATION

ASSESSMENT OBLIGATION

ASSESSMENT COLLECTION

BOARD DECISION MAKING

BOARD MEETINGS

BOARD-ADOPTED OPERATING RULES

CC&R ENFORCEMENT, ARCHITECTURAL CONTROLS

CC&R ENFORCEMENT, GENERALLY

CORPORATE SUSPENSION

DISCLOSURE

FAIR HOUSING ISSUES

GOVERNING DOCUMENT AMENDMENTS

GOVERNMENT PERMITS

INDEMNITY

INSURANCE

LEGAL STANDING

LIABILITY

LITIGATION, CONSTRUCTION DEFECT

LITIGATION, GENERALLY

MAINTENANCE

NUISANCE

PROTECTED SPEECH

RECORDS INSPECTION

RENTAL RESTRICTIONS

STATUTE OF LIMITATIONS

VOTING AND ELECTIONS

Index

A

B

C

D

E

F

G

H

I

J

K

L

M

N

O

P

Q

R

S

T

U

V

W

Z

Notes

Notes

Notes

Notes

Notes

Notes